**Alma College
Library**

LONGING

LONGING

Narratives of Nostalgia
in the British Novel,
1740–1890

Tamara S. Wagner

Lewisburg
Bucknell University Press

© 2004 by Rosemont Publishing & Printing Corp.

All rights reserved. Authorization to photocopy items for internal or personal use, or the internal or personal use of specific clients, is granted by the copyright owner, provided that a base fee of $10.00, plus eight cents per page, per copy is paid directly to the Copyright Clearance Center, 222 Rosewood Drive, Danvers, Massachusetts 01923. [0-8387-5600-X/04 $10.00 + 8¢ pp, pc.]

Associated University Presses
2010 Eastpark Boulevard
Cranbury, NJ 08512

The paper used in this publication meets the requirements of the American National Standard for Permanence of Paper for Printed Library Materials Z39.48-1984.

Library of Congress Cataloging-in-Publication Data

Wagner, Tamara S., 1976–
Longing : narratives of nostalgia in the
British novel, 1740–1890 / Tamara S. Wagner.
p. cm.
Includes bibliographical references and index.
ISBN 0-8387-5600-X (alk. paper)
1. English fiction—19th century—History and criticism.   2. Nostalgia in literature.   3. English fiction—18th century—History and criticism.   4. Autobiographical memory in literature.   5. Loss (Psychology) in literature.   6. Memory in literature.   I. Title.
PR868.N67W34 2005
823'.809353—dc22   2004010450

PRINTED IN THE UNITED STATES OF AMERICA

Contents

Acknowledgments	7
Longing, Yearning, Pining: An Introduction to Nostalgia	11
1. The Aesthetics of Affliction in the Novel of Sensibility	33
2. Headaches or Heartaches: Clinical and Romantic Nostalgia in Jane Austen's Novels	85
3. Childhood Lost: Dysfunctional Domesticity in Charles Dickens's Novels	125
4. Homesickness and the Longing for "Other" Places in Victorian Domestic Novels	162
5. Nostalgia and Men of Sensibility in Wilkie Collins's Novels	190
Conclusion: Nostalgia Revisited	216
Notes	235
Bibliography	270
Index	293

Acknowledgments

THE LONGING TO WRITE A BOOK ON THE CREATIVE, POSITIVE, AND most importantly, literary aspects of nostalgia had been with me for some time. It was first not more than just that: a vague longing to defend nostalgia from simplifications and derogatory comments. It had first occurred to me when I was writing an undergraduate dissertation on Tennyson's "In Memoriam" in 1998; it eventually became my PhD proposal. Although repeatedly revised, *Longing: Narratives of Nostalgia in the British Novel, 1740–1890* is essentially based on the doctoral thesis that grew out of this initial impulse, reflecting my growing interest in the histories and discourses of nostalgia: "Fictions of Nostalgia: Loci of Longing in the Late Eighteenth- and Nineteenth-Century English Novel" was written for the Faculty of English at the University of Cambridge between 1999 and 2002, very appropriately for a thesis on the passing of time, at the turn of the millennium. Subsequently, the manuscript followed me literally across the globe to be completed while I was holding a research fellowship at the National University of Singapore. The many people who have helped to make this book possible include scholars from various disciplines and universities as well as my friends and housemates in Cambridge, whose emotional support and intellectual stimulation have been invaluable for all my projects. In particular, I am indebted to my PhD supervisor, John Harvey, for his constant encouragement and feedback on various drafts of my thesis, conference papers, and articles. Equally important, Nigel Leask, Gillian Beer, Robert Douglas-Fairhurst, Leonee Ormond, Heather Glen, Herbert Foltinek, Mariadele Boccardi, and John van Wyhe have read and commented on the initial proposal and/or parts of the manuscript at its various stages. I am also grateful to members of the C-18 List server, whose stimulating discussions have fed into the final revision and the new conclusion I wrote in the summer of 2003, to my colleagues at the National University of Singapore, in particular John Whalen-Bridge, for their advice on publishing processes, and to my fiancé, Chai Kah Hin, for his constant flow of thought-provoking criticism.

This book would not have been possible without the scholarships and fellowships I have received since my undergraduate studies and I am deeply indebted to the Arts and Humanities Research Board (AHRB) in the UK, the University of Cambridge, Churchill College (Cambridge), the Cambridge European Trust, the ERASMUS Programme, and the Austrian Ministry of Education. The final work on this manuscript was funded by a research fellowship for George Landow's *Victorian* and *Postcolonial Web* projects in 2002 and by the junior (postdoctoral) fellowship at the Department of English Language & Literature at the National University of Singapore, which I took up in 2003.

Parts of the final chapter were originally published in a different form as "Overpowering Vitality: Nostalgia and Men of Sensibility in the Fiction of Wilkie Collins," in *Modern Language Quarterly* 63, no. 4 (2002): 473–502. The section on Burney's *The Wanderer* in chapter 1 and part of the introduction appeared as "Nostalgia for Home or Homelands: Romantic Nationalism and the Indeterminate Narrative in Frances Burney's *The Wanderer*," in *Cardiff Corvey: Reading the Romantic Text* 10 (2003) <http://www.cf.ac.uk/encap/corvey/articles/cc10_n03.html>. Reprinted with permission.

LONGING

Longing, Yearning, Pining:
An Introduction to Nostalgia

WHEN ARNOLD BRINKWORTH, THE TEARFUL, HELPLESS, BUT LOYAL hero of Wilkie Collins's sensation novel *Man and Wife* (1870), indulges in "the hot tears that told of the heartache, and that honoured the man who shed them,"[1] the display of his distress is presented as commendable. It is a sign of moral superiority. Far from resembling the ridiculed "model young Briton of the present time" (68), Arnold stands in sharp contrast to the strong, muscular villain, Geoffrey Delamayn, who spurns attachments of and to the past. The crucial difference between the two men indeed primarily rests in their attitudes to love and the significance of the past—in short, to longing, specifically nostalgic longing. Arnold is bitterly disappointed by his friend: "The one friend he possessed, who was associated with his earliest and happiest remembrances of old days— . . . had left him deliberately, without the slightest expression of regret. Arnold's affectionate nature—simple, loyal, clinging where it once fastened—was wounded to the quick" (274). In lacking Geoffrey's obtuse brutality, Arnold moreover comes close to the nostalgic ideal upheld by old Sir Patrick, his fiancée's uncle and "a gentleman of the byegone [sic] time" (57). Nostalgia has thus a dual function in the novel: nostalgic characters are regarded with nostalgia. The new men of feeling in Wilkie Collins's late novels, in fact, raise intriguing questions about changing attitudes to nostalgia as well as to tearful men.

As the main plot of *Man and Wife* is predominantly set in the mid-nineteenth century, Sir Patrick's nostalgically recalled youth must have coincided with the late-eighteenth-century cult of sensibility. The novel thereby carefully contextualizes different fashions of feeling. Both weepy Arnold and old-fashioned Sir Patrick are eventually rewarded with a happy marriage, while the strong villain's moral and physical demise is detailed with relish. Clearly, crucial shifts in attitudes to emotional pain have taken place between Sir Patrick's youth in the previous century, the rise of a muscular male ideal in the mid-nineteenth century, and the publication of Collins's late novels. His fiction indeed repeatedly reflects on such changes in attitudes to the past and the preferences of the past, suggesting that feelings alter as they go in and out of fashion, and that new ideals are not necessarily better simply because they are the latest innovation. As he nostalgically restores an old-fashioned conception of emotional afflictions as evidence of moral superiority, Wilkie Collins deliberately writes against the grain of Victorian ideals of health, enterprise, and self-help. Even when he sets out to expose laws and institutions in need of reform, he combines such nostalgia with a critical outlook on the present and an essentially skeptical hope of the future. But what does this ambiguous combination say about the positive and creative, indeed hopeful, aspects of nostalgia? A close look at its changing representations and functions in the eighteenth- and nineteenth-century British novel promises to shed intriguing new light on this ambiguity.

As fiction uses and muses over a condition that first received detailed attention in Britain at the beginning of the eighteenth century and repeatedly came under scrutiny in literary as well as medical writing, it provides invaluable insight into nostalgia's history as well as its misinterpretations or misuses. Often dismissively treated as a sentimental affectation or pose, nostalgia is, in fact, a frequently misunderstood emotion and way of remembering. Its history and particularly its literary history provide a key to its changing conceptualizations. In an attempt to reassess common misinterpretations of nostalgia as a cloying sentimentality or an emotionally distorted memory, the present study traces its uses in the traditional, "classic," novel. The ways the genre reflects and, more importantly, contributes to new attitudes to the past and to personal longing, and ultimately also to a nostalgic way of reviewing events and emotions are central to this analysis, and it therefore focuses on the far-reaching changes that took place from the mid-eighteenth century onwards. Retrospection and individualism had of course also been important aspects of the early British novel, but in the second half of the eighteenth century, nostalgia, together with a range of similar emotional states, became the subject of repeated analysis. Influenced by clinical theories of psychophysical maladies, the eighteenth-century novel of sensibility idealized such afflictions as symptoms of virtue and refinement.[2] Nostalgia was welcomed as an emotional experience and a virtuous condition.

The genre's excesses have undoubtedly created persisting suspicions about nostalgia, but it has also been the means of recuperating an emotional state that had been diagnosed as a disease a hundred years earlier. Yet, as the novel of sensibility was ridiculed after its heyday in the late-eighteenth century, nostalgia suffered with it. In the following decades, longing (like sensibility in general) came under close scrutiny. In Victorian literature, nostalgia was redirected to the interior spaces of bourgeois domesticity and appropriated as an essential part of the age's child cult. This sentimentalized version of personal longing was far removed from the controversial, even radical, uses of nostalgia at the end of the eighteenth century as well as from the equally contentious redefinitions of sensibility, and indeed all emotional indulgence, in the first decades of the nineteenth century. Nostalgia's privatization, as it were, in bourgeois homes appeared to render it innocuous.

Even in its most sentimentalized versions, however, nostalgia was never straightforward nor even necessarily conservative or bourgeois. On the contrary, as its personal and private aspects became its most lauded attributes and effects, nostalgia for an ideal space increasingly gave rise to fantasies of particularly eccentric homes, as many of Dickens's fictional homes show. Towards the end of the nineteenth century, new scientific discoveries and clinical conceptualizations of the nerves and the brain complicated attitudes to nostalgia as a longing for bygones and a psychophysical state. When tearful men were nostalgically recalled in Collins's novels, the treatment of nostalgia had come full circle, leaving in its trail a range of contradictory cultural myths or, as Laura Brown has put it, "fables" of and attitudes to nostalgia.[3] As it reassesses these intriguing changes, the present study takes eighteenth-century novels of sensibility as its starting-point and concludes with Collins's last works. This broad span shows how nostalgia has shaped the novel genre and how its literary history not only reflects, but forms, an important part in the formation of Western modernity. The period that saw the novel's rise also witnessed the consolidation of the middle classes, the expansion of a consumer society, and crucial re-conceptualizations of gender, madness, happiness, and personal pleasure as a worthy goal—indeed of individuality, as we know it.

What has been termed the "affective revolution" of the late eighteenth century took place during an age of revolutions that included the French Revolution and the American War of Independence abroad and radical breaks in definitions and ideals of society at home as well as the beginning of the Industrial Revolution.[4] The "invention," as it were, of individuality and personal happiness moreover could not have taken place without crucial changes in the understanding of emotional afflictions. As Lynn Hunt and Margaret Jacob have emphasized in a recent article, the term "affective" combines the internal or emotional with the external or physical and thereby usefully encompasses the intersections and overlaps that characterized explorations of both mind and body at the time.[5] New ideas of privacy or pleasure clearly did not spring into being in isolation. They formed part of a series of changes that stretched across the nineteenth as well as the second half of the eighteenth century. The invention of nostalgia as an emotion and a form of memory was part and parcel of this affective revolution, and the British novel a vital document of its influence and development. Nostalgia's literary history shows how its original meaning was extended to go beyond an emotional affliction to become a creative, wistful as well as comforting, way of remembering. From its inception as a clinical term in the seventeenth century to its flexibility and creativity as a fond yearning and wistful memory, nostalgia slowly accumulated additional meanings that reflected changing attitudes to personal longing at the time.

Origins of Nostalgia

The term "nostalgia," coined in a medical treatise in 1688, was at first used exclusively to describe the physical symptoms of extreme homesickness. In his "Dissertatio Medica de ΝΟΣΤΑΛΓΙΑ oder Heimwehe," the Swiss physician Johannes Hofer analyzed "stories of certain youths, thus afflicted, that unless they had been brought back to the native land, whether in a fever or censured by the 'Wasting Disease,' they had met their last days on foreign shores."[6] In search of a medical term for this malady, he combined Greek νοστος "return home" and αλγος "pain," diagnosing nostalgia as a disease caused by "the sad mood originating from the desire for the return to one's native land."[7] Possible alternatives included "nosomanias" and "philopatridomania." This affliction, Hofer emphasized, had to be taken seriously. It could even end fatally and it needed a name. In most cases, this newly discovered disease was literal homesickness: its victims were primarily soldiers, sailors, and young men and women who had just left home. Their intense desire to return resulted in physical pain. Hofer's choice of terms reflects the disease's aetiology: nosomanias is an insane or maniac desire to return home; philopatridomania an insane love for the fatherland; nostalgia the pain caused by longing for a return home. Leaving out the "maniac" element in his choice of nostalgia, Hofer significantly decided to set it apart from insanity. What is more, he included a case study of a young country girl who had been taken to hospital after a fall and pined there for a return to her parents' house. As homesickness took hold of her, "she wailed frequently, groaning nothing else than 'Ich will heim; Ich will heim,' nor responding anything else to questions than this same 'Ich will heim.' [I want to go home.]"[8] When her parents took her home, she got well within a few days "entirely without the aid of medicine."[9] Not only had the girl never left her fatherland, but she clearly recovered without medical interference. On the contrary, it was her removal from the hospital that cured her. This ambiguity in the understanding and, even more importantly, treatment of nostalgia became central in literary representations of both nostalgic longing and physical homesickness.

Nevertheless, nostalgia was not only quickly taken up as an organic disease, but also associated with patriotism and particularly with the Swiss, whose longing for their native land allegedly indicated the greater freedom of their nation. As he was writing his *Anthropology from a Pragmatic Point of View* (1798) more than a hundred years after Hofer had published his dissertation, Immanuel Kant stressed the dependence of nostalgia on a time rather than a place by a reference to this "Swiss disease." A return home, he argued, cured nostalgia in that it simply dispelled the illusions it had created. He emphatically set his concept of nostalgia as a longing for the past, or a past home, against the prevailing understanding of patriotism as well as homesickness at the time:

> Later, when they visit these places, they find their anticipation dampened and even their homesickness cured. They think that everything has drastically changed, but it is that they cannot bring back their youth. It is remarkable that such homesickness befalls peasants of a penniless province, where there are strong family ties, and it strikes them more deeply than it does these who are busy earning money and who take for their motto: *Patria ubi bene*.[10]

In his *Anatomy of Melancholy* (1621), Robert Burton had similarly dismissed nostalgia as "a childish humor:" "'Tis a childish humor to hone after home, to be discontent at that which others seek; to prefer, as base Icelanders and Norwegians do, their own ragged island before Italy or Greece, the gardens of the world.... All places are distant from heaven alike."[11] As a longing that only imitated a melancholy affliction, it could easily be dismissed as unworthy of further investigation. By the last decades of the seventeenth century, however, physicians had clearly begun to take homesickness so seriously that it needed a clinical term. In the latter half of the eighteenth century, it was not only a well-known and widespread affliction associated with patriotic feeling, but increasingly also a Romantic longing. In his tellingly titled poem "Home-sick" (1799), Samuel Taylor Coleridge referred to the healing effects of the homeland's air, suggesting that homesickness was a disease that could be cured by a return home—in short, a clinical nostalgia—while he simultaneously treated it as a Romantic yearning: "Thou Breeze, that play'st on Albion's shore!"[12]

Hofer had diagnosed nostalgia for "the pleasant breeze of the Native Land" as a disease arising from an afflicted imagination.[13] Kant agreed with Burton and Hofer in dismissing nostalgic idealizations as a delusion, but by the time both Kant and Coleridge wrote, nostalgia had become linked to Romantic ideals of memory as well as to patriotism. At the same time, however, medical treatises on nostalgia perpetuated its clinical meaning even after it had been appropriated as a part of Romantic melancholy, and Coleridge's description of his pining for Albion nicely exemplifies this simultaneity. In "Home-sick," homesickness may be "a wasting pang" as well as a longing that shows the speaker to be a melancholy Romantic, but promises of a cure are "in thy wings, / Thou Breeze" (ll. 15–16). These wings can make Albion's breezes available abroad as whiffs of the English coast carried across the Channel. Clearly, not only returns can cure nostalgia, but nostalgic indulging in the sought (or imagined, for that matter) aromas of a desired place or time may, too.

This longing for a shore, and indeed any shore, had already become the subject of medical discussions of nostalgia. As eighteenth-century nosologies show, it was common among sailors; with a desire to touch land often standing in for a more specific homesickness. In his *Observations on the Scurvy* (1792), Thomas Trotter wrote of "scorbutic nostalgia" as a disease that regularly broke out on board ship. It was a physical illness caused by unbalanced nourishment: "The cravings of appetite, not only amuse their waking hours, with thoughts on green fields, and streams of pure water; but in dreams they are tantalized by the favourite idea; and on waking, the mortifying disappointment is expressed with the utmost regret."[14] Nutritional deficiency was diagnosed as a cause of longing, but emotional affliction continued to play an important role in nosologies. Trotter pointed out that scorbutic nostalgia was rampant on slave ships where despair was expectedly rife.[15] The emphasis on its organic causes such as vitamin deficiency moreover did not prevent writers from treating it poetically. As Jonathan Lamb has recently shown, "this pathological state of the nerves"—whatever its cause—was largely responsible for Utopian descriptions of new discoveries, as explorers were "keyed up to overreact" at the sight of land.[16]

Increasingly, however, nostalgia's pathology itself became the subject of poetic treatment. Scorbutic nostalgia, Lamb suggests, is the theme of Coleridge's "The Rime of the Ancient Mariner" (1798): the figure of Death is a montage of scorbutic symptoms, while the intense descriptions of extreme disgust and pleasure echo eighteenth-century clinical descriptions of nostalgia.[17] The sweet breeze that takes the Mariner back moreover anticipates the wings of Albion's breezes in "Home-sick:" "like a meadow-gale of spring" it feels "like a welcoming" (ll. 459–61). Samuel Rogers's *The Pleasures of Memory* (1792), a collection of poems on a variety of nostalgic attitudes, similarly includes a poem on a homesick Swiss who "guards a foreign shore" and eventually "Melts at the long-lost scenes that round him rife, / And sinks a martyr to repentant sighs."[18] Reviving the myth of the easily homesick Swiss, it suggests that this regretful longing can be fatal, yet what is much more striking is that his nostalgia is listed among the "pleasures of memory." It is poetically treated as a wistful remembrance as well as a painful pining with physical, potentially fatal, results.

Eighteenth- and nineteenth-century travel writing similarly contains repeated references to nostalgia as a common disease among explorers and colonialists and increasingly also as a wistful longing that makes the absent home even more precious. Joseph Banks wrote of nostalgia as a disease that had broken out on James Cook's *Endeavour*, and which was cured as they left the coast of New Guinea in haste in September 1770: "The sick became well and the melancholy looked gay. The greater part of them were now pretty far gone with the longing for home which the physicians have gone so far as to esteem a disease under the name of nostalgia."[19] The sight of land was not enough to cure the crew. They needed to return home. Even more pointedly, when Charles Darwin embarked on the *Beagle* in 1832, he found that only the physical discomfort caused by seasickness was allayed when he reached land, while his constant comparisons of tropical countries with a nostalgically remembered British countryside only exacerbated his homesickness. As Ann Colley's detailed reading of the *Beagle* diaries has shown, for Darwin, tropical trees contrasted unfavorably "with the vigour of an English oak," and the Welsh mountains of his nostalgic imagination appeared to loom larger than the Andes.[20] Victorian scientific explorations served primarily to provide new insight into geological formations and species at home. Progressively, descriptions of nostalgia moreover fed into idealizations of domesticity. Eighteenth- and nineteenth-century domestic novels map a similar movement, as absences in exotic places are used to highlight the significance of home. As the following readings show, its centrality is part of a nostalgic narrative that underlies the development of the British novel.

A parallel shift occurred in nosologies of nostalgia. More and more often, it became an (emotional) affliction that could be experienced at home. That Hofer had already included the homesickness of a girl in hospital had largely been forgotten, and it was only slowly that physicians rediscovered the range of nostalgia. But as the temporal aspect of this longing, which Kant was so quick to point out as he railed against patriotism's delusive nature, was further investigated, absence became irrelevant. To be away from home was no longer seen as a necessary precondition of nostalgia. As a similar psychophysical malady, it soon became conflated or confused with melancholia or hypochondria. In his *Dissertation on the Influence of the Passions upon Disorders of the Body* (1788), William Falconer, for example, set out to distinguish carefully between hypochondria, melancholia, and nostalgia, but had to admit that the latter was "said to begin with melancholy, sadness, love of solitude."[21] These symptoms were moreover also those of love, which Falconer classified as a passion and not a disease. This distinction shows the ways in which these categories were seen to overlap. Love could result in fever, epilepsy, or an aneurysm of the aorta.[22] In *Observations on the Nature, Kinds, Causes, and Prevention of Insanity, Lunacy, or Madness* (1782), Thomas Arnold similarly wrote of "invincible *love*, that has made more Madmen in every age and nation than any other passion beside" and proceeded to emphasize that nostalgia—"this unreasonable fondness for the place of our birth"—closely resembled both grief and love.[23] This resemblance was not confined to their symptoms, as nostalgia was also a result of and, to an extent, a synonym for lovesickness. "[T]he inconsolable grief of disappointed love, which gradually consumes the vital flame, preys upon it unceasingly till it be extinguished, and is termed by the English a *broken heart*," was a common cause of nostalgia.[24]

Broken hearts had to be taken seriously, physicians argued and proceeded to treat love and particularly lovesickness, as Helen Small has shown in her perceptive study of "love-madness," as well as melancholy and nostalgia as forms of derangement that often required clinical treatment.[25] Increasingly, however, it became vital to distinguish emotional distress from madness. Nostalgia was among the first of these psychophysical conditions to be recuperated from such associations with insanity, yet as the proliferation of its definitions in nosologies show, its meaning as a disease and an emotion continued to fluctuate. Its poetic treatment mirrored this simultaneity. In "The Disease of the Soul," the Victorian poet Arthur O'Shaughnessy, for example, used "nostalgy [*sic*]" to describe a longing for the past that causes physical uneasiness: "The nostalgies of dim pasts seize me."[26] Likewise, in his "Lectures on Medical Jurisprudence," delivered at the University of London in 1837, A. T. Thomson listed symptoms common to melancholia and nostalgia to caution against possible misdiagnoses. Confining the nostalgic in an asylum, he argued, could prove fatal: "If *hypochondriasis* may be confounded with melancholia, that disease which has been termed nostaglia [*sic*] is much more likely to be so; and when this occurs, and confinement in a lunatic asylum takes place, death is the inevitable result."[27] Nostalgia was a strong emotion that could result in physical symptoms. "In no disease," Thomson wrote, "is the influence of mind over body so strikingly displayed as in nostalgia."[28] He provided a list of symptoms that neatly summarized the concept of a clinical nostalgia, but also highlighted the indeterminacy of its definition:

> Nostalgia may be mistaken for melancholia, by the restlessness and want of sleep which accompanies the disease, and the strong tendency to selfdestruction [*sic*] which attends it when the desire of revisiting the country which is longed after, cannot be accomplished; life becomes then a burden, and the taedium vitae leads to real insanity, terminating in suicide. From what has been said, the necessity for distinguishing nostalgia from insanity, when the distinction may prove serviceable, must be sufficiently obvious.[29]

According to the *Oxford English Dictionary*, nostalgia has two main sets of meaning: firstly, having preserved its pathological connotation, it is a "form of melancholia caused by prolonged absence from one's home or country; severe home-sickness." Secondly, in its transferred usage, it is defined as "[r]egret or sorrowful longing *for* the conditions of a past age; regretful or wistful memory or recall of an earlier time." Both definitions arose from the vibrantly interacting medical and literary discourses of the eighteenth century. The idealization of psychophysical affliction as the occupational malady of the refined, sensitive, upward-moving middle classes assured that nostalgia retained its pathological properties, while just such pathos (and pathology) became a sign of superiority.

A crucial awareness of discontinuity moreover created a new understanding of history as linear and premised on a break from a stable former order. Building on Foucault's influential account of "this whole sudden conversion of Western memory at the end of the eighteenth century," scholars have subsequently dated the birth of history, or "modern" history, at this point of disjuncture. As Laura Brown has pointedly put it, in historiography, modernity was distinguished by an act of historical differentiation that changed not only attitudes to the past, but also to the present and the future: it drew attention to the novelty of the present and made possible ideas of progress and improvement.[30] Nostalgia for more than a stable past was part and parcel of this new concept. Robert Miles pointedly speaks of the birth of nostalgia as well as of history.[31] A new interest in the individual turned these explorations of history and memory additionally towards personal recollections. When William Wordsworth wrote that "[a]ll good poetry . . . takes its origin from emotion recollected in tranquillity," he formulated a definition of literary production that emphasized the creative aspects of a specifically nostalgic way of recalling events and emotions and moreover associated it with a revolution in poetry that came to be known as Romanticism.[32]

Influenced by Romantic poetry, the fiction of the time shared its idealization of longing and increasingly reflected interest in historical differences, yet it also tended to depict pining protagonists within a realist plot, offering sympathetic insight into their yearnings *and*, from the mid-eighteenth century onwards, an almost clinical description of their symptoms. Protagonists observe as well as experience emotions. Nostalgia is always at once critically described and evoked. As I analyze the nuances of this flexible and at times ambiguous feeling and remarkable cultural phenomenon, I shall show that nostalgia has never completely lost its associations with literal homesickness and that its idealization as a wistful memory is an important eighteenth-century development that comes under careful scrutiny in post-Romantic debates on emotional indulgence and personal happiness.

To suggest that nostalgia has been replaced by a purely temporal interpretation divorced from its origins is clearly misleading. David Lowenthal has pointed out that nostalgia lingered on as an organic malady: it featured in prize-winning treatises in the late-Victorian age and was still used in the 1950s.[33] Even more revealingly, in an extensive study of the medical history of these "related clinical syndromes," Stanley Jackson not only shows that "in the terms *melancholia* and *depression* and their cognates, we have well over two millennia of the Western world's ways of referring to a goodly number of different dejected states,"[34] but also classifies love-melancholy and nostalgia as specific forms of melancholia, reviving them as useful terms for contemporary discussions of these psychophysical states.[35] In the majority of cultural studies, however, nostalgia is simply seen as a regressive obsession with the past, at odds with its origins as well as with its creative potential in structuring narratives and inspiring literature, even though this potential had after all been recognized early in its history without interfering with its clinical definitions. On the contrary, nostalgia's status as a psychophysical affliction was intrinsic to its idealization in late-eighteenth-century literature, as my reading of popular fiction of the time will show.

Nevertheless, critics of nostalgia have routinely swerved away quickly from accounts of its "invention" and subsequent "demedicalization" to stress instead its role as a partisan perversion of the past that helps to commercialize it or, even more damagingly, serves a political, usually conservative, agenda.[36] In a study of Britain's heritage industry, Robert Hewison thus deplores the vogue for historical re-enactments that commercialize the past. The nostalgia it fosters, Hewison argues, is entropic and decadent, even though he admits that it can have an integrative effect as a means to cope with change.[37] Yet critics rarely acknowledge this integrative aspect. As David Lowenthal puts it, nostalgia is "a topic of embarrassment and a term of abuse. Diatribe upon diatribe denounces it as reactionary, repressive, ridiculous."[38] Literary scholars have even gone so far as to devise their own definition of nostalgia in order to highlight its reactionary or repressive tendencies. In the introduction to *Nostalgia and Sexual Difference: The Resistance to Contemporary Feminism*, Janice Doane and Devon Hodges, for example, have composed an intriguingly one-sided and obscure definition of "nostalgia." They speak of "a frightening antifeminist impulse," which they term "nostalgic:" "Nostalgia, as we define it, is a retreat to the past in the face of what a number of writers—most of them male—perceive to be the degeneracy of American culture brought about by the rise of feminist authority."[39] Raphael Samuel's work stands out among cultural studies of nostalgia: he suggests that conservatives dread nostalgia's drive to turn out subversives just as radicals fear its domestication of the past.[40] Nostalgia is by no means inherently conservative and has indeed always had a Utopian component. As Hofer put it in 1688, nostalgics "picture themselves enjoying this [the home]" once again.[41] Nostalgia for an absent ideal can never be simply pre- or "con-servative," as it is emphatically not the *status quo* that is desirable. Its flexibility, in fact, makes it useful to opposed ideologies, and this accounts for much of its popularity as well as its abuses.

Studies of nostalgia that stress its creative aspects have remained rare and sketchy at best. Linda Hutcheon tentatively suggests that nostalgia's aesthetics might express dissatisfaction with the present.[42] Both Jonathan Lamb and Winfried Schleiner have emphasized nostalgia's role in Utopian narratives.[43] Postcolonial studies have similarly rethought nostalgia's creative rearranging of memories of traumatic dislocation, but tend to emphasize the dangers of a fraudulent ideology of "home" that exacerbates feelings of homesickness and homelessness. Homi Bhabha has stressed "the *heimlich* pleasures of the hearth" that are poised against "the *unheimlich* terror of the space or race of the Other" in orientalist writing,[44] while Ban Kah Choon speaks of the creative energy of nostalgia, which, he argues, informs postcolonial revisions of the past.[45] In her study of the "politics of home," Rosemary Marangoly George perceptively suggests that homesickness "can cut two ways: it could be a yearning for the authentic home (situated in the past or in the future) or it could be the recognition of the inauthenticity or the created aura of all homes."[46] Such studies have helped to pave the way for a re-examination of nostalgia that highlights its creativity and flexibility, and my approach posits a similar multivalency, but with the crucial difference that the present study also seeks to pay attention to the much-neglected significance of nostalgia's history.

Susan Stewart's semiotic study, *On Longing: Narratives of the Miniature, the Gigantic, the Souvenir, the Collection*, is so far perhaps the most extensive exploration of nostalgia "as a structure of desire,"[47] and her focus on nostalgia's narrative potential comes close to my own emphasis on its creative as well as flexible elements. Although she joins the critics of the heritage industry in referring to "the social disease of nostalgia" and in positing an inherent inauthenticity, her reappraisal of longings for origins, for the exotic, or the antique as well as the past, testifies to nostalgia's flexibility.[48] Most significantly, Stewart sketches nostalgia's changing role in the rise of the novel—a function that is central to the present study. Building on Ian Watt's seminal work, she has argued that confidence in the circularity of history is broken with in a "new kind of realism and a novel kind of 'psychological' literature."[49] But while Stewart quickly moves on to a semiotics of longing by studying cultural phenomena in general, I wish to take up her references to nostalgia's role in emerging ideals of privacy and its significance for the new interest in individual experience in the second half of the eighteenth century.

By revealing the origins of common misunderstandings about nostalgia, this study shows that nostalgia creatively fosters an imaginative and personal memory. As it explores the ways in which nostalgia shifts between corporal, psychological, and emotional definitions, it attempts to use a series of potential conjunctions among various schools and orientations. It takes the medical history of psychophysical conditions into account and situates the reassessment of nostalgia's cultural as well as more specifically its literary history within the projects of new historicism and cultural materialism. It firmly locates the development of nostalgia and its narratives in their historical contexts, but without losing sight of its main focus on nostalgia's literary role as a central narrative in British fiction. Where this study principally differs from earlier accounts of nostalgia is both in the emphasis on its creative and versatile aspects, and in this focus on the historical contingencies of its functions in the eighteenth and nineteenth centuries. The remainder of the introduction sketches the interdisciplinary context of the following close readings of literary texts.

Nostalgia and the Novel: Contexts and Methodology

Nostalgia's redefinition in the British novel was part of the eighteenth-century "affective revolution:" it was at the centre of domestic fictions that revised the role of colonial places and imperial ventures in the British novel; it became increasingly significant after the industrial revolution; it built on and helped to develop new ideas of privacy and individuality. Above all, it has had a formative effect on the novel's development. In situating nostalgia and the novel genre in their cultural contexts, this study is indebted to Ian Watt's influential *The Rise of the Novel*, while it also draws on studies of medical history and colonial representations, on gender studies, and in particular on the new field of masculinity studies. The interdisciplinary context of this study is a tribute to nostalgia's flexibility and versatility, and underlines its central role in the important revolutions that coincided with the novel's rise. The changing treatment of nostalgia and different trends in the novel can, in fact, be seen as mutually illuminating developments. Nostalgia formed an important cultural force in the formation of fiction, while the novel at once reflected and influenced the changing definition of nostalgia. Both were significant for a new understanding of personal feeling, individuality, and private ways of remembering.

According to Ian Watt, the novel genre interests itself much more than any other literary form in the development of its characters in the course of time.[50] Watt influentially suggested that the traditional novel reflected a "growing tendency for individual experience to replace collective tradition."[51] This rise of individuality paved the way for a realist genre that focused on the particularity of everyday life and promoted individual modes of retrospection. More recent studies of the novel have modified, extended, or refined Watt's argument. Making lesser known texts available for discussion, they have increasingly emphasized that novels need to be read against a broad context of cultural materials. Michael McKeon's dialectic approach has contributed significantly to these revisions in emphasizing the vital functions of the novel's "precursors," such as the romance genre, and the ways they became incorporated into the emergent genre. Narrative, he argues, was particularly suitable for the representation of the opposed aristocratic and middle-class ideologies at the time, and the novel genre needs to be understood as a cultural instrument designed to confront intellectual and social crises.[52] J. Paul Hunter likewise sees the need to read novels against "a far broader context of cultural texts and materials" as central to his project.[53] John Richetti's work evinces a similar interest in the novel's precursors and in non-canonical authors as he reconsiders the novel's rise.[54] More recently, Catherine Gallagher and Margaret Anne Doody have newly addressed its emergence and the problematics of its ideological function. Despite their different theoretical approaches, they share an emphasis on the importance of the novel's contexts.[55]

At the same time, studies of eighteenth- and nineteenth-century social history have drawn attention to the interactions of economic and cultural developments that shaped print-culture at the time, regulated modes and means of consumption, and at once registered and formed the development of Western modernity. Most influentially perhaps, Benedict Anderson has analyzed the role of print in the creation of "imagined communities." The novel, he argues, functioned as a "device for the presentation of simultaneity."[56] According to Anderson, the idea of the nation arose at a time when the Enlightenment's "own modern darkness" demanded promises of a "secular transformation of fatality into continuity,"[57] and the novel helped to form such a sense of continuity by engendering an imagined community of readers. Its interest in the individual's personal emotions and their recollection of course appears to conflict with this emphasis on shared, or communal, experience. Recent reassessments of the novel's rise have, however, suggested that these apparently conflicting interests in the communal and the individual are not necessarily contradictory. J. Paul Hunter has suggested that it is precisely because novels probe the subjectivity of one individual that they generate sympathy: readers can vicariously experience the described emotions.[58] In her study of early women's fiction, Catherine Gallagher has similarly argued that the characters' fictiveness induces readers to sympathize with them, that the stories of fictive individuals can create the sense of shared experience best. Gallagher speaks of "nobody's stories" that are more easily perceived as everybody's story.[59] An interest in individual experience can overlap with the desire to experience vicariously. Readers' tearful consumption of sentimental novels in the mid- and late-eighteenth century accentuated this sense of sharing.

Nonetheless, primary interest still rested on the individual. Notwithstanding the common practice of reading out to others in familial communities, novel reading remained a private, even solitary, affair. As Hunter has put it, despite its societal concerns and its later role as Victorian family entertainment, the novel was still "an essentially individualistic and isolationistic form."[60] The solitude encouraged by novel reading very revealingly gave rise to deep concern at the time. Its notoriety as a promoter of solitary pleasures, in fact, explains the importance of medical discourses for the novel's consumption and further development. As Thomas Laqueur and Roy Porter have influentially shown, in the eighteenth century, novel reading was associated with unproductive pleasure and sedentary as well as reclusive habits: solitary reading could directly result in hypochondriac or hysterical complaints. Masturbation was a related fear. Porter has suggested that "to loll on sofas reading lubricious romances" was seen as encouraging sedentary habits and inflaming the imagination.[61] From the mid-century onwards, novels made a point of distinguishing themselves from romances, yet they were of course likewise fictitious and moreover increasingly excelled in evoking emotional reactions in their sentimental readers. They also fostered the same solitariness as romances did. What is more, the central point of criticism was not so much a question of being caught up in fiction and not being able to tell fantasy apart from reality, but whether the fictional quality of the characters in a novel or a masturbatory fantasy made them more real and compelling. Laqueur speaks of the danger of "representational excess."[62] Like masturbation, fiction was accused of failing to lead to anything productive, except pleasure, and of causing debility and disease. Both novel reading and the "solitary vice" of masturbation were conceived as a threat to sociability.

Despite its promotion of "imagined communities," the novel genre clearly continued to be associated with solitary pleasures and vices and became increasingly domestic as well. In a recent study, Suvir Kaul pointedly identifies the "partial retraction from its colonial origins" as an important feature of the novel's rise. In contrast to the works of Aphra Behn, Defoe, and Swift, later novels reassessed the relation of centre and margins by asserting a new focus on domesticity. While this did not mean that they disavowed concern with the world overseas, they instead displaced or sublimated it.[63] This shift to domestic concerns rendered the novel genre appropriate for bourgeois consumption.[64] John Richetti has similarly emphasized this movement away from concerns with public life and masculine heroism to the interior and private lives of individuals and to the "feminine" realm of domesticity. The novel's parallel promotion of the values intrinsic to individualism further promoted this shift. In most novels that come to mind, Richetti stresses, "particular persons in their individualized immediacy are presented as being more important or more immediate than communities or cultures," and these novels are consequently "most often about the clash between such individuals and the larger social units that necessarily produce them."[65] This double shift to the individual and the feminine engendered an emphasis on "quirky individuality," a representation of eccentricity alert to a modernity of personal expressiveness.[66] Throughout the present study, the novel's promotion of individuality and its gendering of domesticity form important undercurrents, while nostalgia's origins in clinical discourses make the significance of medical history sufficiently obvious. Recent studies of the consumption of fiction have further paved the way for my readings of nostalgic narratives, especially as they close the gap between analyses of colonial discourses on the one hand and the intersections between literary and medical writing on the other. As it impinges on representations of "home" and the "other" as well as of emotions and the psychophysical effects of emotionalism, nostalgia clearly necessitates such an interdisciplinary approach. Throughout this book, I seek to combine theory with close readings of individual texts, and within their contexts, recent developments in the history of science with reassessments of the colonial, or orientalist, undercurrents of domestic fiction.

The functions of the "other" in domestic fiction have of course been amply studied ever since the publication of Edward Said's influential *Orientalism* and *Culture and Imperialism*, but nostalgia has remained largely absent from these works.[67] Nonetheless, my analysis of domesticity's changing role in the British novel is deeply indebted to recent studies by Nigel Leask, Laura Brown, and Felicity Nussbaum as well as to the seminal work of Edward Said and of Raymond Williams before him.[68] In his influential *The Country and the City*, Williams, in fact, drew a significant connection between the fantasies of colonialists or explorers and the idealization of "home," of domesticity as well as the English countryside. Working in tropical or arid places abroad became linked to the acquisition of embowered estates at home, thereby creating a cultural myth which the novel helped to form. Williams wrote of "a marked development of the idea of England as 'home,' in that special sense in which 'home' is a memory and an ideal."[69] This study will show the conflicted, critical, and above all, creative ways in which British fiction of the eighteenth and nineteenth centuries reflected and promoted this novel idea of home.

Most importantly, in his opening chapter, Williams spoke positively of nostalgia and linked a longing for "Old Englands" to childhood nostalgia, which he termed "universal."[70] Novelists, Williams showed, were quick to capitalize on this connection between domesticity, prolonged absence in the name of empire or, more narrowly, business, and the idealization of childhood. Arguing that domesticity was "essentially a nineteenth-century invention," John Tosh has more recently suggested that there was a "special poignancy" in Victorian narratives of return as home was "identified with childhood, innocence and roots—indeed with authenticity itself."[71] This identification of a nostalgically recalled childhood with authenticity created its aura of a universal longing. The bourgeois home especially came to be regarded as a common focus of nostalgic longing. In Victorian domestic novels, home is a sanctuary from the business world, from the dangers of business ventures abroad particularly, but also from the workplace in the city. Accentuated by the Industrial Revolution, this split into workplace and shrinking familial communities in the cozy home had its roots in the eighteenth century, partly coinciding and tying in with the affective revolution and the steady progress of the middle classes. While my argument is deeply indebted to Williams's nostalgic invocation of the permanent significance of "universal and persistent" nostalgia and the connection he drew between inheritance plots in domestic novels and offstage colonies,[72] I situate my analysis of nostalgia within more recent historical studies of childhood (and childhood nostalgia) as well as of domesticity and its "others."

Childhood as we know it was an invention of the late eighteenth century. It was part of the affective revolution and inextricably involved with simultaneous developments. (Pre-)Romantic nostalgia for "original innocence" emphatically connected this new interest in the child to idealizations of the countryside as well as of the past. In 1796 Friedrich Schiller wrote of a longing for "humanity's infancy *prior to the beginning of culture*" and suggested that nature symbolized "our lost childhood, something that remains ever dearest to us, and for this reason [it] fill[s] us with a certain melancholy."[73] The subject of poetry and the target group for educational fiction, the child achieved unprecedented importance. It came to symbolize innocence and, as Tosh has pointedly put it, "authenticity itself." By the mid-nineteenth century, the "Romantic child" had been turned into an icon of bourgeois domesticity.[74] My analysis of mid-Victorian novels looks at this development in more detail, as they trace redefinitions of nostalgia and particularly its subversive potentials at the time. In this context, it is important to note that in the course of the second half of the nineteenth century, the child became associated with interior, bourgeois, spaces. Wild, "exotic," spaces came to serve as a contrast to safe domestic home spaces. Susan Stewart speaks of a link between "the primitive as child and the primitive as an earlier and purer stage of contemporary civilization."[75] This link was a (pre-) Romantic invention, and it was increasingly questioned in the course of the Victorian age. As Suvir Kaul has pointed out, in the eighteenth century, the novel negotiated a shift onto domestic concerns, marginalizing "other" spaces, or reducing them to metaphors.[76] This movement became more pronounced in the following century. In the mid-Victorian novel, exotic spaces are offstage, or a site of homemaking. They are rarely celebrated for their "primitive" qualities, and the same counts for wild landscapes in Britain.[77] Roy Porter speaks of the "new noble savagery in landscaping" that characterized late-eighteenth-century consumption of the countryside;[78] for the Victorians, savage "Nature, red in tooth and claw," as Alfred Tennyson was to put it in "In Memoriam" (1850), was deeply disconcerting.[79] New scientific discoveries had unearthed exciting, but also frightening, aspects of nature.

The Victorians had an increasingly anxious relationship with the past and the future, and their expressions of nostalgia cannot be seen apart from their attempts to come to terms with evolutionary science. The continuous despoliation of the countryside, a steady acceleration of change, and an increased mobility all contributed to a prominence of nostalgic narratives, but the impact of Darwinian science initiated a decisive shift that has been as significant for the novel as the affective revolution of the eighteenth century. Lyell and Chambers's geological discoveries in the 1830s and 1840s already triggered acute religious crises, but such instances became more widespread after Darwin's cataclysmic publications.[80] In one of most famous accounts of such a blow to Victorian self-confidence, J. A. Froude's *The Nemesis of Faith* (1848), this new sense of spiritual emptiness is revealingly alleviated by a belief in childhood. The longing for paradise and childhood nostalgia are the same, but nature is left out. The spiritually isolated narrator speaks of a comforting, even redemptive, longing for "our own Paradise, our own old childhood, over which the old glories linger—to which our own hearts cling, as all we have ever known of Heaven upon earth."[81] Like the invention of the nation, the countryside, and transcendent r/Romantic love, childhood was an attempt to create a sense of continuity in the aftermath of the Enlightenment's secular darkness.[82] Thirty years ago, George Steiner wrote in his *Nostalgia for the Absolute* that the "political and philosophical history of the West during the past 150 years can be understood as a series of attempts—more or less conscious, more or less systematic, more or less violent—to fill the central emptiness left by the erosion of theology."[83] Imagined ideal homes are at the centre of these attempts. In the late eighteenth century, Novalis significantly called philosophy homesickness, the urge to be at home everywhere.[84]

A legacy of Enlightenment secularism, the cultural crises that went hand in hand with new searches for continuities achieved new heights (and pitfalls) in the Victorian age, as the Darwinian imagination transformed culture and literature. The seminal works of Gillian Beer, George Levine, and Sally Shuttleworth have initiated important reassessments of Darwinian science and Victorian psychology and opened up "classic" Victorian novels to studies of cultural homologies.[85] A similar interdisciplinary interest in the intersections between science and literature has characterized eighteenth-century studies in the last two decades, paving the way for an analysis of nostalgia that stretches across the eighteenth and nineteenth centuries.[86] The extensive work of George Rousseau, Roy Porter, and Thomas Laqueur significantly takes them more and more beyond the eighteenth century. Similarly, feminist critics have fruitfully crossed boundaries across eighteenth- and nineteenth-century studies in pointing out the persistence of what Elaine Showalter has called a "pervasive cultural association of women and madness,"[87] or in tracing Victorian treatments of female madness to eighteenth-century cults of sensibility, as Helen Small has done in her study of "love-madness."[88] More recently, masculinity studies have contributed significantly to reassessments of gender definitions and associations of male emotional display with effeminacy or madness.[89] Building on Foucault's works, they treat sexuality as well as madness and the "normalcy" of emotional experience as discursively constituted.[90] I shall draw on and seek to contribute to this new field of "men's studies" as I trace representations of nostalgic men (as well as women) from ideals of the, in George Haggerty's words, "lachrymose male" in late-eighteenth-century fiction to Victorian ideals of "muscular Christianity" and their subsequent rejection at the end of the nineteenth century.[91] To pursue nostalgia's changing representation across this crucial period of change is vital for an understanding of nostalgia as a cultural phenomenon and a new condition that slowly became a recognized emotion in its own right.

The new centrality of feeling in the late-eighteenth-century novel of sensibility makes it a good starting point for this analysis. Chapter 1, "The Aesthetics of Affliction in the Novel of Sensibility," shows how the genre participated in discourses on sensibility that dissected and fostered an association of affliction and virtue. The idealization of psychophysical conditions fed on nostalgia's somatic symptoms, while it contributed to the reformulations of its pathology. John Mullan's pioneering article, in which he argued that novels of sensibility might productively be set against eighteenth-century medical texts on sensibility, has initiated a fruitful line of inquiry.[92] My chapter builds on such reassessments of the vital intersections between medicine and literature. Although I look at instances of male and female pining in fiction, I furthermore emphasize their different treatment. As Thomas Laqueur has pointedly put it, "sometime in the eighteenth century, sex as we know it was invented."[93] The biological gender differentiation that emerged in the course of the century revised the understanding of the masculine and the feminine, while the late-eighteenth-century cults of sensibility came up with a "feminine" culture of feeling that seemed to collapse the new gender differences.

From sketching nostalgia's central role in the sentimental aesthetics of affliction, chapter 1 moves on to investigate the difference in treatment when pining men or women are the object of virtuous distress. I draw on a wide variety of mid- to late-eighteenth-century texts in order to indicate the neglected heterogeneity of the genre as well as an indisputable sameness. The nostalgic memory in Frances Sheridan's *Sidney Bidulph* (1761) clearly stands out in the way in which it divorces somatic effects from emotional suffering and a forgiving nostalgic memory. Frances Burney's novels instead negotiate a struggle for a proper degree of sensibility that then becomes central to Austen's fiction, while mapping a shift from love- to homesickness. Domestic homes come to form the happy solution to the heroine's suffering. This development culminates in Burney's last novel, *The Wanderer* (1814), which reacts critically to the radical sensibility of the 1790s, and even more pointedly, to new nationalist discourses. It is an intriguing document of the increasingly poignant contrasts between individual longing and domestic communities of friends and family on the one hand and a new nationalist nostalgia on the other. I take Charlotte Smith's *Desmond* (1792) as a revealing example of pro-revolutionary fiction to highlight the ways in which Burney's novel crucially differs from earlier fiction.

The second chapter, "Headaches or Heartaches: Clinical and Romantic Nostalgia in Jane Austen's Novels," sheds important new light on the representation of personal and communal needs and desires in Austen's novels. The bullying of Fanny Price in *Mansfield Park* (1814) and the novel's consequent combination of clinical and Romantic nostalgia have formed the original impulse of this reassessment, but a careful reading of Austen's novels reveals their significance for ongoing re-conceptualizations of psychophysical conditions and nostalgia's centrality in the heroines' afflictions. Fanny Price's headaches have of course given rise to repeated ridicule among generations of critics, as they see her virtuous debility as an unhappy departure from the comparative robustness of Austen's livelier heroines. In showing how Fanny's symptoms rehearse clinical nostalgia, while her creative use of memory reflects the "domestication" of the Romantic imagination in domestic novels, I point out the treatment of group-pressure in the novel and underline similar instances in Austen's other novels. More controversially, I highlight the somatic suffering of her lively heroines. Close readings reveal not only that loss of home repeatedly serves as a starting-point or underlying threat in the novels, but that even Elizabeth Bennet, unarguably Austen's liveliest heroine, succumbs to psychophysical conditions, and that her love for Darcy and his estate is a nostalgic love. The heroines' private, often secret, longing is, in fact, central throughout Austen's novels.

Chapter 3, "Childhood Lost: Dysfunctional Domesticity in Charles Dickens's Novels," reassesses Dickens's representations of the ideal home. While his bourgeois ideals of privacy and domestic order seem to sit uneasily with his interest in the underprivileged, and nostalgia for childhood in his fiction has a tendency to lapse into sentimentality, nostalgic longing and the fantasies of home it engenders are subversive. They serve to reveal absences, lack, or mismanagement in dysfunctional households and domestic politics. Dickens's social criticism is moreover fed by his belief in post-Romantic child cults, which presupposes an almost occult understanding of nostalgia. The chapter takes a close look at the ways in which nostalgic longing in his novels contributes to an exposure of domestic ideologies and realities in Victorian Britain.

The novels analyzed in the last two chapters deal with nostalgia by dissecting it critically. They situate it in the contexts of Victorian ways of mapping space at home and abroad and within medical discourses on nervous disorders and emotional illnesses. In these texts, nostalgia and indeed Romantic sensibility in general are considered outmoded or dangerous, but become desirable and eventually worthy of being recuperated. Chapter 4, "Homesickness and the Longing for 'Other' Places in the Victorian Domestic Novel," looks at two mid-Victorian novels in detail, while situating them in the scientific as well as literary discourses of the time. Both present a unique reconciliation of conflicting desires, anxieties, and hopes. The description of homelessness in Charlotte Brontë's *Villette* (1853) sketches a somatic understanding of fervent longing, but the novel significantly proceeds to undermine the codes of Victorian sickroom narratives. It creatively questions domesticity as a desirable end. By contrast, Elizabeth Gaskell's last and unfinished novel, *Wives and Daughters* (1866), offers a hopeful fusion of Utopian and nostalgic longing. Engaging with new evolutionary ideas, it creates a "New Man" who is a new romantic hero, an alternative to mid-Victorian ideologies of "muscular Christianity," and a solution to Victorian anxieties of degeneration. The final chapter, "Nostalgia and Men of Sensibility in Wilkie Collins's Novels," shows how Collins's critical engagement with the medical and (pseudo-)scientific ideas of the time draws the new clinical understanding of emotions and memory into question as it openly attacks popular crazes. His late novels specifically offer a revaluation of nostalgia as a constructive emotion and way of remembering and imagining. In sharp contrast to earlier alignments, in which medical and literary ideas coincided, Collins's defense of emotional memories and emotional excesses is set against prevailing medical, and increasingly also psychological, discourses.

Longing: Narratives of Nostalgia in the British Novel, 1740–1890 presents a literary history of nostalgia and a reassessment of its imaginative potential. While tracing its changing representation, the study sheds new light on its treatment and definition in the eighteenth and nineteenth centuries, reveals its creative and indeed versatile aspects, and stresses the ways in which it shapes the novel genre rather than just operating in it as a theme. The chronological sequence of the chapters traces nostalgia's formative influence on narratives and the nuances of this ambiguous feeling and way of remembering as it mutates from a pathology to a virtue in the eighteenth century and comes under new scrutiny after the excesses of the sensibility cults. The close readings aim to provide insight into the neglected history of nostalgia and its role in the development of the British novel. They show how reconceptualizations of nostalgia reflect and form part of far-reaching changes that took place in the eighteenth and nineteenth centuries. Above all, they aim to underline the creative attributes of the nostalgic imagination, while emphasizing the historical contexts of its narratives.

1
The Aesthetics of Affliction in the Novel of Sensibility

NOSTALGIA IS A CENTRAL, POTENT, AND MOST IMPORTANTLY, WELcomed emotion in the late-eighteenth-century novel of sentiment or sensibility.[1] As the genre developed its symptomatic aesthetics of affliction by combining moral discourses on distressed virtue with a relish in bodily details, it contributed significantly to ongoing redefinitions of nostalgia as well as of hypochondria and melancholia. Operating within bourgeois ideals of refinement that figured psychophysical diseases as the occupational ailments of the sensitive and the intellectual, it sold emotional display to a class-conscious readership. Its emphasis on the marketability of emotions, its often lurid exhibition of physical symptoms, and its deliberate titillations of the reader have revealingly been targets of the genre's most persistent criticisms from its beginnings. That the emotions celebrated in it—nostalgia not the least prominent among them—have suffered with it is not at all unexpected and has indeed been crucial for the representation of emotions in subsequent fiction. The novel of sensibility has amply contributed to a general impatience with detailed descriptions of emotions and specifically idealized emotional distress. To a considerable extent, it was the genre's exaggerations that have given the described emotions a bad name.[2] A detailed analysis of the feelings that are described, or more often prescribed, in the novel of sensibility, however, promises to cast new light on its significance for nostalgia's changing representations and functions.

Drawing on a wide range of examples, I hope to salvage the innovative elements of eighteenth-century literary sentimentalism from the syrupy emotionalism and the lapses into lachrymosity that form an undeniable aspect of sentimental fiction. In detailing the changing treatment of longing in late-eighteenth-century "pre-Romantic" novels, I also aim to highlight their legacies for Romantic fiction and the post-Romantic British novel in general. As Clara Tuite has pointedly put it, during the 1790s "the novel genre was so strongly identified with the sentimental novel that the categories of novel and sentimental novel are to a large extent mutually definitional in this period."[3] Its excesses significantly influenced the treatment of feeling in fiction for the next century. What I wish to highlight here is, firstly, the idealization of psychophysical illnesses at the time and its impact on the treatment of nostalgia; secondly, the telling combinations of love- and homesickness in medical and fictional writing and the consequent interchange of symptoms as well as directions of longing in novels; and thirdly, the simultaneity of nostalgia's representations as a cause of physical pining and a pleasurable form of memory. Above all, this chapter outlines ideals of emotional distress—what I shall term the aesthetics of affliction—and their importance for literary representations of nostalgia.

Physical Pining and the Aesthetics of Affliction

In the cult of sensibility of the eighteenth century, nostalgia and its related afflictions formed a central preoccupation as medical interest in psychophysical distress met a fashionable craze for high sensitivity. Physical and mental affliction was understood as a moral qualification for heroes and heroines of feeling, and idealizations of virtuous suffering frequently employed medical details. In fiction, distress figured as an expression and a result of sensibility. As it is put in Frances Burney's *Camilla* (1796), "innocence [is] oppressed through its own artlessness, and inexperience duped by villainy."[4] In an influential study of the genre, R. F. Brissenden has rightly singled out the "notion not that virtue is rewarded but that virtue invites its own punishment" as a paradigm cliché in novels of sensibility.[5] While it is true that this popular plot development was often ironically evoked, irony or even self-parody hardly ever detracted from its narrative appeal. Geraldine, the heroine of Charlotte Smith's *Desmond* (1792), admits that those novels "delighted [her] most that ended miserably, and, having tortured [her] through the last volume with impossible distress, ended in the funeral of the heroine."[6] Despite her self-ironic attitude, Geraldine virtuously undergoes a range of distresses, re-affirming the cliché: "Is it that I set out in life with too great a share of sensibility? Or is it my lot to be particularly wretched?" (129). In short, the novel of sensibility truly made a virtue of loss and longing, prescribing them as the preconditions of sensibility. Somatic susceptibilities were praised for aesthetic and moral reasons. In Henry Mackenzie's symptomatic *The Man of Feeling* (1771), Harley's "notions of the καλον, or beautiful" center on a tear at a moving tale.[7] "Καλον" means both good and beautiful, and Harley's emphasis on beauty pinpoints the conflation of moral virtue with aestheticized tearfulness. Mackenzie's novel significantly provided the sentimental crying and fainting hero with a lasting epitaph. The man of feeling's tearful resistance to the ways of the world and his capacity to wallow in distress came to represent the standard virtues of sensibility.

Low or depressed spirits were clearly considered a virtue and an aesthetic asset at the time and, in the context of what cultural historians have termed a "nexus of genius and disease," a sign of intellectual superiority as well.[8] This association of illness with virtue was progressively cultivated in the eighteenth century and eventually culminated at the turn of the century only to be carefully reassessed in the aftermath of the sensibility cults. In 1733, George Cheyne wrote in *The English Malady* that it "is a common Observation (and, I think, has great Probability on its Side) that *Fools, weak* or *stupid* Persons, *heavy* and *dull Souls*, are seldom much troubled with Vapours or Lowness of Spirits."[9] Similarly linking great faculties and great suffering, Immanuel Kant remarked in his *Observations on the Feeling of the Beautiful and Sublime* (1764) that a "man of melancholy frame of mind cares little for what others judge, what they consider good or true; he relies in this matter simply on his own insight. . . . He is a strict judge of himself and others, and not seldom is weary of himself as of the world."[10] Frequently conflated, nostalgia as well as related psychophysical maladies such as melancholy and hypochondria were linked not only to high sensibility and virtuous weakness, but also to intellectual powers.[11] As late as the 1830s, A. T. Thomson emphasized that "it is frequently, although not always, in the highest and most cultivated persons that [nostalgia] displays itself.[12] By that time, however, the link between illness and virtue had considerably weakened. As the lower classes aspired to them, this "democratization" of nervous afflictions vulgarized them. They became increasingly the subject of satire. Mrs. Musgrove's famous "large fat sighings" in Jane Austen's *Persuasion* (1818) are evidence of the changing perceptions of sensibility's physical symptoms at the time, and I shall come back to Austen's redefinition of her heroines' sensible sensibility and the ways in which they contrast with the emotional displays of minor characters.[13]

It is indeed vital to note that by the mid-nineteenth century a new interest in physical and emotional firmness had replaced idealizations of weakness, at least as far as men were concerned. In addition, the definition of psychophysical afflictions radically changed, and treatments with them. In the early thirties, Thomson singled out nostalgia as an emotional state that was neither a form of insanity (like melancholy) nor a fanciful affectation (like hypochondria).[14] By contrast, at the height of the sensibility and sickness cults, John Hill asserted in his *Hypochondriasis* of 1766 that to call hypochondria "a fanciful malady, is ignorant and cruel."[15] He posited a causal connection between intellectual pursuits, nobility of mind, and a susceptibility to this ailment:

> The finer spirits are wasted by the labour of the brain.... Greatness of mind, and steady virtue; determined resolution, and manly firmness, when put in action, and intent upon their object, all also lead to it: perhaps whatever tends to the ennobling of the soul has equal share in bringing on this weakness of the body.... From this we may learn easily who are the men most subject to it; the grave and studious, those of a sedate temper and enlarged understanding, the learned and wise, the virtuous and the valiant.[16]

When Hill wrote of the "ennobling" of the "learned and wise," he emphatically underscored the bourgeois ideologies at work in idealizations of such "intellectual" maladies. While it had been in accordance with a classical tradition derived from Aristotle that melancholia and, to an extent also hypochondria, were seen as the occupational illnesses of genius in the Renaissance,[17] in the latter half of the eighteenth century psychophysical conditions that now included a much vaster range of newly coined maladies (such as nostalgia) were increasingly enlisted to indicate bourgeois refinement. As Robert Markley has shown, in the discourses of sentimentality, hypochondria was equated with moral sensitivity, and both combined to form "a half-willed performance, a theatrics of the bourgeois soul" aimed to underline the middle class's claim to moral self-promotion.[18] Positing an innate moral authority rendered visible by psychophysical ailments that were now increasingly traced to nervous complaints rather than to traditional humoralism, the discursive practices of sensibility allowed the middle classes to "outrefine" the aristocracy. These practices embraced a hierarchical social structure of sensibility and moral sentiment, but rendered it accessible to the studious, self-ennobling, socially rising, middle classes. In the process, they crucially redefined notions of the gentleman and, as a result, also emotional conditions and changing attitudes towards illness and medicine.[19]

Pioneering interdisciplinary works by George Rousseau, John Mullan, and Roy Porter have shown how this bourgeois promotion of a sensibility of the nerves manifested itself in literary and nonliterary genres, and how explorations of this intersection between medical and literary writing can prove enlightening.[20] The long neglected cults of sensibility and sentimentality stand revealed as vital developments that reflected and crucially contributed to the rise of the middle classes and conceptualizations of bourgeois ideologies, to developments in consumption and anxieties about luxury. They played a crucial part in the formation of new definitions of personal happiness and expressions of individuality, and they changed attitudes to emotional display. Porter has significantly pointed out the important connections between a new "sociology of illness" in which depression figured as "a life-style disorder" and the rise of consumer society.[21] As a new consumer culture created an atmosphere of cultural pluralism and artistic tolerance, the cultivation of sensibility and self-expression, and ultimately also a "new hedonism" that promoted the pursuit of *personal* pleasure became more acceptable.[22] Nostalgia as a personal longing was part of this invention, as it were, of individual happiness.

Throughout his extensive work on illness and medicine in the eighteenth and nineteenth centuries, Porter has influentially related newly developed medical theories to the exploration of feelings that became fashionable in the cults of sensibility and formed part of the Romantic cultivation of retrospection. In *Bodies Politic: Disease, Death and Doctors in Britain, 1650–1900*, he refers to a "Romantic connection between hypochondria and talent."[23] Not only was melancholy "a silver spoon or a pass-port to high places," as Porter has pointedly put it in an earlier study, it came to be seen as a *social* malaise that called for the Romantic reinstatement of solitude.[24] Accounts of nostalgia's history that argue for its complete "demedicalization" and its divorce from the set of psychophysical illnesses that included hypochondria and melancholy, seldom face the significance of this far more extensive shift in perceptions. The sociology of illness singled out conditions that were already questionable organic diseases at best and linked them to sensibility, bourgeois self-definition, and Romantic self-realization. What Porter has termed "new hedonism" not only sanctioned the right to individual happiness within the consumer society, but also the championing of individualism.[25] As psychophysical illnesses were diagnosed as indicators of sensibility, the promotion of personal happiness as a worthy goal linked them to idealizations of solitude and self-expression. Caused by society, Romantic melancholy essentially defined new experiences of individuality.

Against the background of this intriguing combination of Romantic individualism with moral aesthetics of affliction, nostalgia split into what have now become its two meanings: painful longing and wistful memory. In its emphasis on the refinement caused and evinced by distress, fiction of the time shuttled between these definitions. Their simultaneity has created nostalgia's flexibility, but also accounts for subsequent misunderstandings. Its developments can, in fact, only be understood in the contexts of late-eighteenth-century redefinitions of psychophysical illnesses. In the novel of sensibility, nostalgia is at once a physical pining that figures strongly in the genre's moralized aesthetics of affliction and a creative, personal, even curative memory that becomes increasingly important in the structuring of the narrative. In Elizabeth Inchbald's *A Simple Story* (1791), for example, high sensibility is praised and resentment emphatically counterpoised by a nostalgic forgiveness, but the nostalgic retrospect is also crucial to the novel's form. The sentimental reader is even invited to experience nostalgia in order to understand better that seventeen years have passed between volumes two and three. Everyone, the text suggests, can draw on a similar experience:

> Throughout life, there cannot happen an event to arrest the reflection of a thoughtful mind more powerfully, or to leave so lasting an impression, as that of returning to a place after a few years absence, and observing an entire alteration in respect to all the persons who once formed the neighbourhood.—To find some, who but a few years before were left in the bloom of youth and health, dead . . . —the firmest friends, changed to the most implacable enemies—beauty faded.—In a word, every change to demonstrate "All is transitory on this side of the grave." Actuated by a wish, that the reflective reader may experience the sensation, which an attention to circumstances such as these, must cause; he is desired to imagine seventeen years elapsed.[26]

Time has elapsed. The regretted changes point to the transitory nature of material things. The described nostalgia is a regretful longing for the past, but this temporal aspect is not all there is to the evoked (and not only described) longing. While the illusionary nature of expectations raised by nostalgia for a place—which Kant was to point out only a few years later[27]—is acknowledged as part of the nostalgic experience, nostalgia is also an emotion that testifies to the protagonists' sensibilities. This wistful longing directly appeals to the reader's emotional experience, evoked precisely in order to create an emotional response that links author, reader, and protagonists in a nexus of welcomed, physically experienced and enjoyed longing and the exquisite pain that is so crucial to the reading of sentimental novels. In thus triggering an emotional reaction in a reader of feeling, nostalgia fulfils the same function as other distresses in the fiction of the time, while it also operates as a good transition between the novel's parts.

The nostalgic's disillusionment does not at all detract from nostalgia's praiseworthiness, and similarly, nostalgia's often suggested loss of its spatial aspect never takes place.[28] On the contrary, it is precisely in the latter half of the eighteenth century that fictional spaces become emotionally charged, and that nostalgia for ideal spaces is minutely and also appreciatively described. Allworthy's Paradise Hall in Henry Fielding's *Tom Jones* (1749), for example, is an ideal estate, but not a nostalgic space. Tom Jones's picaresque journeys lead him back to discover his origins, but in his flamboyance he never finds time to indulge in homesickness. In Charlotte Smith's *The Old Manor House* (1793), by contrast, the uncertain fate of the house of the title culminates in the hero's at first cruelly disappointing homecoming. The deprivations Orlando undergoes during the war in America nourish his nostalgia for "all he had left, his Monimia, his family, the Hall, the rural happiness he had enjoyed in his native country," which are forcibly "in contrast to the wretchedness around him."[29] At his return, he encounters only "the spectre of departed happiness" (501). The nostalgic is disillusioned, but only temporarily. His persistent retracing of the remembered places eventually reclaims them. The novel ends by evoking a nostalgic "re-collection" of the past. Such a re-visioning of past spaces has revealingly made the enjoyment of the present as well as remembered happiness even more precious: "With what grateful transports did he now walk with Monimia over the park, and talk with her of their early pleasures and of their severe subsequent sufferings! And how sensible did these retrospects render them both of their present happiness!" (515). As we shall see in a more detailed reading of Smith's first novel, Emmeline in the eponymous story is likewise "greatly affected" when she has to leave the childhood home where she "had known, in that period of unconscious happiness, many delightful hours which would return no more."[30] Mary Hays's *Memoirs of Emma Courtney* (1796) contains an even more poignant contemplation of nostalgia's power. The heroine remembers the poignant sense of loss she felt at being forced to leave home:

> I wandered over the scenes of my past pleasures, and recalled to my remembrance, with a sad and tender luxury, a thousand little incidents, that derived all their importance from the impossibility of their renewal. I gazed on every object, *for the last time*—What is there in these words that awakens our fanaticism? I could have done homage to these inanimate, and, till now, uninteresting objects; merely because I should *see them no more*.[31]

What similarly changes at the time is the selection of nostalgic spaces. It becomes increasingly a matter of personal choice. The chosen home as a new idea begins to displace the straightforward reclaiming of inherited estates. In *Montalbert* (1795), also by Charlotte Smith, the heroine, Rosalie, dwells in nostalgia on a happy childhood away from "home:" "Those were my days of unalloyed felicity; it was my golden age, and every scene has imprinted itself deeply on my memory."[32] Anticipating Austen's Fanny Price in *Mansfield Park* (1814) by almost twenty years, Rosalie is an exile in her parents' house, "a cypher [sic] at home; and rather suffered as one of the family, than seeming to make a part of it" (16). Nostalgia for her childhood and a childhood home becomes the foundation of her love for Montalbert: "I perfectly remember you, and the days I once passed with you at Holmwood made an impression on me that never will be effaced. It has ever appeared to me since the very happiest period of the happy hours of my childhood." (49) Expectedly, Rosalie and Montalbert contrast decisively with their heartless relations, who fail to understand the virtues of longing and remembrance. Before I look at the importance of personally chosen homes and ways of being happy in more detail, I shall analyze the fascinating variety of nostalgia's different representations as an affliction and an asset in late-eighteenth-century novels. It is significant to note what idealizations of longing mean in the contexts of the gender split that occurred at that time and the ongoing revisions of the sensibility cults. I shall start with a short novel by Charles Lamb that idealizes virtuous distress and wistful remembrances of the past. It is a straightforward example of the twofold sentimental use of nostalgia and thus forms a summary of its virtues as well as a good point of entrance to its further discussion.

These Petty Topics of Endeared Remembrance: Lamb's *Rosamund Gray*

In *Rosamund Gray* (1798), a short novel by the poet and essayist Charles Lamb, nostalgia and melancholy are the prerogatives of the innocent. The relatively short tale lists a plethora of losses, and nostalgic retrospection shapes its framestories, while it also forms a central theme. In the course of his narration, the unnamed first person narrator loses his bosom friend, with whom he is reunited in a tearful scene of sentimental restitution; the village of his childhood, which he revisits twice in the text; and his parents. He is not the only orphan in the novel. The grief of Allan and Elinor Clare, the bosom friend and his sister, underlines the relationship between the siblings, which denotes the death of motherly Elinor as another parental loss. In addition, Rosamund and her blind grandmother display a simplicity that invites distress. The villain, Matravis, by contrast, is "cold and systematic in all his plans," a calculating man of the world.[33] His rape of Rosamund is not the result of uncontrolled passion: his "very lust was systematic" (97). But it is his rejection of nostalgic remembrance, even more than his general lack of sensibility that condemns him: "O ye *Matravises* of the age, ye know not what ye lose, in despising these petty topics of endeared remembrance, associated circumstances of past times" (79). The incapability to experience nostalgia marks the callous villain.

Nostalgia, however, is central to the novel's structure as well as to its interrelated stories. A regretful and wistful remembrance of the past opens the narrative and indeed suffuses it as the narrator counts his friends' and his own losses. He embraces his feelings of loss and longing, nurturing a wistful memory that distinguishes him from the obtuse villain. The parents of orphaned Rosamund "had once known better days:" Their story, "their failure, their folly, and distresses, may be told another time. Our tale hath grief enough in it" (6–7). It is a tale of loss. After a brief description of old blind Margaret and her granddaughter and the growing love of Allan and Rosamund, death, rape, and sickness disrupt their happiness. Matravis rapes Rosamund; Margaret dies the same night; the raped and bereaved girl falls into a stupor and slowly dwindles away, dissolving into tears and incoherence in the style of Ophelia, predictably ending in an early death.[34] Her body articulates the unspeakable: "She expired in the arms of Elinor—quiet, gentle, as she lived . . . expressing by signs, rather than words, [her] gratitude" (13). The narrator's general nostalgia for the idyllic village and his own childhood subsumes her retrospectively rehearsed story.

When raped Rosamund pines away, affliction is expectedly idealized. Dwindling away is the only way out for the abandoned heroine. The prototype of the fading maiden in English fiction is of course Samuel Richardson's Clarissa in the eponymous novel (1747–48). The gradual wasting away of the heroine may be presented as shocking, but it is nonetheless endorsed by the text that edits her written self and embodies a textual witness of the dissolution of her body.[35] Claudia Johnson has significantly shown that the death of raped as well as seduced women is an important cliché of conservative sentimental fiction,[36] but Rosamund almost grotesquely abides by the sentimental cult of melancholy and the ideal of a delicately feeble heroine to the extent that her pensive fondness for affliction precedes her actual suffering. She is "grave or melancholy," rebuked by her grandmother who delivers "sprightly lectures about good humour and rational mirth," even though "to the great discredit of her lecture," she tends to "fall a crying herself" (13). These tears "endear . . . her the more to Rosamund" (13). The "pensive and reflective" heroine, in fact, embodies the moral and aesthetic beauty of a persistent depression (12–13). Rosamund is "the most beautiful young creature that eyes ever beheld. . . . There was a sort of melancholy mingled in her smile" (13). Not only is suffering a sign of virtue and excessive sensibility a putative ailment that is fashionable and enviable, its bodily effects are attractive. In any case, the nostalgic's "love of quietness and lonely thinking" (112) is clearly exemplary. While death is the only solution for this abandoned woman, her story serves to provide food for the melancholy contemplations of those who remain behind and notably of the voyeuristic narrator. Without a melancholy history of his own, he feeds on her death. The tale of Rosamund's affliction is framed by his nostalgia for "that *State of Innocence*" of his childhood, a state symbolized by the virtuously dead woman. Memories of Rosamund lead him to the churchyard, where he can seek solitude and indulge in remembrance:

> I prayed, that I might be restored to that *State of Innocence*, in which I had wandered in those shades. Methought, my request was heard—for it seemed, as though the stains of manhood were passing from me, and I were relapsing into the purity and simplicity of childhood. I was content to have been moulded into a perfect child. I stood still, as in a trance. (113)

Driven by "a strong desire to revisit the scenes of [his] native village—of the young Loves of Rosamund and her Clare," he returns to the places of the past where "the memory of old times [becomes] vivid, and more vivid" (108). This regression or "relapsing" constitutes a nostalgic celebration of the past. The return to idealized bygones has a purging effect: it cleanses the returned narrator from the "stains of manhood" (113). Adjectives describing the restoration of perfection ("restored," "content," "perfect") abound. This sentimental topos of childhood's purity exemplifies what Peter Coveney has influentially termed the Romantic child, an embodiment of "original innocence" that prevails in (pre-) Romantic literature. Such versions of the child-figure are nostalgic idealizations.[37] In Lamb's text, the narrator revealingly longs to be "moulded into a *perfect* child [italics added]" (113). His nostalgic return creates a *perfected* past. The re-enactment is entrancing, channeled through remembered music: "Past associations revived with the music—blended with a sense of *unreality*, which at last became too powerful" (110). The "mysterious charm" of the place's "glooms and its solitude" nurtures a "love of quietness and lonely thinking" (111–12). Yet the narrator also rather flippantly refers to retrospective idealization. He articulates his musings in the churchyard in a curiously tongue-in-cheek way: with "that kind of levity, which will not infrequently spring up in the mind, in the midst of deep melancholy" (116). The language of cultivated sensibility collapses into a self-ironic analysis of the gravestones' "pious" sentimentalization of the past:

> I read of nothing but careful parents, loving husbands, and dutiful children. I said jestingly, where be all the bad people buried? Bad parents, bad husbands, bad children—what cemeteries are appointed for these? . . . Or is it but a pious fiction, a generous oversight, in the survivors, which thus tricks our men's epitaphs when dead? (116–17)

The self-irony that permeates expressions of longing is perhaps the most intriguing aspect of eighteenth-century sentimentalism.[38] Parodies range from the contrast between romances and novels that is central to Charlotte Lennox's early self-reflexive novel, *The Female Quixote* (1752), to the redefined Gothic of Jane Austen's *Northanger Abbey*, published posthumously in 1818 but written in the 1790s. Repeatedly and emphatically, protagonists, situations, and sensibilities are not as they are in romances or "other novels." Arabella, Lennox's female quixote, grows up with the fictional heroes and heroines of romances. She embarrassingly mistakes fiction for accurate histories. As B. S. Hammond has put it in an article on quixotism in eighteenth-century literature, to write prose fiction after 1750 was "to be involved in an enterprise that was increasingly self-aware."[39] The horrors Catherine Morland encounters in *Northanger Abbey* are not those Gothic novels have led her to expect, though critics have stressed that the terror she is subjected to in fashionable society is no less menacing.[40] Most importantly, sensible sensibility tends to be even stronger than the censured or parodied pretentious emotional exhibitionism, and thus far from diminished by too much sense. In Frances Burney's *The Wanderer* (1814), for example, Aurora's sensibility is "not of that weak romantic cast, formed by early and futile love-sick reading, either in novels or poems."[41] A close look at the functions of nostalgia will not only highlight the ambiguities of works that appear to subscribe fully to the cult of exquisite sensibility, but also the role of longing in novels that critically explore sentimentalism. Their treatment of longing casts a different light on the changing ideals of sentimentalism, its manners, and mannerisms.

Longing and the Pale Blushing Hero

On one of her romantic rambles through the picturesque countryside the heroine of *Emmeline; or, The Orphan of the Castle* (1788), the first novel by the prolific novelist Charlotte Smith, encounters an interesting stranger. This frail, pale young girl, Adelina, has been abandoned by one of the libertines who so numerously populate the novel. She turns out to be the sister of Emmeline's future lover, who is thus, at the end of the second volume, mentioned for the first time and only makes his appearance in the third volume. *Emmeline* contains an intriguing engagement with both love- and homesickness and moreover with a series of desirable men of feeling, anticipating such contrasts as that between Willoughby and Colonel Brandon in Jane Austen's *Sense and Sensibility* (1811), perhaps the canonized parody of novels of sensibility, although Emmeline's Godolphin is of course not as demure as the Colonel. By creating a hero who is both manly and full of sensibility, Smith's novel, in fact, attempts to solve anxieties about effeminacy that frequently accompany idealizations of male pining. In many novels of the time, in fact, the distress of their female protagonists conforms to sentimental aesthetics of affliction, while a prevailing association of sensibility with femininity complicates the heroes' emotional expressions.

The emerging field of masculinity studies has revealingly found the eighteenth century a particularly fruitful point of entry. Michel Foucault's work on sexuality and power has been an important impetus for cultural historians who see both sexuality and gender as discursively constituted and have detected crucial shifts in their definition in the eighteenth century. John Tosh and Michael Roper have been actively trying to promote a new field of "men's studies," but Thomas Laqueur's work on sexuality, Eve Kosofsky Sedgwick's on the representation of the homosexual and the homosocial, and work on the redefinition of the gentleman and on the anxieties about effeminacy generated by a new consumerism in the eighteenth century more generally have likewise been crucial for this reassessment of men's roles. George Haggerty's recent *Men in Love: Masculinity and Sexuality in the Eighteenth Century*, Claudia Johnson's *Equivocal Beings: Politics, Gender, and Sentimentality in the 1790s*, and Michele Cohen's *Fashioning Masculinity: National Identity and Language in the Eighteenth Century* have made important contributions to a historical view of masculinity and its indeterminacies. As Haggerty puts it, the "very notion of 'masculine' and 'feminine' were sites of cultural conflict throughout the century," as "only gradually did 'feminine' behavior become the exclusive domain of the female."[42]

In *The Culture of Sensibility: Sex and Society in Eighteenth-Century Britain*, G. J. Barker-Benfield has influentially linked the new fashion for "luxury" goods that formed an important result of the consumer revolution to the luxury of feeling of the eighteenth-century culture of sensibility. It was basic, Barker-Benfield emphasizes, "to the consumer psychology the polite and commercial economy required."[43] Such new investigations of the representation of gender and gender alignments importantly modify interpretations that see sentimental men of feeling as nothing more than voyeurs, as Mackenzie's Harley and Sterne's Yorick, or as we have seen, also the vicarious voyeur in Rosamund Gray undoubtedly are.[44] Not only are men in women's fiction the subject of a female voyeurism, but more importantly, aestheticized male feebleness complicates gender alignments. Novels of sensibility exploit and foster this indeterminacy. As Patricia Meyer Spacks has put it in her study *Desire and Truth: Functions of Plot in Eighteenth-Century English Novels*, gender terms loom large in eighteenth-century discourse, and they underlie the action of many novels.[45]

Lovesick pining and nostalgic longing for lost happiness are closely linked in novels of sensibility, and they both generate psychophysical symptoms. Adelina's physical delicacy sentimentalizes her moral frailty by accentuating the somatic signs of her distress, marking her out as beautiful and interesting: "If it were possible to personify languor and dejection, it could not be done more expressively than by representing her form, her air, her complexion, and the mournful cast of her very beautiful countenance" (220). As in most novels of sensibility, the good characters, men and women alike, suffer acutely from unconsummated desire. They succumb to physical pining with all its beautifying paraphernalia such as pallor and delicacy. But while the representation of male and female displays of high sensitivity is continuously reassessed in the fiction of the time, the ways in which they are remodeled differ crucially. While the heroines ultimately arrive at a sensible sensibility as they endeavor to balance moral delicacy with emotional susceptibility, their heroes have to conform to an increasingly gendered sensibility without becoming effeminate. At the same time, the ideal sentimental hero also often stands in as a "home" for the distressed, frequently homeless and homesick, heroine. To qualify, heroes have to unite a promise of stability, an ability to take care of their heroines, with an adequate sensibility that makes them interesting as well.

Emmeline is a particularly revealing novel, as the heroine's homesickness is central to the plot. It is only in the course of the third volume that her love for a suitable hero complements her nostalgia for her home and her longing to know her origins. Even though courtship and inheritance plots often involve searches and longings for (a) home, this emphasis on nostalgia and a comparative neglect of a central love-interest stands out. The novel opens with the heroine's enforced dislocation from her childhood home. The fate of Mowbray Castle and Emmeline's questionable legitimacy are closely connected. An orphan, she has been brought up by servants in a castle that begins to be sadly in need of restoration. Remote from society, "the innocent Emmeline," "the last of the race of [the] ancient benefactors" (289), enjoys a happy childhood, only vaguely overshadowed by the mystery of her birth. Having to leave Mowbray Castle when it is taken over by greedy relatives, Emmeline is "greatly affected.... There she had passed her earliest infancy, and had known, in that period of unconscious happiness, many delightful hours which would return no more" (42). Alone in her nostalgia, she is not only deprived of her home, but practically disowned by her relatives, whose doubt of her legitimacy ostracizes her. As "a being belonging to nobody" (10), Emmeline is thrust into what is, in sentimental fashion, termed "the cruel, unfeeling world" (285). Her afflictions and longings contrast with the insensitivity of more worldly characters. Her uncle's feelings have been "blunted by having never suffered in his own person any uneasiness which might have taught him sensibility for that of others," which explains, if not excuses, "the apathy which prosperity had taught him" (22). As in most sentimental novels, prosperity and lack of distress desensitize, but ultimately, and perhaps rather incongruously, a reclaimed fortune is the reward of the virtuously distressed after all.

Marriage to a man of feeling who restores her inheritance and helps to reassert her legitimacy doubly ensures Emmeline's domestic happiness. The active help he renders her in reclaiming her childhood home further underscores the nostalgic plot, but it also singles him out as one of the most perfect heroes in late-eighteenth-century fiction. Since many women writers at the time preferred to create faulty, though redeemable, and also endearingly weak heroes, as a manly man of feeling who is practical and sensitive, Emmeline's Godolphin is almost an anomaly. This sensitive, but practical, hero boosts his eligibility by displaying his personal qualities and by re-establishing the heroine's claims to belong to men and women of quality. He shares her "silent admiration" of sublime scenery and "the pleasure it gave her, [mingled with] a soft and melancholy sensation" (366). Yet Godolphin's appreciation of longing and low spirits does not reduce him to displays of "the melancholy of the market-place."[46] In contrast to the majority of pale heroes of late-eighteenth-century fiction, he is even unfashionably weather-beaten. He "had passed the greatest part of his life at sea. The various climates he had visited had deprived his complexion of much of its English freshness.... His whole figure was such as brought to the mind ideas of the race of heroes from which he was descended" (289). He conforms to an older ideal, one that is more reminiscent of romances than of realist fiction.

The novel indeed carefully prepares for his introduction. In its search for an ideal hero, it offers an interesting panorama of men and their expression of love and longing, before it settles for a nostalgically recalled romantic hero. As her alleged illegitimacy obscures her social status, Emmeline's would-be suitors can even stretch across class divides: they include the impudent steward Malony, the dull tradesman Rochely, the pretentious would-be man of fashion Elkerton, and the foppish Chevalier Bellozane as well as her cousin, Delamere, to whom she at one point even becomes engaged. As Godolphin does not appear before the third volume, the displacement of Delamere is an intriguing shattering of expectations. Although the latter has been called a "threateningly odious suitor [who] has about him an incestuous air of familiarity,"[47] he is a believable hero. He is not more violent in his afflictions than Mr. B. in Samuel Richardson's *Pamela* (1740), Faulkland in Frances Sheridan's *Sidney Bidulph* (1761), or Werther in Goethe's *The Sorrows of Young Werther* (1774), whose fate he discusses with Emmeline: "You might have learned the danger of trifling with violent and incurable passions" (184). His "violent passion" (302) and "ardent and impetuous temper" (25), however, are not sufficiently tempered by the graces of the man of feeling. Weather-beaten Godolphin may be descended from a "race of heroes," but most heroes in novels by women writers at the time are more indebted to the sentimental antiheroes created by Sterne and Mackenzie. To maintain a careful balance between extremes, the novel lashes out with equal vehemence at insensitivity and aggressive emotionalism. A compromise, Godolphin is "a fortunate compound of the insinuating softness of Fitz-Edward [Adelina's seducer] with the fire and vivacity of Delamere" (389). Godolphin's complexion is, in fact, apologized for rather than praised. The heroine's longing for a manly hero that can rescue her tends to conflict with the attractiveness of a languishing hero of hypersensitivity.

Despite these ambiguities, novels of sensibility continue to cultivate ailments associated with extreme susceptibility. As beautifully distressed heroines and heroes prove popular protagonists, it remains both virtuous and becoming to be prone to physical debility. Smith's Emmeline is physically affected by any emotional disturbance: "Her sensibility of mind was so great, that when she suffered any poignant uneasiness, it immediately affected her frame" (125). Althea in Smith's *Marchmont* (1796) is similarly "always delicate and interesting."[48] "[It is] your misfortune to have too much sensibility to be happy," Arabella writes to Emily in Frances Brooke's *Emily Montague* (1769). Emily's "elegant form has an air of softness and languor, which seizes the whole soul in a moment."[49] This idealization of physical delicacy is not at all confined to women. In *The Excursion* (1777), also by Brooke, the desirable hero, Charles Montague, has suffered from an illness brought on by lovesickness that leaves "a paleness which rendered his countenance, if possible, more interesting than ever."[50] His beauty-enhancing pallor exemplifies the eroticization of the delicate, tearful man of feeling, as women writers at the turn of the century redeploy sentimental anti-heroes as desirable romantic heroes.

This reconfiguration of the man of feeling engenders a plenitude of frail, pale heroes who swoon, weep freely, blush exuberantly, and proudly nurture "feminine" susceptibilities. The physical frailty of desirable heroes excuses even their moral fallibility as long as they "take hysterically to their beds," as Claudia Johnson puts it in her analysis of emasculated avuncular figures in Frances Burney's *Camilla*.[51] Reformed rakes deploy similar strategies. In *Emmeline*, Adelina's seducer, Fitz-Edward, who "contracted his loose morals by being thrown too early into the world" (33), pines in remorseful lovesickness. Returning "thin, pale, emaciated, looking as if he were unhappy" (518), redeems him. Such rewarded weakness is eerily reminiscent of Richardson's Lovelace, who deliberately makes himself ill by taking "a few grains of ipecacuanha; enough to make [him] retch like a fury" to impel Clarissa's sympathy. She falls into the trap: "One cannot, my dear, hate people in danger of death, or who are in distress or affliction."[52]

The reaffirmed men of sensibility, however, are frequently "pale" heroes in that they are literary types, stylized Grandisonian figures, redeemed Lovelaces, or men of tears in the style of Mackenzie's Harley in the tellingly titled *The Man of Feeling*, though with his childishness stripped off and instead invested with erotic possibilities. Gerard A. Barker has shown the influential role of the exemplary hero of Richardson's *Sir Charles Grandison* (1753–54) as "a viable prototype for the idealized hero."[53] Grandison, Barker rightly points out, "seemed tailor-made to fit the needs of the burgeoning feminine novel," yet his analysis is misleading when he calls him "the prototype for the gentle, sensitive, but *manly* hero [italics added]."[54] More to the point, John Mullan speaks of the "strange status of virtuous masculinity" in the novel, suggesting that after Richardson had "gendered sensibility" in *Pamela* and *Clarissa*, he set out to create a paragon of virtue who functions as a "locus of all feminine aspirations."[55] This project to rehabilitate male sensibility becomes central in novels by women writers, whose heroes unite, or tragically fail to unite, masculinity and sensitivity. Evelina, the heroine of Burney's first novel, eulogizes Lord Orville's feminine delicacy: "So steady did I think his honour, so *feminine* his delicacy, and so amiable his nature!"[56] Counterpoising his feminine qualities with "a countenance open, manly, and charming," and without "an air of vanity or impertinence" (281), he is indeed "all that is amiable in man" without lapsing into effeminacy, nor into the "unmanly" behavior of brutes (312).

The tearful, lovesick, and longing hero's attractiveness and the sentimental conflation of tearfulness with virtue continue to complicate the creation of an ideal man of sensibility. In Inchbald's *A Simple Story*, the reader is cautioned not to interpret Lord Elmwood's apparent coldness as a sign that he is not duly affected by the death of his estranged wife: "Nor let the vociferous mourner, or the perpetual weeper, here complain of his want of sensibility—but let them remember Lord Elmwood was a man—a man of understanding" (178). Yet even "the perpetual weeper" is quickly reassured that Elmwood (the gentle Dorriforth of the novel's first half) is still, though outwardly indifferent, a man of feeling. The novel proceeds to detail his trembling hands, how "he once or twice wiped the tears from his eyes," and that eventually "the tears flowed fast down his face" (184). Despite his long-suppressed tears, "manly" Lord Elmwood still contrasts unfavorably with the boyish Rushbrook, who even outdoes Matilda, Elmwood's sensitive daughter, in torrents of tears and symptoms of lovesick pining. Even though she wastes away in her physical nostalgia for her father's house, Matilda "possessed too much of the manly resentment of her father" (224). This characterization neatly foregrounds the gendering of emotions. Elmwood's resentment stems from a high, though aggressive, sensibility, and is indeed in sharp contrast to Rushbrook's attempts to implore his forgiveness. When "a shower of tears" covers the young man's face (90) during their quarrel, an old priest intervenes, declaring that "he is but a boy" (81), whereupon Rushbrook, far from resenting this description, throws "himself upon his neck, where he indeed sobbed like a boy" (85). Not only boyish, but "feminine" in his sensibility, Rushbrook joins Matilda and her mother as well as countless other eighteenth-century sentimental protagonists (most of them admittedly female) in the list of physically pining characters. Conforming to eighteenth-century nosologies, his lovesickness develops into a high fever:

> Rushbrook suffered so poignant an uncertainty, that he became at length ill, and before the end of the week which his uncle [Lord Elmwood] had allotted him for his reply, he was confined to his bed in a high fever. . . . Divided between the claims of obligation to the father, and tender attachment to the daughter, his sickness was increased by the tortures of his mind, and he once sincerely wished for that death, of which he was in danger, to free him from the dilemma into which his affections had involved him. (220)

Rushbrook's physical delicacy, though laudable, prevents him from taking up a very heroic role. When a licentious lord abducts Matilda, her suddenly repenting father rescues her, while Rushbrook is ordered to stay at home. He dutifully, and not very heroically, obeys. When Elmwood allows them to marry, Matilda finds this lovesick antihero "with his head reclined against a book case, and every limb extended with the despair that had seized him" (293). Needless to say, Matilda does not sentence this irresistible lovesick man of feeling to misery. In cultivating melancholy, tearful, and lovesick (anti-) heroes as desirable romantic heroes, novels of the 1790s, predominantly written by women, develop new ideals of male sensibility and of literary heroes, but also reflect concerns with "proper" manliness that seem to be part and parcel of men's expressions of longing.

The propagation of male hypersensitivity and sentimentality perhaps expectedly leads to fears of effeminacy. In *The Theory of Moral Sentiments* (1759), Adam Smith articulated this cultural anxiety when he wrote that "the delicate sensibility required in civilized nations sometimes destroys the masculine firmness of character."[57] In his *Anthropology*, Kant expressed similar concern with the effeminacy of certain emotions and particularly those that result in tears. Laughing is masculine, he suggested, while weeping is "feminine (effeminate in the case of men)."[58] In its idealization of torrents of tears, shed companionably by heroes and heroines, the late-eighteenth-century novel of sensibility of course writes against the grain of such alignments. Intriguingly, this egalitarian "feminization" of the hero has led feminist critics to remark that the cult of sensibility disrupts gender codes, "leaving women without a distinct gender site."[59] Novels of sensibility grant equal rights to aestheticized affliction. This equality does not necessarily imply that the ideal pale blushing hero is emasculated, nor that he violently usurps domestic space by becoming feminized or domesticated, though it is his "feminine" occupations such as crying and sitting in boudoirs that the parodied effeminate antihero becomes notorious for.

In Austen's last finished novel, *Persuasion*, the privilege Anne Elliot claims for her own sex "is that of loving longest, when existence or when hope is gone" (235). Her desirable hero vehemently disputes this privilege, asserting equal rights to suffer from nostalgia. His ability to combine the masculinity of a rising naval officer with expressions of lovesick nostalgia in the most Romantic novel by an author famous for her dissections of sensibility forms the culmination of such explorations of male expressions of lovesick pining. He is neither a weak pining creature nor a passionately ranting hero in love with his own fervor to the point of suicide, nor is he one of those particularly dull monitor figures that become eligible in the conservative plots of anti-Jacobin writers. In Mary Brunton's unfinished *Emmeline* (1819), a heavily moralized story of a divorced wife's second marriage, for example, the deserted husband is a good, but dull, supportive, but moralizing, and significantly marginal character.[60] The most active and also most obnoxious monitor figure in earlier fiction is perhaps Edgar Mandlebert in Burney's *Camilla* (1796), who indeed tracks the heroine's every move. When he temporarily loses sight of her, he only discovers her on her lonely sickbed. Harleigh in *The Wanderer* (1814) closely resembles Edgar, but his inability to help the heroine, of whose problems he indeed knows nothing, only makes his repeated intrusions oppressive. As Claudia Johnson has said of Austen's Mr. Knightley, he "is not nearly so wise and all seeing as he appears to think."[61] In Austen's novels, would-be monitor figures such as Edmund Bertram or Mr. Knightley are always also at fault themselves. As in Burney's fiction, the main interest rests emphatically on the heroines. At what occasions "lovely Man" should dwindle away and when to exert himself becomes a marginal concern. In *Persuasion*, however, Wentworth's countenance and his change of color—at one point "he looked quite red" (175)—become significant once more, as the heroine tries to trace his remembrance of the past and the revival of their past love.[62] The most desirable heroes of late-eighteenth- and early-nineteenth-century novels are, in fact, praised for their longings, while they are also the strong object of the heroines' cherished lovesickness. The conception of the lovesick hero is then doubly created by nostalgia.

With What Delight Do I Recall:
Frances Sheridan's *Sidney Bidulph*

Frances Sheridan's *Memoirs of Miss Sidney Bidulph* is a remarkable novel in many respects. A retrospective and primarily very sad story about distressed virtue that is never rewarded, it is also very funny. Its lively heroine is virtuous and, unfortunately for her, dutiful without being dull. Written with the purpose to expose poetic justice as a sentimental fallacy, the novel anticipates Austen's *Persuasion* in showing how a heroine of feeling is condemned to unhappiness because she has been persuaded into prudence. While most eighteenth-century heroines are either punished for their imprudence (like Miss Milner in *A Simple Story*) or rewarded for their suffering (like Matilda, Miss Milner's daughter or double), Sidney is "punished" for being dutiful. Even while virtue under attack is a topos or, as Brissenden has put it, cliché of the novel of sensibility,[63] virtuous heroines are commonly recompensed at least at the end of the novel. Sheridan outdoes Richardson in his rewriting of *Pamela*'s theme of "virtue rewarded" by showing how a dutiful daughter is denied a happy end because she has renounced the attractive suitor and married the Mr. Solmes of the book instead. Her virtue "to all human appearance, *ought* at last to have been rewarded even here—but her portion was affliction."[64] Yet far from feeling resentment, Sidney indulges a nostalgia that prevents her stoic resignation from lapsing into unfeeling indifference. This treatment of nostalgia as an antidote to resentment requires a partial "demedicalization." Published in 1761, *Sidney Bidulph* predates the rewritings of pining heroines that take place in the novels of Burney and Austen and is therefore an intriguing early example of a novel that treats nostalgia as an emotionally restructured form of memory divorced from its somatic symptoms.

Sidney's "memoirs" are presented as a retrospectively collected journal composed of nostalgically preserved letters to a childhood friend. The rewriting and rereading of repeated reflections on the past and the effects of the past on the present are both a central theme and a structuring pattern. In her article on "Frances Sheridan: Morality and Annihilated Time," Margaret Anne Doody has suggested that the novel's "most signal quality is its reiterated presence of the past."[65] But it is not so much the past *per se* that conditions the present, but the persistent rereading and rewriting of the events and the emotions of the past. Dated fifty-eight years before its publication, Sidney's journal, as well as the copies of letters enclosed in it, has already undergone a selective process: Cecilia has copied only a part of them and arranged them in a continuous narrative. The "editor" admires their pathos and decides to publish them for the edification, or tearful enjoyment, of a sentimental readership. This emphasis on the "re-collection" of the past underwrites the novel's preoccupation with memory as well as with (mis-) representations.

A displaced letter forms the missing link in the novel's juxtaposition of representations and interpretations. Deliberately concealed from Sidney at the time, it is dramatically revealed to the reader only when she discovers it: "Read it, and see by what a fatality we have been governed" (57). Sidney comes across this repeatedly misquoted letter after she has undergone a series of afflictions and losses; this discovery caps her distress: "My heart must, upon this full conviction of Mr. Faulkland's honour, sigh at recollecting the past" (340). Faulkland is the fallible Grandisonian hero who is vilified as a Lovelace because his letters tend to fall into the wrong hands. A dismissed footman steals a compromising letter, written by a Miss Burchell to Faulkland, and uses it to blacken his reputation. While the journal quotes this letter at an early stage, Sidney's over-fastidious mother conceals Faulkland's explanations of his one-night encounter with the lusty Miss Burchell, "a sly rake in petticoats" (387). When his letter is revealed, it is too late to counteract her misrepresentations. The consequent revision of the past is essentially a retrospective and regretful enterprise, in which nostalgia ultimately manages to counteract resentment.

In rewriting the familiar plot-patterns of the villainous seducer, the innocent victim, and the death of the disappointed heroine, the novel effectively dismantles literary expectations without becoming a parody. Faulkland is not so much a reformed rake as a misunderstood one. "Made up of contrarieties," he is neither a Grandison nor a Lovelace, though he can only be one or the other in the rigid imagination of Sidney's literal-minded mother, of whom even her all too dutiful daughter remarks that, "as you know she is not extremely penetrating, and in general, but a superficial observer" (325).[66] Sidney's "full conviction of Mr. Faulkland's honour" (340) is helped by the vices of her ostensibly staid husband. The Mr. Solmes of the book, Mr. Arnold is the literary type of the dull, narrow-minded, conservative suitor. Compared to this epitome of boredom, it is Faulkland's passionate lovesickness that redeems him, setting him up not only as a dedicated man of feeling who shares the fate of Goethe's Werther, but also as a desirable hero, whose loss is nostalgically commemorated. In Charlotte Smith's *Desmond*, unhappily married Geraldine compares her fate to that of "poor Sidney" and bewails her own lack of such a disinterested supporter: "Perhaps there is a little similarity in our destinies—But *I* have *no Faulkland!*" (320) Needless to say, she finds one in the titular hero, Desmond, whose fate parallels that of Faulkland, but eventually comes to a happier end, thus reinstating the sentimental plot critiqued in *Sidney Bidulph*. Faulkland eventually commits suicide, leaving Sidney to her virtuous distress.

One of the most remarkable features of Sheridan's novel is the exposure of the stereotype of the seduced woman. Miss Burchell is Faulkland's seducer, but claims to be his victim. This is of course a much more believable role for a young, attractive female in a sentimental novel. When Sidney finally puts the question to Miss Burchell whether "Mr. Faulkland [has] been just in his representations" (304), she freely admits that it was her own lust that made her throw herself at him. A misrepresentation that abides by the familiar structures of a sentimental seduction-plot, however, has already supplanted Faulkland's letter: Miss Burchell has presented Lady Bidulph with the story she expects and wishes to read. The abandoned woman has her role thrust on her and simply proceeds to conform to the desired narrative pattern: "She led me into a justification of myself, so great were her prejudices against Mr. Faulkland. Or, perhaps, having already disposed of you [Sidney] in marriage, in vindication of this step, she did not wish to be undeceived" (307). As Sidney puts it, her mother "has a sort of partiality to her own sex, and where there is the least room for it, throws the whole of the blame upon the man's side; who, from her own early prepossessions, she is always inclined to think are deceivers of women" (112). Sidney's brother George, Faulkland's best friend, has also slept with the promiscuous Miss Burchell and consequently "laughs exceedingly" at Lady Bidulph's plan to "protect" this putatively victimized seducer of men: "He says his mother ought not to be surprised at Faulkland's falling into the girl's snares, since she herself has done the same; but he supposes my mother thinks she is doing a very meritorious action, in affording an asylum to this injured innocence" (50). The novel expectedly forms an intriguing challenge to feminist scholars. Pointing out that Miss Burchill reinvents herself as a recognizable cliché, Doody has even suggested that Sheridan "has, in what looks like a feminist novel, taken us beyond feminism."[67] The dismantling of newly formed literary clichés is without doubt the novel's most intriguing aspect. It emphasizes incongruities precisely to expose the distorted nature of more straightforward plots and more easily recognizable villains and victims.

However, even while Miss Burchell deliberately exploits prejudices, Lady Bidulph does not so much rely on general clichés—though they nicely reinforce her bias—but on her own unhappy experience. We are told that the "memory of [her] own first disastrous love wrought strongly on her mind" (340). When Miss Burchell's letter shatters her ideal picture of the eligible Faulkland, Lady Bidulph is forcefully reminded of the letter that wrecked her own happiness. At her first wedding day, a letter arrived instead of the groom, in which he presented a prior engagement in a most melodramatic style. This pathetic epistle was "so expressive of a mind overwhelmed with despair, that [she] was exceedingly shocked at the reading of it" (31). Created by the personal resentment of one man, her bias imposes a specific interpretation on another's attempts to vindicate himself: "I own I had not patience to read [Faulkland's] letter through. To say the truth I but run my eye in a cursory manner over it; I was afraid of meeting, at every line something offensive to decency" (45). Lady Bidulph's resentment and the ways in which it interferes with her daughter's happiness highlight the past's governing influence and the importance of a more forgiving and comforting way of remembering.

Her mother's obsession with past wrongs counteracts Sidney's loyalty, but ultimately it is Sidney's nostalgia that prevents her from succumbing to resentment. Nostalgia, in fact, pervades the novel, and it is a comforting rather than a painful emotion. While Sidney bears her loveless marriage with stoic resignation, she indulges in recollections of her childhood: "With what delight do I recall the days of my childhood, which I passed here so happily! You, my dear Cecilia, mix yourself in all my thoughts; every spot almost brings you fresh into my memory." (265–66) Perceptively diagnosing the mixture of pain and pleasure inherent to nostalgia, Sidney embraces them as "exquisite" feelings: "Oh, Cecilia! How exquisite are the pleasures and the pains that those of too nice feelings are liable to!" (266). While her strict sense of virtue prevents her from expressing regret over having married the wrong man, she freely bewails the loss of her maiden name. To the friend of her youth, Cecilia, she writes:

> Our names, our virgin names, I find cut out on several off the old elm trees: this conjures up a thousand pleasing ideas, and brings back those days when we were inseparable. But you are no longer Rivers, nor I Bidulph. Then I think what I have suffered since I lost that name, and at how remote a distance you are from me; and I weep like a child. (266)

In *Sidney Bidulph*, nostalgia is a longing for the past and for unrealized possibilities, a cause of virtuously shed tears, and an emotion unconnected to somatic symptoms. In this, the novel stands out among novels of sensibility. The illness Sidney succumbs to early in the novel significantly precedes her "disappointment" and is the result of a cold that develops into "an ugly sore throat" (35). It is only during her recovery that she hears of a scandal involving her fiancé. Although her mother expresses concern that her health might be endangered by the discovery of Faulkland's "baseness" (40), Sidney dutifully "suppresse[s] the swelling passion in [her] breast" (49): "I am really in pretty good spirits, and bear my disappointment (as I told you I would) very handsomely" (55). Contrary to expectations, she has no relapse, but as her illness might nonetheless "be imputed to the disappointment" (78), her mother rushes her into marriage with Mr. Arnold, an ostensibly staid, because dull, but it turns out, more fallible man. Sidney's dutiful suppression of her lovesickness leads to the destruction of all her hopes. After the discovery of Faulkland's comparative innocence, nostalgia suffuses the novel. Distinct from the somatics of longing, it instead engenders wistful memories. Published at the height of the sensibility cults, *Sidney Bidulph* is unique among the fiction of the time in openly critiquing the somatics of sensibility. Nostalgia in the novel is a comforting emotion that counteracts resentment, not the abandoned woman's last lingering illness. By contrast, Frances Burney's heroines are afflicted with vaguely defined psychophysical illnesses that call for a pathological interpretation of longing, while her novels also show a significant shift from an emphasis on courtship plots to a new interest in childhood homes as well as their reconstruction in an ideal marital union.

Scarcely but by Retrospection Is Its Happiness Known: *Evelina, Cecilia, Camilla*

Frances Burney's novels move away from panegyrics on lovesick yearning, but not simply to advocate a moderated sensibility as an alternative to emotional excess. Instead, they exhibit sentimental idealizations of home and family and often let their heroines pine just as excessively for a lost home, as protagonists in radical novels strive for (frequently illicit) love. Sensibly sensitive heroines always end up in stable, happy homes, safely married to eligible heroes who double as guardians or monitor figures, but the temporary absence or loss of such a domestic environment causes extreme distress. It is moreover possible to trace a shift from lovesickness to a longing for home in the succession of Burney's novels. Homesickness ultimately replaces love as the source of the most distress, and the solution is a nostalgic return rather than a surprising proposal. A return to or re-enactment of safe childhood homes heals raving and pining heroines.

The suffering of the heroine of Burney's first novel, *Evelina; Or, The History of a Young Lady's Entrance into the World* (1778), stands in the tradition of detailed lovesickness. Evelina longs for Lord Orville while at home; her longing is mapped on her body. In *Cecilia; Or, Memoirs of an Heiress* (1782), the distraught heroine is both homeless and lovesick. The loss of her childhood home causes her insecurity and much of her unhappiness. In the tellingly subtitled, *Camilla; Or, A Picture of Youth* (1796), emerging cults of childhood evoke a lengthy and idealized description of the heroine's childhood home. The plot's love-interest moves into the background as the destruction of a happy family and the self-abandoned heroine's physical pining for a return home become the novel's climaxes. *The Wanderer*, Burney's last novel, published only in 1814, has distanced itself from the late-eighteenth-century preoccupation with radical and sensible sensibilities and details instead the clash of personal nostalgia with new nationalist ideologies of communal "memories" and fatherlands. A close reading of these shifts in its representation casts an intriguing light on the continuing centrality and changing functions of nostalgia in the British novel.

Closely conforming to the clichés of the novel of sensibility, while critiquing the fashions of the time, *Evelina* describes the entrance of an innocent young woman into the marriage-market. Brought up in rural retirement at Berry Hill, which Harold Bloom has aptly described as "vaguely pastoral" and "an appropriate environment for elderly, slow paced wisdom," Evelina, Sir Belmont's unacknowledged daughter, leads a sheltered existence.[68] It is her innocence or ignorance of the manners or rites of "polite" society and her position as an observing outsider that mark her as a foil to its absurdities and cruelties.[69] Her fate threatens to become identical to her mother's. Caroline Evelyn's entrance into society, told in retrospect, has ended tragically, and her abused innocence is recollected in nostalgia. Evelina's parallel, but ultimately more fortunate, fate retrieves an idealized Golden Age, the happy past before the seduction of her grandfather and the ruin of her mother, and shows innocence rewarded after all. Evelina's remuneration is a financially and morally profitable marriage that grants her a return to the lost stability of a childhood retreat coveted in nostalgia. Lord Orville is a suitably paternal figure and quixotic hero: "An excellent subject for Quixotism, [he] is almost as romantic as if he had been born and bred at Berry Hill" (369). At the end of the novel, Evelina is safely installed with this chivalrous and patronizing father-figure in a surrogate return to a childhood retreat.

In returning to the protected stability of her childhood, Evelina foregoes the fatal pining that has been her mother's and also her grandfather's fate. Unlike the heroine, they both die of lovesickness. After a rash marriage to an inferior woman, Mr. Evelyn struggles against "shame and repentance . . . feelings which his heart was not framed to support" (14). His daughter,

Evelina's mother, similarly dies after her husband has deserted her, as "her sufferings were too acute for her tender frame" (15). However, even though Evelina is fortunate enough to recuperate from her misguided disappointment in Lord Orville, she closely conforms to the convention of the physically pining heroine. Made to believe that Orville can behave dishonorably, she returns home, "looking pale and ill" (258). Her "gravity . . . dejection, and falling away" (260) lead to physical illness, which, like Clarissa's final illness, remains unspecified, although Evelina's letters admit it to be a psychophysical affliction. As a journey to Bristol is proposed, Evelina writes that she is sent "upon an errand to the success of which I was totally indifferent, the re-establishment of my health" (268). Her belief in Orville restored, she is cured at once: "Lord Orville is still himself! . . . Your happy Evelina, restored at once to spirits and tranquillity, is no longer sunk in her own opinion, nor discontented with the world;—no longer, with dejected eyes, sees the prospect of passing her future days in sadness, doubt, and suspicion!" (278).

Still, Evelina's journey towards a re-created home is fraught with embarrassments that are trifling compared to the combined home- and lovesickness her half-brother, Macartny, has to face. A man of passionate and melancholy feelings, he acts out the somatic symptoms of excessive sensibility. His story indeed exhibits all the melodrama and clichéd difficulties that Evelina's more mundane distresses lack. The first time Evelina encounters him, she is struck by his "profound and melancholy meditation" (176) and believes him on the brink of suicide. It is at a crucial moment, when Evelina feels compromised by her relationship with the vulgar Branghtons and sees her own position reflected in their disparagement of Macartny's poetic effusions. Yet Macartny is of course treated much worse. He is more indigent and altogether more desperate than Evelina. Truly illegitimate, while Evelina is only suspected of it, he has not merely been ignored by their father, but has almost killed him unknowingly in a duel, and while Evelina has been lovingly raised by a surrogate father and respected by their neighbors, Macartny's disgraced mother is shunned by her family.

A pale, blushing hero, Macartny casts his "melancholy eyes" (188) up and down and repeatedly changes color. While Evelina's illness is a quiet "falling away," he exhibits the delirious raving that becomes central to the heroines' crises in Burney's subsequent novels. Lovesick and believing to have fallen in love with his own sister, he faints and succumbs to a protracted illness: "My senses, in the greatness of my misery, actually forsook me, and for more than a week I was wholly delirious" (228). At the novel's happy end, when origins and relationships are revealed, mistaken identities resolved, and all acknowledged children united in familial reunion, Evelina happily "own[s] such an outcast for a brother" (363). Polly Green, an unconscious impostor and the only child (mistakenly) acknowledged by Sir Belmont, is married to his illegitimate son on the same day that the real Miss Belmont becomes Lady Orville. Although both Macartny and Evelina are prevented from succumbing to any suicidal tendencies—including a propensity to "waste away" as well as to risk robbery—through the fulfillment of their longing, they both suffer physically from their lovesickness.

In the later novels, the heroines' physical lovesickness, somatics of desire, and even temporary insanity are minutely detailed, while their heroes only increase their propensity to sermonize. Both Camilla and Cecilia lie languishing and hallucinating among strangers. In the anonymity of the sprawling London streets, they are at once concealed and exposed in the bedroom of an inn and above a pawnshop respectively. They experience a modern loneliness, while they are reduced to socially indeterminate spectacles of emotional display. Even more pointedly, newspapers advertise both Cecilia and Juliet, the heroine of *The Wanderer*, as lost lunatics. While their intense experience of love- and homesickness causes extreme physical, emotional, and mental unease, being thus marked as insane moreover serves to criticize a society that restrains women as they attempt to act independently. In a feminist reading, Julia Epstein points out that Camilla is at one point perceived as mad because she unwittingly transgresses social norms. As she enters one shop after another, asking for the same directions in order to enable her unqualified chaperon, Mrs. Mittin, to view goods without buying them, the shopkeepers make wagers on whether they are simply thieves or mentally deranged. The vacant gaze of "absent and absorbed" Camilla is read as an indicator of insanity (607). According to Epstein, this episode dramatizes the "circumstances of her liminal social position,"[70] yet it also highlights the shifting lines of demarcation between, and the consequent confusion over, the symptoms of sensibility and insanity in sentimental fiction.

Burney's novels argue for a restrained sensibility, as the monitor figures repeatedly point out. They promote a domesticated sentimentality rather than radical sensibility. But in letting sympathetically portrayed heroines suffer melodramatically as the result of their feelings, which contrast with the insensitivity of worldly and frequently frivolous characters, Burney eats her cake and has it, too. As Claudia Johnson has pointed out, in conservative sentimental plots, imprudent and abandoned heroines need to die, and their increasing physical brittleness redeems their too-active or energetic behavior. Burney's heroines, however, not only survive, but their distress is as much the result of misfortune as of their own imprudence.[71] In addition, the homeless wandering of a deranged protagonist who has lost her identity, status, home, lover, and family underlines the connection between loss of societal status and the danger of being advertised as a lunatic, inviting a feminist reading. As we shall see, *The Wanderer* carefully exorcises these protofeminist sympathies in the character of Elinor Joddrell, the heroine's radical antiheroine, but Burney's earlier, prerevolutionary, novels are more at liberty to sympathize with the eccentric as well as with the suppressed.

In *Cecilia*, Mr. Albany, the heroine's eccentric advisor in matters of charity, is described as "singular" by fashionable society, where it is rumored "that he was certainly confined, at one part of his life, in a private mad-house."[72] The poor, however, cherish him, and to Cecilia "the remains of insanity which [seem] to hang upon him [are] affecting without being alarming, and her desire to know more of him [grows] every instant stronger" (294). *Cecilia* explores society's definitions of conformity, fashion, and "singularities," while it also shows how suppressed lovesickness can drive a sensitive heroine mad when she tries to conform to conventions and to adhere to her principles. A novel about homesickness, it details an orphan's struggle with her three uncongenial guardians and an heiress's vacillation between the forfeiture of her name or of her lover. Her homelessness, combined with lovesickness, plunges her into a madness that can be traced back to clinical nostalgia in its last stage as well as to lovesickness:

> Her head was by no means in a condition to bear this violence of distress; every pulse was throbbing, every vein seemed bursting, her reason, so lately returned, could not bear the repetition of such a shock, and from supplicating for help with all the energy of feeling and understanding, she soon continued the cry from mere vehemence of distraction. (899)

Although the result of immediate distress, this plunge into distracted raving has been carefully prepared for. The novel opens with a description of Cecilia's "tears of recollecting sorrow," which "filled her eyes, and obstructed the last view of her native town which had excited them" (5). In London, the changes fashionable society had effected in her childhood friend "cruelly depressed and mortified" (33) her. Subsequent events prove conducive to increasing depression. Among the foppery and affectation of the "insensiblists" and the "jargonists," who are the men of *ton* currently in fashion (279–80), she encounters gallant young Delvile. Her lovesickness robs her "of all power of receiving pleasure from what was passing" (283). But a condition in her uncle's will stipulates that she needs to retain her surname if she wants to keep her inheritance. Her lover's proud family finds this unacceptable, and she eventually needs to forfeit her fortune, with her guardians acting as monitor figures gone awry. Her difficulties culminate in melodramatically detailed physical symptoms of emotional distress. Running through the streets of London in search of her husband, "disconsolate and helpless," she is taken for a lunatic "broke lose from Bedlam" (898) and restrained. Her "unspeakable" agony is interpreted as "the ravings of a mad woman" as she calls out in "frenzy, and desperation" to the "beloved of [her] heart" (899). The novel, however, stops short of letting her die of men's financial foibles. She overcomes her lovesickness and homesickness neither through a blunting of her feminine sensibilities nor through any successful attempts to take her affairs in her own hands, but through her husband's return and the acquisition of a new home. While this domestic ending neatly goes around any radical critiques of patriarchy, it intriguingly shows how the longing for a home supplants lovesickness in the novel, and how the homeless heroine raves in utter abandonment, but is healed once her husband's family accepts her and he can take her home.

In *Camilla*, nostalgia for the childhood home completely displaces lovesickness as the main cause of the heroine's pining. Its ending is consequently the more sentimental and the more domestic. Romantic cults of the child engender idealized descriptions of the heroine's childhood and her childhood home: "The tide of youthful glee flowed jocund from her heart.... Every look was a smile, every step was a spring, every thought was a hope, every feeling was joy!... The early felicity of her mind was without allay" (13). Yet, as in most domestic, even if not outspokenly anti-Jacobin, novels written in the wake of the French Revolution and the Terror, ideas of education safely domesticate the "Romantic child." Such novels are wary of unbridled sensibility and cautious about presenting untaught, impulsive behavior as intrinsically praiseworthy.

Maria Edgeworth's *Belinda* (1801) perhaps most emphatically exposes the dangers of Rousseau's primitivist ideals of original innocence and natural education. Children feature strongly in the novel, but most importantly, in a subplot, a man of the world is tired of fashionable women and decides to bring up an innocent, unspoilt, and uneducated wife for himself. In a wood he encounters a lovely girl who has never seen a man. He renames her Virginia after St. Pierre's *Paul and Virginia* (1789) and continues to conceal her from the world. Even though Virginia turns out to be "so innocent to look at" (312) and displays "exquisite sensibility and ardent imagination" (359), he ultimately decides that he finds her childishness rather insipid, even tedious, and marries the novel's better educated, but nonetheless unspoilt, titular heroine instead.[73]

As I shall show in more detail in the following chapter, Austen's *Mansfield Park* (1814) treats the fears and hopes of the dislocated child Fanny Price with sympathy, but the main point of its childhood passages is similarly a focus on education: the Miss Bertrams' "wonderful memories" confine themselves to facts and figures, sharply contrasting with their cousin's nostalgic memory.[74] While Fanny undoubtedly has innate qualities, she has also had the advantage of Edmund's guidance. He is a faulty monitor figure, and as we shall see, this is precisely where Austen goes beyond conservative plots, but there is clearly no sentimentalization of natural innocence in her novels. Their focus on education is distinctly different from the "inheritance" of childish insight that Dickens was to idealize in *David Copperfield* (1850).[75]

Published in 1796, *Camilla* needs to be read in the contexts of anti-Jacobin reactions to the excesses of the French Revolution, for which the sensibility cults were partly blamed. As recent work on anti-Jacobin novels has show, they were far more prevalent than had been thought. Even while conservatives remained suspicious of the novel as a radical genre, once they realized "the potential boost the novel could give their cause," as M. O. Grenby has convincingly argued, "they were content to cease attacking it and even to endorse it."[76] While they formed a self-conscious reaction to pro-revolutionary fiction that attempted to oust them from the literary market, radical writers such as Mary Wollstonecraft and the lesser known, but more prolific Charlotte Smith continued to publish. I shall look at *Desmond* as one of the most explicitly pro-revolutionary novels of the time and then proceed to *The Wanderer* as an important retrospective reworking of Jacobin and anti-Jacobin plots. In *Camilla*, the French Revolution and its repercussions are not an explicit concern, but the novel's moralizing stance, its minute dissection of the heroine's behavior, and the question of bad influence align it with anti-Jacobin revisions and reuses of sensibility.

Its exposure of childish adults guards against the idealizations of "eternal children" that became so important, and so securely domesticated, in sentimental Victorian fiction. In the late-eighteenth century, associations with Rousseau and revolutionary French excesses still loomed large. Sir Hugh, Camilla's childish uncle, causes irrevocable damage and serves to contrast sharply with the comparative maturity of the most responsible children such as young Edgar Mandlebert, a paragon of virtue even at an early age. Nostalgia for childhood in the novel is premised precisely on the passing of such childhood innocence and not, as in Dickens's fiction, for example, on a desire to retain and foster childlike qualities. As we shall see in subsequent chapters, in mid-Victorian fiction, children are aware of the blessings of childhood, and the good adults try to preserve this inheritance. In *Camilla*, by contrast, this happiness cannot last and can only be known in retrospect: "O blissful state of innocence, purity, and delight, why must it fleet so fast? Why scarcely but by retrospection is its happiness known?" (13).

Instead, the novel's childhood passages primarily serve to establish the heroine in a happy domestic environment and to highlight his parents' excellence. The first chapter is entitled "A Family Scene." Camilla resides in "the bosom of her respectable family" (8). The respectability of this bosom is more important than its cheerfulness, and yet it is sentimentally, even longingly, described. The loss of home functions as the central crisis of the novel. In a chapter symptomatically entitled "The Workings of Sorrow," Camilla realizes that her debts have contributed to the destruction of her family: "Peace and ease are no more for me!— My happiness was already buried" (786). In "The Operation of Terror," she dreads her mother's "malediction," ready to escape through the window at her approach: "'O that I could die! That I could die!' she cried, madly advancing to the window, and throwing up the sash, yet with quick instinctive repentance pulling it down, shuddering and exclaiming: 'Is there no death for me but murder—no murder but suicide?'" (828). Although the concomitant loss of the good opinion of her would-be lover, the overly fastidious Edgar, exacerbates her loneliness, the emphasis remains on her nostalgia for the childhood home. It is Camilla's visit to the deserted house that nearly drives her insane: "To leave thus a spot where she had experienced such felicity; to see it naked and forlorn, . . . gave her sensations almost maddening" (878). Homeless, she stays at an inn, an illustration of depression: "wrapt up, coveting the dark, and stifling sighs that were rising into sobs" (893). The final return home at least partly, and to a large extent thanks to nostalgia, recaptures the happy past. Camilla's sickbed-reunion with her lover ends in a wedding, not a funeral, but it is her reunion with her family that constitutes the desired homecoming to "primeval joy:"

> Camilla, whose danger was the result of self-neglect, as her sufferings had all flowed from mental anguish, was already able to go down to the study upon the arrival of Mr. Tyrold: where she received, with grateful rapture, the tender blessings which welcomed her to the paternal arms—to her home—to peace—to safety—and primeval joy. (855)

In Burney's novels, lovesick heroines fall homesick and can be reclaimed by a return home. Their stories follow the patterns of clinical nostalgia. The importance of returns to, or also reconstructions of, home indeed cautions us not to read their pining simply as lovesickness. In her study of "love's madness," Helen Small has emphasized the centrality of lovesickness in nineteenth-century literature and perceptively pointed out the significance of eighteenth-century cults of sensibility for subsequent literary as well as medical treatments of love-mad women. But what Small does not discuss is that the survival of lovesick heroines in late-eighteenth- and early-nineteenth-century novels is interestingly often brought about by a return home or its reconstruction in an eligible estate. The sentimental hero doubles as the nostalgically desired "home" of the pining heroine, but progressively the home itself becomes more important as well.[77] In *Evelina*, marriage to Orville forms a return to a life as tranquil and quixotic as the heroine's childhood home. Likewise, in Burney's next novel, Cecilia recovers from illness and even madness once her lover's family accepts her. Although she forfeits her inheritance for his sake, the original loss of the childhood home precedes her lovesickness. Delvile rescues her from a state of most intense homelessness, as he takes her home with him. This homecoming undercuts tentative critiques of patriarchy and instead reinstates the importance of domesticity. *Camilla* most clearly shows the transition from a central love-interest and the concomitant lovesickness to nostalgia for childhood and childhood homes, although childhood simplicity is safely contained in the exposure of the dangerously childish uncle.

The Wanderer takes this interest in the "domestication" of nostalgia further by poising an individual's personal homesickness against ideologies of the homeland. Published almost twenty years after *Camilla* and written against the background of the French Revolution and the Terror, Burney's last novel is far removed from the light-hearted parody of fashionable society in *Evelina*. It is a reaction to the radical fiction of the 1790s and even more pointedly, to new nationalist ideologies. It is indeed helpful to consider its juxtaposition of national and personal nostalgia in the context of earlier works, and in the next section, I shall emphasize Charlotte Smith's ambiguous representation of the Revolution and its repercussions in what is her most pro-revolutionary novel before returning to Burney's reworking of such radical plots.

Restoration, Reform, and Revolution in Charlotte Smith's *Desmond*

Charlotte Smith's only epistolary novel, *Demond* (1792), is a self-avowedly radical novel. As the titular hero alternately admires picturesque ruins and reformed estates, however, he exhibits a disturbing self-contradiction. The nostalgia Desmond feels at the sight of decaying buildings, ivy, gnarled trees, and more pointedly, castles and (admittedly deserted) convents runs counter to his political posture, throwing his alignment of ideologies and aesthetics into confusion and the novel's radicalism into sharp relief. His interest in practical improvements, in the reform of estates and, by implication, states, clashes rather embarrassingly with his fondness for ruins. While he heaps ridicule on Burkean reactions to the French Revolution, he proposes ideals of reform that were championed by conservatives as well. The novel, in fact, nicely documents Smith's ambiguous use of sentimental clichés and radical ideas,[78] as it shuttles between pro-revolutionary radicalism and an interest in preservation and reform.

Doubles partly solve this ambivalence as they live out the proposed progressive attitudes to patriarchal structures and oppressive systems, while the main characters remain personally exempt from the repercussions of such behavior. On the brink of adultery throughout the novel, the heroine never wavers from her virtuous resolutions. A young French lady stands in as her double in bearing Desmond's child outside wedlock. Eventually, her boorish husband's fortuitous death leaves her free to marry Desmond after all. The happy marriage contemplated at the end of the novel effectively dismantles its critical engagement with the predicaments of unhappily married women. What is more, even though Desmond's illicit love for a married woman is part and parcel of its radical exposition on sensibility and society's strictures, the neatly resolved love-story tends to disrupt the political theme, or rather, at times Desmond "seems to force himself upon political affairs, (about which, till a few months since, he was totally indifferent) in order to escape from naming

[Geraldine]" in his letters (345). Patricia Meyer Spacks reminds us that the "most important development in the treatment of politics and society by novels of the 1790s was an emphasis on analogies between private and public experience, for example between the situation of individuals within families and that of citizens within a nation."[79] In this context, Desmond's discussions of politics usefully frame debates on the constitution of domestic happiness, and despite all its self-contradictions, *Desmond* remains perhaps Smith's most explicitly pro-revolutionary novel. As Smith puts it in the preface, "if those in favour of one party have evidently the advantage, it is not owing to my partial representation but to the predominant power of truth and reason, which can neither be altered nor concealed" (5–6). The incongruities of *Desmond* are clearly not retractions of this proudly proclaimed stance. They are concessions to sentimental clichés and particularly to the popular marriage plot.

Still, even while the fortuitous removal of all obstacles sadly diminishes the triumph of his hopeless love, the novel clearly defends Desmond's quixotic idealism—an idealism that includes his politics. He is called "an English Werter" who is "far gone in this species of insanity" (282). Bethel, his former guardian, wonders how he "could ever take up such a notion, as of an unchangeable and immortal passion, which is a thing never heard or thought of, but by the tender novel writers, and their gentle readers" (88). The detractors of sensibility, however, are either dull (like Bethel) or unfeeling brutes (like Geraldine's husband). When the latter makes "Desmond's quixotism the subject of his ridicule," he displays "a talent which he manages generally so as to attract ridicule himself" (198). As the basis of radical politics as well as Desmond's chivalry, quixotism fits very neatly into the novel's subversive agenda.

In eighteenth-century fiction, Cervantes's impoverished gentleman of La Mancha, who imbibes a plethora of romances of chivalry and goes forth as The Knight of the Woeful Countenance to accomplish idealistic deeds in the chivalric tradition, undergoes an important metamorphosis from a buffoon into a Romanticized figure.[80] As critics have shown, parodies increasingly make way for idealizations of the quixotic figure as an embodiment of virtue tragicomically tilting definitions of reality. Quixotism becomes part of a nostalgic idealization of lost innocence and even lost illusions. Sarah Fielding's David Simple in the eponymous novel (1744), for example, pursues "a Scheme which was never capable of entering the Brain of one in his Senses; namely, of hunting after a real Friend," and is described as "in this Point only as mad as *Quixotte* [sic] himself."[81] In Burney's

Evelina, Lord Orville shows that a quixotic figure can also be a desirable romantic hero.[82]

In Smith's novel, Desmond's quixotism is at once nostalgic and Utopian, expressed by his "dreams of what *might have been*; as if to embitter the sad reflection of *what is*" (361). It brings out the best in him. It is ultimately rewarded and moreover linked to his enthusiasm for the Revolution. The suggestion that pro-revolutionary sympathies are quixotic is not really an accusation at all. On the contrary, his pro-revolutionary attitudes are simply further evidence of his laudable quixotism. Desmond is revealingly our main source of information on the Revolution, and his opinions are never discredited, just as his quixotic chivalry is triumphant, as he saves Geraldine's life and ultimately reaps his reward after her husband's death. In his letters from France, he exposes the "malignant fabrications" circulated in England (52). Burkean rhetoric is denounced in a stylistic parody as sublime as Burke's own eloquence:

> I will not enter into a discussion of it, though the virulence, as well as the misrepresentation with which it abounds, lays it alike open to ridicule and contradiction.—Abusive declamation can influence only superficial or prepossessed understandings; those who cannot, or who will not see, that fine sounding periods are not arguments—that poetical imagery is not matter of fact. I foresee that a thousand pens will leap from their standishes (to parody a sublime sentence of his own) to answer such a book. (155)

Reactions to Edmund Burke's influential *Reflections on the Revolution in France* (1790) of course recur in the fictional and nonfictional texts of the 1790s. Burke's idealization of the aristocracy and his reverence for old buildings that symbolize established institutions—and Burke even describes the Bastille as a venerable castle—crucially complicate the functions of nostalgia and the picturesque in radical novels of the time. Mary Wollstonecraft emphatically rejects a veneration of the ancient when she questions the point of restoring old buildings that have outlived their function: "[W]hy was it a duty to repair an ancient castle, built in barbarous ages, of Gothic materials?"[83] In many novels written in the wake of the French Revolution, however, architectural metaphors such as Maria Edgeworth's rackrent castles indicate a necessary refurbishing, rather than a violent revolution, of political systems. Even the self-avowedly pro-revolutionary *Desmond* propagates reform rather than revolution, and this is where its central ambiguity rests. The Marquis de Montfleuri, "though born a courtier, is one of the steadiest friends to the people" (79) and exemplary in improving his estate.[84] In sharp contrast to the unreformed gloomy residence of the Comte d'Hauteville, the "*chateau* of Montfleuri is an old building, but it is neither large nor magnificent—for having no predilection for the gothic gloom in which his ancestors concealed their greatness, he has pulled down every part of the original structure, but what was actually useful to himself" (79).

This preference for improved estates, however, is by no means as clear-cut as it may seem at first. Desmond's admiration continues to shift and remains deeply self-contradictory throughout the novel. In a sense, the uncertainties of his divided self aptly display the turmoil created by opposed calls for reform as an alternative to revolution and for the suppression of all radicalism in Britain. His pleasure in viewing picturesque ruins further confuses his ideals of a reformed, but preserved, (e)state. While Desmond's own estate in England is his nostalgically idealized, but nonetheless modernized, childhood home, he delights in his friend's ruins more than in his improvements. When he describes how he "repaired the old house" and "procured modern comforts" (276) on his own inherited estate, his ideals are eminently practical. He is more concerned with modernization, and indeed modern comforts, than with preservation, and yet, he commences his friendship with Montfleuri by embarking on a tour of the picturesque landscape near the old-fashioned chateau. A delightful view of a ruin is its main attraction: "On the top of one of the highest of these hills is the ruin of a large ancient building, of which the country people tell wonderful legends" (80). Desmond "rejoice[s] that Montfleuri . . . will now be able to preserve it in its present romantic form" (80). After the dispersal of a neighboring convent, the estate can even boast a picturesque hermitage. It "exactly correspond[s] to the ideas [Desmond] had formed of those sort of habitations from Don Quixote or Gil Blas" (85), reminding him not at all unpleasantly of the artificial abodes of "a hired [or] a wax hermit in some of our gardens" (85). Montfleuri may have pulled down a dysfunctional ancestral seat, but political radicalism does not at all disrupt the good characters' aesthetic appreciation of ruin and decay. On the contrary, Desmond is in raptures:

> I, who love, you know, every thing ancient, unless it be ancient prejudices, have entreated my friend to preserve this structure in its present state—than which, nothing can be more picturesque: when in a fine glowing evening, the almost perpendicular hill on which it stands is reflected in the unruffled bosom of the broad river, crowned with these venerable remains, half mantled in ivy, and other parasytical [sic] plants, and a few cypresses, which grow here as in Italy, mingling their spiral forms among the masses of ruin. (80)

The decaying ancient building supports parasitic plants and has to be preserved from the "neighbouring hinds" (80) who carry off materials to reuse them. Nothing, however, is made of this inviting metaphor for decadent institutions that ward off a useful restructuring. The preserved ruin is even a place for romance as well as a Romantic site. Josephine, Montfleuri's unhappily married sister, relates her story sitting on a fallen column. That Desmond only thinks of "the similarity of her fate to that of Geraldine" (123) underlines Josephine's function as her double. This projection of sensuality, and ultimately adultery, parallels the divorce of the estate's symbolic function from its aesthetic effect. As Diana Bowstead has pointed out, this scene could not have been written for Geraldine.[85] The novel's heroine can thus remain chaste, while her double acts out the desired betrayal of a tyrannous husband. Similarly, Desmond can indulge in modern comforts and contemplate the aesthetic pleasures of wax hermits at home, while he vents his enthusiasm about ruins and dilapidated cottages abroad.

The site of Montfleuri's ruin is quiet, tranquil, viewed by sunshine. It is far removed from the frightening ruins of castles or abbeys that are usually characteristic of Gothic novels. A pleasant background to romantic tête-à-têtes, picnics, and tours, it lacks "all the horrors that a building such as 'what one reads about' may produce," as Catherine Morland was to put it in Austen's *Northanger Abbey*.[86] In Ann Radcliffe's early Gothic novel *The Castles of Athlin and Dunbayn: A Highland Story* (1789), by contrast, the ruins of an abbey are the site of abduction, hostile confrontations, and a sublime storm. Like the ruin on which Josephine tells her story, the abbey has "fallen to decay, and [is] overgrown with ivy," but its "broken arches and lonely towers arose in gloomy grandeur through the obscurity of the evening."[87] The sunny tête-à-tête in Smith's novel, however, is a sensual moment. Its brightness obscures Josephine's tale of her wrongs, and in this, the scene contrasts sharply with a later episode in which Desmond and Geraldine nightmarishly wander inside a fortified manor, an aristocratic stronghold in revolutionary France.

This distinction between ancient ruins and Gothic castles moves away from the simple effects of earlier Gothic fiction and instead anticipates a similar juxtaposition in Radcliffe's *The Mysteries of Udolpho* (1794). The heroine, Emily St Aubert, repeatedly admires ruins in the course of her picturesque journeys, but while the remains of classical buildings engender pensive feelings and melancholy musings on "the deserted plains of Troy," the greenish, overgrown ruins of a Gothic chapel through which Emily later attempts to make her escape are terrifying. Montoni's castle symbolizes the most frightening aspects of an aristocratic stronghold: "Silent, lonely and sublime, it seemed to stand the sovereign of the scene, and to frown defiance on all, who dared to invade its solitary reign."[88]

In her recent introduction to the novel, Terry Castle has significantly drawn its status as a Gothic novel into question, as "[g]reat swatches of the text—too much of it to ignore—have little to do with Montoni or his villainies."[89] However, Castle suggests not only that the novel anticipates Austen's parody of the genre in *Northanger Abbey* and, ultimately, the genre's revisions by linking the effects of Gothic trappings to a mundane Gothic of domestic bullying, but also that the world of the novel, *including* the picturesque passages that make up its first half, is haunted despite the rational explanations that seem to explain away the supernatural. To be haunted, Castle convincingly argues, is proof of a sympathetic imagination as the "other" functions as the self's ghostly reflection.[90] Elsewhere, she speaks of "the supernaturalization of everyday life:" the Gothic displaces the supernatural it appears to explain into the realm of the everyday.[91] George Haggerty and Robert Miles have similarly traced the significance of this new phenomenology of self and other to a profound disjunction that manifests itself in the haunted consciousness of Gothic fiction. Miles speaks of a "broad agreement that the Gothic represents the subject in a state of deracination, of the self finding itself dispossessed in its own house, in a condition of rupture, disjunction, fragmentation."[92] New interest in nostalgia was not only part of the same shift in perceptions, but additionally grew out of the dialectic of homeliness and otherness that became highlighted in Gothic fiction.

The centrality of homelessness in the Gothic novel, in fact, accentuates the relationship between nostalgia and the uncanny, between longings for the *heimlich* and the *unheimlich*. In *The Architectural Uncanny: Essays in the Modern Unhomely*, Anthony Vidler investigates an important "slippage between what seems homely and what is definitively unhomely."[93] This slippage reveals the uncanny as the counterpart to nostalgia within a dialectic of self and other. The uncanny, Vidler argues, links the "unstable nature of 'house and home' [to] questions of social and individual estrangement, alienation, exile, and homelessness."[94] Sigmund Freud influentially linked the *heimlich* [homely] to the *unheimlich* [uncanny] in his essay on "The Uncanny": Freud suggested that "there is a doubling, dividing and interchanging of the self" in uncanny experiences, pointing to the displacement of the *heimlich*, the origin, the lost first home of the womb.[95]

Nostalgia is premised on a perception of homelessness or unhomeliness, and it thereby generates representations of the "unhomely" in order to underline the homely.

Without necessarily subscribing to Freudian criticism, literary critics have extended this interpretation of the "unhomely" to juxtapose descriptions of home with that of homelessness and to show that such contrasts operate as influential, even formative, cultural fictions. They are central to the concepts of alterity that have shaped Western modernity. As we have seen, Homi Bhabha speaks of "the *heimlich* pleasures of the hearth" and "the *unheimlich* terror of the space or race of the Other" to point out the reverse side, as it were, of "imagined communities."[96] In a reading of Walter Scott's fiction, Janet Sorensen similarly links the "containable '*heimlich*' space" into which Scott tends to turn historical landscapes to nostalgia and to the *unheimlich* as "the uncanny double produced by nostalgia."[97] As they represent private experience and subjective anxieties as external reality, the Gothic novel gives new impetus to these emerging perceptions of self and other, the homely, or nostalgic, and the unhomely, or uncanny.[98]

Margaret Anne Doody's seminal article on the development of the Gothic novel still contains the best account of the significant connections between this new phenomenology and the genre's ambiguous political aspects. Tracing its beginning to descriptions of dreams in earlier novels, Doody sees Gothic fiction as an important stage in the novel's evolution. In it, she argues, men as well as women have nightmares, as dreaming is no longer associated with female instability and male villainy, and the trappings of the phantasmagoria become real objects, real events. It is in the Gothic novel, Doody shows, that women writers first question masculine control as part of the falsehoods and disorder of the "real world" and thus pave the way for "the novel of feminine radical protest."[99]

More recently, critics have extended this focus on the Gothic's feminist potential to describe it as an inherently "queer" genre that is deeply concerned with lines of demarcation between the normal and abnormal, the "proper" feminine and masculine, and the rebellious and the reactionary. Haggerty has addressed the importance of nightmarish imagery in Gothic fiction to emphasize that it seems at odds with the emerging concept of novelistic realism, but that the terms of what is real ultimately shift to include subjective fantasy. Gothic novels thereby give imaginative worlds external reality and in the process underscore the prevalence of individual subjectivity. Their phantasmagoria is an attempt to answer "the philosophical question of how the mind transforms the external world into private experience [as they] give imaginative worlds external and objective reality."[100] The genre leans towards radical redefinitions of normalcy, although literary critics have emphasized that many Gothic works *hesitate* between the revolutionary and reactionary and often leave the potential conflicts unsolved.[101]

It is in this context that the besieged manors, deserted convents, and improved estates in *Desmond* need to be read, even though their decorative functions can account for much of their incoherence or ambiguity. Recent discussions of picturesque aesthetics have suggested that the political oppression represented by a castle or its ruin is displaced backward into former times and thereby rendered innocuous.[102] In a section on Gothic fiction in *Commerce, Morality and the Eighteenth-Century Novel*, Liz Bellamy has similarly argued that the Gothic novel constitutes a critique of the conservative, Burkean, celebration of feudal order, but that its location in the past or in foreign countries and thereby in places that are "other" moderates, if not disrupts, the criticism of contemporary British society.[103] Bellamy, however, proceeds to make a distinction between "the Gothic novel" and "the Jacobin novel" that deploys Gothic elements within its political thematic. Jacobin fiction, she argues, dismantles the suggestion that oppression and despotism are something of the past or limited to foreign countries.[104] While a back-projection of castles' or convents' political significance is precisely Desmond's self-justification when he admires decayed buildings, the novel not only counters picturesque ruins with functional despotic strongholds, but again and again links developments in France to a social critique of British society. Reduced to decorative items, Desmond argues, castles and convents are no more dangerous than a wax hermit. In pointed contrast to their decorative, even domesticated, function, the phantasmagoria of the Gothic castle with its real-life banditti poses a very real danger. Even more fascinatingly, while most Gothic novels use a back-projection of contemporary injustices to externalize them in a dreamlike landscape located in a past age, *Desmond* takes Gothic elements into the present: while the ruins of the past are limited to a decorative effect, the strongholds of tyrannous French aristocrats are still the site of violence and chivalrous rescue.

Nostalgia's role in the novel is therefore doubly ambiguous. Desmond derives a "kind of pensive and melancholy pleasure" from admiring "every thing ancient, unless it be ancient prejudices" (81). This distinction is significant, as he self-consciously divorces the nostalgia he feels at the sight of pretty ruins from the tyrannies of the past. He admires classical and Gothic ruins, but not former political systems or the lack of "modern comforts" in past ages. Still, the theme of improvement remains confused and self-contradictory. Nostalgic childhood memories influence Desmond's preservation of an avenue of graceful chestnut trees on his own estate and induce him to deplore their sacrifice to modern improvements in France. His "early impressions" form an excuse for what he terms his "gothic and exploded taste . . . I know this betrays a very gothic and exploded taste, but such is the force of early impressions, that I have still an affection for the 'bowed roof'" (80–81). Even more incongruously, Bethel invokes nostalgia for lost family estates to defend the nobility. He deplores that "estates that had been in his family since the conquest, now lent their names to barons by recent purchase" (24), and that his own former steward, now Sir Robert Stamford, "improves" the estate he has obtained from Geraldine's spendthrift husband by cutting down a "beautiful little wood which overshadowed the clear and rapid rivulet" (167), since it has no productive, only picturesque, value. Stamford belongs to the "mushroom nobility" of "nabobs and rich citizens" (24). At the same time, however, an old French Count rails against the common people, calling them "a mushroom, a fungus" (106), ironically using the same words as Bethel. The theme of improvements in Britain and France remains confused, as the desirability and extent of change is drawn into debate.

With a similar irony, Montfleuri's reforms have rendered Gothic elements innocuous, but the new comfort of the preserved ruin in an improved landscape leads to his sister's seduction. This affair is liberating, as indeed is the dispersal of the convent and its subsequent reduction to a decorative item, but it is quickly relegated to the margins of the narrative. As Josephine is whisked away after her disgrace, Desmond leaves her and the decorative ruin behind to rescue Geraldine from a truly Gothic location set in present-day France. Even in this, Smith's most outspokenly political novel, ideological allegiances are never clear-cut. The protagonists' personal longings for "what *might have been*" (369) become involved in discourses on revolutions and reforms that express tyrannies at home as well as abroad, but are at odds with the fond descriptions of nostalgically recollected childhood homes and picturesque ruins. While the majority of Gothic novels go around contemporary controversies by projecting them into the past and thereby rescue radical sensibility by converting it into a "sympathetic imagination," as Castle has put it, that engenders a supernaturalization of their surroundings, Smith's most radical novels are set in the present, redeploy Gothic trappings in minutely detailed, contemporary landscapes, and openly defend a high, radical, sensibility. The heroes and heroines of Radcliffe's fiction display their laudable sensitivity in their susceptibility to hallucinations, but Smith's protagonists speak out against present-day oppressors. In later novels, representations of the revolution become further conflicted by an anti-Jacobin "witch-hunting" and the conservative narratives it engenders.[105] As the following sections will show, Burney's retrospective novel stands out. It transcends the predictable plots of anti-Jacobin novels that argue for a restrained sensibility and sentimental restorations of the threatened institutions and moreover takes on new controversies.

Nostalgia for Home or Homelands: Romantic Nationalism and the Indeterminate Native in Frances Burney's *The Wanderer*

The Wanderer; Or, Female Difficulties (1814), Frances Burney's last novel, opens with the flight of a nameless heroine in search of her "loved, long lost, and fearfully recovered native land" (751). Born in Wales and raised in France, the Wanderer flees to England in the aftermath of the French Revolution, attempting to find a safe haven in a location she has been made to think of as her home only to discover that she is marked as "a poor destitute Wanderer" (49), considered foreign by the insular Englishmen she encounters. Homelessness and the longing for home are central themes in the novel. They are inextricably involved with the potentials and pitfalls of a rising Romantic nationalism as well as with retrospective reassessments of the radical 1790s. In juxtaposing prejudices based on "memories" of a national past with personal longings for home, friends, and family, *The Wanderer* takes up and further conflicts the struggle between self and society that informs Burney's own earlier novels as well as pre-Romantic fiction in general and becomes invested with new possibilities and complications in the full-blown Romantic novel. With its intriguing exposure of the new nationalist nostalgia of the early nineteenth century, Burney's last novel casts a different light on the elusive genre of Romantic fiction and the uses (and abuses) of nostalgia by the Romantic nationalisms that are both supported and critiqued in the literature of the time. As the dramatic fate of the wandering orphan heroine dismantles ideologies of the homeland, the novel evokes and then dismisses the concept of a shared national nostalgia. The longing for belonging is instead granted by an alternative ideal community, a family that transcends national borders. In this, the novel suggests a domestic, anti-nationalist solution to the warring desires of self-fulfillment and social acceptance that plague the Romantic self. It is fruitful to read *The Wanderer* as a reaction to the nationalist agenda that informs a number of Romantic novels and as an alternative to straightforward Burkean reactions to the French Revolution.

By contrast, early-nineteenth-century regional novels or national tales wholeheartedly endorse the new nationalist ideology of the homeland and create a communal "nostalgia" for places invested with the allure of the exotic. It has been suggested that Walter Scott creates a Highland Arcadia in *Waverley* (1814) in which the hero's "romantic reservoir" lives up to his expectations after all.[106] In Maria Edgeworth's *Ennui* (1809), *The Absentee* (1812), and in Lady Morgan's *The Wild Irish Girl* (1806), estates in Ireland figure as repositories of down-to-earth attachments and ancient customs, as colonial spaces neglected by absentee landlords, and as the true home, in sharp relief to England, which is metonymically represented by the corrupt city of London. In *The Absentee*, for example, Lord Colambre's return to "his mother earth" evokes "the early associations of his childhood, and the patriotic hopes of his riper years."[107] *The Wild Irish Girl* describes Ireland as "a colonized or a conquered country."[108] The "diminutive body of our worthy steward" appears to be "the abode of the transmigrated soul of some *West Indian* planter" (23). Yet the hero's original bias—his expectation of an "*Esquimaux* group" (1)—is displaced by his belief that there is "no country which the Irish at present resemble but the modern Greeks" (182). In this land of antiquity, but refreshing climate, Horatio can shed the "pining atrophy" (58) he suffers in London. Like Glenthorn in Edgeworth's aptly entitled *Ennui*, Horatio is "devoured by ennui, by discontent" (131) until he rediscovers "emotions of a character, an energy, long unknown to [his] apathised feelings" (45) in a landscape that is exotic and replete with communal nostalgia for a new homeland. In these novels, a personal quest coincides with a new patriotism; rebirth with the regeneration of the rediscovered nation.

It is this concept of a communal memory that *The Wanderer* exposes so brilliantly. The ideal or, in Benedict Anderson's useful phrase, "imagined community" created by Romantic ideologies of the homeland is not always a viable option, as Burney's wandering heroine has to discover. Anderson has suggested that in its focus on the simultaneity of events, the classic novel presents a "shared" memory of common experiences that could be used to fill in the emotional void left by the retreat, disintegration, or unavailability of real communities and networks.[109] Thomas

Nipperdey has further argued that nationalism was set up as a promise of a community rooted in a "common culture" and thus a product of a nostalgia for lost stability, caused by the dissolution of tradition and the concomitant uncertainty and homelessness of the individual.[110] Such nostalgia might have been useful, Anderson and Nipperdey have argued, in the construction of nationalist ideologies. As a medium with an increasingly widespread readership, the novel could promote it. This appropriation of a nostalgic longing for belonging by a nationalist understanding of "imagined communities" engendered national tales and also regional fiction, but soon writers reacted more ambiguously. They came to capitalize on the incongruities that nationalist fiction had left out.

As Romantic nationalism created an ideology of belonging through the "othering" of those outside the "imagined community," on its borders or margins, it had, in fact, already a dual and inherently contradictory relationship with its counterpart, Romantic orientalism. While fictional creations of Highland Arcadias or a rediscovered "mother earth" play with the exotic while fostering an awareness of a national heritage, descriptions of the "other" also serve to define the borders of the imagined nation. Based on notions of exclusivity as well as containment, the writing of the nation necessitates the absorption or exorcism of the other.[111] In that the literary creation of such national spaces conjures up places that are meant to be "exotic," it also undercuts the shared longing for a home or homeland. The "nostalgia" these regional novels create is therefore more akin to a longing for exotic sites. As Nigel Leask has pointed out, in Romantic literature, oriental places "displace the Arcadian *locus amoenus* of neo-classicism from a Mediterranean 'Golden-Age' to a 'contemporary eastern site.'"[112] Both oriental sites and untamed nature in Britain qualify as new ideal sites that contrast with, but also rival, the classical "antique lands" of the Mediterranean. In her recent *The Invention of the Countryside: Hunting, Walking and Ecology in English Literature, 1671–1831*, Donna Landry speaks of the "countryside packaged as a literary phenomenon, a reading experience for urban audiences," a development she links to the beginnings of ecology as well as to a new cult of country-walks and the re-conceptualization of hunting at the time.[113] Edgeworth's national tales as well as Scott's historical novels feed on this new consumption of the countryside and on an interest in the exotic as they cater specifically for readers unfamiliar with the depicted landscapes. Recent criticism of orientalism has amply shown that idealizations of the exotic tend to distort its representation, and as Janet Sorensen has shown in her analysis of Scott's *The Bride of Lammermoor* (1819), the same applies to British marginal landscapes. Scott, she argues, transforms history into landscapes that are romantically "other" to the English reader, but emasculate the Scottish people.[114] Lady Morgan's *The Wild Irish Girl* describes Ireland as "a colonized or a conquered country;" and while the novel succeeds in creating sympathy with the colonized as well as the colonizer, the described landscape similarly reduces it to a contained, cozy, and exotic space.[115] In Edgeworth's *The Absentee*, this connection between orientalism and the inner colonies is comically exemplified by the "picturesque" decorations at Lady Clonbrony's gala night, which include a Chinese pagoda, a Turkish tent, and Alhambra hangings.[116]

While this confusion of orientalism and orientalized homelands turns the nostalgic places of these texts into exotic backdrops, Romantic individualism further conflicts with the new interest in "communal" memories. In *English Fiction of the Romantic Period*, Gary Kelly significantly speaks of the villain society as he analyses the conflicting longings for individual self-fulfillment and the creation of a new community or nation in the Romantic period.[117] This contradiction is an essential aspect of "pre-Romantic" cults of sensibility and sentimentalism, as heroes and heroines of feeling advocate a highly individualist focus on their own emotions while simultaneously depending on an ideology of empathy. Anne Mellor has suggested that women writers attempted to solve this problem by praising an individual subjectivity that located its identity within a human nexus, such as the family. Their work offers an alternative, Mellor argues, to exclusively male manifestations of Romantic sensibility.[118] The domestic Romantic fiction of Burney and Austen, in fact, sheds particularly intriguing light on the disjunction between personal longings and the need of belonging that plagues the Romantic self: *The Wanderer* by directing the stateless heroine towards a familial community, and Austen's novels, as we shall see in the following chapter, by showing how heroines maintain private longings and spaces even while surrounded by "a neighbourhood of voluntary spies," as it is famously put in *Northanger Abbey*.[119]

The Wanderer's subtitle "Female Difficulties" not only promises a treatment of proto-feminist issues, but also a focus on the peripheral participants in historical events in the tradition of Walter Scott. Yet it goes much further in its emphasis on the domestic effects of historical cataclysms, leaving revolutionary France behind very quickly to detail the difficulties experienced by the persecuted heroine at home. *The Wanderer* has consequently been described as "not a novel at all, but a dissertation on the inequalities of the sexes."[120] Its plot can admittedly be seen as submerged by references to current issues and their underlying ideologies. Set in the 1790s but published only in 1814, it has even been dismissed as "a belated novel, striving to have the last word on controversies no one cared about."[121] As a retrospective narrative, however, it significantly draws the nationalist project of writing the past into debate. At the same time, it recycles the collapse of radical sensibility in the 1790s to pinpoint the impact of the resulting xenophobia on nineteenth-century attitudes to the foreigner, to a migrant "other" whose nostalgic memories and longings are radically different from Burkean reactions to the Revolution.

In a recent analysis of the "Burkean themes of migrant maternity, disinheritance, and sexual improprieties of multinational proportions" in early nineteenth-century novels by women writers, Deidre Lynch has significantly suggested that they redeploy Burke's themes in a more radical context by marking their heroines as "by and large irredeemably hybrid."[122] Lynch, however, does not proceed to explore the impact of these alternative narratives of longing and belonging on the writing of nostalgia and the construction of both nationalism and nostalgic places themselves. In her eclectic study of nostalgia as a cultural phenomenon, Svetlana Boym highlights a crucial difference between personal nostalgia and a nostalgia that has turned political, that has become a state policy: "The official memory of the nation-state does not tolerate useless nostalgia, nostalgia for its own sake."[123] *The Wanderer* analyses the effects of longings that have been turned into state policies and their clashes with the heroine's personal needs and desires, casting a different light on both nationalism and nostalgia.

Written in the aftermath of the French Revolution and nearly confiscated by a police officer at Dunkirk in August 1812, *The Wanderer* is the product of warring French and British forms of nationalism and their impact on the lives of those caught up in between.[124] Frances Burney, by that time married to the *émigré* Constitutionalist Alexandre d'Arblay, had first-hand experience of British and French nationalist xenophobia, and her last novel offers insight into the production of fiction about the French Revolution. Instead of detailing the horrors of Robespierre's Terror, the novel briefly refers to the heroine's flight to England and then proceeds to describe her predicament in her "native" country. Juliet *alias* Ellis flees on a boat across the channel and, her money stolen, she arrives as an "itinerant Incognita" (208). She is both perceived as and feels "foreign:" "I feel myself, though in my native country, like a helpless foreigner" (214). In her exile as an outcast at "home," she is "thus strangely alone—thus friendless—thus desolate—thus mysterious" (102). As a nameless, apparently stateless, and homeless heroine, she is seen to wander through the class-system, in which she is judged and treated according to her changing appearance, her apparel, and her shifting monetary and therefore societal status. The idealized England of her imagination clearly fails to supply the sought succor, investing Juliet's raptures on her arrival at the English coast, when she darts "forward with such eagerness" (22), with irony. Her wanderings only commence in her "native" land, become particularly poignant inside English Great Houses, and are further conflicted when she meets the blood relations she cannot claim while retaining her anonymity. Returning "home" from war-torn France offers neither welcome nor safety.

The homelessness and homesickness the Wanderer endures in her "native" country brings the incongruities of nationalism home, transposing it into a domestic context, while at the same time declaring the homeland as an ideologically constructed concept. Gary Kelly has stressed the duality of Romantic nationalism in the 1790s, pointing out that while Britain was at war with a militantly nationalist France, nationalism was also used to block solidarity between French revolutionaries and the Jacobins in Britain.[125] In *The Wanderer*, personal nostalgia stands in stark contrast to the nationalism of post-revolutionary France and the nationalist xenophobia in Britain. When her fellow passengers on the boat that takes her to England discover her confused national and social status, they unanimously agree that Juliet "should hasten to return whence she came" (815). Her upbringing in France additionally underscores the indeterminacy of her national allegiances and her longing for a home. In fleeing France and a potential "home" with a Frenchman who has acquired power during the Terror, Juliet also leaves her childhood home and her only protector, guardian, and father-figure, a Catholic Bishop. Reunited with him, she cries out in French: "My guardian! My preserver! My more than father!—I have not then lost you!" (857). "Home" is exposed as an elusive space and the notion of a fixed home or place of origin as contingent at best. Juliet becomes homesick as soon as she arrives in her "native" land. The place of her nostalgic desire shifts from a long forgotten place of birth to France, the country of her childhood: "Oh hours of refined felicity past and gone, how severe is your contrast with those of heaviness and distaste now endured!" (429).

The dramatized political reactions of the boatload of representative Englishmen she encounters during her flight additionally exacerbates the Wanderer's exilic condition at "home." The presentation of the ostensibly particularly English chivalry of which the Admiral appears to be so proud is almost comical: "You appear to be a person of as right a way of thinking, as if you had lisped English for your mother-tongue" (23). The reaction of the young men to a racially "other," unprotected girl is even more revealing with regard to "female difficulties" and imperial race relations. Dismissive racism—"What, is that black insect buzzing about us still?" (27)—is topped by aggressive desire: "Poor demoiselle . . . wants a little bleaching, to be sure; but she has not bad eyes; nor a bad nose, neither" (27). Harleigh's quixotic knight-errantry is merely a different way of expressing his sexual interest. Elinor Joddrell, the self-contradictory radical antiheroine, comments on his "maimed and defaced Dulcinea . . . this wandering Creole" (50). If a defaced "other" attracts him, she "won't lose a moment in becoming black, patched, and penniless" (28). This "general persecution against such afflicted innocence" (556) exposes British insular xenophobia. Intriguingly, reactions to the Revolution are depicted from the point of view of an unclassified exile, whose disguise as a "native" additionally invokes the incongruities and injustices of both French and British imperial ventures.

Much has been made of Juliet's disguise as "a francophone African," which can be seen as an arraignment of French and British colonial enterprises, and her escape from marriage to one of Robespierre's commissaries.[126] Alternately a spectacle and a scapegoat, this object of charity, suspicions, and sexual desire is exploited for self-serving purposes and has to engage all her powers of resistance "in refusing to be stared at like a wild beast" (54). It is Elinor's "spirit of contradiction" that fixes "her design of supporting the stranger" and "whom she exulted in thus exclusively possessing, as a hidden curiosity" (55). Her strategic display of this exotic curiosity in her own pseudo-liberal revolutionary agenda turns out to be more damaging than the xenophobia of the narrow-minded, largely ignorant, defenders of propriety. The representation of the native "other" in the novel is, in fact, deeply ambiguous and conflicted. It has been shown that blackness serves as a metaphor that connects the heroine's plight to that of slaves, but also that this alterity is altered through what Sara Salih has termed an "epidermic transformation," which converts the unfathomable other into a reassuringly native subject.[127] Claudia Johnson has pointed out an additional ambivalence in the treatment of "the homologous inflections of race, class, and gender."[128] The suggested solidarity with the racially oppressed, from which radical criticism might emerge, is undermined by the ridicule of Mrs. Ireton's slave Mungo, whose status is lower than that of an Incognita who is not "really" black.[129] Juliet undergoes various forms of "enslavement," whereby her change of skin-color can be seen as subverting criticism of racial subjugation by reducing the function of slavery in the novel to a metaphor. This use includes descriptions of the ordeal Juliet undergoes as Mrs. Ireton's "humble companion" and of her attempts to earn her living as an exploited music-teacher or in the confinement of a milliner's shop as well as her escape from the "bonds" of matrimony. The metaphorical connection between enforced marriages and slavery is overtly, even bluntly, put. Juliet flees from a wife's place in her husband's home—a state she describes as the life of "a bond-woman" (848), "destined to exile, slavery, and misery" (863).

The complications of this simultaneous reduction and expansion of "otherness" through such metaphorical uses, however, play a significant role in the novel's eventual assertion of familial domesticity, instead of a national community, as the desired home. In her excellent study of the representations of women in eighteenth-century fiction, *Torrid Zones: Maternity, Sexuality, and Empire in Eighteenth-Century English Narratives*, Felicity Nussbaum shows in detail how the invention of the "other" woman of empire enables the consolidation of a new cult of domesticity as women became associated with the exotic or savage and exotic places were feminized. The resulting domestication of empire tended to reduce it to a metaphor.[130] Burney's *The Wanderer* reacts against earlier representations of "otherness" and redeploys contrasts of nationalist and personal or domestic nostalgia. The theme of confused national identities and the search for home permeates its engagement with metaphorical subjection, eventually letting discourses of racial and national "otherness" re-emerge.

The multivalent deployment of the word "native" in the text pinpoints the Wanderer's shifting status. At first disguised as a "native" dislocated from an undefined "native" land by French imperial politics—and the issues of miscegenation are implied in the discussion of her assumed origins—she employs a camouflage of being at once a "native" and a racial "other," while attempting to reach her "long lost, and fearfully recovered native land" (751), her place of birth, which then turns out to be simply another place of persecution. In questioning ideals of the natural and the innate, Burney plays with the meanings of "native." Considered as French by the English, the Wanderer is termed their "native enemy" (25), yet she also upholds her "native dignity" (51). It is one of the novel's incongruities that while it exposes the suppression sanctioned by class-systems, innate nobility stands nonetheless affirmed. Juliet shares this aristocratic superiority with the similarly exiled Gabriella, her "earliest friend, the chosen sharer of her happier days . . . , restored to her in the hour of her desolation" (395). This foreigner is Juliet's only acknowledged connection in her so-called "native" land. Both have been "driven, without offence, or even accusation, from prosperity and honours, to exile" (390). Both their wandering at once pinpoints and displaces the significance of their origins by representing their experience of exile and consequently their nostalgia for a home elsewhere as identical.

Their parallel predicaments render Juliet's questionable Englishness a mere coincidence, while the characteristics that mark her as "foreign" or "other" indicate the indeterminacy of such categories as Englishness, or Britishness. In particular her accent undercuts her nationality, even though her direct speech is interestingly presented in immaculate "standard" English, as opposed to the various sociolects in the novel. Having been brought up in France, she has "acquired something of a foreign accent" (643). While her "epidermic transformation" externalizes the indeterminacy of her status as a "native other," her accent and attire are the skin-deep categories that deny her the status of a native of England. Accents as marks of ambiguous nationhood significantly recur in the fiction of the time. For the boorish Hughson in Charlotte Smith's *Montalbert*, for example, Montalbert's accent obscures, even denies, his Englishness: "Why, you can't speak much now, Sir. . . . I suppose by your accent, Sir, that you are a foreigner."[131] The Wanderer "understands English on and off at her pleasure" (16), but, unlike Madame Duval's deliberate masking of her lower-class background with a French accent in *Evelina*, her use of assumed and camouflaged "otherness" is not meant as a social imposture. It is purely a means of survival.[132]

In Burney's fiction and increasingly in her later novels, family ties stretch across national borders. Madame Duval's false Frenchness exemplifies Burney's early and primarily comical use of French and "hybrid" characters. In the wake of the French Revolution, representations of the French expectedly become more conflicted. In *The Wanderer*, Juliet's parenthood may be purely British, involving only "transgressions" across class boundaries, but she has two families for whose re-integration she longs. As Lynch has succinctly put it, she remains "irredeemably hybrid."[133] Her "adoptive" family comprises an imprisoned Bishop, his sister, and her unhappily married daughter, who mourns for her dead child and bewails her exile. The head of Juliet's English family as good as refuses to acknowledge the relation, and her anonymous encounter with her half-brother is fraught with the possibilities of incestuous rape. Eventually, however, Lady Aurora and Lord Melbury happily acknowledge the half-sister whose identity, legitimacy, and worth—in a monetary as well as moral sense—have been proved. These two paragons of noble sensibility form the ideal familial community of her nostalgic imagination, evoking "all her tenderest affections" (754). Her connections allow her to receive the offer of marriage she longs for, ending her wandering in a familial community.

Although the Wanderer's search for a home amidst contending nationalisms seems in part to enact the rhetoric of Burke's influential *Reflections on the Revolution in France*, the mixed nationalities of her families effectively dismantle such nationalist alignments. Burke extolled ideological strategies to give the "frame of polity the image of a relation in blood" by

> binding up the constitution of our country with our dearest domestic ties, adopting our fundamental laws into the bosom of our family affections, keeping inseparable and cherishing with the warmth of all their combined and mutually reflected charities our state, our hearths, our sepulchres, and our altars.[134]

The Wanderer's hybridity subverts this fiction of a nation of relations. Instead, the novel ends with the realization of a domestic alternative, at once evading and transcending nationalist ideologies of the homeland. Burney's retrospective novel is of course far removed from radical endorsements of a revolutionary agenda. The chastised antiheroine, Elinor, is a proto-feminist, pro-revolutionary, suicidal atheist who is shown to proclaim her ideological leanings primarily out of a "spirit of contradiction" (55). Various critics have considered Elinor the result of a misreading of Mary Wollstonecraft. Julia Epstein has pointedly called her Juliet's "protofeminist revolutionary alter ego," whose suicide attempt rescues the heroine "just as Bertha Mason would later rescue Jane Eyre."[135] While the novel treats the migrant's difficulties with sympathy, Elinor is, in fact, deeply tainted by her eccentric and, it is emphasized, inherently selfish appropriation of such sympathies with the suppressed. It is this twist that complicates an anti-Jacobin reading, singling out the novel as an essentially, and indeed fascinatingly, ambiguous treatment of the repercussions of nationalist and radical ideologies and their abuse of sympathies and longings.

As Frances Burney's last novel reacts against the concept of a British nationalist counter-ideology to the expansionist French nationalism, it takes the domestic novel into the realm of a more politically conscious genre without lapsing into the openly proclaimed agenda of nationalist literature. Romantic nationalism as founded on a shared culture is instead shown to clash with a personal past; the xenophobia nurtured by Jacobin as well as anti-Jacobin ideologies with the heroine's hybridity; and a manufactured nationalist heritage nostalgia with homesickness. Ultimately, the antiheroine's false liberality and eventual breakdown undercut the liberal, even radical, attitudes that underlie this representation of a woman pursued by her husband, of the racism directed against a (seemingly) black refugee, and the treatment of an employee or hired companion. The heroine herself is not only safely married, but revealed to be white, legitimate, and a member of the British upper classes after all. Nonetheless, *The Wanderer* provides an alternative to pro-revolutionary novels and anti-Jacobin reactions, and offers an exploration of imperialist and nationalist economies and ideologies at home. As such, it sheds a different light on the heterogeneity of Romantic fiction and the writing of the French Revolution and forms an apt conclusion to an analysis of radical and conservative approaches to nostalgia at the time.

2
Headaches or Heartaches: Clinical and Romantic Nostalgia in Jane Austen's Novels

F ANNY PRICE, JANE AUSTEN'S QUIETEST AND SHIEST HEROINE, IS REpeatedly being bullied, which singles out *Mansfield Park* (1814) as the Austen novel that contains the most violence and distress. Deliberately as well as carelessly inflicted, the violence might not be physical, but it has telling physical results, as strategic reminders of this poor relative's lowly position in the household cause low spirits and bad health as well. As Aunt Norris, whose own role in the Great House of the title is never as central as she would like to have it, repeatedly points out, Fanny has to remember that wherever she is, she "must be the lowest and last" (221). A comical, but nonetheless sinister persecutor of innocence, Aunt Norris relishes putting Fanny back into her place by deliberately "depressing her spirits too far, to make her remember that she is not a *Miss Bertram*" (10). Depression is central in a novel that not only subjects its heroine to suppressed lovesickness, but also to the effects of repeated physical dislocation and a group-pressure that both mirrors and complements patriarchal tyranny instead of replacing or dispelling it. This is not the only shift in the representation of emotional distress in the novel. Fanny's headaches conform to an attitude towards physical symptoms of longing that is at the heart of novels of sensibility, parodied after the genre's heyday, but then channeled into a Romantic idealization of nostalgia as a form of emotional memory. This development is traceable in Austen's novels. A reassessment of the clinical and Romantic nostalgia of the much derided heroine of *Mansfield Park*, in fact, sheds a revealingly different light on Jane Austen's significance for the changing representation of feeling and specifically Romantic longing in the British novel.

Fanny's life at Mansfield is never stable or secure. Her shifting status significantly undermines the alleged stability or even stolidity of the house (and of the novel). From the beginning, the Bertrams leave the possibility open that they might easily get rid of their adopted poor relative at any time "should her disposition be really bad" (10). The coincidence that Fanny is eventually sent back to her parents for an extended visit of unlimited duration exactly after she has displeased her uncle shows that the frequent reminder of her precarious position in the household is no idle threat. Her final resistance as she refuses the eligible single man of good fortune, defies her uncle, goes against her aunts' wishes, and proceeds to ignore even the advice of the two men who really care about her and whom she loves, her brother and her cousin, is the crucial moment in which her passive resistance becomes more active or at least more overtly assertive. For once Fanny refuses to succumb to the advice of those who consider themselves her "betters." She proceeds to go against her cousins' group-pressure as well as her uncle's exertion of patriarchal prerogatives. While she might have given up her horse and agreed to act against her wishes, she will not marry one man while she loves another. Interpretations of the novel that only stress the moral stance that undoubtedly also underlies her refusal of the obnoxiously charming Mr. Crawford are, in fact, misleading in that they fail to see how her persistence—Sir Thomas refers to an "independence of spirit" that he terms "perverse" (318)—in holding on to her true love ties in with the money-versus-love theme that runs through Austen's novels. This theme accounts for much of her continued popularity, but critics have instead focused on her parody of excessive emotionalism and invalidism as the nadir of sentimentalism or, alternatively, on imperialist undercurrents. What I aim to show in this reading of her novels is the precise nature and significance of her treatments of sensibility and the clash between personal longing and communal pressures.

The heroines' private and often secret longing is central to the romance or courtship plots of all of Austen's novels, but their succession displays a shift in the representation of feeling and, I shall argue, specifically of nostalgia. *Persuasion*, her last finished and posthumously published novel, undoubtedly represents her most direct and most affirmative engagement with Romanticism, but it is in *Mansfield Park* that an understanding of longing as a set of symptoms merges into a Romantic appreciation of memory and nostalgia. Fanny Price's main objection to Crawford is her secret love for another. She is not only correct (and fortuitously proved right) in her estimate of his character, but she is shown to be right in choosing love over money. Turning down an eligible offer, she instead endorses a Romantic, specifically nostalgic, love that is secret, to some extent unrequited, and rooted in the past. Nostalgia for a childhood attachment has nourished this love. It has grown out of her homesickness and it pinpoints nostalgia's role in the representation of true love and the right lover in Austen's novels. Fanny's nostalgia results from and supports her endeavors to hold on to original, and then much more remarkably, transposed loyalties while under the continuous threat of further dislocations. At the same time, her physical delicacy links her experience of nostalgic longing to the somatics of distress exhibited by eighteenth-century heroines and heroes of sensibility. Her headaches both mask and express emotional pain:

> Fanny went to bed with her heart as full as on the first evening of her arrival at the Park. The state of her spirits had probably had its share in her indisposition; for she had been feeling neglected, and been struggling against discontent and envy for some days past. As she leant on the sofa, to which she had retreated that she might not be seen, the pain of her mind had been much beyond that in her head; and the sudden change which Edmund's kindness had then occasioned, made her hardly know how to support herself. (74)

Fanny's headache evokes an entire tradition of literary heartaches as well as headaches. As she dwells on her suppressed love for Edmund and her irrepressible jealousy of Miss Crawford, who has taken away the horse Edmund had meant to be Fanny's and seems now bent on taking Edmund as well, she symptomatically rehearses her first traumatic experience, the dislocation from the childhood home that has brought her to Mansfield. Homesickness as the original meaning of nostalgia is indeed the central emotion in the novel. Fanny suffers from a clinical nostalgia that eventually converges with her lovesickness, just as her love for Edmund grows out of her gratitude for his help in alleviating her original homesickness. In the course of the novel, this clinical home*sickness* changes into a creative Romantic nostalgia. It is a survival strategy, an incentive to resist group-pressure, and a cherishing of solitude.

Fanny's resilience, even resistance, is easily the novel's most controversial aspect. Her stubborn self-sufficiency does not quite fit the astonishingly persistent image of the prim creep-mouse that detractors of the novel have conjured up. Ever since Lionel Trilling's sweeping generalization that "[n]obody, I believe, has ever found it possible to like the heroine of *Mansfield Park*" and notably because of the "alienating . . . state of the heroine's health" in his 1955 essay, literary critics have rather uncritically rehearsed and intensified this dismissal.[1] In the early eighties, Nina Auerbach declared that "few would contradict this epitaph today" and proceeded to call the entire novel "unlikeable" and its heroine a "killjoy."[2] John Wiltshire refers to an "impatience that one inevitably feels," implying a reader-analysis that never takes place. Even while he tentatively suggests that from one point of view, Fanny is "an interesting psychological study in the manners and attitudes of a radically insecure and traumatized personality," this is hardly more than a slight moderation of what he sees as the usual and natural reaction to the quiet heroine.[3] More sympathetically, Elaine Jordan points out that it is astonishing how few readers give "any recognition to this disadvantaged girl's resistance."[4] Even though Tony Tanner already suggested that Fanny had to exert a form of passive resistance, the sheer wealth of derogatory comments on Mansfield's stolidity has swallowed up this tentative recognition of her difficulties.[5]

A close reading of Fanny's affliction has remained remarkably absent from the plethora of recent reassessments of this, Austen's most controversial, novel. As I shed new light on its representation of nostalgia, I shall also provide a different reading of Fanny's resilience as well as of the headaches and heartaches of Austen's livelier heroines. Before returning to *Mansfield Park*, I shall start with Marianne's clinical lovesickness and homesickness in *Sense and Sensibility*, move on to pinpoint the afflictions that threaten even Austen's most resolute and sensible heroines, and then underline particularly Elizabeth Bennet's sick headaches in *Pride and Prejudice* as perhaps the most surprising psychophysical complaint in early-nineteenth-century fiction.

Moving House and Home in Austen's Plots

There have been various accounts of the shifting treatment of sickness and sensibility in *Sense and Sensibility*. Written between 1795 and 1798, though not published until 1811, it is surely Austen's most direct reassessment of the changing attitudes to sensibility. It is perhaps *the* canonized parody of the sensibility cults. Admittedly, Austen's critical reaction to the relish in medical detail displayed in earlier novels at first sight appears to suggest a preference of sense over sensibility and also that the conspicuously sarcastic parody of Mrs. Musgrove's famous sighs in *Persuasion* can be taken as a typical example of Austen's attitudes to feeling in general. Her novels, it is has been argued again and again, rewrite sentimental plots and refrain from engaging fully in the rising Romanticism not only by securely remaining in a domestic setting, but also by treating emotional effusions with suspicion. As a result, they have been canonized as novels about, rather than of, sensibility if not necessarily as mere parodies.

But nostalgia forms a central and not necessarily mocked emotional experience. Its treatment becomes particularly interesting as the clinical meaning of homesickness meets Romanticized idealizations of longing. The defense of nostalgia forms an important twist in *Mansfield Park* and, even more pointedly, in *Persuasion*. Restoring nostalgia as a private longing, these, Austen's most Romantic, novels work around excesses of affected sensibility *and* its conservative critiques. This shift seems strangely at odds with the exposure of sentimentalism in Austen's earlier fiction, but what is less obvious is that her heroines all have to contend with the threat the community poses to the individual, and that submission to propriety is not always as laudable as it is often made out in conservative fiction. While the resulting clash of communal and private prejudices is frequently comical, what is perhaps the most enduring attraction of Austen's fiction is after all precisely the triumph of personal desire and marrying for love over communal pressures.

Austen's treatment of her heroines' longings is indeed neither unequivocally ironical nor ever completely supportive. Many critics have consequently remained confused as to the precise meaning of her revisions of literary clichés. Ignoring Austen's indebtedness to novels of sensibility, Nicholas Dames has recently argued that her fiction displays "a modern sentimentality and poignant yearning" that is supposedly communal and no longer either physical or isolating.[6] In *Jane Austen and the Body*, John Wiltshire, however, suggests that it is especially in the later novels that the question of health becomes central.[7] He links what he sees as a growing concern with illness to the contrast between "a character's experience in and of the body and other's readings of it:" a "feigned sensibility of fashionable currency" complicates representations of the real sensibility of suffering, while it also accounts for much of the novels' comedy.[8] In 1812 an anonymous review of *Sense and Sensibility* notably already pointed out that the novel was about the "proper quantity of sensibility."[9] As we have seen, this was a popular theme in fiction at the time, a reaction to the most memorable excesses of the sensibility cults. Marianne Dashwood "detest[s] jargon of every kind" as it is "worn and hackneyed out of all sense and meaning,"[10] a sentiment also articulated by the titular hero of Charlotte Smith's *Marchmont* (1796), who suggests that there ought to be a new word for sensibility: "I hate the word, it is so prostituted" (52).

So far from simply breaking away from a homogenous sentimental genre by parodying or inverting it, Austen's novels reuse the plots as well as the literary conventions of earlier as well as contemporary fiction to strip off their overused trappings and to reclaim feeling from affectation. Longing and specifically, though by no means exclusively, love-interest are undeniably the central themes of Austen's novels, and while she pokes fun at the affected languages of sentimentalism, her engagement with literary conventions is never unequivocal. Historical and interdisciplinary approaches, combined with the rediscovery of long-neglected women writers, have done much to revise Austen's role within the literary productions of her time. Maaja Stewart's *Domestic Realities and Imperial Fictions: Jane Austen's Novels in Eighteenth-Century Contexts* and Mary Waldron's *Jane Austen and the Fiction of her Time* are among the most recent revaluations of her writing that set it emphatically in its cultural and political as well as literary contexts. Stewart's insightful study participates in ongoing reassessments of the oblique references to colonial properties and imperial contexts that have been spotted in Austen's novels ever since Said's influential analysis of *Mansfield Park*. *The Postcolonial Jane Austen*, edited by You-me Park and Rajeswari Sunder Rajan, has even more recently addressed the problematics and potentials of such readings.[11] Waldron has instead focused on literary contexts, presenting Austen as a radical innovator who challenged the literary conventions of her time to transform fiction.[12] Clara Tuite's *Romantic Austen: Sexual Politics and the Literary Canon*, by contrast, situates Austen within reconfigurations of Romanticism as she sets late-nineteenth-century concepts of Austen as a novelist of "green England" against the little-understood anticipation of this association in her novels.[13] Although such contextual studies build on Marilyn Butler's influential *Jane Austen and the War of Ideas*, they seek to strike a balance between interpretations of Austen as an essentially conservative writer and the equally extreme views taken by the "subversive school" of critics who see her as flaunting irony to evade and disrupt emotions.[14]

The best account of the much-discussed ambiguities of Jane Austen's supposed "Tory conservatism," however, remains Claudia Johnson's *Jane Austen: Women, Politics, and the Novel*. When Austen applies her parodic style to the "stuff of conservative fiction," Johnson convincingly argues, she engages in "a kind of piracy [that] commandeered conservative novelistic discourse."[15] The clichés Austen ridicules are as frequently the conventions of anti-Jacobin conservatism as of radical writers. Sensibility was after all not only the rallying cry of radicals, as Burkean authors deployed it as part of their conservative agenda as well. Austen's reassessments of sensibility reflect this ambiguity. Indeed, as Johnson has argued elsewhere, Austen's parodies of literary conventions react against *conservative* clichés when they dismantle the ideological frameworks of women's redemptive debility and refuse to grant the abandoned heroine her deathbed scene.[16] While the physical exertions of her liveliest heroines—Elizabeth

Bennet's dirty petticoats spring to mind—echo the vehemently derided health of chastised heroines in conservative fiction, in *Sense and Sensibility*, the abandoned woman's refusal to die graciously, like Clarissa did so influentially, marks the novel as a parody of conservative, not radical, uses of sensibility.[17] Johnson's influential reading of the novel as a "dark and disenchanted novel" has indeed cast a remarkable light on Austen's ambiguous use of literary conventions and specifically on her representation of feeling. *Sense and Sensibility* complicates the simpler world of Burkean fiction by exposing institutions of order (patrimony, marriage, and family) as promoters of avarice and oppression. Love of money is moreover the principal vice, as it is in many radical novels of the time.[18]

As Jane Austen's seemingly most clearly structured novel, *Sense and Sensibility* has expectedly been at the center of such reassessments. The most fruitful points of inquiry have been the contrast between Elinor and Marianne's love-interests and the way they deal with their disappointments, yet increasingly also Colonel Brandon's tumultuous past. Despite the novel's pithy title, which may easily mislead the reader to approach the novel "much as Mary Bennet would, as dramas of moral correction," as Claudia Johnson has pointedly put it, there is no clear opposition.[19] The sisters do not serve as embodiments of sense or sensibility. Mary Waldron has even gone so far as to suggest that Marianne "has really done no more to deserve the calamity which has befallen her than Elinor."[20] While there clearly is a difference in the sisters' behavior, it is important that the more prudent sister crucially misinterprets her seemingly steady lover, just as Willoughby's resemblance to the "hero of a favourite story" (43) misleads Marianne. Elinor moreover feels her disappointment, though more secretly than her sister, and it is this ability to feel that redeems her even in the eyes of a reader of sensibility: she cannot suppress her lovesickness or reason it away, but only conceal her pain. While she thereby conforms to polite etiquette, she also needs to shirk the sociability of intimacy: "She was stronger alone" (141). She might be more prudent, but she is also more withdrawn and more unsociably solitary. Still, she does not additionally enhance her emotional experience, as her sister seems to be doing when she "courted the misery which a contrast between the past and present was certain of giving," (83) "in all probability not merely giving way to as a relief, but feeding and encouraging as a duty" (77).

"In all probability," however, draws any simple conclusions into question. In Austen's novels, we always have to be wary of taking either self-representations or interpretations by other characters at face value. Marianne is never guilty of affectation. Although she would consider "composure a disgrace" after her first parting from Willoughby, her "sensibility was potent enough" to prevent it without any artificial means (83). Elinor suffers more secretly, perhaps more discreetly, when she seeks solitude to be "at liberty to think and be wretched" (135), but she suffers nonetheless, and ultimately it remains unclear whether her concealment has not given just as much pain as its expression would have. Her mother is mortified to find "that she had erred in relying on Elinor's representation of herself" (355). A reliance of the protagonists' representations of themselves or others is almost always misleading in Austen's novels and particularly in her parodic passages.

Accounts of Colonel Brandon are of course so contradictory as to puzzle characters and readers exceedingly. Recent reassessments of the novel have expectedly focused very often on his apparent dullness, his tempestuous past, and his role as the object of Marianne's second attachment. In sentimental fashion, he recounts embedded stories of excessive lovesickness when he details the stories of his lost love and her daughter. Their offstage suffering follows the familiar pattern of the abandoned heroine of sensibility, and they can be said to suffer by proxy for Marianne. Brandon means his story as a warning, but this conservative narrative is mediated within the novel: indirect speech renders its presentation curiously detached. The story of the two abandoned Elizas is, in fact, not an embedded sentimental story at all, but a synopsis. Its melodramatic potential is skimmed over.

Taking the novel as Austen's reaction to "the sentimental love-madness vogue" of the late-eighteenth century, Helen Small has interestingly remarked that Brandon stands "very much in the eighteenth-century tradition of the man of feeling," but also cautioned that his story's "classically sentimental content ... sits rather oddly within a novel otherwise highly critical of sentimentalism."[21] Melodramatic scenes in *Sense and Sensibility* are always mediated, and they are moreover invariably told by men. Claudia Johnson has intriguingly shown how Brandon's story of the first Eliza fits the clichés of conservative fiction. As he suggests that it would have been better for Eliza to die of her disappointment than to survive only to sink further into sin, Johnson argues, his expectation of both the first Eliza's and Marianne's death subscribes to the same cliché as Willoughby's "reassuring act of ventriloquy" when he envisions a deathbed scene starring himself as the object of Marianne's last regrets.[22] This is of course very different from what actually happens. The novel refuses to grant a sentimental death. Against all expectations, Marianne recovers. The second Eliza similarly lives to bear Willoughby's child in secrecy, apparently unmolested by either his visits or the intrusion of virtuous lady-visitors in the ilk of Lady Bidulph in Sheridan's novel.

Yet two happy marriages modify this sturdy recovery of abandoned heroines, granting a more conventional happy end. When Brandon marries the recovered Marianne, he follows an essentially nostalgic impulse and thereby brings his own more melodramatic story to a close. Tentatively hinting at the role of nostalgia in his revived love life, Maaja Stewart speaks of his "atemporal perspective" as the "memory of the dead Eliza is thus imposed upon the living Marianne."[23] Glenda Hudson has similarly suggested that his love for Marianne is more "like a transfer or resuscitation of his former passion for Eliza."[24] This happy conclusion to his nostalgically transposed lovesickness has largely been responsible for the mixed reactions to Brandon in recent criticism. Clara Tuite terms him a man of feeling who is also "a reformed rake, a man with a past" and a voyeur, and Mary Waldron singles him out as "the nearest approach to a romantic figure among the men" in the novel.[25] Waldron indeed stands more traditional interpretations on their heads by suggesting that Brandon's past renders him not so much Marianne's "acceptance of second-best," but rather "the reality of the vision . . . she has misread in Willoughby," and that Marianne need not change in any essential way as she and Brandon are alike in their sensibility.[26] Could it be that Austen has gone so far in denying a conservative sentimental narrative of moral chastisement as to go against expectations of the heroine's change as well?

In a similar way of course, Elinor and Edward do not change: the circumstances that unite them are out of their control. Lucy Steele's scheming machinations as she "pursu[es] her own interest in every thought" (357) and her much more suitable second attachment to Edward's more congenial, i.e., as nasty as Lucy, brother fortuitously free Edward. It is to no credit of either Elinor or Edward that they are able to marry. Similarly, a series of coincidences saves Marianne from further temptations and she becomes Brandon's "reward" not because he has done anything to rescue her, but simply because he has assisted Edward by giving him a living, which renders the alliance additionally suitable. Marianne of course appears calmer, less fervent, after her illness, but the narrator slyly indicates at the end that ultimately, her whole heart will be as much and, we can safely assume, as fervently involved in her love for Brandon (379). Their similar history of suffering thereby denotes their second attachment as a romantic, and indeed a nostalgic, ending after all. Marianne marries "a man who had suffered no less than herself under the event of a former attachment" (372). So far from overcoming the past and denouncing fervent feeling, they can console each other and revive the keenness of emotions that have almost deadened under their first disappointments. They might not be alike in their sensibility, as Brandon is as quiet, almost muted, and introspective as Marianne is expressive, but they do share a nostalgic longing for love:

> Colonel Brandon was now happy, as all those who best loved him, believed he deserved to be;—in Marianne he was consoled for every past affliction;—her regard and her society restored his mind to animation, and his spirits to cheerfulness: and that Marianne found her own happiness in forming his, was equally the persuasion and delight of each observing friend. Marianne could never love by halves; and her whole heart became, in time, as much devoted to her husband, as it had once been to Willoughby. (379)

Their second attachment holds a nostalgic reward for both of them. When he rediscovers in Marianne a likeness to his lost love, Brandon's lovesickness converges into a nostalgia that is so happily transposed that it does not even leave room for allegations of a betrayal of his first love. A fondness for nostalgic recollection moreover links Brandon and Marianne together early in the novel. Marianne praises nostalgia, asserting that she "love[s] to be reminded of the past, . . . whether it be melancholy or gay, I love to recall it" (92). Her nostalgic attitude brings the image of his own nostalgically recalled first love to Brandon's mind, even while he admits that his own recollections are fading: "If I am not deceived by the uncertainty, the partiality of tender recollection, there is a very strong resemblance between them, as well in mind as person" (205). Eventually, Marianne's recovery not only serves as a resuscitation, as it were, of the lost Eliza, but her own lovesick and homesick longings are cured by the gain of an eligible estate belonging to nostalgic Brandon. It makes up for the loss of the original home, the nostalgically commemorated Norland.

Literal homesickness and the loss of the family home are central themes in the novel, as they are indeed in most of Austen's novels.[27] *Sense and Sensibility* opens with the heroines' eviction from their ancestral estate: "The family of Dashwood had been long settled in Sussex. Their estate was large, and their residence was at Norland Park, in the centre of their property" (3). After its loss, nostalgia suffuses the novel. Whatever may be said about other emotional or psychophysical afflictions, homesickness is always sympathetically treated in Austen's fiction. Marianne's panegyric on the missed autumnal beauties of "dear, dear Norland" may induce her sister to ridicule her "passion for dead leaves" (87–88), but it is much more than a rehearsal of picturesque jargon.[28] What it does rehearse is Marianne's last evening at home, the origin of nostalgia in the novel:

> "Dear, dear Norland!" said Marianne, as she wandered alone before the house, on the last evening of their being there, "when shall I cease to regret you!—when learn to feel a [sic] home elsewhere!—O happy house! could you know what I suffer in now viewing you from this spot, from whence perhaps I may view you no more!—and you, ye well-known trees!—but you will continue the same.—No leaf will decay because we are removed, nor any branch become motionless although we can observe you no longer!" (27)

Marianne's effusions recall the equally nostalgic panegyrics of the more dramatically isolated, homeless heroines of Gothic fiction. In Radcliffe's *The Mysteries of Udolpho*, Emily similarly evokes the happy hours of her childhood spent in a peaceful home: "O, peaceful, happy shades!—scenes of my infant delights, of parental tenderness now lost for ever!—why must I leave ye!— In your retreats I should still find safety and repose. Sweet hours of my childhood—I am now to leave even your last memorials!" (114). Marianne's regrets parallel Emily's very closely. Her eulogy is not sufficiently different to qualify as a mere parody. What brings about Emily's panegyrics is moreover not simply the contrast between Gothic entrapment and tranquil retreats. On the contrary, she indulges nostalgic recollections long before Montoni enters the story. Remembrance of the dead father suffuses her nostalgia, as it does Marianne's. Like the bereaved Dashwood sisters, Emily meets with social mortifications: "Remembering the delicacy and the tenderness of St Aubert, the happy, happy days she had passed in these scenes, and contrasting them with the coarse and unfeeling behaviour of Madame Cheron, and with the future hours of mortification" (112), Emily deplores a change that is still far removed from her confinement in the castle, but clearly foreshadows this experience. Fashionable and unfeeling Madame Cheron has moreover much of Mrs. John Dashwood and Mrs. Ferrars in her. Sudden indigence, homelessness, and social mortification are the fate of the Dashwood sisters, and subsequently, of Fanny Price and Anne Elliot in Austen's later novels as well as of Emily St Aubert in Radcliffe's novel or Emmeline in Charlotte Smith's. Marianne is perhaps least fervent in succumbing to nostalgic pining as she already envisions a possible cure: it is a matter of time, she admits even in her first nostalgic pangs, that she will come to feel at home elsewhere, to form a second attachment, as it were, to another home.

A nostalgic mood permeates the novel despite the indisputable irony that works against many of the evoked literary clichés (conservative and radical alike). Willoughby's absence impels Marianne to wander "about the village of Allenham, indulging the recollection of past enjoyment and crying over the present reverse" (83), but her affection for Allenham is more than just lovesickness. The Great House at Allenham has, in fact, sparked off the girls' curiosity long before Willoughby makes his first appearance. It reminds them of home: "on one of their earliest walks, [they] discovered an ancient respectable looking mansion, which, by reminding them a little of Norland, interested their imagination and made them wish to be better acquainted with it" (40). It can be said to have fed into her love. Very pointedly, Brandon's Delaford is "a nice old fashioned place" (196) that eventually takes the place of both Norland and Allenham. At the end of the novel, not only Brandon, but also Elinor and Edward reside in or near Delaford. It is Marianne's "visits at Delaford [that assist in] bringing Marianne and Colonel Brandon together" (378). The new home thus replicates the lost one and thereby heals Marianne's homesickness. The novel's structure, I wish to argue, is built on the nostalgic's dislocation, affliction, and return, and as the novel carefully sets true suffering apart from affectation, such nostalgia is taken seriously and its curative properties underlined.

Marianne's illness is as much a clinical nostalgia as the result of a disappointment in love. As she lies ill, she desires to be taken home to her mother, even though she cannot actually return to the original home. That her succumbing to physical illness delays her return home is to her the worst exacerbation: "the idea of what to-morrow would have produced, but for this unlucky illness, made every ailment more severe; for on that day they were to have begun their journey home; . . . were to have taken their mother by surprise on the following forenoon. The little that she said, was all in lamentation of this inevitable delay" (308). In her delirious rambling, she recurs again and again to the desire for a return home and her fears that her mother might not reach her in time if she, incongruously, "goes round by London" (311), the place where Marianne has suffered her crucial disappointment and her most ardent homesickness. The nostalgic's geography is an emotional reconstruction of actual places, revealing their subjective significance.

Marianne's eventual return to the neighborhood of Barton, their new home, in the vicinity of both Allenham and Delaford even more pointedly, evokes recollections that are "peculiar," the mixture of pleasure and pain that is intrinsic to a nostalgic return: "as they approached Barton, indeed, and entered on scenes, of which every field and every tree brought some peculiar, some painful recollection, she grew silent and thoughtful, and turning away her face from their notice, sat earnestly gazing through the window" (342). But her feelings for the landscape near home are sympathetically presented: Elinor "could neither wonder nor blame" (342). The return cures the psychophysical effects of nostalgia by rendering nostalgic recollection at first "peculiar" and then increasingly less painful. Eventually, Marianne can even look at the spot where she first encountered Willoughby "with so little pain" (344).

Marianne's illness is clearly not a parody. The imputed rejection of the physically pining heroine of sensibility as a sentimental cliché is, in fact, neither as extreme nor as new as it has often been made out. Marianne's fever might be the result of a neglected sore throat as well as of lovesickness and ultimately also a clinical nostalgia, but her danger is real and presented as an important crisis or turning point in the novel. *Sense and Sensibility* shifts away from the conservative sentimental plot of the victimized imprudent heroine by letting her recover and form new attachments and, even more markedly, by showing her most dangerous imprudence to be no more than the "imprudence of sitting in her wet shoes and stockings" (306). But her fever is nonetheless a psychophysical affliction that is carefully prepared for. Her cold serves as a convincible catalyst that counteracts possible dismissals of the sickbed scenes as exaggerated or unrealistic. Suspense and disappointment weaken Marianne. She is "very much plagued lately with nervous head-aches" (219) and "has had a nervous complaint on her for several weeks" (227). After her disappointment in love she yearns to go home, but needs to acknowledge that they owe Mrs. Jennings some more weeks of their company. The yearning for home revives original homesickness and exacerbates regrets for a lost love, and these combined sources of nostalgia at first materialize as its clinical variant before the traditional cure, the return home, sees the nostalgic healed.

The shifting nature of Marianne's longing indeed strikes at the heart of the indeterminacy of nostalgia and lovesickness as clinical terms as well as emotions, while they also reveal the ambiguity of the novel's representation of psychophysical affliction.[29] By contrast, Frances Sheridan's earlier *Sidney Bidulph* much more emphatically rejects the cliché of the physically lovesick heroine. As we have seen, Sidney's sore throat precedes her disappointment. Still, at least her hero ultimately succumbs to lovesickness. Claudia Johnson has suggested that Marianne's failure to conform to the deathbed scenes imagined for her by both Brandon and Willoughby shows a radical reversal of a conservative narrative,[30] but Willoughby commits the same "incivility in surviving [Marianne's] loss" (379). Although he regrets his financially sensible choice, he finds "no inconsiderable degree of domestic felicity" (379). Unlike the suicidal heroes of earlier novels, including Sheridan's Faulkland and the would-be suicide Delamere in Smith's *Emmeline*, he leads a comfortable, apparently quiet, domestic life with his breed of horses and dogs. The narrator quickly defies readers who expect a more dramatic end for the pitiable villain: "But that he was for ever inconsolable—that he fled from society, or contracted a habitual gloom of temper, or died of a broken heart, must not be depended on—for he did neither" (379). Ironically, this failure to show sufficient evidence of remorse undercuts any sympathy, and Marianne is therefore free to marry someone else. Much of the comedy of the novel's end rests in this happy disposal of all protagonists: even the nasty characters enjoy a degree of domestic happiness. Lucy Steele's second choice is more suitable for herself as well as convenient for Elinor and Edward. Similarly, Mr. Collins's choice of Charlotte Lucas frees Elizabeth Bennet from further maternal pressure in *Pride and Prejudice*, but also guarantees a comfortable arrangement for Charlotte and himself.

Economic considerations are central to the inheritance and courtship plots of Austen's novels, displacing, most emphatically in *Northanger Abbey*, a more Gothic terror. Financial prudence remains the choice of villains and boors, although more rarely also of unromantic sensible young women like Charlotte Lucas in *Pride and Prejudice* or Mrs. Norris in *Mansfield Park*, while the novels' heroes and heroines usually deem an affective marriage worth while a risk despite all warnings. Elinor Dashwood accepts Edward Ferrars even though his new living has just been declared enough for a single man, but not enough for him to marry Lucy, as the latter prudently acknowledges by transferring her affections to Edward's financially independent brother. Yet, throughout the novels, the loss of home and the need to seek out a comfortable establishment as a way to make up for this loss at least financially are a central driving force. The affective marriage as an ideal has to compete with economic ideas of comfort. In *Pride and Prejudice*, Mrs. Bennet lives under the constant fear of being turned out of her house after her husband's death and frantically tries to marry off her five daughters. Although urged to marry "from the pure and disinterested desire of an establishment,"[31] Elizabeth refuses obnoxious Mr. Collins despite her mother's hysterical pleas and is horrified when her friend Charlotte accepts him to secure "a comfortable home" (108).

Increasingly, economic necessities and not only ideas of comfort begin to influence the heroines' decisions. Catherine Morland might be one of a superabundance of children, but she is made welcome at home after her return from Bath and Northanger Abbey. Her lovesickness inclines her to a "loss of spirits," which her unsentimental mother diagnoses as a "getting out of humour with home because it is not so grand as Northanger" (240–41), but she is expected to settle back in at home. The lack of raised expectations at her departure for the fashionable world is after all an essential part of the novel's parodic aspect. Similarly, Marianne can look forward to quiet "pleasures in retirement and study" in her mother's cottage (379) after her return home, and the Bennet sisters are not indigent yet. Nobody really forces them to accept any man with a good fortune, and Elizabeth's choice of Darcy causes more astonishment than pleasure. Mr. Bennet wishes to "advise [her] to think better of it" (376). Her rather mortified, but essentially self-possessed, opposition to her father's advice and, more pointedly, her spirited dismissal of Lady Catherine, in fact, rework a popular sentimental cliché. At the end, Lady Catherine has to condescend to "wait on [Elizabeth] at Pemberley, in spite of that pollution which its woods had received, not merely from the presence of such a mistress, but the visits of her uncle and aunt from the city" (388). Elizabeth is a self-possessed and, despite her interesting headaches, a vitally healthy heroine who comically defies parental pressure. It is true that she is emphatically set against her youngest sister Lydia, whose unafraid stoutness and consequent sexual prowess take Elizabeth's physical energy to more dangerous extremes, but Elizabeth's rejection of Collins, her defiance of her mother, and her spirited dismissal of Lady Catherine are the more remarkable when read against the anti-Jacobin plots of the time.

Admittedly, parental opposition in Austen's fiction is often a very watered down, even comically presented, version of patriarchal tyranny. In the later novels, this subtly changes. Sir Thomas's project to break Fanny's spirits in order to render Mr. Crawford's estate more eligible in *Mansfield Park* exposes the respectable, self-righteous paterfamilias as a pompous bully whose ideas of a marital alliance contrast with his niece's new-fangled notions of an affectionate, companionate marriage. Her financial dependence on her uncle underscores this plot. Elizabeth can smugly point out to the condescending Lady Catherine that her own affairs are none of her ladyship's concerns, and Mr. Darcy can afford to displease his aunt. Even Anne Elliot has only Lady

Russell's uneasiness to fear when she goes against this maternal surrogate's wishes for an alliance with Mr. Elliot in *Persuasion*. Her father is indifferent, as "he had no affection for Anne, and no vanity flattered" (248). Lady Russell is therefore the "only one among them, whose opposition of feeling could excite any serious anxiety . . . Lady Russell must be suffering some pain in understanding and relinquishing Mr. Elliot, and be making some struggles to become truly acquainted with, and do justice to Captain Wentworth. This however was what Lady Russell had now to do" (249). Her earlier parental interference has deprived the lovers of eight years of happiness; now she has to overcome her prejudices. The pithy comment that this is simply what she has to do now is one of the most emphatic dismissals of parental displeasure in the fiction of the time. I shall come back to the revision of first attachments in *Persuasion*, but it is important to note that Anne, though dependent, is by no means threatened by poverty, and in this her situation is very different from that of Fanny Price in *Mansfield Park* or Emma Watson in the earlier, unfinished novel *The Watsons*. There, an economic threat is vital to the plot. Reversals in the family's financial situation constitute the choice of partners.

The beginning of *The Watsons* sees the heroine, Emma Watson, return to her family after her aunt's unfortunate second marriage. Having never known what it is like to be one of a superfluity of sisters who all need to secure a husband, Emma experiences a psychological exile in an estranged home, prefiguring the fate of Fanny Price, Anne Elliot, and Jane Fairfax in subsequent novels. Emma is truly shocked when she hears of her sisters' rivalries: "To be so bent on Marriage—to pursue a Man merely for the sake of situation—is a sort of thing that shocks me; I cannot understand it. Poverty is a great Evil, but to a woman of Education & feeling it ought not, it cannot be the greatest."[32] Her eldest sister, however, thinks she "could like any good humoured Man with a comfortable Income" and that Emma has been brought up "rather refined," which "will not be for [her] happiness" (318). Written between 1803 and 1805, the fragment of *The Watsons* was left unfinished. One of the most convincingly argued explanations for Austen's abandonment of the manuscript has revealingly been "the evil of having placed her heroine too low, in a position of poverty and obscurity."[33] After Mr. Watson's death, his daughters would have been dispersed as dependent relatives in search for a new home. Fanny Price's situation in *Mansfield Park* is reminiscent of this displacement, but Emma Watson's homelessness clearly promises to be much more extreme than that undergone by any other Austen heroine.[34]

The wealthy and independent heroine of *Emma* (1816) is a notable exception. The richest, healthiest, and also most fallible of Jane Austen's heroines, she need not marry to secure an establishment. The opening sentence sums up her fortunate position: "Emma Woodhouse, handsome, clever, and rich, with a comfortable home and happy disposition, seemed to unite some of the best blessings of existence."[35] Her search for true love is untrammeled by the need of a home. As a result, she is free to assess the men around her more critically. This is a luxury that very few heroines can boast. Even Mr. Weston's manners come under scrutiny, as Emma's imagination conjures up an available man *like* him (since he himself is taken) and then dissects his qualities: "She liked his open manners, but a little less of openheartedness would have made him a higher character. General benevolence, but not general friendship, made a man what he ought to be.—She could fancy such a man." (320).

The novel is indeed remarkable for the list of scrutinized men and their foibles. They range from Mr. Elton's affected sentimental silliness and Frank Churchill's "professions of openness and simplicity," which ultimately turn out to be "a system of hypocrisy" (399), to John Knightley's domestic qualities, which are spoilt by his bad humor and contrast with his brother's truly gentlemanly behavior. Emma's match making is at once premised on, and encourages her to speculate on, men's various advantages and disadvantages. As Claudia Johnson has convincingly argued, Emma's privileged position and the ways in which her own entitlement to independence and power "poaches on what is felt to be male turf" express a radical attitude that invites feminist readings,[36] but the contrasting variety of assessed, dismissed, and revaluated men is similarly of great interest to masculinity studies. The happy arrangement of the novel's end brings these explorations of powerful women and patronizing men together. Having discovered the man she can "fancy" (320) in Mr. Knightley, Emma's only worries about the home she neither needs nor desires to leave are solved when he decides to move to Hartfield, her home. This move is truly extraordinary and even eccentric, as Mrs. Elton, another patronizing woman, is quick to point out: "Poor Knightley! poor fellow!—sad business for him— She was extremely concerned; for, though very eccentric, he had a thousand good qualities. . . . Shocking plan, living together. It would never do" (469).[37]

Jane Fairfax's outset in life, however, counterpoises Emma's good fortune. Gary Kelly has aptly termed her Emma's "shadow." Jane is a sickly orphan whose financial dilemma is the result of homelessness.[38] While Emma has to learn to pay more attention to others without falling into the opposite extreme and become as patronizing as Mrs. Elton or the tyrannous Mrs. Churchill, who rules her husband and adopted son with her hypochondria, Jane has to attend too much to others' whims. Her lack of solitude in "[s]uch a home [with] such an aunt" (363) secures her Emma's compassion, but her forlorn situation marks her too much out as the victimized heroine of a sentimental plot to become much more than the object of Emma's speculations. In the unfinished *Sanditon*, Charlotte Heywood, a healthy heroine amidst the various invalids collected at the eponymous seaside resort, similarly finds that she "could not separate the idea of a complete Heroine from Clara Brereton.... Her situation with Lady Denham so very much in favour of it!—She seemed place with her on purpose to be ill-used. Such Poverty & Dependence joined to such Beauty & Merit, seemed to leave no choice in the business."[39] Anticipating *Sanditon*'s exploration of new health cults, *Emma* contains perhaps the most complex representation of psychophysical afflictions in Austen's completed novels. Mr. Woodhouse's valetudinarianism has emasculated him; Isabella Knightley's fussing over her children is treated with ridicule; Jane Fairfax's ill health is made so notorious by her fussy aunt that it disguises her real suffering. Yet, when Frank Churchill's rich aunt fortuitously takes her hypochondria so far as to die from it, Jane's self-suppression and consequently her headaches can end. Pallid, homeless Jane reminds Emma of "the difference in woman's destiny.... The contrast between Mrs. Churchill's importance in the world, and Jane Fairfax's, struck her; one was every thing, the other nothing" (384). This juxtaposition of real suffering and affectation as an abuse of power, however, remains marginal. Mrs. Churchill's off-stage tyranny and Mrs. Elliot's presumptuous sociability primarily serve to define Emma's different management of power, rank, and sociability. By contrast, *Mansfield Park* and *Persuasion* choose sensitive, even sickly, heroines and show that they can be assertive despite their lack of physical sturdiness. Before I look at the representation of nostalgia as a physical affliction and a Romantic longing in these later novels, however, I wish to point out that even Austen's liveliest heroines experience psychophysical headaches and heartaches.

Eliza Bennet's Sick Headache

The heroine of *Mansfield Park*, Fanny Price, whose rejection of a financially prudent offer of marriage isolates her and even drives her into literal exile, surely is the most vehemently persecuted heroine of Austen's novels, yet such persecutions or persuasions threaten the love-interests of less vulnerable heroines. While much critical comment and also much derision have been unleashed on Fanny's sick headaches, Elizabeth Bennet's tears and headaches in *Pride and Prejudices* have escaped attention. Yet her succumbing to low spirits is far more marked than Fanny's consistently suppressed desires.[40] Although the romantic disappointment is relegated to her sister Jane, it is the concealment of Elizabeth's nostalgia for a love only realized after its loss that requires self-isolation and the suppression of the symptoms of unhappiness. Jane's disappointment in Bingley is open to the neighborhood's speculations. Her mother certainly makes the most of it, petulantly suggesting that Bingley might be—presumably like Lovelace—punished by Jane's death: "Well, my comfort is, I am sure Jane will die of a broken heart, and then he will be sorry for what he has done" (184). As in the case of Elinor Dashwood in *Sense and Sensibility*, it is her "good sense" that prevents Jane from indulging in clinical nostalgia or love-madness: "[S]o fervently did she value his remembrance, and prefer him to every other man, that all her good sense, and all her attention to the feelings of her friends, were requisite to check the indulgence of those regrets, which must have been injurious to her own health and their tranquillity" (184). Her exertions, however, do not completely prevent her from feeling the psychophysical effects of her disappointment, and her happy acceptance of Bingley after a lengthy separation show that her love has by no means abated. Like Elinor Dashwood's, Jane's lovesickness is moreover resolved, rather than cured, as circumstances outside her control remove all obstacles. Marianne's cure, as we have seen, is similarly prepared by Brandon's own nostalgia and sanctioned by her family. Elizabeth Bennet, however, has to engage in a reordering of her memories and a restructuring of her former prejudices before she can acknowledge that she is in love with Darcy. As she only discovers her love when it seems too late, it is doubly a nostalgic recognition.

The first sight of Pemberley famously makes Elizabeth conclude "that to be mistress of Pemberley might be something" (196). Falling in love with a desirable home, she starts feeling "something like regret" (197) for having rejected Darcy's first offer. In a Victorian study of the novel, Sarah Tytler already emphasized that "Elizabeth is disinterestedly delighted" with the estate.[41] Alistair Duckworth speaks of Elizabeth's "spatial recapitulation of her association with Darcy."[42] Similarly, Isobel Armstrong suggests that Elizabeth "literally revalues her experience with Darcy by re-vision."[43] Her love is genuine, despite the ironic coincidence of her re-vision of Darcy's eligibility. I wish to argue that the revision Elizabeth's views undergo is a nostalgic "recollection" of her memories. The estate is full of telltale signs of Darcy's presence; it has his character stamped on it. A tour of the grounds does not so much provide Elizabeth with new information, but crucially reorders what she already knows. Looking into his portrait's eyes, "she thought of his regard with a deeper sentiment of gratitude than it had ever raised before; she remembered its warmth, and softened its impropriety of expression" (200). Her love *is* nostalgia: "[A]nd never had she so honestly felt that she could have loved him, as now, when all love must be vain" (221). After Lydia's elopement with Wickham has potentially put an irrevocable bar to further intercourse with Darcy, this honest feeling changes into conviction: "She was convinced that she could have been happy with him; when it was no longer likely they should meet" (311).

While nostalgia enables her to acknowledge her love through a reordering of memories that softens the picture she has made of Darcy, it is not the only emotion that is expressed by tears, headaches, and a craving for solitude. Elizabeth's psychophysical complaint is even more interesting perhaps than Marianne's or Fanny's because it is unexpected. Her anxiety on Jane's behalf parallels her disappointment in Wickham very closely, combining to dampen her own spirits, while she worries about her sister's: "When to these recollections was added the development of Wickham's character, it may be easily believed that the happy spirits which had seldom been depressed before, where now so much affected as to make it almost impossible for her to appear tolerably cheerful." (173–74) When she hears of Darcy's role in Bingley's "desertion" of Jane, the "agitation and tears which the subject occasioned, [brings] on a headach [*sic*]" (154). This psychophysical reaction compels her to seek solitude. Like Marianne, she cherishes solitary rambles "in which she might indulge in all the delight of unpleasant recollections" (173). The recurrence of words describing processes of memory and its revision—recollection, reflection, remembrance—focuses the significance of a rethinking of first impressions in the novel.

The next letter Elizabeth receives from Jane causes even more dramatic psychophysical reactions, and this time Darcy arrives in time to observe her first musings on the subject of Lydia's elopement. What follows is a display of agitated sensibility and Darcy's reading of Elizabeth's symptoms. In accordance with the literature of sensibility, language breaks down, as physical reactions instead embody emotional meaning. It is a touching scene that brings Darcy and Elizabeth closer than ever and subsequently plays a role in their reordering of the past. Her "pale face" (276) makes Darcy start. He has to "recover himself enough to speak" and exclaims "with more feeling than politeness" (276). This is a very different Darcy from the quiet, proud man of their first meetings. Elizabeth is similarly "so breathless" that she is "almost unintelligible:" her "knees trembled under her" and "she sat down, unable to support herself, and looking so miserably ill, that it was impossible for Darcy to leave her, or to refrain from saying, in a tone of gentleness and commiseration" (276). After bursting into tears, she is unable to "speak another word," leaving Darcy to observe her "in wretched suspense" and "compassionate silence" (277). While literary critics have tended to ignore this dramatic, and indeed not at all ironic, display of sensibility and sympathy, endless reworkings of this scene in continuations of and sequels to Austen's novels, written between 1850 and the early twenty-first century, are a good indicator of its popularity among readers.[44] This tête-à-tête is crucial in establishing Darcy as a man who expresses sympathy with more feeling than politeness. It moreover becomes a nostalgic memory. Elizabeth dwells on Darcy's qualities after her sister's misbehavior appears to have wrecked all; Darcy only thinks of Elizabeth when he proceeds to help Wickham and Lydia. When Darcy eventually brings forth a *revised* proposal, the revision of the past is complete. Suggesting that her rejection of their first attempts ought to be forgotten, Elizabeth stresses that remembrance should be pleasant:

> The feelings of the person who wrote, and the person who received it, are now so widely different from what they were then, that every unpleasant circumstance attending it, ought to be forgotten. You must learn some of my philosophy. Think only of the past as its remembrance gives you pleasure. (293)

This philosophy of forgetfulness stands in sharp contrast to the tendency towards resentment of which Darcy used to be so proud and ties in neatly with the novel's successful exposure of pride and prejudice. Yet a complacent retelling of the past can also become an easily ridiculed lapse of memory. The fickleness of the communal memories circulated in the small town of Meryton becomes particularly glaring when it changes its opinion of the hitherto universally popular Wickham: "Every body declared that he was the wickedest young man in the world; and every body began to find out, that they had always distrusted the appearance of his goodness" (234). Similarly, in *Emma*, Frank Churchill's teasing revival of the pain he and, more unwittingly, Emma inflicted on Jane Fairfax is premised on a form of forgetting that shows that he has not improved at all. As he glosses over the mortifications his past behavior caused, Jane opposes his delight in remembering his jokes and foibles: "How you can bear such recollections, is astonishing to me!—They *will* sometimes obtrude—but how you can *court* them!" (480) Emma's feelings are "chiefly with Jane" (480) on this point, and she proceeds to compare Frank unfavorably with Mr. Knightley. Frank's dismissal of his culpable conduct indeed contrasts significantly with Emma and Mr. Knightley's careful and considerate revision of the past when they go over their former quarrels about Harriet Smith's choice of a husband (473–74).

In *Persuasion*, Anne's snobbish sister Elizabeth can similarly forget the past when it suits her to invite presentable gentlemen. Sir Walter and Miss Elliot not only go to mortifying extremes to court their titled cousin and quickly forgive Mr. Elliot for his past trespasses, but they ignore their past snubbing of Wentworth now that he has made his fortune: "The truth was, that Elizabeth had been long enough in Bath, to understand the importance of a man of such an air and appearance as his. The past was nothing. The present was that Captain Wentworth would move about well in her drawing-room" (226). As the concluding section to this chapter will show, this forgetting is pointedly opposed to the nostalgic remembering of Wentworth and Anne, for whom the past is everything and significantly revives their future. In *Pride and Prejudice*, Elizabeth's new self-scrutiny prevents her from inventing false memories: "But no such recollection befriended her" (168). Her nostalgic "philosophy" is about pleasurable remembrance, not indiscriminate forgetting. This contrast between communal forgetting and a careful reordering of past interpretations anticipates Fanny Price's unheeded recollection of Mr. Crawford's misbehavior and Anne Elliot's disregarded preferences for a love of the past.

But Alas! It Was Not Such a Home: From Clinical to Creative Nostalgia in *Mansfield Park*

Fanny Price's retiring character focuses the desire to keep personal longing private. At the same time, it is also fruitful to see her homesickness as a reflection on colonial concerns with forceful dislocation. Fanny's transference of homesickness during her exile at home has been seen as evidence of a preoccupation with differentiated spaces of alterity and imperialist cultural productions ever since Edward Said's influential analysis has re-inscribed the novel within the geopolitical discourses of its time.[45] Implicitly evoked anxieties of empire in the novel shed light on the domestic or micropolitics of imperialist homemaking and their changing function in fiction. Sir Thomas Bertram's expedition to Antigua and his treatment of a dependent niece of course seem to invite such analyses. Even though Franco Moretti has recently suggested that Sir Thomas goes abroad "not because he must *go there*—but because *he must leave Mansfield Park*,"[46] as his absence is crucial to the development of the plot, imperialist attitudes and absentee landlordism undoubtedly underline the centrality of economic relationships in the novel. Considering it "expedient to go to Antigua himself, for the better arrangement of his affairs," Sir Thomas views the "necessity of the measure in a pecuniary light" (32). When Fanny turns out to be the "daughter he truly want[s]" despite all his stratagems, he self-complacently accepts her as a "rich repayment" for his "charitable kindness" (472).

Miss Price's loss of home and consequent homesickness are undeniably bound up with the economics of the estate and even more importantly, with medical theories on the effects of dislocation through her uncle's use of home*sickness* as a "medicinal project upon his niece's understanding" (369). Taken from her parents' overcrowded house, she has been brought up by a self-congratulatory, pompous West Indian planter. Not conforming to his ideas of a suitable match for her, she is sent "home" into exile. The confrontation with her parents' comparative poverty is to "teach her the value of a good income," to "incline her to a juster estimate of the value of that home of greater permanence, and equal comfort, of which she had the offer" (369). Sir Thomas freely admits to himself that "his prime motive for sending her away, had very little to do with the propriety of her seeing her parents again, and nothing at all with any idea of making her happy" (369). Counting on what he terms "wholesome regrets" (366), he wishes her to be "heartily sick of home before her visit ended" (369). The connection he draws between regret, the need for a comfortable home, and different versions of homesickness pinpoints the flexible nature of nostalgia. Fanny is indeed alternately sick *of* and sick *for* home, though not for Mr. Crawford's estate. In one aspect Sir Thomas's project turns out to be almost too successful:

> [H]ad he known all, [he] might have thought his niece in the most promising way of being starved, both mind and body, into a much juster value for Mr. Crawford's good company and good fortune, [but] he would probably have feared to push his experiment farther, lest she might die under the cure. (413)

Sent back to her childhood home in Portsmouth as a form of punishment, Fanny is soon in a fair way of wasting away from clinical nostalgia. Struggling against the effects of "her foreign education" (390), she falls homesick for the absent home. Nostalgically, she heaves sighs and looks increasingly languid: "[S]he often heaved a sigh at the remembrance of all her books and boxes, and various comforts" (398). There is no doubt about the nature of her affliction. Fanny suffers from homesickness: "Her eagerness, her impatience, her longings to be with them [at Mansfield], were such as to bring a line or two of Cowper's Tirocinium for ever before her. 'With what intense desire she wants her home,' was continually on her tongue, as the truest description of a yearning which she could not suppose any school-boy's bosom to feel more keenly" (431). The keenly felt yearning is associated with poetry and described as a Romantic longing.

At the same time, however, Fanny is also physically homesick as she tries to cope with lack of air, exercise, and adequate nourishment. They are the direct results of Sir Thomas's "medicinal project," her exile from the chosen home. As in *Sense and Sensibility*, in which Marianne's psychophysical afflictions coincide with her sore throat, the cause of Fanny's increasing pallor is her low spirits and the unsanitary squalor in her parents' house, which is aptly illuminated by "a stifling, *sickly* glare [italics added]" (439). Greasy butter and unwholesome puddings "with such accompaniments of half-cleaned plates, and not half-cleaned knives and forks" (413) partly account for her ill health, but unhappy heroines seldom display a healthy appetite. In this, they contrast with their affected counterparts such as Mary and Mrs. Musgrove in *Persuasion*. Fanny is "out of spirits" (413), suffering from "dejection" (413), and has "lost ground as to health" (409). There is no affectation in Fanny's affliction. Indeed, no-one at Portsmouth would notice if she were to display her distress more openly.

This clinical nostalgia—Sir Thomas's cure of what he considers her forgetfulness of her economic position—ironically reveals to what extent Fanny has already suffered from a forceful dislocation. When her "homecoming" is first proposed, she misunderstands it as a cure for her homesickness: "The remembrance of all her earliest pleasures, and of what she had suffered in being torn from them, came over her with renewed strength, and it seemed as if to be at home again, would heal every pain that had since grown out of the separation" (370). This reminder of the original loss of home briefly rehearses the first chapters of the novel, in which the child Fanny is the unhappy object of her rich relatives' charitable plan. They take her from her familiar home to a "grandeur [that] astonished, but could not console her" (14), and expect her to show a proper display of gratitude. Separated from "the brothers and sisters among whom she had always been important as play-fellow, instructress, and nurse" (14), she feels awkward and shy. Her cousins quickly dismiss her as undersized, uneducated, and unfashionably clothed. Her ostracized position in an attic room aptly defines her status as being "so near Miss Lee [the governess], and not far from the girls, and close by the housemaids" (10). Remote from the house's centre, the attic reflects and conditions her isolation: "Nobody put themselves out of their way to secure her comfort" (14). It is only when Edmund systematically tries to cure her homesickness by helping her to re-establish contact with her old home (by giving her the means to write to her brother) and by making her new home more congenial (by filling the vacant role of elder brother) that Fanny begins to settle in, "learning to transfer in its favour much of her attachment to her former home" (20).

Nevertheless, Fanny's position at Mansfield Park remains unstable and indeterminate, preventing her from feeling completely at home. The threat of being sent to stay with Mrs. Norris after only five years at Mansfield is a reminder that Fanny's new home is never secure. This plan, which is unsurprisingly connected to Sir Thomas's reduced financial situation, isolates Fanny further as even Edmund fails to see her objections to the unwanted dislocation. Her relatives' inability to understand her longing for a *home* as a place of belonging and not just a residence is at times almost comical. As her Aunt Bertram puts it, "you are sure of a comfortable home. It can make very little difference to you, whether you are in one house or the other" (25). It is only Mrs. Norris's unwillingness to bear the expense of Fanny's further upbringing that saves her. After the Crawfords' arrival, her position becomes increasingly uncomfortable as their sociability further accentuates her marginality. When Miss Crawford's definition of Fanny as "not out" (51) is taken up by her cousins, she is more than ever shut out from the newly formed clique's activities. Fanny is literally marginalized, enviously watching merriment from afar: "[T]he sound of merriment ascended even to her. It was a sound which did not make *her* cheerful; she wondered that Edmund should forget her, and felt a pang" (67).

Two significant episodes in the novel, the excursion to Sotherton and the staging of private theatricals, reveal Fanny's treatment during the patriarch's absence. As Sir Thomas leaves for Antigua, his home estate slips into unruly disorder, and as the weakest, Fanny only suffers anew under the new rule of unpredictable group-pressure. Although Edmund manages to include Fanny in the excursion to Sotherton, he then forgets her on a bench while he saunters off into a wilderness with Miss Crawford, and I shall return to the significance of landscapes in the novel. Fanny's role in the theatricals is even more pointedly ambiguous. Like Edmund, she refuses to act, but while his infatuation with Miss Crawford eventually outweighs all his principles and inclinations, Fanny does not change her decision, though her cousins and aunts do everything in their power to change it for her. The significance of this episode is not simply the moral corruption of Edmund as he acts knowingly against his conscience, but the bullying of Fanny, who is denied the right of refusal, anticipating her attempts to reject Mr. Crawford without taking her economical position into account. "Let her choose for herself as well as the rest of us" (147), Edmund suggests. But this only prompts Aunt Norris to remind Fanny that she is "very ungrateful indeed, considering who and what she is" (147). While Julia Bertram can ignore the theatricals after she has been denied the desired part, Fanny is not granted the easy opting out available to her cousin. What has been glossed over in analyses of Fanny's refusal is the fact that the controversy surrounding it is not only about the moral qualities of private theatricals, but about the dependent relative's denied right to make her own decisions.[47]

Group-pressure is indeed the cause of most of Fanny's distress. The patriarch's absence is clearly not liberating for everyone, and this exposure of communal tyrannies has generated so much unease among readers of the novel. Yet, it is a convincing description of bullying and revives a Romantic need of solitude. By contrast, in the second half of *Northanger Abbey*, the patriarch's displeasure outdoes the Thorpes' group-pressure in causing the heroine distress. In the other novels, fathers are either dead (the fathers of all central protagonists in *Sense and Sensibility* and both Darcy's and Wickham's fathers in *Pride and Prejudice*), neglectful of responsibilities (*Pride and Prejudice* and *Persuasion*), or simply weak (*Emma* and *The Watsons*). But Sir Thomas is absent throughout most of *Mansfield Park*, and it is during his absence that Fanny suffers most. Even her "exile" is the result of Mr. Crawford's insinuating charms and her inability to expose him without implicating her cousins. A return home to Portsmouth seems at the moment particularly welcome because it entails a separation from "all mention of the Crawfords" (370).

Previous to her renewed experience of its realities, Portsmouth is the nostalgic space, the home of her homesick longing. The negative experience of homecoming is one of the most intriguing twists in the novel. What is not granted within the strictly hierarchical structures of Mansfield is Fanny's suppressed desire to be "in the centre of such a circle, loved by so many, . . . to feel herself the equal of those who surrounded her" (370). But her return is a mockery of such dreams of equality and self-importance. Instead, it is a parody of the nostalgic's ideal homecoming. Before Fanny's first week at "home" is over, "it was all disappointment" (388). Instead of being the beloved center, which is to compensate for her peripheral position at Mansfield, she finds herself stumbling through a narrow passageway and forgotten in a dark parlor. In short, Portsmouth is "in almost every respect, the reverse of what she could have wished" (388). It is ironically at "home" that Fanny fully realizes the results of her original loss of home: "She was at home. But alas! It was not such a home, she had not such a welcome, as—she checked herself; she was unreasonable. What right had she to be of importance to her family? She could have none, so long lost sight of!" (382). Her realization that "home" is elsewhere eventually counterpoises the traumatic homelessness.

Sir Thomas's projection of this transposition, however, creates an additional irony. He has cleverly anticipated her disillusionment and her need to transfer her homesickness, but her choice defeats his project because it is not confined to economic reasons and instead informed by memories of childhood, personal reminiscences, and a nostalgic lovesickness. Marilyn Butler has, in fact, rightly pointed out that Fanny's "implicit alternative home" is Everingham, Henry Crawford's fashionably improved estate.[48] The desired nostalgic return to Mansfield is at first not an offered option. At one point, Fanny even perceives Crawford's unwelcome visit to Portsmouth as a link to the lost home and his departure as "a sort of renewed separation from Mansfield" (413). As he attempts to impress her by suggesting practical improvements to his estate, she is "on the point of giving him an approving look" (404), but is then "frightened off" (404) by the recollection that, firstly, she is to be one of the improvements, and secondly, that she has witnessed his ideas of improvement at Sotherton, which primarily consisted in the seduction of its future mistress. This moment of relenting is nonetheless significant in that it reveals the extent to which Fanny is already sick of home and longing for a return to her former friends and family. Sir Thomas's medicinal use of clinical nostalgia almost pays off. But instead of regretting Everingham, the estate that comes with the eligible offer of marriage, Fanny longs for a return to an idealized Mansfield:

> When she had been coming to Portsmouth, she had loved to call it her home, had been fond of saying that she was going home; the word had been very dear to her; and so it still was, but it must be applied to Mansfield. *That* was now the home. Portsmouth was Portsmouth;

Mansfield was home. They had been long so arranged in the indulgence of her secret meditations. (431)

This transposition of home is a revealing moment in the novel, disclosing suppressed longings and shedding light on the failures and the ultimate triumphs of nostalgic idealization. It is only in retrospect that Fanny yearns for her "various comforts" (398) at Mansfield. What she remembers—and remembers in nostalgia—is the comfort and the space that her exile lacks. Portsmouth has failed to be the home of her homesick longings. As the reverse of the desired home, it usefully figures as its foil: "Such was the home which was to put Mansfield out of her head.... On the contrary, she could think of nothing but Mansfield, its beloved inmates, its happy ways" (391). Fanny resourcefully relocates her ideals of home. She lives on memories, on letters from home, and on hopes of a return. In the noisy overcrowded Price household, she dwells on memories as "her private regale" (431), creating a private space, a sanctuary of and for the imagination. The reconstruction of a quiet space in Portsmouth, a private room in the midst of bustling disorder, where she can indulge in nostalgia, proves the resistant adaptability that Fanny derives from what can be termed her nostalgic strategies. She re-creates a part of Mansfield in the cold room she shares with her sister: "They sat without a fire; but *that* was a privation familiar even to Fanny, and she suffered the less because reminded by it of the east-room" (398). A familiar privation is the focus of her nostalgia. It is cherished as a memory in a way in which the empty grate is not appreciated during her Mansfield days. Nostalgia is introduced as a clinical condition consciously abused by her imperious uncle, but triumphantly restructured as a very creative survival strategy. Eventually, Fanny is needed back at "home" at Mansfield and united with her beloved cousin.[49]

In Fanny's rewarded resistance to the pressures exerted by patriarchal authority and the community, her Romantic appreciation of memory, nature, and a seemingly hopeless love, Austen's reassessment of sensibility seems to have come full circle. It is, in fact, repeatedly stressed in the novel that Fanny's resolution not to marry Crawford has less to do with her assessment of his money or his morals and more with her incapability to marry without love, and this is clearly significant in the economic contexts of her homesickness. Sir Thomas revealingly associates Fanny's attitude to love and marriage with "that independence of spirit, which prevails so much in modern days," a tendency to "decide for yourself," which he terms "wilful and perverse" (318). He is partly right. Unlike Charlotte Lucas in *Pride and*

Prejudice, who is content with Mr. Collins's situation in life, even if that means putting up with the man as well, and unlike Maria Bertram, who marries Rushworth to spite Crawford and get a house in town, Fanny will not marry without love. For her uncle, the marriage contract has very little to do with love: "He who had married a daughter to Mr. Rushworth. Romantic delicacy was certainly not to be expected from him" (331). Crawford undoubtedly has the ability to please whoever he wishes by acting the proper part, and it is suggested that he might have stood a chance "had not Fanny's heart been guarded in a way unsuspected" (231):

> [F]or although there doubtless are such unconquerable young ladies of eighteen (or one should not read about them) as are never to be persuaded into love against their judgment by all that talent, manner, attention, and flattery can do, I have no inclination to believe Fanny one of them, or to think that with so much tenderness of disposition, and so much taste as belonged to her, she could have escaped heart-whole from the courtship . . . had not her affection been engaged elsewhere. (231)

Fanny's loyal lovesickness gets its reward. The happy end sees her enjoying the man and the home of her choice. Nostalgia has prevented her from accepting the other available home at Everingham together with its corrupt owner.

Nostalgia's function in her return home to Mansfield's environs is, however, twofold. The real improvement Mansfield sees at the end of the novel is additionally premised on a nostalgic revision. Fanny's return restores Mansfield Park to a less obtuse tranquility, turns the neglected Thornton Lacy into a home, and ultimately even reclaims Mansfield Parsonage. Mrs. Norris is removed; the spendthrift heir reformed; Sir Thomas content with the marriage of the dependent niece to one of her cousins. Thornton Lacy, having escaped the fashionable "improvements" suggested by the Crawfords, becomes what a parsonage ought to be. Henry Crawford's advice to Edmund how to "raise [Thornton Lacy] into a *place*" (244), in fact, exposes his superficial interest in a fashionable fad that has very little to do with practical improvements. Likewise, Mary Crawford's idea of improving Edmund's future living is to modernize the building radically and to disguise its original function as a clergyman's residence. In the "picture she [forms] of a future Thornton," she contrives "to shut out the church, sink the clergyman, and see only the respectable, elegant, modernized, and occasional residence of a man of independent fortune" (248). When Edmund and Fanny eventually move to Mansfield Parsonage, they reclaim even that dreaded space by modernizing it sensibly, albeit not as fashionably as the Crawfords might wish it. After having been occupied by the malicious Aunt Norris and then by the insinuating Crawfords, it becomes a home that is so improved that even uncomfortable recollections are accepted in nostalgia:

> [T]he parsonage there, which under each of its two former owners, Fanny had never been able to approach but with some painful sensation of restraint or alarm, soon grew as dear to her heart, and as thoroughly perfect in her eyes, as every thing else, within the view and patronage of Mansfield Park, had long been. (473)

The right extent of improvements as of sensibility is of course one of the recurring themes of Austen's novels. Henry Austen remarked that his Aunt Jane "was a warm and judicious admirer of landscape, both in nature and on canvas. At a very early age she was enamoured of Gilpin on the Picturesque."[50] Her deliberately ambivalent critiques of the picturesque as a fashion to be discussed by protagonists rather than as a descriptive mode, however, reveal a more creative use of cultural crosscurrents.[51] While Marianne's genuine nostalgia for her lost home in *Sense and Sensibility* vindicates her "passion for dead leaves," Edward falls into another affectation by trying to avoid an affected appreciation of the picturesque: "Because he believes many people pretend to more admiration of the beauties of nature than they really feel, . . . he affects greater indifference and less discrimination in viewing them himself than he possesses. He is fastidious and will have an affectation of his own" (97). Austen, in fact, consistently poises genuine feelings against affectations. The former are usually excusable or understandable if not always praiseworthy; the latter objects of ridicule. Marianne admits "that admiration of landscape scenery is become a mere jargon" (97). *Pride and Prejudice* similarly parodies the confused raptures of "the generality of travellers" (154), but shows Elizabeth eager to store memories that are to bid "disappointment and spleen" adieu, and not to return "like other travellers, without being able to give one accurate idea of any thing (154). Her picturesque journeys significantly lead her to Darcy's carefully improved estate, where she then engages in storing and reordering of memories.[52] In *Mansfield Park*, improvement is a vital concern that often works not necessarily against, but with, nostalgia.

The excursion to Sotherton, the old-fashioned estate of Maria Bertram's fiancé (the heavy, slow Rushworth) exemplifies this use of attitudes to fashionable trends as moral indicators perhaps best. An "old place, and a place of some grandeur" (56), Sotherton abounds in "walls of great promise" (90). Expectedly,

Fanny prefers to see it "in its old state" (56). The proposed artificial opening up of a "fine prospect" by cutting down "two or three fine old trees" induces her to quote nostalgic lines from Cowper's poetry: "Cut down an avenue! What a pity! Does not it make you think of Cowper?" (55–56). Although Fanny is disappointed when she fails to find signs that "a Scottish monarch sleeps below" in the chapel, which has "nothing awful . . . , nothing melancholy, nothing grand" (85–86) about it, her rhapsodies are never ridiculed.[53] Her genuine interest contrasts with the idle indifference displayed by most of her companions and Miss Crawford's civil appearance of listening to Mrs. Rushworth, which only masks her boredom.[54] Maaja Stewart has suggested that the "characterizations of Sotherton, London, and Portsmouth disguise the similarity of Mansfield to all these spaces," thereby subverting its idealization.

The novel's pattern of contrasting spaces, however, further includes the offstage Everingham, Thornton Lacy, and, most controversially, plantations in Antigua. Attitudes to these spaces as well as to landscaping are used to indicate the protagonists' moral capacities. Yet Fanny's creation of a private sanctuary in the crowded spaces of Portsmouth moreover shows that real improvement is possible and not always tantamount to corruption. While critics have tended to question the improvement in Mansfield's restoration, they have given Fanny more credit for her appropriation of the original east-room, the deserted schoolroom at the Park, which she later replicates in Portsmouth. Such tentative appreciation, however, is usually qualified by an emphasis on her unobtrusive, even sneaky, claiming of that space. As her personal space within Mansfield, it prefigures much of its eventual revision.

The east-room is a place of self-improvement and solitary reflections, where Fanny reads Cowper's poetry or travel accounts of China, surrounded by sketches of landscapes and the memorabilia of the past. It is a room of and for memories and certainly much more than a storage space for souvenirs. A solitary place decorated with memorabilia, it has been seen as specifically Romantic.[55] It is, like Fanny's little white attic, remote from the central rooms of the Great House. Miss Crawford has difficulties finding it (168); and even the sight of Edmund causes considerable surprise (261). But Fanny makes a virtue out of this lack and a "nest of comforts" (152) out of a deserted space. As the abandoned schoolroom, it moreover figures as the empty space that stands for the Misses Bertrams' superficial education. They are "blessed with wonderful memories," but "entirely deficient in the less common acquirements of self-knowledge, generosity, and humility" (19). Fanny's nostalgia depends on another form of selective memory, but one that is preferred over the Misses Bertrams' wonderful memories of facts and figures. Choosing the space of self-improvement, Fanny claims "what nobody else want[s]" (151). As Fanny contemplates its history, she realizes that "the whole was now so blended together, so harmonized by distance, that every former affliction had its charm" (152). Such a nostalgic revision later restructures the environs of Mansfield Park.

As a nostalgic space, the east-room even inspires in Miss Crawford a (however short-lived) "reverie of sweet remembrances" (358) as she thinks back to her flirtation with Edmund under the cover of a rehearsal. Yet she dismisses her reminiscence quickly as "a little fit" (359). In her lack of sensibility, she serves as Fanny's double: "She had none of Fanny's delicacy of taste, of mind, of feeling" (81). Her "acknowledged disinclination for privacy" (255) could be no more poignant contrast to Fanny's fondness for solitary and quietly shared reveries. As Fanny rhapsodizes over "the sublimity of Nature" (113) when gazing at the stars with Edmund, he is lured away by Miss Crawford's singing of a glee. As Fanny remarks on the growth of a shrubbery and is led on to muse over the "wonderful . . . operations of time, and the changes of the human mind" (208), Miss Crawford remains untouched and inattentive:

> "If any one faculty of our nature may be called more wonderful than the rest, I do think it is memory. [It] is sometimes so retentive, so serviceable, so obedient—at others, so bewildered and so weak—and at others again, so tyrannic, so beyond controul [sic]!—We are to be sure a miracle every way—but our powers of recollecting and forgetting, do seem peculiarly past finding out." Miss Crawford, untouched and inattentive, had nothing to say. (208–9)

The cultivated thriving of the hedgerow is an analogy to Fanny's growth. Having "so naturally and so artlessly worked herself into [Mansfield]" (151), she grows from an unappreciated, freshly transplanted, puny little girl into what Sir Thomas is most happy to accept as having naturally grown on his estate—almost forgetting what she was before.

Her fondness for nature moreover contrasts sharply with the Crawfords' interest in fashionable "improvements" as well as with purely economic interpretations of nature's value, as grotesquely evinced by Mrs. Norris's sponging of cream cheeses, pheasants' eggs, and a young heath from Sotherton. Miss Crawford moreover not only uses foliage as a mere accessory when she poses at the harp, but she freely admits that she is incapable of seeing any "wonder in this shrubbery equal to seeing [her]self in it" (210).[56] The Crawfords' use of nature as ornament and a display of wealth, together with Mrs. Norris's frugal interest in its consumable products, serve to highlight Fanny's delight in observing nature and her nostalgic fondness for familiar spaces. Referring to Fanny's rhapsody on the "powers of recollecting and of forgetting" in the shrubbery, Tony Tanner already suggested that "in a way there is a little of the artist about her: she speaks for the value of literature, of memory, of fancy; she alone reveals a true appreciation of nature."[57] Yet Jay Clayton has cautioned that even while Fanny "possesses many of the qualities of a fine Romantic heroine . . . the attempt to turn Austen into a closet Romantic obscures the true significance of the few Romantic elements in her fiction."[58] Nonetheless, Clayton admits that "Fanny's nostalgia can be seen as part of a larger state of consciousness, the familiar mood known as Romantic melancholy," an alignment that unfortunately contributes to the persistent confusion of nostalgia with melancholy.[59] Even while this nostalgia is never parodied or criticized, the extent of *Mansfield Park*'s Romantic elements admittedly remains debatable, not least because Austen's engagement with Romanticism results in a specifically domestic Romantic novel. Domestic preoccupations more than settings function as deliberately evoked interruptions, which account for much of the novel's comedy. Thus, the intrusion of the tea things undercuts the melodrama of Fanny's struggles as she is almost bullied into accepting Mr. Crawford: "[B]ut for the occupation and the scene which the tea things afforded, she must have betrayed her emotion in some unpardonable excess" (335).

Despite their allusions to British imperialism, Austen's novels are primarily domestic. In his recent analysis of Patricia Rozema's 1999 adaptation of *Mansfield Park*, John Wiltshire speaks of the Goyaesque horrors depicted in Tom's plantation sketchbook and the ways in which this introduction of imperialism corresponds to the emphasis on the novel's Antigua-subplot in literary criticism, but significantly proceeds to point out that the real violence of the novel remains domestic: "There *is* a heart of darkness in Austen, but it lies elsewhere, often in the psychological violence of woman against woman, like Mrs. Norris's persecution of Fanny, or Emma's half-inexplicable burst of spite."[60] In Austen's novels, the struggles between self and society, the suppressed and the dominant, are acted out at home, anticipating what has been called the "domestic Gothic" of the Victorian sensation genre.[61] Most damaging to *Mansfield Park*'s Romantic aspects is perhaps the exposure of group-pressure as democracy's dark double and also the return of Mansfield's tranquility at the end of the novel. Its solidity seems grotesquely embodied by Lady Bertram's "sofa-bound inertia."[62] This blemish, if it is one, is repaired in *Persuasion*, as it rewrites the Great House plots and abandons the eligible estate altogether in favor of the sublime sea.

The Natural Sequel of an Unnatural Beginning: New Spaces for Lost Love in *Persuasion*

Anne Elliot is easily Jane Austen's most depressed heroine, outdoing even Fanny Price in her solitary reveries. At the outset of *Persuasion* we learn that her spirits have never been high since her disappointment. Her protracted pining for lost love has left her looking worn out, but this psychophysical affliction has not been the result of imprudence, nor has Anne become inured to emotional agitation. On the contrary, prudent persuasion has ruined her happiness, and the novel's beginning sees the faded heroine of twenty-six nostalgically longing for lost love. The story then opens with the impending loss of her home, adding literal homesickness to Anne's lovesick nostalgia. Her peripheral position within that home, reminiscent of Fanny Price's or Emma Watson's, prefigures her literal dislocation. It prepares her for the restoration of the other, potential, home that would have been hers had she married Fredrick Wentworth. The "general chill . . . , cold composure, determined silence [and] heartless elegance of her father and sister" (226) contrast unfavorably with the Harvilles' makeshift, but happy home and the Musgroves' indiscriminate sociability. This awareness of her family's shortcomings, combined with the loss of Kellynch Hall, gradually shifts Anne's ideas of "home." Listening to Lady Russell's comments on her new home in Bath, she realizes "how much more interesting to her was the home and the friendship of the Harvilles and Captain Benwick, than her father's house in Camden-place" (124). Her choice of words is significant. Like Fanny, who is exiled in her family's *house*, while her thoughts dwell on her *home* at Mansfield, Anne thinks of her father's *house*, but of the Harvilles' *home*.

The Great House's loss recedes to the margins of the narrative. Anne is fond of the places she has to leave behind and cherishes their remembrance in nostalgia. With her "domestic habits" (29), she is averse to dislocation and truly regrets missing the sad autumnal months in the countryside, but other places accumulate nostalgic value as well: "Scenes had passed in Uppercross, which made it precious. It stood the record of many sensations of pain, once severe, but now softened" (123). Such nostalgic recollections and the softening of pain enable Anne to relocate her nostalgia, while retaining a stable self. By contrast, in *Mansfield Park*, Fanny Price has to dismiss Portsmouth as unworthy of a nostalgic imagination. When she leaves it for the second time, there is no nostalgia for her parents' home; she has transferred all to Mansfield Park. In *Sense and Sensibility*, Norland similarly disappears from Marianne's homesickness. What she yearns for in London is a return to their home in Barton Cottage, near Delaford. Anne, however, is able to unite her different experiences, and their recollection, in a coherent self. The many years of solitary reflection on a past happiness have shown her the value of remembrance and that she can take memories with her wherever she goes: "She left it all behind her; all but the recollection that such things had been" (123).

Her accumulative nostalgia contrasts crucially with her family's reverence of an ancestral form of "memory," which primarily manifests itself in a rather unpleasant "Elliot pride." Sir Walter Elliot finds consolation in reading the Baronetage. The escapist impulse that makes him take up his favorite book more and more frequently exacerbates his neglect of present problems: "there any unwelcome sensations, arising from domestic affairs, changed naturally into pity and contempt, as he turned over the almost endless creations of the last century" (3). Lady Russell similarly "had prejudices on the side of ancestry; she had a value for rank and consequence, which blinded her a little to the faults of those who possessed them" (11); it is this bias in favor of old families that prompts her to persuade Anne to refuse a young naval officer. Such ancestral, or "heritage," nostalgia is premised on a method of deliberate forgetting and opposed to the careful cherishing of remembrances that structures Anne's personal nostalgia. A contemplation of former grandeur not only induces Sir Walter to forget at least momentarily all about the estate's present danger, but blocks remembrance of embarrassing events of the past as well. As far as Anne's disappointment is concerned, a "general air of oblivion" prevails in the family: they "seemed almost to deny any recollection of it" (30).

When Anne ultimately discovers that her nostalgic cherishing of past love has not been in vain, her reunion with her lover clashes with Lady Russell's wish to see her restored to Kellynch Hall as the next Lady Elliot. For both Sir Walter and Lady Russell, ideas of home are confined to vanities of situation; for Anne the "charm of Kellynch and of 'Lady Elliot' all fade[s] away" (160) when she compares the presumptive heir with her former lover,

Captain Wentworth. The return home that an alliance with Mr. Elliot would facilitate is of course tempting to the nostalgic heroine, and "[f]or a few moments her imagination and her heart were bewitched:" "The idea of becoming what her mother had been; of having the precious name of 'Lady Elliot' first revived in herself; of being restored to Kellynch, calling it her home again, her home for ever, was a charm which she could not immediately resist" (160). The charm of such a return, however, quickly loses its "bewitching" allurements as soon as she recollects that she would have to accept Mr. Elliot as well: picturing "Mr. Elliot speaking for himself, brought Anne to composure again" (160). Regardless of his eligibility as the heir, he does not come up to her standards: "Her early impressions were incurable" (161), and "[n]o one had ever come within the Kellynch circle, who could bear a comparison with Frederick Wentworth, as he stood in her memory" (28). While Lady Russell contemplates "the desirableness of the alliance" (159), Anne nostalgically dwells on the comforts of an affective marriage.

Meanwhile, the defection of the spendthrift baronet has clearly improved Kellynch Hall. Its tenants, Admiral Croft and his wife, Frederick Wentworth's sister, refurbish the house by reducing the number of ornaments (especially looking-glasses) and making practical changes, adding a further dimension to the ambiguous representation of improvement in Austen's novels. Fun is poked at the two generations of Musgroves, who are "like their houses . . . in a state of alteration, perhaps of improvement," the parents "in the old English style, and the young people in the new" (40). The "proper air of confusion" demanded by fashion creates "an overthrow of all order and neatness" (40). The Crofts' alterations, on the other hand, include a better place for keeping umbrellas and the repair of the laundry door, which is "the greatest improvement the house ever had" (127). The Crofts' practical care of the house and the estate reconciles Anne to Kellynch's loss, as she feels assured that it "had passed into better hands than its owners" (125): "In such moments Anne had no power of saying to herself, 'These rooms ought to belong only to us. Oh, how fallen in their destination! How unworthily occupied! An ancient family to be so driven away!'" (126). Her appreciation of the Crofts precludes "that pain which Lady Russell would suffer in entering the house again" (125). Anne's nostalgia has detached itself from ancestral grounds. The eventual outcome of such improvements, however, remains unsolved.[63] She has to find new space for past love, as the Great House fails to be miraculously bequeathed to the novel's deserving couple.

Most critics have agreed that Anne Elliot's sensibility, her melancholy, and—although it has received comparatively little attention—her nostalgia are affirmed in a way that the more ambivalently presented infatuations of the earlier heroines are not.[64] Her nostalgic recollection of the past and past attachments is indeed carefully defined against its negative counterparts, including her father's self-congratulatory, forgetful worship of his family's history and the affected melancholy displayed by Mrs. Musgrove or Captain Benwick. Anne's psychophysical affliction has resulted in "an early loss of bloom and spirits" (28). As a genuine effect of suffering, it contrasts with Mary Musgrove's tendency to think "a great deal of her own complaints" (33) and with Mrs. Musgrove's "large fat sighings" (68) over a "pathetic piece of family history" (50): her "comfortable substantial size was infinitely more fitted by nature to express good cheer and good humour, than tenderness and sentiment" (68).

However, while sentimental conventions deny a "large bulky figure [to have] as good a right to be in deep affliction, as the most graceful set of limbs in the world" (68), what really subjects Mrs. Musgrove's sudden recollection of a lost sailor son to such sarcasm is the fact that nobody had cared for him while he was still alive. Without retracting the ridicule from Mrs. Musgrove's big sighs, the narrator's comments on the unfairness of associating body size with degrees of affliction highlight the deceptive nature of appearances, which forms an underlying theme in the novel. Sir Walter is ridiculed for judging all his acquaintance according to their looks; Mr. Elliot is suspiciously pleasing; and above all, Anne is the apparently resigned spinster who turns out to be not only consistently nostalgic, but ultimately able to marry her lost love.

Captain Benwick significantly has "a pleasing face and a melancholy air, just as he ought to have" (97). Unlike coarse Mary and substantial Mrs. Musgrove, he looks his role. Indicative of a broken heart, his gloominess renders him "perfectly interesting in the eyes of all the ladies" (96). Yet he seems altogether too much "pleased with [Anne's first] allusion to his situation" (101). Even more pointedly, his sudden transference of his love shows him to be "a little man" (97) in more than just his physical delicacy. His much-professed eternal mourning has not lasted very long: We meet Benwick for the first time in November and are told that his fiancée died in June and that Wentworth had informed him of her death in August; at the beginning of February, Anne receives a letter that announces his engagement to Louisa Musgrove. Rather unfeelingly, Benwick commissions the brother of his dead fiancée, Captain Harville, to set the miniature originally meant for her for another.

This display of insensibility prompts Anne's discussion with Harville about the comparative fickleness of men and women and this further induces Wentworth to compose a letter to Anne that is at once hopeful and nostalgic, declaring his love once more. Benwick's sudden recuperation thus serves as more than just an example of affected melancholy. The contrast between the easy transference of his affections and the nostalgically nurtured love of Anne and Wentworth brings the latter together. Claiming men's rights to be equally nostalgic as women, Wentworth writes that "weak and resentful I have been, but never inconstant" (237). Unlike Benwick, he has never forgotten his first love, although his resentment has to change into nostalgia before he can soften painful recollections. The passage of time is irrelevant, as the reduction of eight years to a mere "nothing" shows:

> Soon, however, she began to reason with herself, and try to be feeling less. Eight years, almost eight years had passed, since all had been given up. How absurd to be resuming the agitation, which such an interval had banished into distance and indistinctness! What might not eight years do? Events of every description, changes, alienations, removals,—all, all must be comprised in it; and oblivion of the past—how natural, how certain too! It included nearly a third part of her own life. Alas! with all her reasonings, she found, that to retentive feelings eight years may be little more than nothing. (60)

On the contrary, true nostalgia grows as time passes. Wentworth can offer Anne "a heart even more your own, than when you almost broke it eight years and a half ago" (237). The novel's "unnatural" beginning builds on an accumulation of regrets and revisions of the past that feeds nostalgia: "How eloquent could Anne Elliot have been,—how eloquent, at least, were her wishes on the side of early warm attachment, and a cheerful confidence in futurity. . . . She had been forced into prudence in her youth, she learned romance as she grew older: the natural sequel of an unnatural beginning" (30). Despite her attempts to reason herself out of her agitation, Anne knows that she may preach "patience and resignation" to Benwick, but that "her own conduct would ill bear examination" (101). Yet, her nostalgia is a praiseworthy quality and instrumental in uniting her experiences of the past in the course of her dislocations. While her father and eldest sister indulge in a snobbish ancestral pride when they pursue titled cousins, Anne revives an acquaintance with a poor invalid, Mrs. Smith, whose kindness to her in the past "could never be remembered with indifference" (152). Their first conversations center on "the interesting charm of remembering former partialities and talking over old times" (153). Ultimately, Mrs. Smith's help is vital in exposing Mr. Elliot's true character. It is Anne's "reward" for honoring the attachments of the past: "She had never considered herself as entitled to reward for not slighting an old friend like Mrs. Smith, but here was a reward indeed springing from it!" (212). Lest we consider Wentworth's fervent letter the impulse of a suddenly revived love, it is important to note how his repeated kindnesses to Anne arise from his recollection of the past:

> It was a remainder of former sentiment; it was an impulse of pure, though unacknowledged friendship; it was a proof of his own warm and amiable heart, which she could not contemplate without emotions so compounded of pleasure and pain, that she knew not which prevailed. (91)

Anne's nostalgia depends on her recollection of the particularity of pain with a fondness for past emotions, and this is important as her physical reactions to Wentworth are slowly subsumed to her wistful memories and nostalgic hopes. Encounters with Wentworth have psychophysical effects on Anne: "For a few minutes she saw nothing before her" until "she had scolded back her senses" (175); "the room seemed full—full of persons and voices—but a few minutes ended it" (59). She is "wearied . . . sick of knowing nothing" (180). During the excursion to Lyme, nostalgia as a mode of memory converges with physical recuperation when her "bloom and freshness of youth [is] restored" (104). She delights in the "high grounds and extensive sweeps of country, and [a] sweet retired bay, backed by dark cliffs," on "romantic rocks," and on the "happiest spot for watching the flow of the tide, for sitting in unwearied contemplation" (95). Wentworth even bestows a half-admiring look on her when he notices Mr. Elliot's interest (104).

When Anne sees the Harvilles' domestic happiness, she is overcome by nostalgic regret. Looking back to unrealized possibilities, she grieves for the loss of what could have been: "'These would have been all my friends,' was her thought; and she had to struggle against a great tendency to lowness'" (98). The ambiguity of her feelings at Lyme is further accentuated by Louisa's accident and Wentworth's subsequent appeal to her (111, 114). Like Kellynch and Uppercross, Lyme is a place that has seen both pain and pleasure and can be recollected in nostalgia to form part of Anne's remembrances and consistent love, indeed her consistent selfhood. When she speaks of her fond recollections of Lyme to Wentworth, she implies an equally nostalgic attitude to their love: "'When pain is over, the remembrance of it often becomes a pleasure. One does not love a place the less for having suffered in it.... [I]n short' (with a faint blush at some recollections) 'altogether my impressions of the place are very agreeable'" (184).

Nostalgia isolates the feeling heroine, but eventually unites the lovers, who are happily "heedless of every group around them" (241), wrapt in their private affective union. Far from being a debilitating disease, nostalgia has strengthened their attachment: they "returned again into the past, more exquisitely happy, perhaps in their re-union, than when it had been first projected; more tender, more tried" (240). If there is a decisive shift in Austen's ambiguous treatment of sensibility, it is one to a new affirmation of personal, private, longing. In order to achieve the affective marriage that forms the underlying ideal of the novels, heroines have to go against the concepts of "alliance" held by Sir Thomas Bertram, Lady Catherine, or Lady Russell. Indifferent Sir Walter can be bypassed easily, but the persuasion of those monitor figures who really care can exert a painful pressure. This has been Anne's fate: "Young and gentle as she was, it might yet have been possible to withstand her father's ill-will...—but Lady Russell, whom she had always loved and relied on, could not, with such steadiness of opinion, and such tenderness of manner, be continually advising her in vain" (27). Eventually, Lady Russell has to learn "to love Captain Wentworth as she ought," and Anne has to put up with "the consciousness of having no relations to bestow on him which a man of sense could value" (251).

While Austen's heroines are never locked up or dragged to weddings against their will by plotting patriarchs, friends and family tend to exert a pressure that easily results in psychophysical afflictions. Yet, in showing the transformation of a clinical nostalgia into a pleasant and hopeful recollection as a form of survival strategy, Austen's novels imbue such stories of emotional distress with an intriguing twist and furthermore contribute significantly to changing representations of nostalgia. Even while minor characters such as sofa-bound Lady Bertram or affectedly sighing Mrs. Musgrove continue to be unashamedly abused, and Romantic rhapsodies interrupted by the intrusion of the "tea things," her novels recuperate genuine feeling from allegations of affectation and free the development of true love from overdrawn literary clichés. This movement away from parodic attitudes to sensibility and its symptoms recalls the nostalgic return to romance of her most mature heroine, who "learned romance as she grew older: the natural sequel of an unnatural beginning" (30).

3
Childhood Lost: Dysfunctional Domesticity in Charles Dickens's Novels

NOSTALGIC PASSAGES IN CHARLES DICKENS'S NOVELS FREQUENTLY dwell on childhood memories or are in some way connected to children and their homes or homelessness. Romance in his novels at once feeds on and into a Victorian romancing of childhood. They reflect and contribute to a sentimentalization of Romantic child cults. But the evoked memories of childhood are seldom happy. They are not even necessarily sentimentalized, and yet their narrated recollection is nonetheless invested with a nostalgic glow or part of a nostalgic recuperation of the "softening memory of sorrow, wrong, or trouble," as it is put in *The Haunted Man* (1848), one of Dickens's Christmas stories.[1] It almost seems as if traumatic as well as happy occasions are recalled with nostalgic regret simply because they are irrevocably past. Most intriguingly, this nostalgic way of remembering has a "softening" influence—and in Dickens's fiction, such a softening is usually a good thing. It generates a nostalgic imagination that tends to dwell particularly on dream homes, ideal sanctuaries for homesick characters. What Dickens terms "the romantic side of familiar things" in his preface to *Bleak House* (1853) invests his fictional good homes with an almost magical aura, which contrasts sharply with the much larger number of bad homes in his novels and is further complicated by the affectionate memories his characters have at times rather incongruously of unhappy homes.[2] Such patterns of opposites recur in the novels, juxtaposing idealizations of happy domesticity and the sordid realities of the literally or metaphorically homeless.

Though qualified by softening memories, the childhood homes of Oliver Twist, Esther Summerson, or John Harmon, Florence Dombey's "wilderness of a home" or "the rigid and unloving home" of Arthur Clennam's childhood are neither ideal nor happy.[3] Yet in that the good home is present through its absence, its negation asserts the need for it more vigorously than the praise of a realized ideal could. Its absence offsets nostalgia for what is lost and longed for. This topos of the "non-home," a dysfunctional household in which ideologies of domesticity impede or stifle what they set out to foster and celebrate, is not only as harrowing as literal homelessness, but moreover undermines the notion of the bourgeois family home as a sanctuary from a dangerous "outside world."[4] At the same time, dysfunctional homes are of particular importance for the fostering of a nostalgic imagination as a survival strategy and an incentive for the reconstruction of nostalgic spaces.

There are surprisingly few studies of nostalgia *per se* in Dickens's works, although the prevalence of idealized child-figures along with his notorious sentimentality has been widely acknowledged. His fiction is prominently associated with the blessings and the bane of sentimentality and the best and the worst of what has been termed "the Victorian romance with childhood."[5] The figure of "the angelic, and preferably dying, child"[6] all too often seems a sentimental tear-jerker, although recent criticism has done much to reassess the "purpose" of depicting child death in Victorian literature.[7] This chapter connects the functions of social criticism in Dickens's fiction to his nostalgia for the child's "freshness, and gentleness, and capacity of being pleased," as he puts it in *David Copperfield* (1850).[8] Descriptions of childhood and childhood memories are indeed prominent in the novel. It famously opens with David's account of his birth and carefully conjures up a young child's perceptions and his emerging selfhood. The retrospection creates a nostalgic atmosphere, and unhappy memories by no means undercut this wistful recollection.

In *The Sense of the Past in Victorian Literature*, Raymond Chapman has rightly diagnosed a tenderness for old abuses in Victorian culture that makes "even those who claim to have had an unhappy childhood . . . look back with a sense of pleasant nostalgia on the years of growing up."[9] The rarity of happy moments makes them more precious. As the heroine of Charlotte Brontë's *Jane Eyre* (1847) puts it when she describes her early childhood as an unwanted dependent relative, "even for me, life had its gleams of sunshine."[10] Yet in Dickens's fiction, nostalgia also actively helps to retrieve the lost happiness. A nostalgic imagination can even recuperate "memories" of a gentleness or comfort that have never been experienced. As I shall show, Dickens draws on the Romantic cult of the innocent and often also inspired child and combines it with theories of mesmerism to show the importance of a way of remembering that is imaginative, creative, and above all, nostalgic.

Idealized children and in particular deprived orphans expectedly play a crucial role in the juxtapositions of loss and longing that structure Dickens's exploration of good and bad homes. In his influential analysis of the functions of the "Romantic child" in Victorian fiction, Peter Coveney has suggested that the child serves as "the symbol of sensitive feeling anywhere in a society maddened with the pursuit of material progress."[11] More recently, Catherine Waters has added that even though orphans had been the heroes and heroines of earlier fiction, the figure of the orphan became a particular source of fascination for Victorian writers because of its utility in representing an anxious relation to the past.[12] Fictional orphans provide not only the most vulnerable version of the innocent child and a literary convention that promises the revelation of mysteries, but they usefully embody a homelessness that strengthens bourgeois idealizations of domesticity. In showing how orphans serve to introduce longings for ideal homes and adoption fantasies as a form of nostalgic wish-fulfillment in Dickens's novels, I hope to develop and reinterpret critical interest in the figure of the orphaned child. Baruch Hochman and Ilja Wachs's *Dickens: The Orphan Condition* has been significant in paving the way for a much-needed revision of the fictional orphan's allegedly purely sentimental role. The "orphan condition," Hochman and Wachs suggest, includes children deprived of a happy childhood by other calamities than the death of a biological parent:

> The orphan condition is not essentially the objective state of growing up without one's real parents, or even of being bruised and battered by wicked stepparents and brutal, exploitative institutions. It is, rather, a state of mind that . . . informs some part of everyone's imagination. It gives rise to a virtually insatiable craving for the warmth and the shelter that have been lost [or that] have never been experienced and, therefore, endlessly tease the imagination.[13]

Orphans in Dickens's novels often turn out to be not real orphans at all. The "insatiable craving" for a home, however, is indeed central to the imagination of literal and metaphorical orphans, and my analysis of Dickens's use of a nostalgic imagination builds on Hochman and Wachs's suggestion that it is particularly subconscious "memories" of a never experienced happiness that become central in the orphans' search for wish fulfillment. Most analyses of Dickens's orphans have emphasized a vaguely defined "poetics of loss,"[14] his "poetry of London, the poetry of darkness and isolation,"[15] and not his treatment of longing, which sheds quite a different light on the functions of nostalgia as well as of the orphan as a figure of loss and longing. Peter Ackroyd speaks of "the poor, the ignorant, the diseased, the wretched" beyond the hearth, who induce us to "enjoy the flames of the Christmas fire more because of the very shadows which it casts."[16] Sentimentalized domesticity sharply contrasts with homelessness. This pattern generates *chiaroscuro*: light is set off by darkness.[17]

Comments on nostalgia's role in this pattern have been surprisingly infrequent and sketchy. In *The Imagined World of Charles Dickens*, Mildred Newcomb even maintains that while Dickens received from his recollections of childhood "those intimations of an earthly paradise that would make of him a humanist and a humanitarian," there is very little nostalgia in his work.[18] In a study of the "grown-up child" in Dickens's novels, Malcolm Andrews speaks rather dismissingly of "a kind of sentimental archaeology."[19] Nostalgia in Dickens's fiction undoubtedly comes close to mere sentimentality—the mellow counterpart to Romantic sensibility[20]—at times propagating a withdrawal into bourgeois homes that oddly undercuts his interest in the underprivileged. His social criticism, in fact, arises from his belief in the Romantic child, yet is ultimately also complicated by his own childhood experience and his humiliation to have been temporarily deprived of the education a middle-class boy could expect. This ambivalent attitude towards the underprivileged child leads to the stark contrasts and ambiguities in his descriptions of idealized children on the one hand and of the harrowing realities of the urban poor in Victorian Britain on the other.

Dickens's orphans are undoubtedly a poignant realization of homelessness. The recurrent pattern of deprivation and restitution that characterizes their lives creates adoption fantasies of happy homes. In my analysis of his representation of the orphan, of dysfunctional homes, and also of the domesticity associated with the idealized Victorian family, I shall discuss several of his novels, taking them in the order in which they relate to these themes rather than according to the chronology of their publication. I shall devote a substantial part of the chapter to a close reading of *Bleak House*, which I consider as a focus point for Dickens's preoccupation with adoption fantasies. I seek to recuperate the creative aspects of nostalgia, emphasizing the importance of the nostalgic retrospect as a means of overcoming regret and resentment. A close look at the juxtapositions of resentful and regretful memories in *Little Dorrit* (1857) will even more strikingly reveal Dickens's idealization of the softening effects of a nostalgic imagination. Throughout his fiction nostalgic forgiveness acts as an antidote to resentment.

Dickens's Orphans: Longing for an Adopted Home

Oliver Twist, Little Nell, Pip, and David Copperfield are or become literally orphaned. But the experience of dysfunctional homes links Florence's cheerless, loveless, and "homeless," though resplendent, abode—the commercial House of Dombey, in which she is considered a void investment—or Arthur Clennam's haunting memories of a stern household to Pip among the graves of the family he never knew and to David's resentment of his changed home and his "new Pa"—"connected with the grave in the churchyard, and the raising of the dead" (*DC*, 37): "What a strange feeling it was to be going home when it was not home" (*DC*, 93). Conversely, there are nostalgic spaces in uncongenial homes as Amy Dorrit's "surviving attachment" (*LD*, 75) to the Marshalsea perhaps most pointedly shows: "I suffer from homesickness.... I long so ardently and so earnestly for home, as sometimes, when no one sees me, to pine for it" (*LD*, 538). The orphan's twofold homesickness as a longing for a past (or never experienced, but only imagined) ideal home and as a being sick of a dysfunctional household or institution is crucial to Dickens's treatment of nostalgia on three grounds. Firstly, the delineation of the abandoned child's predicaments ties in nicely with the popularity of sentimentalized suffering children in Victorian fiction. Secondly, it is the absent ideal home that teases the imagination and therefore stresses the need for a cozy domesticity even more. Dickens's polarized opposites largely feed on this emphatic presence of an absent ideal. Thirdly, "memories" of what has never been experienced indicate an innate longing for and even remembrance of an ideal, usually bourgeois, home. These instances truly testify to the romantic side of familiar things. Oliver Twist, perhaps Dickens's most idealized abandoned child, dwells on "dim remembrances of scenes that never were, in this life; which vanish like a breath; which some brief memory of a happier existence, long gone by, would seem to have awakened; which no voluntary exertion of the mind can ever recall."[21]

This nostalgia is repeatedly described as innate in *Oliver Twist* (1838). It is invoked by "a strain of gentle music, or the rippling of water in a silent place, or the odour of a flower, or the mention of a familiar word" (*OT*, 216), testifying to a recurring Romanticism in Dickens's fiction. At the same time, such descriptions of unconscious or subconscious memories of what has never happened in this life also reflect Dickens's interest in popular Victorian theories of mesmerism. In *Dickens and Mesmerism: The Hidden Springs of Fiction*, Fred Kaplan speaks of Oliver's "mesmeric sleepwalking" and "mesmeric consciousness," drowsy states that are comparable to trances, which put "us in touch with hidden springs of the self that are inaccessible to us in our waking states."[22] One of the questions such trances promise to answer for Dickens, Kaplan suggests, is the "relationship between childhood and the life-energy potential of the adult," a connection that is central to Dickens's nostalgia for childhood and the much-valued perspicacity with which he credits children.[23] His idealization of "the power of observation in numbers of young children" and the importance of retaining this capacity as an "inheritance they have preserved from their childhood" (*DC*, 11) in *David Copperfield* has revealingly been read as an obstruction of the *Bildungsroman*'s progress.[24] But while nostalgia for childhood is undoubtedly often sentimentalized in Dickens's novels, their representation of nostalgia emphasizes its constructive qualities.

In *Oliver Twist*, nostalgic "memories" of ideal homes are evidence of Oliver's innate goodness and ultimately rewarded or fulfilled. Waking in the Maylies' domestic paradise, he is touched by dreamy glimpses "of scenes that never were, in this life" (*OT*, 216). Rose's tears dropping on his face reinitiate a "maternal" link: "The boy stirred, and smiled in his sleep, as though these marks of pity and compassion had awakened some pleasant dream of a love and affection he had never known" (*OT*, 216). This restoration of broken family ties through a dreamy unification of two orphans consummates a pattern of fantasies of origin and wish-fulfillment. Another, very similar, instance in the same novel is the reunion of mother and child through the mysterious portrait in the similarly blissful Brownlow household. The recognition, during which Oliver most aptly swoons, is subconscious. It has the nature and the logic of a dream. In his illness he dreams of his mother's "face [looking] sweet and happy" (*OT*, 77); during his convalescence he is confronted with her likeness, which is so very much like him. He wakes in an earthly paradise of plenty and pictorially framed smiles, which offers an orphan's fantasy with dreamlike completeness as well as abruptness: "This is not the place I went to sleep in" (*OT*, 76). His longing for this domestic heaven connects him to universal "memories." It is what—magnetically—draws him "home."

In accordance with Romantic child cults and new mesmeric theories, such insights and "memories" are the prerogatives of the susceptible, of children and those who have preserved their "inheritance" (*DC*, 11), as it is put in *David Copperfield*. As Kaplan has shown, Dickens uses mesmerism to boost the credibility of his characters' visionary revelations and innate goodness. Alison Winter has even argued that mesmerism provides a good "diagnostic tool to study Victorian culture" and further pointed out Oliver's mesmeric insight into his enemies' evil machinations.[25] A similar revelation takes place when Tom Pinch plays the church-organ in *Martin Chuzzlewit* (1844): as he conjures up "grand tones" that seem "to find an echo in . . . the deep mystery of his own heart . . . down to its very lightest recollection of childhood,"[26] he not only achieves insights into his own life as well as into grander mysteries, but ultimately exposes Mr. Pecksniff's hypocritical schemes (*MC*, 486–92). Like the similarly childlike heroes in novels of sensibility, Pinch is "a poor, shy, awkward creature [and] not at all a man of the world" (*MC*, 487–88). While he is only the novel's antihero, he is more than a comic foil. He is an endearing character whose musical abilities help to preserve his good nature—not least because of the mesmeric components of his performance.

The main function of mesmeric passages in Dickens's fiction is without doubt to render credibility to memories of a never-known happier existence, but at the same time, descriptions of such ways of remembering come surprisingly close to an almost Proustian episode. They are reminiscent of the moment when the flavor of a tea-soaked biscuit triggers a series of vivid memories of Marcel's childhood in Proust's novel: "The whole of Combray and its surroundings, taking shape and solidity, sprang into being, town and gardens alike, from my cup of tea."[27] Association as the way memory and in particular recollections of childhood work is an important theme in Dickens's novels and indeed in Victorian fiction in general. In *Nicholas Nickleby* (1839), Smike, another "orphan" whose lost parent is rediscovered too late, adopts "the spot where the happiest years of [Nicholas's] life had been passed" together with its happy "old associations" as his chosen home and final resting place.[28] David Copperfield and Pip speak at length of their earliest "associations."

In his discussion of psychological associationism and its influence on Victorian fiction, Rick Rylance comments on the "associationist romance" of *David Copperfield*.[29] Its form and themes, Rylance convincingly argues, depend on memory and the way it was thought to work through association. Nicholas Dames has similarly shown that the words "association" and "associated" persistently recur in the novel to serve as "the pivot to countless passages that describe the shifts and routes of memory"— a mnemonic mode that he contrasts with Proust's "pure memory."[30] However, not only is Dames's identification of amnesia and nostalgia as forms of forgetting flawed, his argument that in the Victorian novel, "immersions in the specificity of the past, ranging from the mundane to the hallucinogenic, are largely barred" is based on sweeping generalizations and fails to take Victorian experiments with mesmerism into account.[31] At the other end of the spectrum, Franco Moretti has suggested that "the typical novelistic 'episode'. . . always contains within itself something of Proust's *madeleine*: it is an experiment with time."[32]

In its indeterminate and changing status, nostalgia as an emotional experience and as a form of (emotional) memory of course lends itself to simplifications and extensions of its definition. In Dickens's novels, nostalgia is an essential aspect of what he calls the "softening memory of sorrow, wrong, or trouble" (*HM*, 189) while the "memories" of something that has never been experienced contribute significantly to the romantic side of familiar things.

Its "softening" influence is perhaps nostalgia's most important effect for Dickens. As it counterpoises resentment, it prevents his much-suffering characters (particularly the deprived orphans) from seeking revenge or becoming embittered. The "softening memory" praised in *The Haunted Man* is nostalgia. In this Christmas story, the loss of emotional associations with the past depraves mankind, reducing it to a subhuman state. Nostalgia satisfactorily turns even unhappy memories into a constructive emotion that is vital to the characters' happiness as well as to their treatment of each other. Most importantly, the story makes it emphatically clear that a nostalgic memory has nothing to do with forgetting. On the contrary, the happiest and most nostalgic character is an old man whose daily prayer is "keep my memory green!" (*HM*, 162). His son proudly boasts of his father's healthy memory: "There never was such a memory as my father's. He's the most wonderful man in the world. He don't know what forgetting means" (*HM*, 161). Redlow, the lonely scientist, wonders at this. He wrongly connects happy memories to a form of forgetting: "Merry and happy—and remember well?" (*HM*, 162). Assuming that everyone would want to forget their sorrows and wrongs, he strikes a bargain with a ghost, his own "evil spirit" (*HM*, 166), to eradicate all his emotional associations, though not his knowledge. As he spreads this emotional amnesia, the people around him become selfish and discontent.[33] Eventually he has to realize his mistake. Having no emotional associations at all is worse than bad memories. A young street-child embodies life without softening memories: this "baby savage, a young monster, a child who had never been a child, a creature who might live to take the outward form of man, but who, within, would live and perish a mere beast" (*HM*, 167), has never experienced the nostalgic dreams that connect Oliver or Smike to idealized bourgeois households.

While such negative examples appear to undercut belief in innate goodness, they serve to show the vitality of nostalgia. Monks, Oliver Twist's half-brother, exhibits the corruption to which Oliver appears to be immune; Monks can therefore be seen as a rejected and damaged child, denounced and disinherited by his weak father, used and abused by his vengeful mother. Still, like the majority of villains in Dickens's early novels, Monks is a static villainous character. There is more sympathy for Steerforth, whose younger self is nostalgically remembered. It has even been suggested that "Steerforth learns his pride and Heep his cloying humility at their mothers' knees."[34] This emphasis on learned or conditioned villainy becomes more and more important in Dickens's later novels: society is to be blamed, but increasingly, a choice is available between bitterness or resentment and a nostalgic forgiveness.

In *Martin Chuzzlewit*, scheming Jonas Chuzzlewit lives up to his upbringing. His maltreated father chuckles to himself in "stealthy glee," muttering "in his sleeve . . . *I* taught him. *I* trained him. This is the heir of my bringing-up" (*MC*, 180). *Hard Times* (1854) takes Dickens's growing interest in an educational system that pays no attention to the needs of the imagination even further. Bitzer does credit to Gradgrindery when he proves that his heart serves only a physiological and certainly not a sentimental function: "'The circulation, sir,' returned Bitzer, smiling at the oddity of the question [whether he has no heart], 'couldn't be carried on without one.'"[35] In *Little Dorrit*, Arthur Clennam re-emerges softened, but somewhat bitter, from the "inexorable discipline" of his childhood: "Nothing graceful or gentle anywhere, and the void in my cowed heart everywhere—this was my childhood, if I may so misuse the word as to apply it to such a beginning of life" (*LD*, 20). Still, it is his "belief in all the gentle and good things his life had been without" (*LD*, 158) that rescues him:

> He was a dreamer in such a wise, because he was a man who had deep-rooted in his nature, a belief in all the gentle and good things his life had been without. Bred in meanness and hard dealing, this had rescued him to be a man of honourable mind and open hand. Bred in coldness and severity, this had rescued him to have a warm and sympathetic heart. (*LD*, 158)

This nostalgic dreaming prevents his initial resentment from embittering him. In this he contrasts sharply with a series of acrimonious characters in the novel: Mrs. Clennam has had her proclivity to "wholesome repression, punishment, and fear" (*LD*, 774) indoctrinated into her by the religious fanaticism of *her* parents, while her husband has been brought up as "a poor, irresolute, frightened chap, who had had everything but his orphan life scared out of him when he was young" (*LD*, 771–72). I shall come back to the significant contrast between Mrs. Clennam's longings for revenge and Arthur's attempts to atone for the past. *Little Dorrit* can, in fact, boast a panorama of remembering and forgetting characters. The dangerously bitter Miss Wade refuses to redefine the hated places of the past: "If I had been shut up in any place to pine and suffer, I should always hate that place and wish to burn it down, or raze it to the ground. I know no more" *(LD,* 22). A pathological case study, Miss Wade's story indeed shares so many elements with Arthur's own life and also that of other characters in Dickens's fiction that her failure to overcome her resentment stands out. The childhoods of both Arthur Clennam, whose orphan experience turns out to be literal, and of Esther Summerson in *Bleak House* are likewise overshadowed by the "taint" of illegitimacy, as has been Miss Wade's. Mrs. Clennam has resentfully reared the illegitimate offspring of her husband's affair. Esther's godmother has carefully concealed her relationship with her sister's child. Esther is her mother's "disgrace . . . orphaned and degraded from the first of these evil anniversaries [her birthday]" and "set apart" *(BH,* 17). It remains confused whether it is innate goodness or a nostalgic forgiveness that preserves Esther and Arthur. Their suffering seems to have only contributed to their goodness, and ultimately, happiness.

Pathological cases such as Miss Wade's, in fact, not only underscore the importance of a softening, or nostalgic, memory, but also prevent Dickens's repeated praise of mistreated and, in accordance with a sentimental logic, therefore virtuous characters from lapsing into a propagation of mistreatment. His idealized "orphans" are good because of their suffering as well as despite of it, almost suggesting that suffering is good for you. One might be tempted to draw the conclusion that something very much like Mrs. Clennam's "inexorable discipline" is perhaps salutary after all. This is certainly far from what Dickens wishes to promote, and the insight he provides into the minds (and more importantly, hearts) of some of his villains serves to counteract any such undesirable alignments. But what does this contrast say about the power of a nostalgic imagination or dream? Is it only innately good characters who experience visions of a better life, or is their allocation more ambiguous? What is noticeable is that in the later novels, a conscious choice between resentment and nostalgia becomes more and more important. As I shall show in more detail in my readings of the novels, Pip in *Great Expectations* (1861) or Arthur in *Little Dorrit* have to overcome their bitterness or resentment. But still, a certain incongruity remains—testifying perhaps most to Dickens's allegiance to the romantic side of familiar things.

This ambiguity extends to Dickens's representations of ideal homes. They are meant to be the restitution for his nostalgically dreaming characters, but they are based on an ideal that becomes doubtful when one considers the prevalence of bad homes in the novels. Although his sentimentalized domestic paradises are one of the most memorable aspects of his fiction, Dickens, in fact, excels particularly in descriptions of dysfunctional domesticity. He thereby undermines the Victorian ideal of the happy home as a sanctuary from the cold, cruel world. Somewhat disturbingly, unhappy homes bring forth virtuous characters and, conversely, those in possession of comfortable homes are not always sufficiently aware of their luck. Still, this distinction is by no means clear-cut. Dysfunctional households are shown to be rife in asocial behavior and there are also—though this is a rare occasion in Dickens—happy people in happy homes. Ultimately, Dickens subscribes to bourgeois ideals of domestic happiness after all. Its rarity makes good homes even more special. As the ideal Victorian home is thought of as a counterpoise to the marketplace, the fear that the hard commercial world might enter domestic space is, in fact, part and parcel of this idealization. In *Sesame and Lilies* (1865), Ruskin revealingly describes "the true nature of home" as

> the shelter, not only from all injury, but from all terror, doubt, and division. In so far as it is not this, it is not home; so far as the anxieties of the outer life penetrate into it, and the inconsistently-minded, unknown, unloved, or hostile society of the outer world is allowed by either husband or wife to cross the threshold, it ceases to be home; it is then only a part of that outer world which you have roofed over, and lighted fire in.[36]

In *Great Expectations*, Wemmick takes this split into his "office life" and "home life" to comical extremes. His home is literally his "castle," a private space equipped with a range of locks and even boasting its own diminutive drawbridge.[37] By contrast, in most bourgeois households of the novels, negative examples of homemaking and family life recur with an astonishing persistence, marking out the good home as a decided oddity. Recent criticism has pointed out that the Victorian dream of domestic shelter can easily lapse into a nightmare of psychological imprisonment, and that retrospective diatribes such as Samuel Butler's are by no means the first accounts of the ideal's failure.[38] In his study of the Victorian family, Steven Mintz suggests that "Victorians often regarded the family as a walled garden, yet the family walled in as much as it walled out."[39] The Victorian home as a place of domestic discord, of a hypocritical concealment of commercial interests, and a deliberate, but ineffectual, shutting out of social wrongs has become a critical commonplace and entered the popular imagination.

Christabel LaMotte, the fictional Victorian poetess in A. S. Byatt's *Possession* (1990), writes that amidst the warmth of the strong house, "brains may shrill in carpet-hush" and "walls break outwards—with a rush."[40] More recently, historical novels about the Victorian age like Sarah Waters's *Fingersmith* and Michel Faber's *The Crimson Petal and the White* (both 2002) have reactivated the focus on a "domestic Gothic" of deceiving harmony and underlying unrest that were the hallmarks of the Victorian sensation novel. They share their interest in madness, sexual exploitation, and the production of cultural fictions with popular novels of the 1860s. Yet what is perhaps more surprising are the ways in which this dismantling of Victorian domestic ideals is anticipated in Dickens's novels—in the same novels that reaffirm nostalgia for a domestic space and happy family life.[41]

The presence of a wide variety of negative homes in Dickens's novels clearly undermines any association of a Dickensian home with harmony. The ways of the commercial world are deliberately "walled in" by Dombey, Gradgrind, and Old Harmon in his Harmony Jail. The Harmon siblings, the rich man's "poor little children,"[42] Florence Dombey, and the Gradgrind children are deprived of a true home. Such families yield ample evidence that it needs neither illegitimacy nor wicked stepparents to make a home sufficiently uncongenial to qualify as a dysfunctional household. Seemingly innocent family events and celebrations can go terribly wrong. The Wilfers' wedding anniversary in *Our Mutual Friend* (1865)—"still celebrated . . . in the bosom of their family," "kept morally, rather as a Fast than a Feast, enabling Mrs. Wilfer to hold a sombre darkling state" (*OMF*, 449)—is a case in point. There is little domestic coziness in a gathering morally kept, chilled by Mrs. Wilfer's frosty formal kisses of her daughters. The gathering of relations in *Martin Chuzzlewit*, like that of the aptly named Pockets in *Great Expectations*, shows a substitution of a purely economic relationship over affection: "Such was the pleasant little family circle now assembled in Mr. Pecksniff's best parlour, agreeably prepared to fall foul of Mr. Pecksniff or anybody else who might venture to say anything whatever upon any subject." (*MC*, 54)

What is fascinating is that Dickens's exposures of failed homes do not even need the dark secrets that become so vital in exposing ostensible respectability in sensation fiction. Some of the worst households are condemned because of their very respectability.

In Dickens's last finished novel, *Our Mutual Friend*, smugly unimpeachable middle class snobbery and self-righteousness are brilliantly summed up as "Podsnappery." Mr. Podsnap's household shows Victorian domesticity at its worst. To Podsnap's young person, domestic stability is somber and stifling: "Miss Podsnap's early views of life being principally derived from the reflections of it in her father's boots, and in the walnut and rosewood tables of the dim drawing-rooms . . . were of a sombre cast" (*OMF*, 134). There is no restitution for its "hideous solidity" (*OMF*, 131). The Podsnap home can boast a dysfunctional domesticity that is worse than literal homelessness. Lizzy Hexam's nostalgia for those moments of falling "asleep together [with her little brother] in a corner, snuggled under a little shawl," in the same novel contrasts forcefully with the depiction of Georgiana Podsnap alone and lost among "massive furniture" (*OMF*, 37, 134). The bourgeois home of the Podsnaps is a decidedly unpleasant experience of stability. Leaving home and its wrongs behind indeed forms an important theme. Orphans need to make their own homes. The father's inheritance becomes problematic: Lizzy's legacy is her illiteracy and guilty feelings for the river; John Harmon inherits dust mounds; Miss Riderhood only a squint, and so on.

Podsnap, like Pecksniff in *Martin Chuzzlewit*, is a comical character whose hypocrisy is his main character-trait. In contrast, there is sympathy for some commercial gentlemen who have put business before family without becoming mere caricatures of their capitalist values. Considering the focus on neglected children in the novels, it is hardly surprising that such sympathy is primarily bestowed on bereaved fathers. While Ralph Nickleby's loss of his only just-rediscovered son Smike fails to redeem him, it nonetheless shows him to be more human than he thought he was. Scrooge's reformation is notably connected to Tiny Tim's possible death. But the most extensive treatment of a suffering business man takes place in *Dombey and Son* (1848). Its full title, *Dealings with the Firm of Dombey and Son, Retail, Wholesale and for Exportation*, underlines the importance of business interests in this domestic novel. The dysfunctional household reflects the effects of capitalism and imperial strategies of appropriation at home, as Jeff Nunokawa has convincingly shown.[43]

Florence Dombey's idea of a father is strikingly similar to that of Podsnap's young person: "The child glanced keenly at the blue coat and stiff white cravat, which, with a pair of creaking boots and a very loud ticking watch, embodied her idea of a father" (*D&S*, 3). But whereas Mr. Podsnap is a grotesque Dickensian character with only blander smugness under his smug, shining surface, there is pity for Mr. Dombey, whose own childhood has been overshadowed by his inheritance of the House of Dombey (*D&S*, ch. 3). After Paul Dombey's sentimentalized death, he grieves as much for the lost Son of Dombey and Son as for the child, and his resentment of his daughter is psychologically convincing. It takes a long list of further disasters before he can acknowledge her worth. While it is true that Mr. Dombey's eventual reformation through his daughter's influence remains doubtful, Mr. Carker's death exorcises the worst aspects of the company's aggressive strategies. Repeated descriptions of Dombey's loneliness and grief have moreover paved the way for a more sympathetic treatment. What strikes *home*—and the choice of words is significant in a novel so much preoccupied with homes and non-homes—is his loneliness, which reflects his daughter's: "By the waning lamp, and at that haggard hour, [his face] looked worn and dejected; and in the utter loneliness surrounding him, there was an appeal to Florence that struck home" (*D&S*, 252). What Florence pines for is a happy home with her father.

In fact, despite Paul's sentimental death and his father's restitution, Florence remains the novel's center of interest. She is a good example of Dickens's "orphans." Neglect only makes her softer and more endearing. Her homesick dreams thrive in deserted rooms, highlighting the hallucinatory nature of fervent longing and the power of a nostalgic fiction as a counterpoise to depressing realities: "As if her life were an enchanted vision, there arose out of her solitude ministering thoughts.... She imagined so often what her life would have been if her father could have loved her and she had been a favourite child." (*D&S*, 313–14). Her nostalgic imagination is a survival strategy. She counteracts resentment with her belief in an ideal home and eventually succeeds in reclaiming it. Dickens's subsequent novels further explore this creative and rewarding rearranging of memories and dreams, as the softening memory of nostalgia becomes a structuring device as well as a theme.

Indisputably Dickens's most autobiographical novel, *David Copperfield* is deeply concerned with the representation of memory and specifically childhood memories. The famous idealization of "a certain freshness, and gentleness, and capacity of being pleased, which are also an inheritance [that is] preserved from ... childhood" (*DC*, 11), disconcertingly opens a novel that deals more with childhood trauma than with happy associations. After his mother's death, David's stepfather sends him to London, where he has to earn money by undertaking menial tasks despite his wishes for an education and a career. This experience is "a period of my life, which I can never lose the remembrance of, while I remember anything; and the recollection of which has often, without my invocation, come before me like a ghost, and haunted happier times" (*DC*, 129). David's writing (and hence the novel as well) is a means to exorcise haunting memories. Repetitive references to "the secret agony of my soul" (*DC*, 133), of "that slow agony of my youth" (*DC*, 145), admittedly invite allegations of self-pity. David's proclivity to emphasize his diminutive size at the time of his ordeal, his repeated astonishment at "what a little creature [he] really was" (*DC*, 150), down to his "childish feet" (*DC*, 145), generates a sentimental pathos that obscures profounder effects of his ordeal. But such fixated dwelling on the small and childish aside, the experience is harrowing, and so is its recollection. The "sordid things" of the past are reworked into an imaginative world, but the self-alienating distance between the narrating self and a pitied "innocent romantic boy" that appears to be no longer a part of the self disrupts the integration of memories:

> When my thoughts go back now, to that slow agony of my youth, I wonder how much of the histories I invented for such people hangs like a mist of fancy over well-remembered facts! When I tread the old ground, I do not wonder that I seem to see and pity, going on before me, an innocent romantic boy, making his imaginative world out of such strange experiences and sordid things! (*DC*, 145)

As it rewrites the self-pity of *David Copperfield*, *Great Expectations* traces ways to overcome resentment through a nostalgic acceptance of the past. Pip is a mistreated orphan whose longing for adoption is at the bottom of his expectations. Eventually, his contrition for past mistakes counteracts resentment of suffered wrong, enabling Pip's synthesis of past selves.[44] As he can neither return to his childhood innocence nor change the past, Pip can only redeem and preserve it by endorsing memories. The revision of his experience of shame, snobbery, and suffering negotiates an acceptance of what has made him what he is. Most importantly, there is very little self-pity in Pip's reassessment of his past. On the contrary, his discovery of "the identity of things" and of himself as a "small bundle of shivers growing afraid of it all and beginning to cry" is striking for the way it eschews sentimentality.[45] The retrospective accounts of having been brought up by hand, by his sister's "hard and heavy hand" (*GE*, 8), supported by the vividly animate "Tickler," are couched in a self-ironic, light-hearted style that repeatedly repudiates any allegations of self-pity. Pip's victimization by the negative parents of the novel—Mrs. Joe, Miss Havisham, "Uncle"

Pumblechook—is detailed with a bitter but comical self-irony: "I was always treated as if I had insisted on being born, in opposition to the dictates of reason, religion, and morality, and against the dissuading arguments of my best friends." (*GE*, 23) His recollection of his sister's "fearful catalogue" of his illnesses is delightfully cynical (*GE*, 28). His retrospection is filtered through an ironic reappraisal that creates nostalgia as well as comedy.

At the same time, the wish fulfillment moves away from the orphan's fortuitous adoption and instead focuses first on repressed desires for revenge before making way for a nostalgic reassessment of the past. While David Copperfield's "vanished" (*DC*, 11) eccentric fairy-aunt provides the sought-for home that liberates him from the Murdstone regime and life as an exploited drudge in London, Miss Havisham is more "like the Witch of the place" (*GE*, 85). Pip's doubles, Magwitch and Orlick, instead act out a desire for revenge. As the hunted convict emerges among the graves of Pip's dead parents and dead siblings, he externalizes his resentment and guilt. When Orlick takes up Magwitch's leg iron, which Pip has helped to remove, Pip symbolically kills his abusive surrogate parent.[46] His doubles indeed express a sense of guilt—a "guilty knowledge" (*GE*, 13), "a guilty mind" (*GE*, 17)—that has already been fostered in him even before he encounters the hunted man. From his imagined delivery by an "Accoucheur Policeman" (*GE*, 23) to his protection of the criminal that adopted him, a sense of guilt haunts him. His futile attempt to save Miss Havisham and his hardly more successful support of Magwitch nonetheless redeem him.

Eventually, the wish-fulfillment fantasy of Oliver's or David Copperfield's "re-adoption" by their relatives is discarded for a mere glimpse of the next generation, of the better home of a second, "reborn" Pip, his namesake, who has taken his place in the original home: "There, smoking his pipe in the old place by the kitchen firelight, as hale and as strong as ever though a little grey, sat Joe; and there, fenced into the corner with Joe's leg, and sitting on my own little stool looking at the fire, was—I again!" (*GE*, 476) This "return" to an idealized version of his lost home forms a restoration of nostalgic space.[47] It materializes like a revitalized memory of the past. The domestic scene is strikingly similar to the original childhood home, but also strikingly different. It is its idealized, happier version. Whereas Joe Gargery, the mild husband of Pip's shrewish sister and the only good parent in the novel, has remained at his old place by the fireside, the formerly dysfunctional home has been purged of the presence of Orlick, Miss Havisham, Tickler, Mrs. Joe, Magwitch, and Pumblechook. Pip assumes the role of the visiting uncle, but unlike obtrusive Pumblechook, he emphatically does "*not* rumple [his namesake's] hair" (*GE*, 477). As Pip's positive double, his namesake acts out an adoption fantasy that is no longer attainable.

Most importantly, unhappy memories can no longer be "forgotten" by being relegated to the vague recollections of an earlier, now estranged self, which is what happens in *David Copperfield*. At the same time, there must not be a lapse into resentment. Pip's feelings of guilt obstruct his nostalgia until his need for revenge is externalized by villains that serve as his doubles, adroitly leaving him to cherish a softening memory of the past. The pathos of Miss Havisham's resentful memory is not only counterpoised by, but also connected to, Pip's ultimately curative nostalgia. He becomes the victim of Miss Havisham's obsession with the past, a holding on to negative memories that contrasts crucially with his contrite attempts to reclaim the home of the past at the end of the novel. Yet, the memory of her elaborate, though futile, endeavors to stop time at the moment just before her devastating disappointment eventually helps him to accept his own loss of home and the unrealized possibilities of the past. Her resentment is sharply poised against Pip's capability to overcome his desire for revenge as well as his disappointment. Seeing Miss Havisham as a travesty of the love-mad woman, Helen Small has rightly pointed out that there is little sympathy for her in the novel. She "should be tragic, but there is a forced quality to her desolation . . . that leaches sympathy from her."[48] Not so much the result of lovesickness than of a general animosity directed at mankind in general and her relatives in particular, Miss Havisham's resentment is indeed the opposite of nostalgia. In dwelling on the bitter aspects of the past, she shuts out any softening memories. She embodies the resentment that Pip needs to expel.

Pip's dilemma throughout most of the novel is, in fact, his deliberate forgetfulness of his past and of the softening memories of his home. They are only revived by a cathartic illness. Joe's maternal nursing recuperates a more nostalgic version of the past: "We have had a time together, Joe, that I can never forget. There were days once, I know, that I did for a while forget; but I never shall forget these" (*GE*, 467). Pip wakes from symbolic death to moral rebirth and is "thankful [for having] been ill," which has been "a memorable time" for him (*GE*, 467). His glimpses of his double's happier home reconcile him to the realization that he cannot really return home, but the homecoming he experiences in his sickroom shows that curative nostalgia heals him. His longings and disappointments result in an emotional and physical affliction that is then cured by his nostalgic memories of a "memorable time" in the sickroom even more than by his salutary suffering itself. The sickroom as a space of emotional reconciliation and metaphorical rebirth of course forms a popular topos. As we have seen, it is important as a place of emotional crisis in eighteenth-century novels of sensibility, parodied as early as Frances Sheridan's 1761 novel *Sidney Bidulph*, and revised in Austen's *Sense and Sensibility*. As it is taken up in mid-Victorian fiction, it forms the true heart of the bourgeois home. In his affirmation of this sickroom topos, Dickens clearly subscribes to Victorian ideals of domesticity. Even though Pip's experience in the sickroom fails to grant a complete homecoming, for most of Dickens's orphans it does just that. Comfortable sickrooms are at the heart of their adoption fantasies.

The Homecoming of the Orphan: The Sickroom as a Place of Restitution

The sickroom in mid-Victorian fiction functions as a place of restitution, familial reunion, and moral redemption—in short, of emotional as well as physical recuperation. In allowing, even indulging, infantile passivity and physical dependence by providing nursing by a (surrogate) parent, it makes up for suffered deprivation and neglect. A sanctuary from or counterpoise to material strife, it is a domestic space of somatic desire. Mid-Victorian sickroom narratives connect a somatic understanding of emotional afflictions to a sentimental treatment of illness that often figures a curative return to infantile helplessness. In the process, nostalgia can become its own cure. When Joe Gargery, the only maternal figure in Pip's childhood, nurses the estranged, adult Pip, he revives associations of the "memorable time" they spent together in the past. The sickroom brings them close once again. As in most Victorian novels, the sickroom is a familial space, and nursing consolidates family ties or, less often, romantic attachments. By contrast, Sairey Gamp, the hired nurse in *Martin Chuzzlewit*, is a patient's nightmare, and indeed came to embody the scandalous malpractices of habitually drunk and largely unqualified nurses who practiced little hygiene and a deplorable bedside manner in Victorian medical discourses.[49] In the same novel, Martin Chuzzlewit's selfishness is cured when he has to nurse Mark Tapley more than when he is nursed by him. Their care of each other creates a domestic space in the swamp abroad and enables them to return home. Throughout Dickens's fiction, friends and family make use of the confines of the sickroom to re-establish or redefine domestic relations.

Our Mutual Friend marks a departure from this association of adequate nursing with domesticity in its praise of a children's hospital: Johnny, the Orphan, would have survived if he had been taken from his poor home in time. The same novel sees the failure of Rogue Riderhood's rebirth, while a marriage takes place at Eugene Wrayburn's sickbed to reclaim an effete gentleman, bleaching bourgeois associations from the sickroom narrative, while domesticating a lower-class girl and an upper-class gentleman. This section will look at the functions of nostalgia in Dickens's sickrooms as they move away from a place of restitution for orphaned children to a romantic space that is nonetheless safely bourgeois.

Oliver Twist tells the story of a mistreated orphan who is richly recompensed as he not only rediscovers family connections, but gets an inherited fortune into the bargain. The novel expectedly contains an abundance of nursing to counterpoise the descriptions of neglect and mistreatment. Tended by Mrs. Bedwin (*Bed*-win), Oliver Twist is "taken better care of than he ever was before" (*OT*, 76) by a maternal surrogate. He imbibes love and food—broth "strong enough . . . to furnish an ample dinner, when reduced to the regulation strength, for three hundred and fifty paupers, at the lowest computation" (*OT*, 79)—under a pictorial likeness of his dead mother. Crucially contrasting with the famous episode in which he asks for more (*OT*, 12), the sickroom topos is realized as a return to maternal sources of nourishment and nursing: "They were happy days, those of Oliver's recovery" (*OT*, 94). Both Oliver and his aunt, Rose, undergo physical illness before they find tranquil happiness in their convalescence. *Oliver Twist* perhaps shows the most straightforward realizations of Dickens's favorite topoi, and this leads to its fairy-tale-like quality. John Lucas has pointedly suggested that Rose's recovery is "too obvious a piece of symbolism."[50] Carolyn Dever argues that the novel is a "complete articulation of the psychologized, sentimentalized plot of the dead mother," which she calls the "predominant domestic topos in the Victorian novel."[51] Like the ideal home, the maternal ideal is, as Dever puts it, honored more often in the breach.[52] Miriam Bailin's *The Sickroom in Victorian Fiction: The Art of Being Ill* provides perhaps the best account of the power of the "sickroom romance." The Dickensian sickroom, she shows, is closely connected to images of paradise and the *locus amoenus* of the pastoral, as it doubles as "the hallowed ground of matrimonial, filial, and self-unification" and "a kind of provisional or preliminary heaven."[53] The Maylies' country retreat in *Oliver Twist* shows this function most clearly. Nostalgia for a happier world saturates its pastoral tranquility: "The memories which peaceful country scenes call up, are not of this world, nor of its thoughts and hopes" (*OT*, 237). Recovering amidst "scenes of peace and quietude" is "a foretaste of heaven" (*OT*, 237). It is at this happy place that Oliver experiences his mesmeric visions of his enemies' sinister plans as well as of his familial connection to Rose.

For the representation of nostalgia in Dickens's novels, the significance of the sickroom topos is threefold. It serves as the background to sentimentalized death scenes, as a place for symbolic rebirths, and as a paradisiacal sanctuary of plenty, in which the deprived orphan is granted the desired nurturing and nursing. This "homecoming" is figured as a return to a lost or, even more poignantly, a never experienced, happy past. Death is regularly identified with such nostalgic returns, and this accounts for the significance of death scenes. The association of heaven and home is not always metaphorical. Slowly dying of consumption, Paul Dombey seeks out the sound of the waves and ultimately death, a place beyond the waves, which he repeatedly calls "home" (*D&S*, ch. 14) in *Dombey & Son*. In *Nicholas Nickleby*, Smike dies in the arms of his long-lost cousin in the pastoral retreat of the lost Nickleby home, at a moment of supreme happiness: "I am quite contented. I almost think that if I could rise from this bed quite well, I would not wish to do so now" (*NN*, 762). Through a further nostalgic transposition he experiences his first and final days of contentment amidst scenes of a happy childhood not his own. The restored home becomes Smike's final resting place, "keeping his memory green," as the refrain goes in *The Haunted Man*: "The grass was green above the dead boy's grave, and trodden by feet so small and light, that not a daisy drooped its head beneath their pressure." (*NN*, 831) The novel ends with a triumph of nostalgia, when the old house as the locus of happy memories is returned to its original owners, and "nothing with which there [is] any association of bygone times [is] ever removed or changed" (*NN*, 830).

Little Nell's death in *The Old Curiosity Shop* (1841) takes this sentimental combination of a pastoral *locus amoenus*, death as homecoming, and a dying orphan or neglected child to its extremes: "Where were the traces of her early cares, her sufferings, and fatigues? All gone. Sorrow was dead indeed in her, but peace and perfect happiness were born; imaged in her tranquil beauty and profound repose."[54] This birth of happiness through death consummates a pattern of opposites in the novel: Little Nell "seem[s] to exist in a kind of allegory" (*OCS*, 20). The pastoral site of her transfiguration sharply contrasts with the urban wildernesses from which she has fled. Robert M. Polhemus speaks of her final home in the church under whose stones she is buried and of which she becomes a part.[55] Most critics, however, have pointed out that Dickens's use of suffering as spectacle can easily become suffused by overdrawn, sensationalist pathos. In particular the tear-jerking description of Little Nell's tranquil fading away and the rhetorical bathos of Jo's last breaths in *Bleak House* have been the subject of repeated criticism.[56] The death of a child is undoubtedly the most easily sentimentalized use of the sickroom and the eroticization of dead and dying children in Victorian fiction notorious, as James R. Kincaid has amply shown in his study of the "erotic child" in Victorian culture.[57]

Nostalgia for childhood is at once disrupted and fostered by this sentimentalization, even eroticization, of the dying child. On the one hand, a child's death symbolizes loss of childhood; on the other, the "spiritual" appearance of sickly children acts out a lingering sentimental aesthetics of affliction. Dinah Craik's *Olive* (1850), for example, eulogizes "the child's pale, spiritual face" as it minutely delineates the childhood of its "slightly deformed" heroine.[58] Her "unchildlike expression" (42) is reminiscent of "old-fashioned" Paul Dombey. Olive is a child who finds it "sweet to be sad, sweet to weep," making "a few delicious sorrows for herself" (39), and who appears as an angel in her unloving mother's dream. As in many of Dickens's novels, the ideal of childhood is cherished, while its realities are touchingly evoked: "O Childhood! Beautiful dream of unconscious poetry; of purity so pure, that it knew neither the existence of sin nor of its own innocence.... Blessed Childhood! Spent in peace and loneliness and dreams!" (38). This is a sentimental description of childhood, unhampered by the fact that Olive's parents perceive her as "a deformity on the face of the earth, a shame to its parents, a dishonour to its race" (14). Contrary to expectations, she survives and grows into a resourceful young woman, an artist, and a happy wife, while the discussion of her health problems recedes to the margins of the narrative.

Dickens's Little Nell and Paul Dombey nevertheless stand in a series of sentimentally dying children, including Helen Burns in Charlotte Brontë's *Jane Eyre* (1847) and Beth in Louisa May Alcott's *Little Women* (1868). Increasingly, however, sentimentality makes way for a sensationalist exploitation of premature death that mixes pathos with sadism. In Ellen Wood's *East Lynne* (1861), sinful Lady Isabel is "punished" at the deathbed of her dying son William, who could never call her mother: "No; not even at that hour when the world was closing on him dared she say, I am your mother."[59] The meticulous delineation of her remorse, rage, and resentment climaxes in the boy's minutely detailed demise. It is this idealization of child-death that Frances Hodgson Burnett's *The Secret Garden* (1911) sets out to eschew. In *East Lynne*, William happily anticipates death: "The time was at hand, and the boy was quite reconciled to his fate.... It is astonishing how very readily, where the right means are taken, [dying children] may be brought to look with pleasure, rather than fear, upon their unknown journey" (484). This resignation is what almost kills Colin, who is subjected to the influence of what is called "the wrong Magic" in *The Secret Garden*: the effect of negative thinking that also mars the life of his father.[60] Before Mary finds him, Colin does not care whether he lives or dies: "He said it as if he was so accustomed to the idea that it had ceased to matter to him at all" (101). The novel explodes the aestheticization of afflicted children.

Children's "magical" return to health in Burnett's fiction, in fact, perhaps most emphatically ushers in the death of the sentimentalized dying child and a rejection of the shut-up spaces of the sickroom. Her reaction to the cults of the beautiful dying child is at times even savage in the denunciation of the attraction of sickliness in *The Secret Garden*, best realized by the ugliness of Colin's "sharp, delicate face the colour of ivory [with] eyes too big for it [and] a lot of hair which tumbl[es] over his forehead in heavy locks and [makes] his thin face seem smaller" (97). In *Secret Gardens: A Study of the Golden Age of Children's Literature*, Humphrey Carpenter has even suggested that sickly Mary is "Cedric Errol reversed," "destroying all the stereotypes of [the] earlier work."[61] The novel's opening unsympathetically describes her "little thin face," "little thin body, thin light hair and ... sour expression" (1). In contrast, *Little Lord Fauntleroy* (1886) sentimentalizes "the beautiful, graceful child's body."[62] The novel subscribes to a sentimental eroticization of children's bodies, but the robust child is already preferred over the intellectually pale and suffering child. In *The Secret Garden*, the children gradually improve in health, spirits, and manners, paralleling the garden's revival.

Late Victorian and Edwardian children's fiction perpetuates a Romantic cult of the child, deriving much of its nostalgia from the identification of children with innocence and nature. As in Johanna Spyri's *Heidi* (1880), an earlier rejection of the idealized death of a child, nature heals the sickness of (indoor) civilization, as the Alps cure Clara of her lameness: "If only I could walk and clamber about with you, Heidi."[63] In the secret garden, Mary finds a realization of the fantasy gardens she imagines in India and a cure for Colin: "Perhaps if he had a great deal of fresh air [and] saw things growing he might not think so much about dying" (118). Through the boy's recovery, instead of his death, his father's grief changes into a recuperative nostalgia. Mr. Craven's memories encapsulate nostalgic spaces—a containment that is represented by the walling in of the garden and the confinement of his child's body. Wherever he is "his mind fill[s] with dark and heart-broken thinking" (220) until he is redeemed by the "Magic" that constitutes a symbolic unlocking of memories as well as a literal re-entry into a nostalgic space: "I almost feel as if—I were alive!" (222). In Kenneth Grahame's *The Golden Age* (1895) and *Dream Days* (1898), childhood is similarly identified with Arcadia, nature, and the imagination. Adults are the "sordid unimaginative ones," while children experience the "germinating touch that seems to kindle something in [their] own small person as well as in the rash primrose."[64] Most importantly, this connection between children and nature emphasizes the natural (physical and emotional) strengths of children, even while the descriptions of gardens and parklands are nostalgic not only because they are connected to the writers' childhoods as well, but also because England's green landscapes are seen as threatened by ongoing industrialization.[65]

By contrast, in Dickens's fiction, as in most mid-Victorian novels, connections between children and nature capitalize on the sentimentalization of afflicted children and usually evoke a pastoral tranquility. Convalescence can admittedly be an alternative to death as a form of recuperative homecoming, but the associations between nostalgic spaces and dying remains striking. Oliver Twist's wakening to love and food in abundance is offered as a recompense for the denied tranquility of death, for "that calm and peaceful rest which it is pain to wake from. . . . Who, if this were death would be roused again to all the struggles and turmoils of life?" (*OT*, 78). Sleeping among the coffins, those epitomes of claustrophobic confinement, he longs for a never-experienced pastoral placidity in "tall grass waving gently above his head, and the sound of the old deep bell to soothe him in his sleep" (*OT*, 29). Jenny Wren's telling invitation to a pastoral retreat high above the roofs in *Our Mutual Friend* similarly pinpoints the link between these longings for tranquility and death: "Come back, and be dead!" (*OMF*, 282). David Copperfield's identification with the infant at his mother's breast moreover underlines the association of a return to the maternal with death. Laying his "head down on her bosom near the little creature" (*DC*, 94), he re-experiences his happy babyhood. Nostalgia for this moment reverberates through the narrative: "I wish I had died then, with that feeling in my heart! I should have been more fit for Heaven than I ever have been since." (*DC*, 94) His childhood self is buried: "The mother who lay in the grave, was the mother of my infancy; the little creature in her arms was myself, as I had once been, hushed for ever on her bosom" (*DC*, 115). In *Our Mutual Friend*, "John Harmon's namesake" (*OMF*, 330), the object of Mrs. Boffin's fantasies of adoption, makes his will, leaving a kiss for a wife "willed away" by Old Harmon, to be delivered when allegedly drowned John Harmon resurfaces again. In *Oliver Twist*, all recompense comes too late for Dick, who dies by proxy for Oliver. It serves as a reminder that not all orphans are as fortunate as this providentially rediscovered foundling. Such death by proxy allows the main protagonists to achieve a healthier homecoming, while it grants a sentimentalized death scene. Such a redemptive death also ends and perfects *A Tale of Two Cities* (1859). No other death in Dickens's fiction—not even Little Nell's—has the same regenerative power or celebrates selfless suffering with the same unsentimental purity as Sydney Carton's death for his double or as double:

> I see that child who lay upon her bosom and who bore my name, a man winning his way up in that path of life which once was mine. I see him winning it so well, that my name is made illustrious there by the light of his. . . . It is a far, far better thing that I do, than I have ever done; it is a far, far better rest that I go to, than I have ever known.[66]

Failures or comical versions of the sickroom's potential sit oddly among examples of its successful realizations. Little Nell's sentimentalized transfiguration coincides with Dick Swiveller's comically detailed moral and physical recovery. His adoption of the "Marchioness," another abused child figure, who inverts parent-child relations by nursing her future protector, realizes an adoption fantasy, while indicating his moral redemption, but Swiveller and the maid he calls the Marchioness remain primarily comical figures. Similarly, in a parodied version of nourishment as restitution, Aunt Betsy administers a series of restoratives, "taken out at random [and tasting of] aniseed water, anchovy sauce, and salad dressing" (*DC*, 166), in *David Copperfield*. David is then washed, fed, and clothed. His primary—physical—needs are attended to in what comes fairly close to a parody of the nursing scenes in *Oliver Twist*. However, after his adoption David is reborn as "Trotwood Copperfield" and embarks on a new life in a new school, "a New Boy in more senses than one" (*DC*, 193). Betsy Trotwood's reappearance marks a shift from childhood trauma to a fairy-tale respite. Her rescue of David is comical, but it is nonetheless a much-needed counteraction to the Murdstones' ideas of parenting.

The one crucial failure of redemptive rebirth occurs in *Our Mutual Friend*, Dickens's last completed novel, which indeed charts a number of crucial changes in the representation of domestic sickrooms and moral recuperation. I have already mentioned the idealization of the children's hospital that admits the Orphan. It is a tranquil place full of toys, kind nurses, and a family of patients. This efficient "family" contrasts significantly with the many failing families in the novel as well as with the much-feared workhouse. *Little Dorrit* partly anticipates this shift as the big child Maggie nostalgically dwells on her stay in hospital as "such a Ev'nly place" (*LD*, 101), and the most important nursing scenes of the novel take place in the Marshalsea. Hospitals and prisons become the locus of effective nursing, as bourgeois homes fail completely to offer a comforting space. Mrs. Clennam's invalid chamber, in which she presides over a big Bible and her delicately cooked oysters, lacks all the trappings of the cozy and comforting sickroom. Her "guilt-promoted paralysis" has rightly been diagnosed as a "psychogenic illness" that is connected to her deliberate forgetting of the past,[67] and I shall come back to her use of resentful memories. She achieves neither redemption nor forgiveness; eventually a crumbling house built on guilty profits collapses on top of her.

The most remarkable redefinition of the sickroom topos in Dickens's novels, however, is Rogue Riderhood's failure to undergo any transformation after his near-death experience in *Our Mutual Friend*. When he nearly drowns in the Thames, his resuscitation parodies not only expectations raised by the introduction of the sickroom, but also adds a comical dimension to the novel's theme of rebirth and recycling. Riderhood's return from the river ties in with the central function of waste matter in its symbolic landscapes, while it also contrasts with John Harmon's alleged drowning, which facilitates his rebirth as someone else. Yet, even as concerned bystanders gather around the dying man to support and cheer on the doctor, the interest raised by attempts to rekindle a spark of life in the "outer husk and shell of Riderhood" evaporates as soon as he is brought back to life (*OMF*, 443). His experience has not effected any changes either in himself or in attitudes to him: "The spark of life was deeply interesting while it was in abeyance, but now that it has got established in Mr. Riderhood there appears to be a general desire that circumstances had admitted of its being developed in anybody else, rather than that gentleman" (*OMF*, 444). The promises of the sickroom topos are comically defeated. Still, Riderhood's eventually fatal drowning partly remedies this failure. As he dies together with the obsessive stalker Bradley

Headstone, his death underlines and indeed helps to facilitate Eugene Wrayburn's symbolic rebirth. This Victorian dissipated gentleman as reformed rake has aptly been called "the Yellow Book Wrayburn" and as such anticipates the *fin de siècle* antihero.[68] His diatribe against energy as a societal ideal poises him against the social climber Headstone, a physically powerful, determined, and dangerous man, whose will power feeds a threatening obsession:

> "Then idiots talk," said Eugene, leaning back, folding his arms, smoking with his eyes shut, and speaking slightly through his nose, "of Energy. If there is a word in the dictionary under any letter from A to Z that I abominate, it is energy. It is such a conventional superstition, such parrot gabble!" (*OMF*, 20)

Eugene's physical altercation with his rival in love results in a cathartic sickroom narrative. Rescued by the woman he loves, he is reborn, purged of his effete languor. In this, the idea of love as the means of redemption complements the struggle for a new selfhood that integrates as well as regenerates past selves. After violent obsessions have been, in the embodiment of Riderhood and Headstone, literally washed down the river, Eugene is reclaimed. As the sickroom topos is reaffirmed after all, his near-death even reconciles his aristocratic father to his son's marriage to a "waterside character." Lizzy Hexam is the daughter of a man who used to make a living out of fishing corpses from the Thames: when she drags out her lover and manages to revive him, she has sufficiently atoned for her inheritance. Eugene's sickroom becomes the site of their marriage, and thus the lower-class woman and the effete aristocrat are brought together in a sentimentalized bourgeois space. They are both domesticated. At the same time, the recuperation of the effete "well-born" (the literal translation of "Eugene") sees a reversal of bourgeois prejudices. While the social climber is brought down, Eugene is the younger son of an old gentry family with aristocratic pretensions; he seems to sport with the affections of a woman who is decidedly lower in rank. Yet he ultimately marries her. This happy union rewrites a similar plot in *Hard Times*, which can boast an early exposure of the self-made man in hypocritical Mr. Bounderby, but reduces the aristocratic lover, Harthouse, to a literary stereotype. The sickroom in *Our Mutual Friend* is a democratic space, but also one that is distinctly bourgeois in its function as a domestic site. Lizzy is at Eugene's bedside both to marry him and to administer the "nourishment he required" (*OMF*, 753).

Homemaking in *Bleak House*

Bleak House the house is a realization of homesick dreams. It is an ideal home built on a powerful nostalgia for origins. It contrasts with a series of dysfunctional homes and offers a pastoral respite remote from the obscuring fog and mud of London, a shelter for orphans, a sanctuary for familial relationships restored through "adoption." Very aptly, it is an adopted house, a house that has remained empty for years and has almost become derelict. Unhappy Tom Jarndyce was once driven to despair in it, when "the signs of his misery [were left] upon it" and "the place became dilapidated" (*BH*, 96), but it is reconstituted by good John Jarndyce, who furnishes it with a family of orphans. It is by no means a typical middle-class house, and it does not house a typical family. Bleak House is "delightfully irregular" (*BH*, 65), and like most of the protagonists, with a bleak as well as with a happy past. Its "bountiful provision of little halls and passages," in which you find, in penetrating more into its heart, signs of past habitation (*BH*, 65), makes it too irregular to become an example of Podsnappian stolidity. It is an alternative to stifling bourgeois houses as well as to homelessness.

Bleak House is a focus-point of Dickens's preoccupation with nostalgia for an ideal and specifically an "adopted" home. The adoption of a deserted house serves as a recompense for all the suffering caused by Jarndyce versus Jarndyce. No homes can resist the questionable allure of this lawsuit. It represents a commercial world that cannot be "walled out." Tom-all-Alone's is a London slum characteristic of Chancery property: "a street of perishing blind houses, with their eyes stoned out" (*BH*, 96). Krook's shop, a storage room of Chancery's discarded documents and the rags of its victims, is a site of death and decay. The rooms above the shop house unhappy victims of various lawsuits. The aristocratic House of Dedlock is connected to the law through Lady Dedlock's lawsuit as well as through her lost lover's new profession as a law writer. It is haunted by the guilty past. Even Bleak House is not immune. A disease bred in Tom-all-Alone's infects two members of the household and threatens the rest. The corrosive influence of the law enters through the dyspeptic lawyer Vholes, who is ready to stifle every natural feeling in his victims. The "hope of expectation on the family curse" (*BH*, 524) destroys Richard Carstone, one of Chancery's wards. He leaves the refurbished Bleak House to embark on an inherited search for imaginary Utopias: "Everything postponed to that imaginary time! Everything held in confusion and indecision until then!"

(*BH*, 527). It needs the doubling with a difference of Bleak House to exorcise the haunting effects of its bleak past. The nostalgic return to the new Bleak House symbolizes a new beginning, into which Richard is reborn as his son and namesake, a child surrounded by the ideal Guardian and two (doubled) caring mothers, and in which the Growlery (or its double) is barely needed. This Richard is to return to the original "older Bleak House," as it "claims priority [for him to] come and take possession of [his] home" (*BH*, 877). Miss Flite liberates her caged birds; and Esther is happily surrounded by her "dearest little pets" (*BH*, 880), two little girls that are the doubled replica of her buried doll and of herself as the infant who died to her mother on her birthday. This new beginning is a nostalgic restoration.

The ideal home is, in fact, restored through reduplication, adoption, and redefinition. The uncanny doublings (of buried babies and dolls, of the three ladies that haunt Jo, of "scraps of old remembrances" that appear like a "broken glass" (*BH*, 250), of the Lord Chancellor's uncanny double Krook) eerily point to the desire for restoration and the resurfacing of the repressed.[69] They create a haunted atmosphere, in which the past refuses to remain buried; and dead babies and dead bodies, like the insufficiently covered corpses in the graveyard where Nemo lies and buried memories of sorrow and guilt, have a tendency to resurface.[70] Yet possibilities of restitution taunt the homesick imagination and displace even the original nostalgia for origins. Esther's mystery of origin is to her primarily a reminder of the sense of shame inculcated into her during her orphan childhood, not, as the ambitious Guppy perceives it, something to her advantage. The adopted home constitutes an aesthetically consummate closure of the searches for origins and (adoptive) parents.

This restoration of the paternal in households of married orphans, overlooked by the bachelor-guardian, is almost uncanny in its pervasive resemblance to the orphan's homesick fantasies. Adoption displaces returns to original homes or parents. Esther's "story of my birthday" (*BH*, 15) is the origin of her homesickness and her homemaking, her need to restore homely spaces: "Often I repeated to the doll the story of my birthday, and confided to her that I would try, as hard as ever I could, to repair the fault I had been born with (of which I confessedly felt guilty and yet innocent)" (*BH*, 18). Esther commences life by being left for dead and by dying to her mother. She is sternly raised by her godmother: "It would have been far better, little Esther, that you had had no birthday; that you had never been born!" (*BH*, 17). The pervasive absence of "mama's grave" (*BH*, 16) reveals to this "orphan" the origin of her unease. It presages the uncanny moments of recognition that link her loss of the maternal inextricably to her mother's losses, whose face at their first meeting is "like a broken glass to me, in which I saw scraps of old remembrances" (*BH*, 250).

Esther's confrontation with an uncannily displaced and obscured mirror-image reflects hidden longings for the lost mother: "*I*, little Esther Summerson, the child who lived a life apart, and on whose birthday there was no rejoicing—seemed to arise before my own eyes, evoked out of the past by some power" (*BH*, 250). It is similar to Oliver Twist's "recognition" of his mother's portrait, which "seems to strike [his] fancy" (*OT*, 80). Such moments of revelation point to the unveiling of the underlying mystery of origins, an unraveling uncannily prefigured in Esther's revealing of her new face from behind a veil of hair (*BH*, 504) after her disfigurement. Her scars obscure the resemblance to her mother, at the same time externalizing her feelings of guilt and shame at her illegitimacy, which mar her selfhood. That she is prettier than ever at the end of the novel (*BH*, 880), after the mystery of her origins is revealed, and the scars of the past are healed, is undoubtedly the most overt sign of the novel's allegiance to the romantic side of familiar things. It is an apt closure for Esther's narrative of the quotidian reality of her orphan condition and its origins: "I was brought up, from my earliest remembrance—like some of the princesses in the fairy stories, only I was not charming—by my godmother" (*BH*, 15). Her story progresses through her adoption into the good home and a family of orphans to an advantageous and happy marriage.

This retrospective first-person narrative, however, alternates with a second narrative, told in the present tense by an omniscient narrator. Hochman and Wachs maintain that the social invective of this third person narrative acts as a medium "venting ... everything that inhabits the orphan condition" by giving "form to what Esther cannot integrate in consciousness."[71] While repression alone cannot sufficiently account for the novel's intriguing form, which is an experiment in narrative techniques that unites the *Bildungsroman* to a present-tense social commentary veering between the journalistic and the essayistic, it is true that this omniscient, disembodied "voice" shows the condition of England to be a societal version of the orphan condition. Society fails as surrogate parent for its wards, for the abandoned like Jo, for the literally orphaned like Charlie and her siblings, for Guster, irrevocably damaged at a baby farm, for the despairing wives of the bricklayers, both mothers of dead children, for the poor, the sick, and the broken-hearted, including Nemo, the nameless law writer and Esther's lost father. Even more than

Dickens's other novels, *Bleak House* is crammed with orphans. Ada Clare and Richard Carstone, the wards of Chancery who fall in love with each other in Bleak House, are orphans. Esther thinks she is an orphan and ultimately becomes one. The little "Coavinses" are similarly orphaned in the course of the novel. Jo, Guster, and Squod are abandoned, possibly illegitimate children. Nemo has no known living relatives; Lady Dedlock and her sister have no parents; Guppy and Allan Woodcourt no father; Prince Turveydrop closely resembles his dead mother; the youngest Rouncewell deserts his widowed mother. Then there are also, as it has been pointedly put, the "little monsters who are so fortunate as to have parents, the little Jellybys, Pardiggles, and Skimpoles."[72] Neglected or bullied, they almost seem to suggest that orphanhood might not be so bad after all.

Domestic discontent, in fact, pervades all spheres of society, ranging from the *ennui* of childless Lady Dedlock to the brutality and penury in the bricklayers' homes. The Jellyby household perhaps most clearly shows that dysfunctional domestic politics can turn bourgeois homes into an example of a larger "orphan condition." There are no real orphans, no deaths, no shady past of illegitimacy in the Jellyby family. The children are numerous and healthy, albeit smudged and ragged, but they are "homeless" in that they have been deprived of a true home through their mother's negligence and their father's resignation. What is repeatedly called Mrs. Jellyby's "telescopic philanthropy" has distracted her attention from the needs of her own family to missionary projects. Such imperialist concerns, the novel suggests, are responsible for the condition of her messy household. To draw a connection to the condition of England is inevitable. These negative examples, however, also highlight the need for better homes and show how the longing for the absent ideal can realize it after all. Influenced by Esther, Caddy Jellyby overcomes her resentment of her mother and transforms her longing for the happy home she never knew into the source of her restitution. She creates a better home than her parents' mismanagement of the wildly thriving Jellyby brood, as she fondly attempts to alleviate the plight of her deaf-and-dumb child. This silent infant recalls the bricklayers' dying babies, the child Esther's mother was made to believe dead and buried, and the death of Esther's father. The discovery of his nameless corpse is a picture of abandonment, highlighted by its juxtaposition with a nostalgic glimpse of "brighter days" (*BH*, 150). Found dead above Krook's shop, he is figured as a mother's lost child:

> If this forlorn man could have been prophetically seen lying here, by the mother at whose breast he nestled, a little child, with eyes

upraised to her loving face, and soft hand scarcely knowing how to close upon the neck to which it crept, what an impossibility the vision would have seemed! (*BH*, 150)

Nemo, or Nobody, dying in obscurity among the innumerable nobodies of the time, exemplifies the orphan condition in its broadest sense. Krook, the sordid proxy of the Lord Chancellor, whose shop is itself "a dirty hanger-on and disowned relation of the law" (*BH*, 50), is "the nearest relation he had" (*BH*, 139). This lack of relatedness links his fate to that of the suicide victim Tom Jarndyce, to Gridley and Miss Flite, drawn to each other through their sufferings—as Nemo is to Jo, in whom he sees his own penury and anonymity reflected. Jo has no proper name and no family. He is not Mr. Snagsby's son; and Mrs. Snagsby's attempts to solve the question of his origins brilliantly parody the novel's detective and inheritance plots. Instead, he embodies the literary figure of the orphan child in its most unromantic realization. Coarse, dirty, and ignorant, he is neither, like Oliver Twist, the born gentleman as mysteriously lost foundling nor, like David Copperfield, a "little gent" (*DC*, 142) in reduced circumstances. Instead he is an uninteresting home-grown savage who munches dirty bread on the doorstep of the Society for the Propagation of the Gospel in Foreign Parts, having "no idea, poor wretch, of the spiritual destitution of a coral reef in the Pacific" (*BH*, 221). Paralleling Nemo's demise, the description of Jo's death arraigns a careless society. Their affection for each other, amidst all the mud and fog, the cruelty and neglect, the homelessness and the dysfunctional homes, is one of the few "parental" relationships in the novels. Like the Guardian's affection for Esther, Esther's interest in Peepy, or Snagsby's kindness to Guster and Jo, it is not prompted by ties of blood, but underlines the novel's fantasies of adoption as a restitution for homelessness and as a form of homesickness or, more precisely, of nostalgia for an ideal of the imagination.

Throughout Dickens's novels, adoption into the good home stands at the very heart of the orphan's longings. One thinks of Oliver Twist discovering middle-class domestic sanctuaries as well as his lost relatives in the Brownlow and Maylie households, of David Copperfield restored to his closest remaining female relative and surrogate mother, who "vanished [in the opening chapter] like a discontented fairy" (*DC*, 22). The adoption of the two Bleak Houses by families of orphans and by a celibate guardian is simply the most extreme version of such wish fulfillment. In the same novel, the strong ties between Miss Flite and Gridley, George and Squod, Nemo and Jo, similarly create familial spaces that make up for the loss of their original relations. The very few intact families are notable for "adopting" such outsiders. George, the prodigal son eventually reclaimed by the mother he once deserted, is moreover a member of the Bagnet family, while Mrs. Rouncewell has motherly feelings for Rosa even before she is to be the wife of her grandson. Most importantly, cozy Bleak House with its "homely, comfortable, welcoming look" (*BH*, 93) serves as contrast and recompense for homelessness and dysfunctional homes.

The failure of respectable domesticity as Pecksniff, Podsnap, Dombey, or the Clennams practise it singles out irregular homes as ideal places of such adoptions, and Bleak House is perhaps the most irregular of all. The Guardian is eccentric and childlike. He plans to induce two of the resident orphans to marry each other, and at one point to marry Esther himself. The homemaking angel in the house is the illegitimate child of a fashionable lady. The irregularity of the house's architecture aptly mirrors the irregularity of its inhabitants' lives. Nonetheless, Bleak House is cozy and comforting, a happy domestic space, even though it subscribes to a decidedly eccentric form of domesticity.[73] It is an extreme version of a series of eccentric happy homes in Dickens's fiction. In *David Copperfield*, for example, Betsy Trotwood shares her house with a man who has been declared mad by his relatives, while her husband only irregularly resurfaces to get at her money. It is not really a very respectable arrangement, as the Murdstones are quick to point out. But there could be no more poignant contrast to the stifling Murdstone household of firmness and order. All the homes David encounters away from home—the ark of orphans in Yarmouth, the grandly pathetic Micawbers, the domestic bliss around Agnes, overshadowed as it is by her father's alcoholism and Uriah Heep's creepy schemes—are despite all their faults more inviting than the orderly Murdstone "home." In *Dombey and Son*, Florence similarly seeks refuge in the quaint world of Solomon Gills, as it offers her the home that the respectable House of Dombey denies her. The mock-pastoral "Happy Cottage" in Bleeding Heart Yard, an artificial idyll in an impoverished part of London, in *Little Dorrit* and Wemmick's "castle" in *Great Expectations* are both lovingly and humorously detailed.[74] While Oliver Twist is adopted into orderly homes that contrast with baby farms, workhouses, and Fagin's parodied family of thieves,[75] the contrast between congenial eccentric and uncongenial stolid homes becomes more and more pronounced in Dickens's subsequent novels. *Little Dorrit* sees the literal collapse of the commercial house, while the heroine's childhood takes place in prison. A brief analysis of her homesickness forms an apt conclusion to a study of Dickens's fictional homes.

Prisoners and Exiles in *Little Dorrit*

Amy Dorrit is homesick for the Marshalsea prison: "For I must now confess to you that I suffer from home-sickness—that I long so ardently and earnestly for home, as sometimes, when no one sees me, to pine for it.... So dearly do I love the scene of my poverty and your kindness. O so dearly, O so dearly!" (*LD*, 538). After her family's sudden aggrandizement has taken her abroad and into a foreign social circle, she nostalgically recollects her life in prison, where she used to be of so much importance to everyone and where she met Arthur Clennam and secretly fell in love with him. Unable to grasp the effect of their sudden wealth on their lives and unwilling to let go of a past that is embarrassing to her father and sister, but the only life she has ever known, she physically pines for a return and stocks up remembrances. Her faded dress, which her sister derides so much precisely because it symbolizes the past, becomes a nostalgically preserved souvenir. It is hidden away and secretly sighed over. When Little Dorrit returns to the Marshalsea to nurse Arthur Clennam at the end of the novel, she triumphantly resurrects it. Their roles reversed, the former prison-child comes to liberate the now imprisoned business man. His nostalgia for the days of her residence in the Marshalsea has induced him to prefer it over the King's Bench, even though the latter would have been considered the more "prestigious" choice, as debtors' prisons go.

As the former prison-child rescues the former exile, the novel's two guiding metaphors meet. Opening up with the description of a Marseilles prison and the effects of confinement on a group of quarantined Englishmen, *Little Dorrit* introduces a contrast between migration and imprisonment as its overarching pattern. A debtors' prison with its changing, migrant, but imprisoned population is its central setting and also the heroine's nostalgically recollected childhood home. Mr. Dorrit is locked up throughout most of his life and eventually trapped in the memories of his imprisonment. A mental collapse makes him think he is back in prison. It is the result of his attempts to suppress the past and very pointedly contrasts with his daughter's homesickness for and real return to the Marshalsea. The bourgeois home of Arthur Clennam's childhood has similarly always been like a prison to him, as it had been for his bullied father. It becomes the site of Mrs. Clennam's guilty self-confinement. Reared in an unhappy, though ostensibly intact and respectable, family, but unconsciously perceiving the brunt of his illegitimacy, Arthur feels orphaned and uprooted: "I am such a waif and stray everywhere" (*LD*, 19). Sent to China as a young man to look after his family's business interests, he has experienced a psychological exile that has literally taken him abroad without doing away with his feelings of imprisonment. Working for the family business abroad, he has been at once an exile and a prisoner:

> Trained by main force; broken, not bent; heavily ironed with an object on which I was never consulted and which was never mine; shipped away to the other end of the world before I was of age, ... ; what is to be expected from *me* in middle life? Will, purpose, hope? All those lights were extinguished before I could sound the words. *(LD*, 20)

The commercial traveler's disappointing homecoming shatters any fantasies of embowered estates in England. Chapter three, ironically entitled "Home," describes a homecoming that is disillusioning because the home has not changed, refusing to grant a sanitizing forgetting. Returning to his childhood home, Clennam is overwhelmed by the negativity of his memories: "All the old dark horrors of his usual preparations for the sleep of an innocent child [seemed] to overshadow him" *(LD*, 36). However, while this yearning seems to invite disappointment, it is a praiseworthy quality that prevents him from becoming embittered. He is disappointed, but not disenchanted. He has hoped against hope, and instead of making him ridiculous, his belief in nostalgic dreams redeems him:

> "How weak am I," said Arthur Clennam, when he [Flintwinch] was gone, "that I could shed tears at this reception! I, who have never experienced anything else; who have never expected anything else." He not only could, but did. It was the momentary yielding of a nature that had been disappointed from the dawn of its perceptions, but had not quite given up all its hopeful yearnings yet. *(LD*, 33)

These "hopeful yearnings" are longings for an ideal home and a love he has never known. In this, he joins incorruptible Oliver Twist with his mesmeric awareness of "scenes that never were, in this life" *(OT*, 216). Arthur's "belief in all the gentle and good things his life had been without" *(LD*, 158) is a nostalgia for something he has never experienced and therefore missed all the more. His inner resources of such creative and sustaining yearnings prevent a succumbing to pathological paranoia or bitter resentment. They have succeeded in "mak[ing] him a dreamer, after all" *(LD*, 40), and his dreams are ultimately rewarded. Just as Little Dorrit's secret love for Arthur Clennam is part of her homesickness for the Marshalsea, his disappointing homecoming leads him to Little Dorrit. She appears as a materialization of his longings:

> "From the unhappy suppression of my youngest days, through the rigid and unloving home that followed them, through my departure,

my long exile, my return . . . , what have I found!" His door was softly opened, and these spoken words startled him, and came as if they were an answer: "Little Dorrit." *(LD*, 158–59)

Little Dorrit's love for Clennam is part of her surviving attachment to her childhood home. "I have not grown out of the little child" *(LD*, 538), she assures him in one of her letters from abroad. The eventual union of these two "orphans" is central to the novel's ambiguous treatment of memory and longing, firstly because nostalgia is shown to be a constructive emotion that is ultimately rewarded, and secondly, because their relationship is a reciprocal "homecoming." It is this reciprocity that saves the novel from lapsing into the sentimental pathos of Wilkie Collins's similar novel, *The Fallen Leaves* (1879), in which a socialist "adopts" and then marries Simple Sally, a girl lost in more senses than one. "His heart ached as he looked at her, she was so poor and so young. . . . She was artlessly virginal and innocent; she looked as if she had passed through the contamination of the streets without being touched by it."[76] Their relationship comes much closer to the unequal, even pseudo-paedophilic, affair of which the marriages of Dickens's fictional child-wives are often accused. Little Dorrit's stunted growth and demure resignation have put off generations of readers. With "her diminutive figure, small features, and slight spare dress," she has the appearance of being much younger than she was" *(LD*, 52). Touched by "her youthful and ethereal appearance, her timid manner, the charm of her sensitive voice and eyes" *(LD*, 252), Arthur longs to offer her the parental protection that neither of them has known *(LD*, 184). Little Dorrit, however, is both mother and child to him. As she nurses him, their roles are reversed in more senses than one. He is now the poor prisoner and the nursling, and it is the child of the Marshalsea who smoothes his way.

Their nostalgia for the Marshalsea as the place that first brought them together reunites them, but nostalgia has an even more important function in the novel. As a softening memory, it not only allows glimpses of ideal homes that have never been experienced in this life, but also restructures the past in a positive, forgiving as well as comforting, way. "Do Not Forget" is inscribed on the watch Arthur Clennam's father bequeaths to his wife on his deathbed. But she interprets it as a warning not to let go of her resentment of past wrongs, and thereby only feeds into her carefully nourished bitterness, while Arthur sets out to retrieve a forgotten past in order to make amends. The watch, in fact, brings out contrasting attitudes to time, the past and ways of remembering and forgetting. To Arthur's father, it once was a reminder and a memento of happier days and a lost love, of which Arthur is the unsuspecting offspring. To the wronged woman, Mrs. Clennam, it simply serves as an excuse for indulging resentment. When she speaks of the past and of the need to remember, she only nurtures bitter memories. Gillian Beer revealingly speaks of Mrs. Clennam's "monomaniac memory."[77] The need for restitution is forgotten. It is an anti-nostalgic memory. By contrast, Arthur's reinterpretation of the inscription leads him to the fulfillment of his own hopeful yearnings, while he can honor his father's memory. His nostalgia eventually helps him to overcome the bitterness of his childhood memories as he counteracts the effects of Mrs. Clennam's resentful memory. Amy Dorrit similarly overcomes her suppressed resentment of her family.[78] Mrs. Clennam's Evangelical interpretation of the need to remember wrongs completely lacks such forgiveness.

The novel carefully analyzes this affirmation of nostalgia. A panorama of different ways of forgetting and remembering contextualizes the potentials and pitfalls of a good memory.[79] Embittered Miss Wade nourishes her anger as her personal agenda, much as Mrs. Clennam considers her resentment a virtue. Her bitterness is repeatedly juxtaposed with the comically presented forgetfulness of easygoing Mr. Meagles. There is something ludicrous about his insistently cheerful suppression of all negativity: "It was an uncommonly pleasant thing being in quarantine, wasn't it?" (*LD*, 187). His lack of empathy with those who do engage with the past renders his cheerfulness often jarring. The Meagles' kindness is without doubt genuine, but it is prejudiced and patronizing. Their exasperating admonition of Tattycoram, another "orphan," is as belittling as the "droll name" Pet Meagles gives her, "playfully pointing [her] out and setting [her] apart" (*LD*, 319). Small wonder that one day she hurls it back and "wouldn't count five-and-twenty" (*LD*, 312). The alternative life with Miss Wade among "waifs and strays of furniture," however, offers little consolation to the Meagles' "broken plaything" (*LD*, 324). Miss Wade and Mr. Meagles are extreme examples, preparing the ultimate affirmation of a more balanced mix of nostalgic memory and forgiving forgetting.

The lovesick nostalgia Arthur Clennam's former love, the now full-blown Flora Finching, puts on display is more complicated. It is important to note that his disappointment in his past love has little to do with the changes time has wrought. On the contrary, the realization that Flora has always been silly shatters his nostalgic idealization: "Flora, who had seemed enchanting in all she said and thought, was diffuse and silly. That was much. Flora, who had been spoiled and artless long ago, was determined to be spoiled and artless now" (*LD*, 143). That "his sense of the sorrowful and his sense of the comical [are] curiously blended" when she makes "a moral mermaid of herself" (*LD*, 147) by taking up their former flirtation shows the wry humor with which Dickens can treat engagements with the past—the obsessive, the traumatic, and the nostalgic. Flora is undoubtedly a comical figure, but her kind-hearted loyalty to Little Dorrit as well as to Arthur disrupts the ridicule heaped on her. A "tender memory" underlies her inadvertently comical enactment of the past: "And still, through all this grotesque revival of what he remembered as having once been prettily natural to her, he could not but feel that it revived at sight of him and that there was a tender memory in it" (*LD*, 147). Similarly, Young John's romantic disappointment is comical, but also brings out his better side, as he helps Arthur Clennam, because he knows Little Dorrit cares about Clennam. Like Flora's flirtation with a past romance, his cultivated melancholy is a source of comedy, while it is also the character trait that makes him endearing.

Throughout Dickens's novels, nostalgia contrasts with a resentful way of remembering as well as with comical versions of obsessive memories. These negative examples underline the importance of an ideal way of remembering, just as dysfunctional homes make the need for good homes all the more felt. Miss Havisham in *Great Expectations* and Mrs. Clennam and Miss Wade in *Little Dorrit* suffer from an obsessive, resentful, indeed anti-nostalgic memory. Their ends are a warning to all characters with an unhappy past. Conversely, when Mr. Dorrit believes he is back in the Marshalsea just before his collapse, he lapses into an amnesiac state that is partly the result of his suppressed nostalgia. Forgetting is a frightening occurrence in Dickens's novels, underscoring the importance of remembering, and of remembering without resentment.[80] *The Haunted Man* shows perhaps most clearly what the absence of nostalgic associations can do, but the softening influence of nostalgic memories and dreams is indeed a recurring theme in the novels. An adaptation of mesmeric theories complements interest in the Romantic child and its abilities, as children and child like protagonists retrieve nostalgic "memories" that they have never experienced, but which connect them to their better selves. In *Little Dorrit*, Arthur Clennam has "deep-rooted in his nature, a belief in all the gentle and good things his life had been without" *(LD*, 158). Most pointedly, while such longings tend to lead to domestic spaces that subscribe to bourgeois ideals, it is increasingly the eccentric home that becomes desirable to a homesick imagination.

4
Homesickness and the Longing for "Other" Places in Victorian Domestic Novels

THE ACCELERATION OF CHANGE, THE PROGRESSIVE DESPOLIATION OF the countryside, and an increase in mobility during the nineteenth century necessitated a more and more prominent and urgent engagement with nostalgia. At the same time, the simultaneity of fears and hopes inculcated by new theories of evolution further accentuated the ambiguity with which Victorian writers regarded the past and the future. Jerome Hamilton Buckley already remarked that the "great polar ideas of the Victorian period" were the idea of progress and the idea of decadence, "the twin aspects of an all-encompassing history."[1] Raymond Chapman similarly spoke of an oscillation between pessimism and faith in the future: the Victorians, he pointedly suggested, looked back to the past with nostalgia and complacency.[2] More recently, Matthew Campbell, Sally Shuttleworth, and Jacqueline M. Labbe have written in their introduction to *Memory and Memorials, 1789–1914* that in this period of change, memory became a "necessary tool . . . , bolstering social progression and the transformation of the past into the future."[3] Nostalgia became a prominent attitude, but also a recurring concern. The Victorian novel increasingly reflected and formed this evolving engagement with continuities and changes, with conflicting and complementary longings for the past and for the future.

This chapter looks at mid-Victorian novels that deal with nostalgia by reassessing it. They mistrust its allurements and dissect its pathology, but ultimately reaffirm much of its potential to direct a journey home or to a new home. Most importantly, they show that nostalgia in Victorian fiction need not be a longing for domesticity or a green England that can only be found in the past. Home remains the desired nostalgic space in Charles Dickens's fiction, even though it is increasingly an eccentric home. Similar longings for idealized homes, particularly childhood homes, are at the center of many other novels of the time, ranging from Olive's "delicious sorrows" (39) when she muses over the absence of happy family life in Craik's *Olive* (1850) to Little Lord Fauntleroy's struggles with "his first feeling of homesickness"

(74) in Burnett's eponymous novel: as the little homesick boy "mak[es] so brave an effort to bear it well" (74), his grandfather softens and even decides to grant the boy access to his mother after all. Eventually, the mean old Earl finds "something he cared for at last—something which had touched and even warmed his hard, bitter old heart" (124). The novel thereby effectively stereotypes the redemptive child.[4] Literal homesickness moreover often serves to underscore the theme of childhood nostalgia. In Burnett's *A Little Princess* (1905), originally published as *Sara Crewe* in 1887, the Indian furniture in the neighboring house gives Sara "a weird, homesick feeling" for her early childhood home in India. This Victorian sentimentalization of the child is a memorable and indeed influential aspect of Victorian literary nostalgia, but by no means the only, or even the most important one.[5] In this chapter, I wish to move away from Victorian child cults, but not by abandoning domestic fiction. On the contrary, it is particularly fascinating to look at mid-Victorian novels that affirm nostalgia without resorting to the topoi of redemptive children and idealized childhood homes.

In a close reading of Charlotte Brontë's *Villette* (1853), I shall emphasize the novel's dissection of the complementary longings for a safe home and for mobility, independence, and individual choice. *Villette* can be read as a post-Romantic realist novel that redeploys Romantic yearnings and critiques the Victorian topos of the sickroom as a bourgeois haven. Its insightful description of the expatriate experience builds on a pathology of homesickness, but ultimately draws the availability and even the desirability of the homecoming as an easy solution into question. This rejection of the sickroom topos decisively bears out the central conflict between the longing for home (and homelands) and for "other" spaces and shows a significant departure from mid-Victorian sickroom narratives. The chapter's second section then looks at the impact of evolutionary narratives on the treatment of nostalgia in domestic novels. After a short overview of Victorian popular fictions of degeneration, a close reading of Elizabeth Gaskell's *Wives and Daughters* (1866) will reveal that this very domestic and nostalgic novel is informed by a post-Darwinian understanding of the ideal home and the effects of scientific imperialism at home. Although both novels include lengthy passages on the heroines' childhoods, children have neither redemptive nor mesmeric powers, and the heroines have to find new homes. As they consciously move away from past homes, however, they ultimately discover that nostalgia plays a crucial role in their choice of a home after all.

Roughly Roused and Obliged to Live: Moving out of the Sickroom in *Villette*

Villette closes with the anticipated homecoming of M. Paul to a flourishing school and a house made ready for his return. But it is left to "sunny imaginations" to "picture union and a happy succeeding life."[6] The invocation of an ominous Banshee successfully subverts a tentative sentimentalization of a domestic haven, which seeps into the last pages of a novel otherwise steeped in emotional turmoil and, most importantly, in a rejection of such subduing domesticity. Emphatically reaffirming the pathetic fallacy, the ills a Banshee is said to have foreboded are repeatedly realized in the novel. Miss Marchmont's death and Lucy Snowe's illness are both anticipated or evoked by such ill-bringing winds. The hopes of "sunny imaginations" are therefore painfully doubtful at best. *Villette* ends on a note of suppressed sadness and, as Jenni Calder has pointed out, "of unresolved and unfulfilled possibilities."[7] This uncertainty forms an apt closure for a story that engages with a choice between stability and the attractions of mobility. What is central to the novel is a vehement, but heartrendingly painful, rejection of the return to a re-enacted past home. This turning away from nostalgic homecomings renders Lucy Snowe's search for a space of her own so poignant.

The longing to escape from claustrophobic quietude and an undirected homesickness that is no longer connected to a stable point of origin or departure are the driving forces of the novel. Real migration both externalizes and solves emotional exile. In rejecting the nostalgic's homecoming as an available or even desirable option, the novel subverts a topos that is at the heart of bourgeois plots. We have seen the persistence of this topos in Dickens's novels: despite occasional parodies, the sickroom's efficiency is indisputable. In Charlotte Brontë's own earlier novel *Shirley* (1849), the heroine's sickroom likewise serves as a place of parental reunion and a cure for lovesickness. Her mother's reappearance saves pining Caroline Helstone, as the fulfillment of a lifelong longing heals a physical disease connected to lovesick yearning. The sickroom offers an infantile cosseting in which nostalgia figures as disease and cure. Nurse and patient share this recuperation: "The dependent fondness of her nursling, the natural affection of her child, came over her [Caroline's mother] suavely: her frost fell away."[8] In *Jane Eyre*, Jane is similarly nursed by fortuitously rediscovered cousins as she collapses at their doorstep, a "poor, emaciated, pallid wanderer" (336). The designs of her self-righteous male cousin, however, disrupt the apparently consummate homecoming, and a telepathic call from Mr. Rochester reminds Jane where she truly belongs. His voice is significantly "known, loved, well-remembered" (417). Almost forgotten, it forces itself upon Jane's remembrance by a supernatural, mesmeric occurrence "like an electric shock" (417). Jane returns to nurse and ultimately marry the emasculated and enfeebled Rochester and they go on to live happily in a domestic setting in the manor-house of Ferndean. Although Jane leaves the cousins who granted her a familial sickroom, the end of the novel sees Rochester domesticated as Jane's patient in a retired, private, home that is "of considerable antiquity" as well as of a "moderate size, and no architectural pretensions" (429). By contrast, the heroine's search of a home in *Villette* is a departure from England, from the cozy spaces of the sickroom, and from the dreams of love in a cottage.

Describing the effects of an expatriate experience and a young woman's daring mobility, the novel explores nostalgic as well as other cravings (or cravings for the other). This analysis of "otherness" is twofold, connecting the "other" inside Lucy herself, her "life of thought" as opposed to "that of reality" (105), to the irascible pseudo-Jesuit M. Paul, one of England's "others." This dual concept of "otherness" sheds light on the rejections, subversions or transformations of nostalgic and "other" spaces in all of Brontë's novels. Sally Shuttleworth has convincingly shown how "the realm of the 'foreign' functions as a site of imaginative projection."[9] The narrative functions of abroad, as of cross-cultural relationships, have, in fact, been at the fulcrum of critical attention, but most scholars have ignored their significance for representations of nostalgia. Brontë's protagonists have been characterized as "outcasts," a description reminiscent of the sense of existential abandonment that Hochman and Wachs have termed the "orphan condition."[10] Cross-cultural and/or cross-class marriage is the outcast's final goal. It is a solution that appears to transcend boundaries, even while it re-establishes stability, as in the domestic, though not necessarily comfortable or cozy closures of *Jane Eyre*, *Shirley*, and also *The Professor*, an earlier version of *Villette*. In the latter, however, this termination of the heroine's search for both stability and mobility remains uncertain, highlighting the conflicts between different longings that are so decisive in her departures: from England, from the stifling rooms of the school, from the sickroom, from conventional roles.

The choice of and by the "other" lover and therefore of the life he represents resolves Lucy Snowe's dual cravings for an eerily re-enacted childhood home on the one hand, and for a different—

"other"—home on the other. M. Paul is a "small, dark, and spare man" (90), "pungent and austere" (179), irritating and easily irritated, French and Catholic, with "certain vigorous characteristics [in] his physiognomy" (532). By contrast, Dr John stands for solidity and stability. Like an English oak and a medieval knight, he symbolizes old England: he is of "a nature chivalric to the needy and feeble, as well as the youthful and fair" (85), with a "firm and equal stride" (133) that inspires trust. This "true young English gentleman" (85) seems lordly to a precipitate expatriate who finds herself in a strange place, unable to speak the language and trying to trace her missing luggage: "He might be a lord, for anything I knew: nature had made him good enough for a prince, I thought" (84). This gentlemanly hero stands in sharp contrast to the quarrelsome, but strangely attractive anti-hero M. Paul—a contrast that parallels the juxtaposition of Lucy's old and new homes.

The attraction of security and stability embodied by solid, firm, and moderately stout John Graham Bretton moreover shows nostalgic idealization at work. His double name reveals the split into the schoolboy of the past and a potential lover. Graham is a "handsome, faithless-looking youth of sixteen.... A spoiled, whimsical boy he was in those days" (20). He is adored by Polly, whom he alternately teases and caresses like a toy— or like the doll she physically resembles with her neck "delicate as wax, her head of silky curls" (10). Lucy cautions her not to worship or idealize (44). Given her later idolization of and nervous infatuation with John, her preaching of stoicism is ironic. In retrospect, the portrait of young Graham becomes invested with romantic possibilities: "Any romantic little schoolgirl might almost have loved it in its frame" (242). Assuming this role, he becomes Ginevra's "Isidore." In a sense, happily flimsy Ginevra acts out not only Lucy's romantic longings, but also fantasies of rejection.[11] Isidore is effectively jilted. His accumulation of names shows the ways in which a romantic imagination can transform a very dull man.

But it is his familiarity that is his main attraction to the homeless expatriate. As he comes to stand for England, he is endowed with knightly qualities for Lucy. His attractions to Ginevra and Polly are decidedly different, and this is where the irony of Lucy's idealization lies. With "the whole world . . . gabbling around [her]" in a language she can neither speak nor understand, she recognizes "the Fatherland accents; they rejoiced my heart" (83). They are not only the familiar tones of her native language, but literally of her childhood home. Such suppressed recognition is at the heart of her infatuation with this English nobleman of her imagination. Secretly she "recognis[es] his very tread" (102) in that of the young doctor and his portrait among the Bretton furniture, which has been so strangely relocated from the "Old England" of her childhood. Her convalescence at La Terrasse, with all its mementoes of the English house at Bretton, clearly seems to promise a metaphorical return to childhood.[12] This fantastic re-enactment of a past home transposes delirious, physically homesick Lucy amidst disconcertingly familiar furniture. Her sickroom actualizes fantasies of "home." It is a seemingly consummate realization of nostalgic possibilities of restitution. Waking in "an unknown room in an unknown house" (237), Lucy recognizes details of a past home. But they grow familiar with a frighteningly hallucinogenic intensity:

> As I gazed at the blue arm-chair, it appeared to grow familiar.... Strange to say, old acquaintance were all about me, and "auld lang syne" smiled out of every nook.... Of all these things I could have told the peculiarities, numbered the flaws or cracks, like any clairvoyante. [There were] elaborate pencil-drawings finished like line engravings: these, my very eyes ached at beholding again, recalling hours when they had followed, stroke by stroke and touch by touch, a tedious, feeble, finical, school-girl pencil held in these fingers, now so skeleton-like. (237–38)

It is a literally delirious return to the novel's childhood passages, evoking memories of the quietude of "the clean and ancient town of Bretton" (5) and the Brettons of Bretton. Lucy's mysterious restoration to its enactment abroad should, according to the codes of the Victorian sickroom topos, represent a perfect nostalgic return. She falls ill in her homeless isolation, succumbing to "a strange fever of the nerves and blood" (122). Prolonged depression culminates, or finds a vent, in physical symptoms: "A sorrowful indifference to existence often pressed on me—a despairing resignation to reach betimes the end of all things earthly" (218). Physical illness releases a crisis of homesickness as a recognizable semiotics of emotional distress, conforming to the dictates of sickroom fiction: "Indeed there was no way to keep well under the circumstances. At last a day and night of peculiarly agonizing depression were succeeded by physical illness" (222). It is not at all unexpected that the transposed childhood home figures as a nostalgic re-enactment of the past: "Where was I? Not only in what spot of the world, but in what year . . . ? For all these objects were of past days, and of a distant country" (238). The distant country is England, but the remembered home has always only been temporary. Lucy's true origins remain obscure; her original home an elusive and ultimately also evaded space. She is not one of the Brettons of Bretton, but a dependent relative. The ultimate failure of the sickroom's potential is the impossibility of her adoption (or marriage) into a desirable old English family.

The return to the objects, if not the spaces, of the English "home" is a teasing enactment. Its phantasmagoric strangeness already foreshadows its inefficiency as a cozy familial space. After she has collapsed in the streets, Lucy is taken to an English family, who turn out to be her relatives. Her sickroom can even boast the Brettons's relocated furniture. There is more of nightmare and disorientation than of wish-fulfillment in this recognition of the relics of a "home" of the past. Recognizing familiar objects in the intensity of their tangible reality makes her "very eyes [ache]" (175). Even though the sickroom temporarily provides a space of quiet, it does not—contrary to the expectations raised by this topos—effect any permanent transfiguration, nor does it offer any form of restitution at all. Lucy cannot remain in her "cave in the sea:" in "a world so high above, that the rush of its longest waves, the dash of its fiercest breakers could sound down in this submarine home, only like murmurs and a lullaby" (258–59). What is important in the delineation of the ensuing sickroom scenes is not the apparent adherence to the codes of the sickroom topos, but the subversion of the efficacy and, more importantly, the desirability of the restitution it commonly offers. There is no consummate return home and no sentimental reunion with the godmother, who, though kind, remains detached. Lucy is attended by a stranger, a native nurse of Villette, whose language she neither speaks nor understands. There are moreover no detailed nursing scenes, neither by the godmother nor by the false physician-lover, who turns out to be neither an ideal lover nor an ideal healer, as his inability to read the languages of emotional distress indicates. Lucy's disorder comprises all the symptoms—insomnia, nervousness, depression—that inform Victorian conceptualizations of "neurasthenia," the new term for "nervous exhaustion" coined later in the century.[13] Dr John speaks of hypochondria. Interestingly, he freely acknowledges the incompetence of the medical profession:

> "Your nervous system bore a good share of the suffering?"
> "I am not quite sure what my nervous system is, but I was dreadfully low-spirited."
> "Which disables me from helping you by pill or potion. Medicine can give nobody good spirits. My art halts at the threshold of Hypochondria: she just looks in and sees a chamber of torture, but can neither say nor do much." (261)

This longing is a homesickness for a home that never existed. There is consequently no return home that might cure it, but neither can it be stifled by medical interference. Dr John admits to this incompetence. In a detailed overview of Victorian attitudes and treatments of different forms of depression, Janet Oppenheim has emphasized that this is "a confession, needless to say, that came more easily to fictitious than to practicing medical men."[14] Dr John is not only unable to heal an emotionally disturbed nervous system, but he also fails to recognize his patient's suppressed lovesickness, indeed her obsession with him, as well as her loneliness, an undirected homesickness exacerbated by the lack of even an absent home. In short, the novel displays emotional longing through somatic distress that is misread by the physician. In her study of Victorian "somatic fictions," Athena Vrettos speaks of "an immediately recognizable and conventional language" of psychophysical afflictions, as illnesses figure as expressions of emotional meaning.[15] Even more pointedly, Sally Shuttleworth suggests that Lucy Snowe opens herself up to Dr John's "reading" skills: "Every outer sign becomes an active invitation to his interpretative penetration."[16] Despite this open invitation, however, he fails to read her needs correctly. M. Paul turns out to be not only more congenial, but also shows that he can read Lucy's character. His use of phrenology reveals an important aspect of their shared "otherness." While slow, solid, rosy Dr John is ideally matched with waxen, doll-like Polly, an affinity of physiognomy between Lucy and M. Paul transcends their other differences:

> I was conscious of rapport between you and myself. [We] are alike—there is affinity. Do you see it, mademoiselle, when you look in the glass? Do you observe that your forehead is shaped like mine—that your eyes are cut like mine? . . . I perceive all this, and believe that you were born under my star. (532)

Phrenology is an important characterization device in Brontë's novels. In *Villette*, it is not only the subject of one of the lively, even antagonistic, discussions that bring Lucy and M. Paul together, but becomes the central aspect of all characterization, even of minor characters. Phrenological analysis ranges from the description of the servant Rosine with her low brow to the "strong hieroglyphics graven as with iron stylet on [the] brow" of the foreign King of Labassecour (303).[17] In its use of phrenology, *Villette* moreover also rewrites the stereotypes as well as the overall plot of *The Professor*, Brontë's earlier version of this story about the expatriate experience of teaching English abroad and the desire to leave stifling households in England. Crimsworth, the first-person narrator of the earlier novel, expresses his contempt for his pupils by sketching their physiognomies. The miscellaneous assortment includes various "nationalities" or races. A "Gorgon-like" Belgian is distinguished by "sullen ill-temper [on] her forehead, vicious propensities in her eye, envy and panther-like deceit about her mouth . . . her large head so broad at the base, so narrow towards the top."[18] Frances, the girl with whom the professor falls in love, by contrast, seems reassuringly English, despite her mixed origins and limited knowledge of the English language. Her wish to improve her English is a laudable "symptom" of her longing for an unknown homing-space. Nevertheless, it is her cranial capacities that attract the professor's clinical gaze: "The shape of her head too was different, the superior part more developed, the base considerably less. I felt assured, at first sight, that she was not a Belgian" (244). In stories of expatriate experience and of falling in love abroad, Victorian concepts of race usually play a pivotal role. *Villette* negotiates a more ambiguous, nonetheless racially determined understanding of "otherness," yet in both novels familiarity with a moralized version of phrenology is taken for granted.[19]

Still, as it opts for the "other" lover, *Villette* subverts the concept of racial, or national, affinity as a criterion for marital compatibility. Eventually Lucy chooses the uncertain fate with a man of equally uncertain temper and uncertain future. The homecoming within the healing spaces of the sickroom is reserved for childlike Polly, who aptly marries a physician. At first presented as resembling "a mere doll," she is reintroduced as a frail, fainted maiden, rescued from the flames and born away in Dr John's strong arms. It is during his attendance in her sickroom that they fall in love, thus recovering their childhood attachment. Lucy rejects what she considers neither attainable nor desirable. Somewhat savagely, she points out the resemblance between Polly and M. Paul's spaniel, Sylvie: "she was very tiny, and had the prettiest little innocent face, the silkiest long ears, the finest dark eyes in the world. I never saw her, but I thought of [Polly]: forgive the association, reader, it *would* occur." (602) In its realization of the sickroom topos, Polly's fate represents one of Lucy's potential futures. Yet Lucy's choice draws the sickroom's desirability into question. Observing the growing attachment between John and Polly with increasing detachment, Lucy renounces the potential restitution offered by such a home. The extremity of her loneliness highlights the poignancy of her decision to reject a return "home" and to choose the challenges of uncertainty and otherness. As she points out to M. Paul, "to be home-sick one must have a home, which I have not" (526). In a Romantic and also sublime episode, a tempest that frightens everyone else has an invigorating effect on Lucy, voicing her right to her otherness, an escape from safe entrapment:

> As for me, . . . I was roughly roused and obliged to live. I got up . . . and creeping outside the casement close by my bed, sat on its ledge, with my feet on the roof of a lower adjoining building. It was wet, it was wild, it was pitch-dark. [Too] resistless was the delight of staying with the wild hour, black and full of thunder, pealing out such an ode as language never delivered to man—too terribly glorious, the spectacle of clouds, split and pierced by white and blinding bolts. (152)

To Lucy, the allurement of a homecoming offers only mock restitution. It lures her into dependence and a false sense of security. The self-deceiving sense of belonging she feels in the Brettons' transposed home would imply a return to the outwardly smooth life of her childhood. In the novel's childhood passages, Lucy is notably quiet, subdued, and peripheral. A lonely expatriate in Villette, marked by her "otherness," she listens to the whispers of "solitude and the summer moon" (149), seeking her private space in nature: "The seclusion, the very gloom of the walk attracted me" (150). She comes to acknowledge and to assert her peculiarities, her "otherness" as the eccentric Englishwoman abroad: "For a long time the fear of seeming singular scared me away; but by degrees, . . . people became accustomed to me and my habits, and to such shades of peculiarity as were ingrained in my nature" (150). Lucy's survival strategy is "to hold two lives—the life of thought, and that of reality" (105). But "the rude Real" has a tendency to "burst coarsely in—all evil grovelling and repellent as she too often is" (153), pinpointing the inconsistencies of Romantic elements in a realist novel that rejects the "sickroom romance," as Bailin calls it, to reaffirm other desires and a longing for the other lover.[20]

Lucy's desired place of belonging is consequently not the tantalizingly offered and then rejected return to England, nor its fake enactment abroad, but the uncertain union with an embodied other in the "other" home. This desire for the foreign home constitutes a deliberate swerving away from Victorian ideals of home, and it is most apt as well as poignantly painful that this "regaining" of a new space is held in abeyance. Romantic longings for distant spaces collapse into M. Paul's probably fatal colonial enterprises; Lucy's search for independence ends in her patient vigil. Nevertheless, the impossibility of accepting the stolid Englishman and his re-creation of England abroad demands a rejection of the comically depicted exclusiveness of expatriate communities. M. Paul sneers at Lucy's social excursions with the Brettons, deliberately barring her potential idealization of an adoptive "homecoming" into the Brettons' recreated home abroad. The impossibility and, more importantly, the questioned desirability of such a return shows that homesickness need not be directed at places of origin. By reworking the effects and conditions of literal homesickness, the novel thus pointedly draws nostalgia's directions into question. By contrast, the next section will look at the ways in which a very different mid-Victorian domestic novel, Gaskell's *Wives and Daughters* engages critically with nostalgia for the past and its projections into the future.

Nostalgia and the New Man:
Victorian Fictions of Degeneration in the Domestic Novel

Elizabeth Gaskell's unfinished last novel, *Wives and Daughters*, was published posthumously in 1866. Like a number of mid-Victorian novels, including *David Copperfield* and *Pendennis*, it is set in the recent past, in the period of the author's childhood and youth, and consciously concerned with ways of representing the past. Spanning the 1820s up to the 1830s, it is an emphatically rural version of mid-Victorian fiction about George IV's reign. The Great House family, Lord Hollingford and the rest of the Cumnors, remain at the margins of the narrative. The account of the former governess's bourgeois emulation of their way of life is mainly comical. The novel creates a nostalgic vision of pre-industrial rural England while it welcomes scientific progress. It leads up to the Victorian era to accentuate its differences, mixing nostalgia and complacency. Most intriguingly, the novel describes the social rise of a new scientist, who re-emerges from an old, declining family of country squires instead of representing a middle-class triumph over the nobility. He unites the best of the past with a better future. This fascinating solution to Victorian anxieties about degeneration is a neglected aspect of the novel, masked as it is by its fond descriptions of a rural town, its social comedy, and its emphasis on domestic concerns. Most critics have seen it simply as a more substantial version of the "much beloved pastoral vignette *Cranford*" of 1851, though more recently also as a social-problems novel that has more in common with *Mary Barton* (1848) or *North and South* (1855).[21] In its contribution to the development of a "New Man" in Victorian fiction, *Wives and Daughters* uses new scientific theories of degeneration and evolutionary progress precisely to point out their effects on domestic life and social structures. Darwinian conceptualizations of physical inheritance invest the courtship plots with particular poignancy, even though love ultimately turns out to be the most reliable factor in the choice of a mate after all, and nostalgia for old families is mercifully honored by a natural evolution of their descendants.

With Roger Hamley, the novel posits a nostalgically recalled new man of old family who is a new scientist, a naturalist who employs physical advantages for intellectual pursuits and, in making up for his elder brother's extravagance, restores domestic unity and the value of the inherited estate. But it does not merely depict the social rise of a naturalist and connects inheritance and courtship plots to a historical interest in the turbulent changes of the 1830s, placidly recollected in retrospect. It engages with new scientific ideas of heredity, spelling out their implications for the inheritance of land and the planning of a suitable heir. In short, *Wives and Daughters* is a domestic novel that incorporates new scientific ideas into the inheritance plot of the traditional British novel and offers a new hero created in response to theories of evolution. In the following sections, I shall argue that fears of degeneration figure strongly in the novel and usefully cast new light on the many ways in which contrasting interpretations of evolution permeate the Victorian novel.

Before analyzing the representation of nostalgia and progress in Gaskell's novel in detail, I shall situate it within the contexts of Victorian evolutionary narratives. In *The Romance of Victorian Natural History*, Lynn Merrill has highlighted the range of Victorian nostalgia(s) by suggesting that nostalgia for a lost rural past "may have served as an impetus for the vogue in natural history."[22] This intriguing thesis sheds a different light on the often misunderstood juxtaposition of nostalgia and scientific progress in Gaskell's novel. In her book on Gaskell's life and writing, Anna Unsworth suggests that *Wives and Daughters* is both about "nostalgia [and about] an objective reality as real as material and scientific progress,"[23] yet as Merrill's study suggests, their simultaneity need not be understood as contradictory. Reading the novel as an important example of a domestic Victorian novel that engages with scientific discourses to solve *domestic* concerns, I shall contextualize it within Victorian fictions of evolution.

In tackling topical issues such as the rise of the naturalist, the link between evolutionary and social change, and the need for a new type of hero, *Wives and Daughters* contributes significantly to the development of a post-Darwinian imagination. The seminal studies of the role of Darwinian "plots" in Victorian fiction, Gillian Beer's *Darwin's Plots: Evolutionary Narrative in Darwin, George Eliot and Nineteenth-Century Fiction* and George Levine's *Darwin and the Novelists: Patterns of Science in Victorian Fiction*, have curiously overlooked Gaskell's creative use of evolutionary theory. The first to hint at the influence of Darwinian thought on *Wives and Daughters*, Deirdre D'Albertis moreover crucially misreads the character of Roger Hamley when she speaks of "Gaskell's concentration on [his] brute strength."[24] On the contrary, he represents a new ideal man who diverges from Regency elegance without simply embodying ideologies of a primarily anti-intellectual "muscular Christianity."[25] This is the novel's true importance as a fictional document of the anxieties and hopes of the time. Roger Hamley provides an ideal compromise to contrasting fashions of manhood and a solution to fears inculcated by Victorian theories of evolution. I intend to trace how this proposed New Man figures within mid-Victorian ideals of "muscular Christianity" and the redefinition of the sentimental hero as well as within issues of inheritance, of the new heir and the new hero.

Victorian stories of evolution and degeneration have opened up new horizons for Utopian as well as Gothic fiction. By the end of the nineteenth century, a post-Darwinian imagination formed an established background to popular culture. Most recent studies have expectedly concentrated on later fiction. Kelly Hurley's *The Gothic Body: Sexuality, Materialism, and Degeneration at the Fin de Siècle* and William Greenslade's *Degeneration, Culture and the Novel 1880–1940*, for example, have pointed out the significance of degeneration theories for literature at the turn of the century. Greenslade speaks of a "loose assemblage of beliefs which can be marked out as 'degenerationism.'"[26] Degeneration, he argues, became an important myth for the post-Darwinian world.[27] Hurley similarly suggests that the implications of Darwinism were perceived "as disastrous and traumatic—one might say 'gothic'—by a majority of the population."[28] This "gothic" aspect was already exploited by sensation novelists in the sixties, though it undoubtedly became more pronounced towards the end of the century.

The literature of the period not only drew on Darwinian science, but reflected a preoccupation with neurasthenia or "nervous exhaustion" as well as with apocalyptic visions of racial suicide, as theories of entropy, first formulated in 1850, informed Dystopian rewritings of ideologies of progress. Linking fears of the end of mankind and racial suicide, medical concepts of the *vis nervosa*, stipulating that the energy of a human body was "a definite and not inexhaustible quantity," as Henry Maudsley put it in *Sex in Mind and in Education*, redefined fears first raised by thermodynamics as threatening to the individual as well as the social body.[29] The increase of nervous exhaustion was seen as paralleling the slow demise of the universe. In "The Death of the Sun: Victorian Solar Physics and Solar Myths," Gillian Beer has emphasized the "urgent propinquity in Victorian thinking" caused by the "contradiction between evolutionary ideas of sustained development and physicists' theories of the dissipation of energy."[30] This debate focused Victorian vacillations between optimistic hope of progress and anxieties of decadence, which came to be manifested by conceptualizations of degeneration as well as by theories of the sun's death.

Late Victorian fictional manifestations of these speculations and anxieties include tales of degeneration such as *The Time Machine* (1895) or *Dracula* (1897) and blueprints of eugenic Utopias that attempt to channel the new wisdom of degenerationism into eugenic blueprints. Expecting to see the realization of confident "visions of Utopias and coming times," the Time Traveller of H. G. Wells's *The Time Machine* neatly summarizes fears of degeneration when he sees his hopeful interpretation of evolution disproved: "The memory of my confident anticipations of a profoundly grave and intellectual posterity came, with irresistible merriment, to my mind."[31] In contrast, Francis Galton's "Kantsaywhere" describes a society where processes of selective breeding are meant to boost physical and mental superiority. As Galton's biographer, Karl Pearson, points out, "we must remember that Galton had set before himself in the last years of his life a definite plan of eugenics propagandism."[32] Those who fail the eugenics examination are "undesirable as individuals, and dangerous to the community, owing to the practical certainty that they will propagate their kind if unchecked. They are subjected to surveillance and annoyance if they refuse to emigrate" (420).

The deportation of undesirables is a familiar "solution" in popular Utopias of the time as well as in subsequent Dystopias. In Edward Bellamy's sequel to his Utopian novel *Looking Backward* (1888), ironically entitled *Equality* (1897), for example, mankind is purged of "uncleanness." Unfit individuals are sentenced to solitary confinement and "absolutely prevented from continuing their kind."[33] In Mary E. Bradley Lane's *Mizora* (1890), the narrator travels to the interior of the earth, where she encounters a "wonderful civilization" populated exclusively by blonde women of robust health: they have eliminated not only the sick and weak, but also all men as well as dark people of both sexes.[34] The impact of these Utopias on subsequent speculative fiction has been immense. The Darwinian imagination clearly initiated a decisive shift that has been as significant for the development of the novel as the affective revolution of the eighteenth century.[35]

In the course of the second half of the nineteenth century, evolutionary terms entered the language. Theories of degeneration and evolutionary improvement informed characterization in fiction. As Beer and Levine have influentially shown, the impact of the Darwinian imagination on domestic novels revealed and strengthened its prevalence. Levine speaks of "a sort of gestalt of the Darwinian imagination" and emphasizes the "counterchronological interpenetration between science and literature."[36] The function of science in literature is, as Beer has similarly put it, not "a one-way traffic, as though literature acted as a mediator for a topic (science) that precedes it and that remains intact after its re-presentation."[37] On the contrary, the relationship is one of interchange and transformation.[38] In positing a conflation of evolutionary narratives and courtship plots, mid-Victorian novels contributed much to the perpetuation of Darwinian myths, while subsuming them to the interests of domestic fiction.

In her seminal *Darwin's Plots*, Beer has already pointed out that "succession and inheritance form the 'hidden bond' which knits all nature past and present together, just as succession and inheritance organise society and sustain hegemony."[39] In *Desire and Domestic Fiction: A Political History of the Novel*, Nancy Armstrong similarly suggests that the sexual contract functions as a narrative paradigm in the British novel and that Darwin's *The Descent of Man, and Natural Selection in Relation to Sex* is based on the same contractual model—a model that becomes imbued with new possibilities in post-Darwinian fiction.[40] Victorian novels were quick to appropriate degenerationism, together with racial theories, phrenology, and the various developments of early psychology, as a form of characterization. In Wilkie Collins's sensation novel *No Name* (1862), for example, Norah Vanstone is described as in almost every way a replica of her mother, with the difference that something seems to have been lost in the transmission (the word is Collins's):

> Inheriting the dark majestic character of her mother's beauty, she had yet hardly inherited all its charms. Though the shape of her face was the same, the features were scarcely so delicate, their proportion was scarcely so true. She was not so tall.... If we dare to look closely enough, may we not observe, that the moral force of character and the higher intellectual capacities in parents seem often to wear out mysteriously in the course of transmissions to children? In these days of insidious nervous exhaustion and subtly-spreading nervous malady, is it not possible that the same rule may apply, less rarely than we are willing to admit, to the bodily gifts as well?[41]

Wives and Daughters similarly subsumes invoked discourses to the story—and I want to stress that it is by no means a novel about evolution or degeneration in the sense that Francis Galton's "Kantsaywhere" is about eugenics. Nevertheless, in contrast to the brief invocation of degeneration in *No Name*, evolutionary narratives run through Gaskell's novel, tying in with its presentation of the social rise of new naturalists. Miss Vanstone in *No Name* is a marginal figure. The interest in her younger sister's more complicatedly arranged character, however, reveals a refusal to bend completely to scientific explanations: "by one of those strange caprices of Nature, which science leaves still unexplained [she] presented no recognisable resemblance to either of her parents" (11). In its juxtaposition of different ideals of manliness and its proposition of a physically strong New Man, *Wives and Daughters*, engages more explicitly with discourses of evolution, bearing out their ramifications for the central themes of the domestic novel—courtship and inheritance. In the process it comes up with a new romantic hero and a solution to fears of mankind's uncontrolled evolution and its dark side, degeneration. In a close reading of the novel, I hope to show how Roger Hamley embodies this new manliness and why this new hero is vital to the reconstitution of an ideal home that is at once nostalgic and optimistic about the future.

Inheritance in the Evolutionary Plot: The Nostalgic Utopia of *Wives and Daughters*

Wives and Daughters maps the decline and restoration of homes and families. The changes in the Gibson household are paralleled by the crumbling of the Hamley family and estate, and the recuperation of both homes rests in the productive union of Molly Gibson and Roger Hamley. With its physically strong, though intellectual, hero the novel proposes a solution to the threat of degeneration and introduces an evolutionary plot into a domestic novel. The creation of this New Man is informed by mid-Victorian ideologies of muscular Christianity as well as by Levine's Darwinian gestalt, while it also redefines ideals of the romantic hero. "Clumsy and heavily built," Roger Hamley is "a tall powerfully-made young man, giving the impression of strength more than elegance;" his face "rather square, ruddy-coloured."[42] His clumsiness at first appears to disqualify him from claims to the role of the hero, but ultimately his physical strength asserts his capabilities as a healthy specimen of the desired New Man. In contrasting physically, intellectually, and morally weak and strong young men—eligible bachelors that pose as romantic heroes for the novel's courtship plot—*Wives and Daughters*, in fact, engages with literary sentimentalism, ideals of muscularity, and the changing fashions of attractiveness as well as with the preoccupations of post-Darwinian Victorian society.

The progress of this New Man is firmly and reassuringly located in the past. *Wives and Daughters* is set in the 1820s and 1830s, half a lifetime in the past for the novel's readers—in "those days before railways" (3), "before the passing of the Reform Bill" (6), and also "in those days, before muscular Christianity had come into vogue" (27). Kathleen Tillotson has pointed out that to read "novels such as *Wives and Daughters* and *Middlemarch* without due recognition of their setting in an England of forty years before the date of writing" is to "miss . . . much of their quality" (92). Gaskell not only reassuringly presents the New Man's generation as having commenced in the recent past, thereby alleviating anxieties about sudden changes caused by evolutionary, social, or scientific progress, but also juxtaposes bygone and emerging ideals of manhood.

By making the hero a scientist, whose success at Cambridge displaces the expected, but unrealized, poetic brilliance of his delicate elder brother and by rooting his success in his physical superiority, *Wives and Daughters* proposes an alternative to an elegant manliness that is increasingly associated with effeminacy and degeneracy. The mid-Victorian ideal of the physically strong male is in striking opposition to the lingering fashion for the genteel, almost girlish, elegance of the sentimental hero—an understanding of the frail body as an indicator of moral virtue—and both are transcended in the figure of the New Man who restores the best of the past. As an intellectually renowned, though at first underestimated, scientist, whose physical stamina proves advantageous in his scientific explorations, Roger Hamley constitutes an important transitional figure in the redefinition of male sensitivities, transcending the brutality and anti-intellectualism not undeservedly associated with the ideologies of muscular Christianity.

In contrast, high-strung sensibility and an ideology of the heart manifest themselves as weak nerves, physical delicacy and, in Osborne Hamley's case, ultimately as aneurysm of the aorta, embodying the death of the sentimental hero while evoking discourses of degeneration and nervous exhaustion. The juxtaposition of a healthy coarseness, still viewed as unattractive in the late 1820s, but rendered more popular by the 1860s, and lethargic elegance is central to the characterization of the Hamley brothers, whose bodies thus represent diverging fashions of male beauty and sensitivity. Each resembles one of their parents in disposition as well as in physical appearance—inherited traits that are expectedly equated. Having a "girl's delicate face, and a slight make," Osborne "takes after madam's side" (70), as his father puts it. His physique explains his proclivity to indulge in "feminine" susceptibilities. Appropriately called after his mother's maiden name, Osborne is "full of taste, and had some talent. His appearance had all the grace and refinement of his mother's. He was sweet-tempered and affectionate, almost as demonstrative as a girl" (40). He embodies the older ideal of the sentimental hero or man of sensibility, but his (mediocre) sentimental poetry cannot compete with his brother's scientific papers, and ultimately his delicacy and elegance are reduced to a physical weakness linked to the threat of degeneration.

In a similar contrast between Margaret Hale's two suitors in Gaskell's *North and South* (1855), a novel about pressing social issues that has little time for nostalgia and little patience with the heroine's homesickness for the rural neighborhood she has to leave behind, the new strong man figures as a counterpart to the questionable progress of industrialization. At the same time, he represents a counterpoise: a good man who makes up for the many drawbacks Margaret has to face in the industrial town in the north, away from her two southern homes in London and in the countryside.[43] The London lawyer Henry Lennox and the northern mill-owner John Thornton thus come to embody old and new types of masculinity. Juggling with these stereotypes, the novel treats the heroine's eventual choice of Thornton as the emergence of a New Man. The description of this "tall, broad-shouldered man . . . with a face that is neither exactly plain, nor yet handsome" and with "such an expression of resolution and power" in it (95) is by no means idealized, but successfully consigns the rather pale characterization of Lennox to the margins of the narrative. The New Man in *North and South*, a sympathetically presented Mr. Bounderby as well as a "muscular Christian" as promoted by Thomas Arnold and Samuel Smiles, the author of *Self-Help* (1859), represents an answer to sociological changes brought about by industrialization and the rise of the self-made man.[44] By contrast, *Wives and Daughters* presents a revised version of the New Man by locating the introduction of a more muscular and less elegant ideal man in the past and by combining his physical strength with both intellectual abilities and a more amiable, even gentle, disposition.

Although it equates bodily and moral or intellectual strengths in its representation of the male characters, *Wives and Daughters* is critical of sentimentalism and muscular Christianity as the two chief suppliers of ideals of manhood and literary heroes.

In sharp contrast to the refinements of his poetic brother, Roger's face is "square, and the expression grave, and rather immobile" (40), yet he is by no means a straightforward incarnation of muscular Christianity. While his strong physique conforms to mid-Victorian aesthetics of the "muscular Christian," his intellectual abilities and scientific career forgo what J. A. Mangan has termed the ideology's "virulent anti-intellectualism."[45] Aware of the allegations brought forward against muscular Christianity and the figure of the physically strong hero, *Wives and Daughters* creates a hero whose intellectual capacity excels in the emerging natural sciences.

The New Man's intellectual and physical strength moreover not only contrasts with the moribund graces of a sentimental man of sensibility, but also with the villain's aggressive physical power. This double, the "tigerish" land agent Robert Preston, is a social climber who is sexually attractive in his bold brutality. Molly's stepsister, Cynthia Kirkpatrick, feels persecuted and mesmerized: "Have you never heard of strong wills mesmerizing weaker ones into submission?" (408). His strong physique, combined with his upward mobility and strong will power, renders him a worthy object of Victorian anxieties of degeneration. Anticipating Wilkie Collins's villainous athlete in *Man and Wife*, Preston is morally weak. His passion is intensely physical and devoid of any sentimentality as well as of any scruples. Yet, ultimately he is unsuccessful in his attempts to marry above his station. Embodying the dangers associated with physical superiority, he is a negative version who serves to underline Roger's intellectual use of his bodily strength.

Although critics have pointed out that the representation of Preston's lower-class body parallels that of African countries in the novel, the function of Africa is more complicated.[46] Both Africa and France, a rival in imperialist conquests as well as scientific discoveries, figure repeatedly, but remain offstage. Africa is both the testing ground of the New Man's ability to survive and a lucrative site of scientific imperialism. The geopolitical implications of a larger body politic play a surprisingly important part in a story that seems at first sight so deeply rooted in the cozy spaces of a provincial town. In his *Atlas of the European Novel*, Franco Moretti cautions that the main function of sites abroad in domestic fiction is sometimes only the convenience that they are offstage.[47] It could therefore be argued that Roger Hamley has to leave the provincial world of the novel in order to be absent during his brother's death—which forces Molly to take an active role in contacting Osborne's concealed wife—as well as during the altercation between Roger's fiancée, Cynthia, and Preston. Roger's long distance relationship with Cynthia is put to the test, faring badly when contrasted with Molly's secret devotion. In short, there is more than one purely plot-based reason why Roger has to be removed to an offstage location. Nevertheless, his expeditions abroad also serve as a test of his endurance and consequently also of his eligibility as the New Man. This representation of an exotic locus of tested manliness feeds on the clichés created and sustained by Victorian racial theories. Bearing Moretti's caution in mind, I shall highlight the functions of race and class in the characterization of the New Man. Roger's homecoming triggers an exhibition of excitement and xenophobia in an early-Victorian provincial town:

"If a young man of twenty-four ever does take to growing taller, I should say that he was taller. As it is, I suppose it is only that he looks broader, stronger—more muscular."
"Oh! Is he changed?" asked Molly, a little disturbed by this account.
"No, not changed; and yet not the same. He is as brown as a berry for one thing; caught a little of the negro tinge, and a beard as fine and sweeping as my bay-mare's tail." (166–67)

The alterations of his body embody Victorian anxieties about activities abroad in a twofold way in that they poise speculation about an "infection"—the catching of "a little of the negro tinge" through colonial activities—against an unwillingness to attribute racial difference to climate alone, a concept that undermines myths of inborn "racial" superiority. The effects of climate on the body, in fact, formed an intricate aspect of eighteenth- and nineteenth-century imperialist discourses, both reaffirming and dismantling concepts of racial distinctiveness. Fears of degeneration or racial suicide were at the centre of ongoing reconceptualizations.[48] In *Somatic Fictions: Imagining Illness in Victorian Culture*, Athena Vrettos speaks of a hermeneutic uncertainty: Victorian racialism conceived the lower classes as well as nonwhite races as less sensitive than the self-image of the "civilized" white middle class. Either hereditary factors or repeated exposures to hardships were seen to have fostered the "savage's" physical resilience. At the same time, however, stamina was also understood as an attribute necessary for evolutionary survival.[49] In *The Complexion of Race: Categories of Difference in Eighteenth-Century British Culture*, Roxann Wheeler has recently provided an overview of eighteenth-century theories on the effects of climate on the body.[50] What they shared was an emphasis on the effects of the weather, food, and in general, the surroundings on the peoples inhabiting different continents. Relocated individuals would quickly be affected by climatic changes. This belief persisted throughout the nineteenth century, although it was at odds with a new racialism that suggested categories of "otherness" were innate rather than derivative from immediate surroundings. Their simultaneity expectedly conflicted Victorian fictions of imperialism and increasingly also neo-imperialism.

In *Wives and Daughters*, ordeals abroad test the New Man's stamina. Roger's struggles to adapt to his new surroundings include a fall and a fever. Eventually he returns strengthened: stronger, more muscular, his beard accentuating matured and tested manliness. His successes abroad and their financial reward increase his value on the marriage market, even while obliquely evoked anxieties about racial "infection" or miscegenation point at submerged concerns with both racial and sexual competition. The ambiguous presentation of evolution and degeneration is highlighted by these fissures in its treatment of race. Roger's expeditions are mapped within the geopolitics of scientific imperialism, which appropriates his interest in and instinctual love of nature as it conquers the exotic terrain that his expeditions categorize for the Geographical Society. In his study of colonial desire and hybridity, Robert Young has emphasized that the identities of metropolitan and colonial societies "needed to be constructed to counter schisms, friction and dissent."[51] Evoking Deleuze and Guattari's geospatial model of global capitalism, he calls racism the best example of group fantasies of desire and of its antithesis, repulsion.[52] Not surprisingly, in *Wives and Daughters,* the monetary aspects of the Geographical Society's appreciation of Roger's surveys are frequently mentioned. His mapping of space abroad provides the necessary funds to improve the estate at home.

However, regardless of the submerged anxieties about forms of infection, about fevers, falls, and sexual encounters, Roger Hamley's successes are viewed favorably. He has brought home botanical, zoological, geographical, and anthropological data, and consequently prestige and substantial remuneration. He is the empire's new scientist. After his first expedition, he is the guest of honor at one of the dinners that Lord Hollingford hosts for internationally renowned scientists. The old squire's family has achieved a new importance. D'Albertis speaks of the "cross-class troika" of Lord Hollingford, the country doctor Mr. Gibson, and the Cambridge-trained naturalist Roger Hamley, and their rising importance in an international and cross-class scientific community.[53] But not only is its internationalism restricted to representatives of the British and French empires, its ostensibly egalitarian optimism is necessarily inscribed by narratives of conquest as well as by capitalist geopolitics.

Despite these ambiguities, however, the novel's happy end is nostalgic and hopeful at the same time, as it celebrates the New Man's success and his impending marriage to the heroine. As a scientific imperialist and a physically strong intellectual, Roger Hamley represents the empire's new man of science, as he conquers new territory in the international community of scientists while mapping terrain abroad. His absence meanwhile facilitates a wealth of plot-developments at home. An imagined sickroom scene acts out Molly Gibson's fanciful fantasies of female nursing and male suffering in "savage lands," thereby bringing the novel's hero and heroine together in a conventional, though imagined, sickroom narrative that offers a nurturing contrast to homeless migrations abroad. Molly's fantasies contrast sharply with Cynthia's comparative indifference and, at the same time, underline her feminine delicacy, as she pictures Roger in want of nursing while not in strong health herself, which "perhaps . . . made her a little fanciful" (84). The eventual prospect of a marriage between the intellectual, though healthy, hero and the motherly, but delicate, heroine says as much about a successful inclusion of evolutionary patterns into a courtship plot as about living in and of nature in an age of science. Most importantly, Roger replenishes inherited lands at home with the financial rewards of his explorations abroad, restoring the position of the oldest family in the county. The chapter's concluding part will take a closer look at the importance of the new heir in the novel.

Old England and the New Heir

As the New Man, Roger is, as is often stressed, "a man of the future,"[54] but he is also a genuine Hamley of Hamley. He stands in a line of proud Saxon squires, whose "mode of life was simple, and more like that of yeomen than squires" (38). This old-fashioned roughness contrasts decisively with Osborne's and the former Miss Osborne's (Mrs. Hamley's) "cultivated" tastes. Their bodily refinement is, in fact, a mock gentility, as the Osbornes have acquired their fortune by trade. Similarly, when compared to the Hamleys, of whom Mrs. Goodenough asserts "with all the slow authority of an oldest inhabitant . . . that there was Hamleys of Hamley afore the time of the pagans" (37), the "Cumnor folk" and Lord Hollingford of Hollingford are a recent introduction: "Where [were they] in the time of Queen Anne?" (71) Having inherited the physiognomy of the Hamleys and in caring for the estate financially and emotionally, Roger Hamley represents the land's natural heir. Squire Hamley significantly asserts his sons' respective claims to gentility by juxtaposing their different physiognomies. Issues of descent articulate the body's manifestation of inherited proclivities and hereditary diseases:[55]

> Osborne has a girl's delicate face, and a slight make, and hands and feet as small as a lady's. He takes after madam's side, who, as I said, can't tell who was their grandfather. Now, Roger is like me, a Hamley of Hamley, and no one who sees him in the street will ever think that red-brown, big-boned, clumsy chap is of gentle blood. Yet all those Cumnor people, you make such ado of in Hollingford, are mere muck of yesterday. (70)

Through a confluence of hereditary lands with inherited bodies, it is the regeneration of the old families and their old-fashioned ways of life with their close connection to and affinities with nature that constitutes the desired restoration: it is epitomized by an "evolution" of the Hamleys. "At any rate," the narrator emphasizes, "the Hamleys were a very old family, if not aborigines" (37). The Old Squire embodies lawful heredity run to seed, resembling the Hamley estate, ill managed due to lack of proper resources and badly in need of regeneration. Nonetheless, the raw material of the old stock is sound. Uneducated and prejudiced, the Squire represents values of the past that are worth preserving. There is "a dignity in his quiet conservatism that gained him an immense amount of respect both from high and low" (38). The natural heir, however, is not always the traditionally or lawfully selected one. Such disregard of nature's claims could not be better exemplified than by the Hamleys' unwholesome petting of Osborne, as they declare his "likes and dislikes [as] the law of the house" (85), while neglecting the younger son. Yet it is this second son, Roger, who renders the improvement of the inherited lands possible.

In thus positing an unpredictable "evolution" of Roger Hamleys, the novel draws primogeniture into question. In his study of late-Victorian degenerationism, Greenslade has shown that propagators of eugenics tended to view primogeniture with skepticism since they wished to emphasize the claims of natural ability. Greenslade's reference to underlying class-issues is a valid point: eugenicists, he shows, had a vested interest in promoting the interests of a professional middle class, from which they had mostly sprung themselves, against the existing hereditary elites.[56] In electing a true Hamley of Hamley as the New Man, *Wives and Daughters* goes around this alignment. On the contrary, as Osborne takes after his mother's class-climbing family, his displacement sees the restoration of the true Hamleys, of old blood after all. More controversially, it is the offspring of Osborne's secret marriage to a French nursery maid who becomes the third Roger Hamley. The heir's foreign and working-class mother infuses fresh blood into the old stock, but also introduces the practical knowledge of a well-trained nursery maid, linking issues of descent to the significance of maternity in evolutionary narratives. The old squire has to combat his xenophobia, and this is important for the novel's repeated parody of different forms of snobbery. Still, what makes the former nursery maid such a good mother is her practical care of the new heir. Osborne's sentimental mother has spoiled him as a true Hamley as much as his inheritance of her physique. Maternal care is as important for the evolution of new men and new heirs, the novel suggests, as their inherited bodies.

In *Wives and Daughters*, the very title of which points emphatically at the absence of the mother, maternity naturally plays a crucial role. The responsible nurturing of offspring, of the heir of the land, is only one facet of its significance. Households lacking in maternal affection are exposed as dysfunctional, as the arrangement of stepmother, unwanted daughter, and nostalgic stepdaughter in the Gibson home plainly shows. Mrs. Kirkpatrick's neglect of Cynthia highlights its importance: "I don't think love for one's mother quite comes by nature; and remember how much I have been separated from mine!" (221). That filial love does not come naturally is vividly exemplified not merely by the estrangement of Mrs. Kirkpatrick and the child long separated from her, but also by Mrs. Hamley's "adoption" of Molly. Having grown into the home of the Hamleys, Molly cherishes "that old bond" in nostalgia: "His mother called me 'Fanny;' it was almost like an adoption" (24). Molly becomes an enactment of the dead daughter, while Mrs. Hamley's death re-enacts the original loss of Molly's mother. It is this double loss that reinforces the bond between Roger and Molly, reanimating "the brotherly kindness of old times" (243). Yet while filial or maternal love may not come by nature, maternal feelings might still be inherited. Mr. Gibson traces Molly's motherly qualities to an unconscious or inborn "memory." Comforting her stepsister Cynthia, Molly employs "a mode of caressing that had come down to her from her mother—whether as a hereditary instinct, or as a lingering remembrance of the tender ways of the dead woman, Mr. Gibson often wondered" (332). Molly's twofold maternal loss becomes connected to her new nostalgia for Hamley Hall and thereby prepares for her transference of affections, while her motherly qualities single her out as a potential mother for more Hamleys of Hamley.

The novel's narrative situation is wistfully retrospective, but a wry ambiguity seems to counteract the nostalgic idealization of the squire's old England. His "quaintness" is at once an "unreasonableness" and a "strong conservatism in religion, politics, and morals" (41). At Hamley Hall, it is "the character of the furniture" to be "old-fashioned, [giving] an aspect of comfort and picturesqueness to the whole apartment" (61). The habits and value-systems of the past, and especially the recent past, are often simply quaint—"droll enough to look back upon" (2). E. Holly Pike consequently speaks of a "gentle mockery of the old ways."[57] Jane Spencer even suggests that "although there is much affection for past ways in the chapters on Molly's childhood, and there is an idyllic quality about her first visit to Hamley Hall, the work is not nostalgic about old England."[58] Anna Unsworth, however, emphasizes that in the idyllic depictions of rural landscapes "we see Mrs. Gaskell contemplating the archetypal scene of old England, "an image representative of a way of life only ended, finally, by the General Enclosures Act of 1845."[59] A fondness for rural England permeates the novel; and that the idealization of the past remains critical does not underscore the sincerity of its affectionate appreciation.

Molly Gibson notably feels more at home at Hamley Hall than in her father's house after her fashionable stepmother has refurbished it beyond recognition. In chapter fifteen, entitled "The New Mamma," Molly returns "home, to the home which was already strange" (171). The renovation discards the old completely, foils nostalgic remembrance, and altogether reflects the new Mrs. Gibson's "superficial and flimsy character" (139). Molly's own room, which she "wouldn't have . . . changed for the world" (151), is altered despite her protests. The "little white dimity bed" that is so fondly delineated in the opening chapter (1) is, together with an "old-fashioned chest of drawers, and her other cherished relics of her mother's maiden days . . . , consigned to the lumber-room" (184). The new mamma rids her new home radically of remembrances of the first Mrs. Gibson:

> Many a time when Molly had been in this room since that sad day, had she seen in vivid fancy that same wan wistful face lying on the pillow, the outline of the form beneath the clothes; and the girl had not shrunk from such visions, but rather cherished them, as preserving to her the remembrance of her mother's outward semblance. Her eyes were full of tears . . . . Nearly everything was changed. (150–51)

Clare, as Mrs. Kirkpatrick, the former Miss Clare and the new Mrs. Gibson, continues to be called by the Cumnors, is most at home at the Towers, where she used to be employed as a governess. Coming "home" from the unprofitable school she unwillingly keeps at Ashcomb, she is conscious of how natural the dainty environment appears to her: "It seemed to her far more like home than the dingy place she had left that morning; it was so natural to her to like dainty draperies and harmonious colouring, and fine linens and soft raiment" (96). One of the very few governesses in Victorian fiction that enjoy their position, she is truly homesick for the Cumnors' Great House, not for her present or, in fact, any other later lawfully assigned home: "She dreaded the end of her holidays as much as the most home-loving of her pupils" (96). Once she has secured Mr. Gibson, she attempts to restructure his home to fit her ideas of an elegant household, modeled on a bourgeois imitation of a more gentrified or even aristocratic lifestyle. Predominantly a longing for the fashionable, Clare's desire for the right kind of home forms the parodic counterpoise to Molly's homesickness, and at the same time exposes a darker side of homemaking: the forceful restructuring of new homes that are the nostalgically preserved homes of other inhabitants.

Like an unwilling colonialist, the new mamma adapts her new home to her own needs. Her preoccupation with food and beds is conspicuous. At the first sight of her future home, the new Mrs. Gibson sees the need to readjust her habitation: "What an old-fashioned bed! And what a—But it doesn't signify. By-and-by we'll renovate the house—won't we, my dear?" (172). Even before her marriage, she feels repulsed by the domestic habits and in particular the diet of the prospective habitat. She abhors cheese as "such a strong-smelling, coarse kind of thing" (126), but Mr. Gibson is significantly very fond of it. Their different appetites and attitudes to proper nourishment result in domestic discord: "I shouldn't like to think of your father eating cheese.... We must get him a cook who can toss him up an omelette, or something elegant" (126–27). The "elegant" omelette embodies her concept of the dictates of fashionable "genteel" decorum. Clare's fondness for savory dainties, especially for the "exquisitely cooked delicacies" (96) served at the Towers, the Cumnors' Great House, indicates her appetite for luxuries and sensual pleasures. Her idealization of the Towers contrasts crucially with Molly's memories of once getting lost on the Cumnors' extensive grounds, which have continued to "[haunt] her dreams ever since her childhood" (289). It is on the other's territory that she has "to face Mrs. Kirkpatrick by herself, the recollection of her last day of misery at the Towers fresh in her mind as if it had been yesterday" (125). The child's experience of acute and little-understood homesickness, when she had been forgotten at the Towers after a social visit, has strengthened her attachment to her childhood home and made her suspicious of Mrs. Kirkpatrick's pretensions to genteel refinement and affected sentimentality.

But what the many juxtapositions of homesickness most insistently show is that living in the wrong place can prove unwholesome. This is not only true for Molly's unhappiness at the Towers and Mrs. Kirkpatrick's longing for its luxuries. For Mrs. Hamley, slowly fading away despite all her love for the Squire, who is "wont to say he had got all that was worth having out of that crowd of houses they called London"—a "compliment to his wife which he repeated until the year of her death" (39)—her dislocation from a more varied life in town eventually proves fatal: otherwise Mrs. Hamley "would not have sunk into the condition of a chronic invalid" (38). Molly is more fortunate as she transposes much of her longing for a return home onto Hamley Hall, just when the childhood home undergoes refurbishments: "She had been so happy there; she liked them all, down to the very dogs, so thoroughly" (148). Leaving the ideal home, which need not be the "original," is painful and unnatural, a disruptive transposition: "She would have to wrench up the roots she had shot down into this ground" (208). Her marriage to the New Man not only brings the novel's courtship plot to a desirable conclusion, but also realizes the nostalgic desire for a restored home.

Much of the novel's narrative interest rests in the question if and when and how this New Man will finally select his perfect partner. The romance and inheritance plots are repeatedly put in evolutionary terms. The subplot involving class-climbing Mr. Preston additionally underscores class issues. Rivals in love, Roger and Preston compete for the hand of alluring Cynthia. Roger temporarily wins the day, but when Cynthia decides to marry a fashionable minor character from offstage London, he eventually realizes Molly's superior qualities. While she shares her stepsister's social inferiority, she is a better match. The allurements of womanly Cynthia are, like those of manly Preston, primarily sexual. As an indicator of reproductive fitness, such attractions are thus exposed as a delusion. Likewise, the courtship of Preston and Cynthia is ripe with sexual energy, but fraught with cruelty. The contrast between Roger's infatuation with Cynthia and his more mature appreciation of Molly can well be termed the difference between lust and love. While the novel puts emphasis on the importance of inherited bodies and temperaments in the choice of a mate and the conception of a suitable heir, it is quick to point out that physical attraction alone can be misleading. Handsome, lower-class, and morally reprehensible, this negative New Man embodies the threats of sexual selection and the drawbacks of social mobility. While his social ambitions are disappointed, the true New Man reinstates the power of an old family. Although Roger's social standing has increased by the end of the novel, he is, in fact, far from being a class-climber. Equally, the healthy young heir, Osborne's son, may be the product of a transgression across class boundaries as well as national borders, yet his resemblance to his uncle and grandfather shows him to be of old yeoman stock. As Anna Unsworth has rightly pointed out, the three Roger Hamleys evoke "an immediately recognisable image" conjured up by "that well-known term, 'the yeomen of England.'"[60] The ideal circumvention of degeneracy, the novel suggests, is the regeneration of the nostalgically commemorated "old stock."

The projected Utopia is clearly less about the introduction of the new than about the renewal of what is preserved or recalled in nostalgia. Evolution, it is suggested, selects the good old families after all. Analogously, the success of rising scientist Roger Hamley and his financial replenishment of his father's estate facilitate what is predominantly a nostalgic restoration. The Hamley estate needs to be restored; and what this regeneration requires is the "evolution" of Roger Hamleys. A hopeful treatment of nostalgia, the novel situates the inheritance plots of the traditional novel within evolutionary narratives of congenial habitats and the survival of the fittest heirs, connecting them to a new emphasis on inherited bodies and reintegrating the concept of evolutionary progress with the preservation of "old England." Nostalgia for pre-industrial landscapes merges with Utopian hopes for both society and nature, as the new scientist is figured as a caring preserver of its fauna and flora. His mapping of the diversity of nature at home and abroad establishes a descendant of the yeomen of England in an international scientific community. Even while the New Man's scientific imperialism and the dismissal of his "savage" double are without doubt disturbing, considered within the constrictions of Victorian perceptions of the foreign and the lower-class body, the novel offers a solution to degeneration without drawing on eugenic discourses or conservative xenophobia. Instead, it suggests a natural regeneration of deserving old families. A domestic novel with a central courtship plot, it propagates love, not Mrs. Kirkpatrick's social ambition, nor Mr. Preston's possessive passion, as the most reliable factor in the choice of a partner. Most importantly, the nostalgically sketched Utopia requires a New Man who successfully represents both progress and nostalgia. Far from contradictory, this nostalgic evolutionary plot disarms the dangers of uncontrolled evolution and degeneration.

5
Nostalgia and Men of Sensibility in Wilkie Collins's Novels

A SOCIETY THAT VALUES PROGRESS AND SELF-HELP DIAGNOSES nostalgia as subversive. Deliberately exposing the alignment of moral with physical strength that underlies these ideologies, Wilkie Collins's novels introduce new men and, less controversially, women of sensibility whose distresses are dismissed as a pathetic self-indulgence, a clinical condition, or a form of sulky defiance by their more energetic contemporaries. But as his later fiction reaffirms an older ideal of sensibility, nostalgia comes to play a dual role. Longing is once more praiseworthy in all its indulgences, while this representation of the nostalgic hero or heroine is nostalgic. The novels written at the heyday of the "sensational sixties" as well as Collins's "mission novels," consciously engage with the sensibilities and sensations of desirable and admirable men of feeling. They nostalgically reclaim older ideals of manliness in propagating a Romantic sensibility divorced from medical conceptualizations of nervous susceptibilities. Tracing the development of the new hero of feeling in Collins's fiction, I shall highlight the shift from an ambiguous treatment of sensitive antiheroes in the early novels to the consummation of a nostalgically recalled ideal.

The glorification of bodily affliction as a sign of virtue was an important aspect of the novel of sensibility in the late eighteenth century. By the mid-nineteenth century, however, the idealization of weakness fostered by literary sentimentalism had been displaced by an ideology of energy and enterprise that discredited lethargy and bodily procrastination. In a medical treatise characteristic of the period, John Barlow asserted that "there's every reason to suppose that where the habit of self-government is strong, . . . nervous affection is not likely to occur."[1] The congruity between the Victorian symptomatology of neurasthenia and a sentimental somatics of longing is indeed striking. In *A Practical Treatise on Nervous Exhaustion (Neurasthenia)*, George M. Beard, pioneer in the exploration of this "Central Africa of medicine"—a metaphor that fed on the Victorian infatuation with exploration—listed frequent blushing, insomnia, appearance of youth, and abnormalities of the secretions as the symptoms of neurasthenia: "In nervous exhaustion, the eyes may become moistened more readily than in health, and under a very slight emotion of pleasure or of pain. The flood-gates seem, as it were, to stand ajar; and on trifling agitation the tears flow forth."[2] This symptomatology echoes the description of a tearful hero of sensibility. This eighteenth-century legacy is recycled in the Victorian sensation novel, especially in Collins's later works.

Recycling the Somatics of Longing in the Sensation Novel

As his most explicit defense of nostalgic insight, *The Two Destinies* (1876), Wilkie Collins's novel about mesmerism, describes a secular spirituality that evokes and is evoked by the sympathy of kindred spirits, or more precisely, of nostalgic lovers.[3] But in a society in which new medical theories dominate the understanding of melancholy moods, and in which mesmerism is a popular, but highly controversial, topic, the "mesmeric" link of two lovers separated since early youth is diagnosed as a delusion caused by a disease of the nerves or of the brain.[4] Childhood friends, George and Mary have been separated because their social positions prohibit a lasting affection. The obstacles in the way of a reunion cover a range of sensational plot devices, including mistaken identities, bigamy, a suicide attempt, a mysterious deformed woman who nurses the hero and falls in love with him, and social stigmatization. The prophecy of Mary's "wild and weird grandmother" ultimately comes true, despite the ridicule of George's father, who mocks both his son's "childish" attachment to his bailiff's daughter and the old woman's admonishments: "For time and for eternity they are united one to the other. . . . You may doom them to misery, you may drive them to sin—the day of their union on earth is still . . . predestined."[5] The memories of their childhood survive in shared dreams or visionary trances, eventually enabling them to live again "as we lived in our first Paradise, before sin and sorrow lifted their flaming swords, and drove us out into the world" (18). Their skeptical contemporaries dismiss George's "phantoms" as delusions. His nostalgia, re-pathologized once more, is considered as a symptom of nervous depression. A renowned physician diagnoses his mind as "unhinged," as he links love and disturbed nerves: "It is in his temperament to take the romantic view of love. . . . The effect is plain—his nerves have broken down; and his brain is necessarily affected by whatever affects his nerves" (189). Intriguingly, George's phantoms closely resemble those described by John Barlow in his treatise on will power and insanity, but his "delusions" are genuine visions.[6] Threatened with medical surveillance and restraint, George needs to escape "like a criminal escaping from prison" (197). But as he indulges his longing "to look once more at the old scenes, to live for awhile again among the old associations" (193), he eventually recovers the love of the past. Nostalgia is triumphant; its clinical conceptualization as the result of a "re-pathologization" of longing and monomaniac memories disproved.

Collins's interest in psychological aberration and in particular in definitions of normality and their impact on representations of a longing that is seen as pathetic or pathological is central to his fiction. The treatment of diagnosed delusions in *The Two Destinies* expresses his defense of "irrational," socially unacceptable, desire most clearly. Similarly, in *The Legacy of Cain* (1888), nostalgically recollected love is the "all-powerful counter-influence" that counteracts jealousy, neutralizes an inheritance of murderous propensities, and thwarts medical discourses on phrenology, hereditary insanity, and nervous breakdowns.[7] Although Collins's defense of nostalgia undoubtedly becomes more emphatic in his later fiction, the dissection of the contingent boundaries of emotional memory and madness is also at the center of his best-known sensation novel, *The Woman in White* (1860), and the different ways of remembering become just as important to the projects of amateur detectives in subsequent novels as nostalgic longings to their love interest.

In *The Woman in White*, Anne Catherick is the Woman in White to honor the memory of the late Mrs. Fairlie, whose kindness has been imprinted on the heightened memory of a backward child. The likeness between the beautiful madwoman and the exquisitely feminine heroine accentuates the identification of sensibility with both femininity and effeminacy and of a too-acute memory with madness. I shall return to the gendered perceptions of nervousness in *The Woman in White*; what is central to its representation of memory is its juxtaposition of nostalgic retrospection with trauma as well as with a legal re-collection of the past. Attempts to reconstruct events, in particular the date of Lady Glyde's departure from Blackwater Park, dramatize the need for a reliable memory of "the troubled and terrible past" that bears forensic investigation.[8] Vague, emotionally distorted, memories are of no legal value: "All hope of fixing that important date, by any evidence of [Laura's] must be given up for lost" (353). Anne's memory of her childhood is as intense as her understanding of recent events is unreliable. As Laura is forcefully thrust into taking up the role of her double, her memory revealingly becomes as confused as that of an inmate of an asylum is expected to be. Laura's recollections of that "troubled and terrible" past are tantalizingly absent from the re-collections that form the novel.

But nostalgia for the happy time before her double imprisonment in an arranged marriage and an asylum heals Laura. Bringing back happy memories and erasing the effects of her incarceration in the insane asylum, it retrieves her sanity. As another form of an emotionally distorted or selective, but also curative, memory, this nostalgia counteracts the brainwashing she has undergone in the asylum. The novel ultimately ends with a happy domestic scene, in which Laura's remaining symptoms are fondly indulged by her protective husband and sister: "Tenderly and gradually, the memory of the old walks and drives dawned upon her; and the poor, weary, pining eyes looked at Marian and at me with a new interest" (361). Collins's fiction repeatedly figures nostalgia as a counter-influence to medical control over happiness.

New Heroes of Feeling: Wilkie Collins's Men in Tears

In the later novels, this defense of his protagonists' nostalgia is complemented by nostalgia for the sensitive heroes of an earlier time. In *Man and Wife* (1870), nostalgic and nostalgically presented old-fashioned Sir Patrick sarcastically summarizes the "cant of the day" (69) that takes "physically-wholesome men for granted, as being morally-wholesome men into the bargain:" "I don't see the sense of crowing over him [the model young Briton] as a superb national production, because he is big and strong, and . . . takes a cold shower bath all the year round" (68). Collins's novels increasingly eschew Victorian fashions of a muscular masculinity, anticipating the rise of the new *fin de siècle* antihero, but also harking back to the sentimental heroes of the novel of sensibility. This shift from heroic masculinity to praiseworthy physical delicacy reaffirms the concept of psychophysical affliction as a sign of moral strength: vital villains contrast with a series of hypersensitive heroes. To understand this development, one needs to take a close look at the mental, moral, and bodily strengths and weaknesses of Collins's heroes and their relationship with formidable, robust women. An analysis of this relationship will shed an intriguing light on gender issues in Victorian fiction and particularly contribute to the recently developed field of masculinity studies. Most importantly, however, by nostalgically reclaiming an older ideal of manliness, Collins's novels doubly promote nostalgia. Indulgence in emotions and emotional memory is, after all, the redeeming quality of his nostalgically recalled men of sensibility.

The legacy of the novel of sensibility as recuperated by the Victorian sensation novel is a fascinating topic that has so far been ignored in literary criticism. The reworking of the sentimental ideal of manliness in this body of literature places in a new light the reactions against mid-Victorian ideals of the muscular hero. There are significant parallels between the late-eighteenth-century heroes of sensibility and the enervated (male) victims of sensation in popular sensation fiction of the 1860s. Sensation novels such as Mary Elizabeth Braddon's *Lady Audley's Secret* (1862) and Charles Reade's *Hard Cash* (1863), written in the wake of *The Woman in White* (1860), create hypersensitive antiheroes who are reconfigured as assertive men possessed of recharged energies. Collins's fiction, however, maps a shift away from this reassertion of energy and will power. While drawing on his extensive oeuvre, I shall focus on *No Name* (1862), written when the "sensational sixties" had reached a peak, and *Heart and Science* (1883), one of his mission novels, which redeploy the techniques and themes of the sensation genre to attack particular issues, such as, in the latter work, vivisection. Both novels discuss fashionable ideals of male as well as female beauty and sensibility and their influence on the creation of post-Romantic romantic heroes and heroines. Their juxtaposition maps the development of a new hero of feeling, as they show the shift from an ambiguous treatment of sensitive antiheroes in Collins's earlier novels to a new ideal of male sensibility. *Man and Wife*, published eight years after *No Name* and thirteen years before *Heart and Science*, provides a useful point of entrance to the recurring theme of what constitutes a desirable hero.

The recuperation of delicate heroes and heroines in Collins's fiction, however, has also to be seen against the background of the changing medical understanding of health and strength at the time. Insanity, the norms of normality, and incarceration in insane asylums or private attics are without doubt the favorite topoi of sensation fiction. But whereas the significance of the genre's representation of subversive women has been studied by feminist critics from the 1980s onwards, the importance of transgressive male protagonists has only recently been brought to the fore. Lyn Pykett has argued that in opening up the transgressive domain of the improper feminine, the sensation novel functions as political activism.[9] The "abnormalities" of the new man of sensibility, however, place such alignments in a different light. Alex J. Tuss's analysis of the "troubled young man" in mid-Victorian literature is one of the few studies that offer "a companion piece for the valuable body of criticism concerned with female writers, their works, and their representation of women."[10]

"Being judged a womanly man," writes Tuss, "was a concern for Victorian males," and "male writers often complained of being feminized."[11] The anxiety about effeminacy is crucial to Victorian critiques of the sensation genre, in which feminized men frequently strive for a reaffirmed manliness. This popular plot invests the defense of hypersensitive men of feeling in Collins's later fiction with additional poignancy. Pykett significantly links the gendering of the sensation genre to a feminization of literature that begins with sentimental novels of the eighteenth century.[12] The defense of nervous antiheroes of sensibility in Collins's fiction is partly a legacy of the sentimental novel as well as a reaction to the more embarrassing and dangerous aspects of Victorian ideologies of energy, enterprise, and muscularity, as is vividly exemplified by Geoffrey Delamayn's moral and then physical demise in *Man and Wife*.

The fascination with the somatics of sickness and sensibility bleeds into the fissures of Victorian discourses on health not only by redefining the healthy male body against the "sickness" of effeminacy, but also by upholding an interest in the sentimental hero that becomes a constituent aspect of a new hero of sensibility. Protesting against the ideologies of physical superiority that ideals of the healthy body come to embody, such subversive narratives redefine the understanding of neurasthenia and demythologize racial imperialism.[13] In these processes of reforming the muscular, the neurotic, and the moral, corporeal categories are reviewed within a physiological and pathological terminology. Linking the politics of fitness to imperialist ideologies and social Darwinism, Athena Vrettos suggests that the related discourses of evolutionary theory, reproductive fitness, and imperialism formed part of a vocabulary that "codifies and genders acts of self- and social definition."[14] In a study of athleticism as an educational ideology, J. A. Mangan has shown that the anti-intellectualism propagated by ideologies of muscular Christianity cultivated distrust of "the intellectual of questionable masculinity."[15]

An anti-intellectual education of the body consequently became increasingly promoted at British public schools[16] and, as Wilkie Collins and Charles Reade show in their novels with delightful sarcasm, at the universities as well. Thomas Hughes's *Tom Brown's School Days* (1857), by contrast, endorses muscular Christianity. Young Tom is "mighty proud of his running, and not a little anxious to show his friend [Master East] that although a new boy he was no milksop."[17] Sixty years later this public school ethos was controversially exposed in Alec Waugh's semi-autobiographical *The Loom of Youth* (1917), which cynically details bullying, bodily abuse, and the hypocrisy with which homosexuality is treated. Laying bear the unhealthy obsession with athleticism and the imperialism that is to be nurtured by them, Waugh exposes the impact of muscular Christianity:

> The Public School system was venerated as a pillar of the British Empire and out of that veneration had grown a myth of the ideal Public Schoolboy—Kipling's Brushwood Boy. In no sense had I incarnated such a myth and it had been responsible, I felt, for half my troubles. I wanted to expose it.[18]

Consciously writing against Victorian ideals of manliness, the public school ethos, and the emphasis on physical competition at the universities, Wilkie Collins embraces controversy in *Man and Wife*, as he begins to set his new heroes apart from the more energetic men of his early fiction. Nostalgic Sir Patrick is a man of wit as well as of honor, of sense as well as of sensibility, a man who wears knee breeches and quotes poetry—in short, "a gentleman of the byegone [sic] time" (57). Arnold Brinkworth, his niece's suitor, comes close to his nostalgic ideal because he does not resemble the "model young Briton of the present time" (68). Arnold's tearful "heartache" testifies to his superiority over his base, but popular, successful and energetic, in short, "modern" friend:

> Left by himself, Arnold's head dropped on his breast. The friend who had saved his life—the one friend he possessed, who was associated with his earliest and happiest remembrances of old days—had grossly insulted him; and had left him deliberately, without the slightest expression of regret. Arnold's affectionate nature—simple, loyal, clinging where it once fastened—was wounded to the quick. Geoffrey's fast retreating figure, in the open view before him, became blurred and indistinct. He put his hand over his eyes, and hid, with a boyish shame, the hot tears that told of the heartache, and that honoured the man who shed them. (274)

As I have shown in Chapter 1, the idealization of the tearful (anti-) hero is at the heart of eighteenth-century literary sentimentalism. The alignment between distress, illness, and virtue is increasingly being reassessed. Although Fanny's physical homesickness and Anne's melancholy moods are treated sympathetically, Mrs. Musgrove's famous "large fat sighings" (68) in *Persuasion* and Mr. Woodhouse's endless gruel in *Emma* already express a reversal of the sentimental mind-body relationship.

Austen's reassessment of the sensibility genre would undoubtedly have been more familiar to Collins than the plethora of eighteenth-century novels that unashamedly affirm, or at the very least reaffirm, this emotional indulgence. In Victorian fiction, an ideology of energy and enterprise that discredits incapacity displaces this idealization of weakness. Fred Kaplan speaks of "a characteristic Victorian triad—energy, will, and power."[19] The gender differentiation that forms an integrated part of the new ideologies of health and strength identifies physical illness with both moral weakness and effeminacy. Tearful heroes consequently have a much harder time in Victorian fiction than their female counterparts.

Victorian sickroom fiction reflects this split. Male protagonists such as Pip in Dickens's *Great Expectations* or Wrayburn in *Our Mutual Friend* find their moral health restored, while sentimentalized somatic decline is often reserved for women and children. In Wilkie Collins's early fiction, physically frail women are, in sentimental fashion, afflicted with nervous and other disorders. Yet big rosy men are also exposed as vacuous giants, while it is increasingly the frail, pale, and nervous men that qualify as new heroes of sensibility. Languid melancholy and even sickliness seem to be the price that men of feeling have to pay for their sensibilities. As in eighteenth-century sentimental fiction, lack of will power, energy, and "masculine firmness," to use Adam Smith's term, is a sign of sensitivity.[20] The alignment of will power, strength, and also emotional control with moral depravity recurs in late-Victorian and Edwardian fiction, as the Victorian health crazes lose their impetus.[21] Gerald dying "broken up in the football match" in E. M. Forster's *The Longest Journey* (1907) takes the light-hearted ridicule of exhausting rowing competitions in *Hard Cash* to its logical conclusion and is reminiscent of Geoffrey's more sensational demise during a footrace in *Man and Wife*.[22] Gerald is a brute and a bully, sharply contrasting with the novel's delicate and disabled hero.

As it revises the novel of sensibility, the sensation novel shares its concern with the "proper" feminine and masculine. Its emphasis on sensual experience engenders anxieties about uncontrollable emotionalism, about emasculated men and mannish women.[23] In many sensation novels, female excess is, as feminist critics have stressed, given free rein, even though it is usually policed and the policing is not always criticized. Male sensibilities are let loose as well, and, in this case, it is more often the system of surveillance and restraint that is exposed. The resistance of the emerging hypersensitive antiheroes casts a different light on the sensation genre and on representations of masculinity.

Wrongful incarceration in insane asylums is of course common in sensation novels. Incompetent or fake diagnoses, ruthless experimentation, and other abuses of power by medical practitioners as well as by scheming relatives become the main ingredients of plots involving critical dissections of the definition of sanity. But in many novels, the victims are not "madwomen in the attic," but young sensitive and delicate men of feeling who fail to abide by ideologies of will power and capitalist enterprise. Sally Shuttleworth has compared limitations that constrained Victorian women to "equivalent constraints . . . imposed upon young men: failure to show sufficient enterprise in the realm of commerce was judged sufficient evidence of insanity."[24] What was considered inappropriate for a young woman was prerequisite for her male counterpart. The hero of Charles Reade's *Hard Cash*, for example, is removed to an asylum because his absence will facilitate his father's financial plots. His physical delicacy and lovesickness provide greedy, easily manipulated, physicians with a welcome excuse. In Braddon's novel, Lady Audley likewise schemes to get rid of her suspicious brother-in-law by suggesting that he is the one who is insane. Collins's novels evince a similar attitude towards the medical profession and its institutions, and as I shall show, his men of sensibility are as easily victimized as women.

At the center of most early sensation novels, however, lies a reassertion of will-power and manly firmness, a restoration of a proper masculinity. In Reade's *Hard Cash*, Alfred Hardie is reminiscent of a sentimental man of feeling. He is "a clever boy, not a cool . . . man of the world."[25] His "feminine suffering [makes] him doubly interesting" (38), as it testifies to his emotional and intellectual potential. In this, he contrasts with his university friends, "who strayed into Aristotle in the intervals of Perspiration" (11). His emotional and intellectual qualities are matched by his physical delicacy. He is a "bloke [who] really has awful headaches, like a girl" (33), prompting two ladies to lend him their smelling bottles, is suspected of shedding tears at college, and sobs heartrendingly in the asylum. Eventually, he exerts himself, and is moreover rescued by the heroine's John Bull-like muscular brother, who has become a fireman to be able to support his impoverished mother and sister. The novel is full of scheming physicians, wrongly incarcerated or mistreated nervous men and women, and poor madmen who cannot get access to an asylum. It also describes a mysterious recuperation from amnesia. With consummate irony, the uncle who has signed the forms that condemn Alfred to imprisonment in a madhouse ultimately turns out to be the only truly imbecile member of the family, and the father's obsession with money is diagnosed as a form of monomania.

In Braddon's *Lady Audley's Secret*, the habits of Robert Audley, "the most vacillating and unenergetic of men," invite Lady Audley to describe him as a nervous hypochondriac and then as a monomaniac.[26] While attempting to read the symptoms of crime and madness, the novel's amateur detective is thus re-inscribed as the sought madman. As Lady Audley accuses her suspicious brother-in-law, it becomes a matter of skillful scheming for him to combat her allegations: "Are you going mad, Mr. Audley, and do you select me as the victim of your monomania?" (266). Eventually, it is the murderous, bigamous, and possibly hereditarily insane Lady Audley herself—and all of these attributes are part of her sensationally revealed secret—who is tricked into lifelong incarceration in an asylum abroad. Robert has to reassert his dormant energies. He investigates his friend's death, saves his uncle from a powerful, willful woman, and woos the good woman he loves. As the enterprising female social climber is successfully captured, the languid male aristocrat has to become interested in a worthy enterprise that demands an exertion of all his energies. This twist in the narrative initiates a rejection of the hypersensitive hero's resistance and reaffirms ideals of vigor and strength.

Similarly, Walter Hartright in Collins's best-known sensation novel, *The Woman in White*, sheds his nervousness as he reasserts a self-confident masculinity through offstage ordeals abroad. Janet Oppenheim has suggested that Hartright is an "important fictional figure from [this] transitional period of Victorian manliness,"[27] yet in a more recent reassessment of the novel, Peter Thoms has convincingly shown that the "transitory period" Hartright spends in a primeval Central American forest functions as "a process of rebirth" and "a crucial period in his growth."[28] Hartright shares this reaffirmation of an assertive manliness with Robert Audley and to a certain extent Alfred Hardie as well as with Collins's other early heroes. As I shall show in detail in the rest of this chapter, it was reserved for Collins's later novels to reclaim love and longing from narratives of sickness and the sensitive hero from allegations of effeminacy and morbidity.

Wilkie Collins's extensive *oeuvre*, in fact, maps the development of the man of feeling both in the way he is treated by society and its institutions and in the novels' treatment of his failures or successes. As early as *Hide and Seek* (1854), ridicule of Victorian health crazes paves the way for the new nervous, nostalgic hero, but at this point the description of the physically strong, cheerful, and careless protagonist is humorous.

Zack is "the perfection of healthy muscular condition," with "a thoroughly English red and white complexion," and "the most thoughtless of human beings.... In short, Zack was a manly, handsome fellow, a thorough Saxon, every inch of him; and (physically speaking at least) a credit to the parents and the country that had given him birth."[29] When he decides to become an artist, he starts by practicing leapfrogs in the studio. Although the nervous, physically delicate hero of *Basil* (1852) anticipates the transformation of masculinity that becomes central in the novels of the 1870s and 1880s, in this early novel, the sensationally detailed transgressions of the sensual woman who deceives the delicate hero displace interest in the proper masculine. Basil falls madly in love with a physically well-developed, fleshy, but emotionally and intellectually insipid woman, who breaks his heart and almost drives him insane. His lovesickness results in physical illness.[30] The experimentation with gender boundaries in the sensation novel marks it as an arena in which active (anti-) heroines and passive (anti-) heroes are played out against each other. As we shall see, Collins's *No Name* exemplifies both the antiheroine's transgressions (and her failure and successful reclamation) and the dismissal of the weak anti-hero in favor of a hero who is both physically and morally strong. In this, it further accentuates a similar alignment in *The Woman in White*, while the later novels show a significant departure from mid-Victorian ideals of masculinity.

Androgyny and Transition

The Woman in White promises to show "what a Woman's patience can endure, and what a Man's resolution can achieve" (9). Hartright's tested fortitude puts him in strong contrast to Laura's effeminate uncle, Mr. Fairlie, who strikingly fails to exert himself to save his niece. Female debility comes dangerously close to madness in the novel, and can therefore be easily mistaken for it. Yet it is interesting, not repulsive, whereas male nervousness is associated with effeminacy, as a contemptible lack of "a Man's resolution." The most nervous man in the novel, Mr. Fairlie is also the most risible. Laura's and Mr. Fairlie's nervous susceptibilities are the same and yet other.[31] Whereas Laura is seen to be "nursing that essentially feminine malady, a slight headache" (31), "Mr. Fairlie's selfish affectation and Mr. Fairlie's wretched nerves meant one and the same thing" (37). His effeminate body is diagnosed as diseased: "He had a frail, languidly-fretful, over-refined look—something singularly and unpleasantly delicate in its association with a man" (36). Hartright returns from his strengthening experiences to save the delicate woman whom he loves, and who has been declared dead, as well as her half-sister, a strong, almost masculine, antiheroine, who has been emaciated and emasculated, as it were, by a fever. In its focus on a transgressing (anti-) heroine and its stereotyping of effeminate peevish men, *No Name*, published two years after *The Woman in White*, subscribes even more directly to this topos. Its idealization of heroic manliness best illustrates the early development of Collins's heroes. Captain Kirke's worth has been tested in the China Seas. He arrives just in time on his aptly named ship, the *Deliverance*, to rescue the strong and scheming, but by now endearingly helpless, heroine. The novel's emphasis on the transgressing woman admittedly pushes the problematics of the hero's manliness to the margins of the narrative, but its juxtaposition of proper forms of femininity and masculinity deserves a closer look.

Like most sensation novels of the 1860s, *No Name* exposes ostensibly ideal family life in Victorian Britain. It concentrates on power in the family, on physical as well as emotional violence at home, on the "domestic Gothic" of the sensation genre.[32] Anticipating Collins's mission novels, it concerns moreover the legal issues of adultery and illegitimacy. In many of his novels, the law, in fact, plays a central role and is attacked for its inconsistencies and inhumanity. The disputation of wills in *No Name*, however, also articulates a struggle of will power—a quality that the effeminate men in the novel lack and the strong, transgressing women have in abundance. The balance between the genders is restored as the disputed inheritance is given to one of the few manly men and the only consummately passive woman, while her transgressing sister is put in her place by an illness that, significantly, leaves her physically weakened and morally chastened.

The opening chapters introduce the emphatically happy household of the Vanstones, an ostensibly perfect Victorian family. Yet after the parents' sudden deaths, the family lawyer discloses a never-suspected dark past. Respectable, florid Andrew Vanstone, a happy husband and fond father of two grown-up daughters, has been guilty of adultery, or more precisely, of a pseudo-bigamous arrangement. Married as a young man to a debauched woman along the lines of Bertha Mason in Charlotte Brontë's *Jane Eyre*, he had been saved at the brink of suicide by one Major Kirke, the father of the novel's hero, who negotiated a pecuniary arrangement with the woman. She then settled in New Orleans, her probable place of origin, which again links her to Bertha Mason. Casting the debauched wife as a type, Collins refuses to make more of her dubious past. Love and lovesickness, however, receive their customary defense: Vanstone returned to England and fell in love with a woman who agreed, as Jane Eyre would not have done, to live with him as his wife despite his prior attachment. After almost thirty years they are finally able to marry on the death of the first Mrs. Vanstone. But in annulling his will, this marriage disinherits their illegitimate children. After Mr. Vanstone's sudden death in a railway accident, his second wife dies while giving birth to a stillborn boy. This series of unfortunate events leaves the Vanstone daughters penniless, "nobody's children" with "no name."

As in many of Wilkie Collins's novels, adultery and illegitimacy are sympathetically treated, while the law and society are the culprits. Vanstone's fortune goes to his elder brother, whom their father disinherited, and then, after his own death, to the brother's sickly son, Noel. While Mr. Vanstone's older daughter, Norah, is resigned to become a governess in a stereotypically nasty rich family reminiscent of those exposed in Anne Brontë's *Agnes Grey* (1847), the younger daughter, Magdalen, vows to reclaim her fortune. As the novel traces her struggles under the "opposing influences of Good and Evil," as it is melodramatically put in the preface, it becomes frighteningly clear that Magdalen will stop at nothing: "It is your [society's] law—not hers. She only knows it as the instrument of a vile oppression, an insufferable wrong. The sense of that wrong haunts her, like a possession of the devil."[33] Although Magdalen's obsession is detailed with sympathy, and there is a tentative admiration of her daring attempts to free "herself from all homedependence, . . . to run what mad risks she pleases, in perfect security from all home-control" (180), they lead to her depravity. By carrying out her ruthless schemes, she loses moral and then physical substance, pathetically dwindling away.

Magdalen's exploitation of Noel Vanstone's admittedly repulsive physical and moral weaknesses shows her at her worst. She plots to marry this "abject mannikin" (291) under an assumed name, and his feebleness is then comically accentuated by the contrast with his emphatically strong wife, who, although only eighteen, is blooming in "full physical maturity, . . . in right of her matchless health and strength" (14): "suffering! . . . I don't know the meaning of the word: if there's anything the matter with me, I'm too well" (15). Yet Magdalen does suffer, after all; as a transgressing woman redeemed, she lives up to her name. In the opening chapter the narrator suggests that her name simply externalizes her "self-contradictory" nature, but this seeming contradiction proves as ominous in foreshadowing her ordeal as her complaint about being "too well:"

> Magdalen! It was a strange name to have given her?... Surely, the grand old Bible name—suggestive of a sad and sombre dignity; recalling, in its first association, mournful ideas of penitence and seclusion—had been here, as events had turned out, inappropriately bestowed? Surely, this self-contradictory girl had perversely accomplished one contradiction more, by developing into a character which was out of all harmony with her own christian [sic] name! (15)

Her "overflowing physical health" and "exuberant vitality" (14) contrast sharply with the moral and physical feebleness not only of the overindulged Noel, but of the man Magdalen is in love with, the spineless sneak Frank Clare. Handsome "in his own effeminate way," Frank embodies the tearful sentimental antihero at his lowest: "His beard was still in its infancy; and nascent lines of whisker traced their modest way sparely down his cheeks. His gentle wandering brown eyes would have looked to better advantage in a woman's face—they wanted spirit and firmness to fit them for the face of a man" (41). Thus furnished, Frank meets with steady ridicule. "Ready tears" rise in his eyes (116). He is "so dull and helpless" in his "sentimental resignation" (76). That "his gentle melancholy of look and manner [has] greatly assisted his personal advantages" counts against him (78). He is lampooned as a "convalescent Apollo" (78), an apt description for most sentimental antiheroes: "His soft brown eyes wandered about the room with a melting tenderness; his hair was beautifully brushed; his delicate hands hung over the arms of his chair with a languid grace" (78).

The explanation for Magdalen's love, whose strength and will disqualify her as a sentimental heroine until both are broken, is equally satiric. As her parents put it, "[s]he is resolute and impetuous, clever and domineering; she is not one of those model women who want a man to look up to, and to protect them—her beau-ideal (though she may not think it herself) is a man she can henpeck" (77). Frank's "small regular features" are, together with his want of "spirit and firmness" (41), denounced as unmanly and revealed as indicators of moral frailty. His delicate beauty does not disqualify him as a desirable hero, but it obscures his petulance. Not blinded by love, Magdalen's sister Norah clearly sees that he "is selfish, he is ungrateful, he is ungenerous" (69). His helplessness is a symptom of his idleness, and his tears are meant to appeal to Magdalen's sympathy.

Noel is Frank's caricatured double. While Magdalen views Frank through the eyes of love, the same physical attributes disgust her in the man she loathes. This "frail, flaxen-haired, self-satisfied, little man," with a complexion "as delicate as a young girl's" and a "weak little white moustache" (281), begins to waste away after his marriage: "The poor weak creature! The abject, miserable little man!" (429). Noel becomes the helpless object of a power struggle between his scheming wife and his "domestic treasure" (205), the old Swiss housekeeper, Mrs. Lecount. This subaltern servant subverts the rule of her English master by manipulating his will. She is in this sense another transgressing woman who masks her power with her domestic functions. The women's struggle over the direction of Noel's dwindling will power and the contents of his last will shows the "mannikin" as a pitiful victim and strong women as perverted.

Both elder Vanstones having died intestate, Noel leaves two wills, one written under his wife's influence and one, literally, at his vengeful housekeeper's dictation. This second will disinherits his "false" wife, leaving her again with "no name:" "No legacy of any kind is bequeathed to her. Her name is not once mentioned in her husband's will" (457). Magdalen's conniving becomes increasingly desperate. She gains entrance to the new heir's house as a parlor maid in a daring scheme that further underlines the subversive stratagems of transgressing women. Magdalen's only redemption is her inability to succeed, which undercuts the fascination with which her plots are delineated and eventually restores her to the novel's deserving hero, Captain Kirke. Ultimately, the inheritance goes to a peripheral character who happens to fall in love with Norah. The resigned sister is thus rewarded. As an ideal of virtuous womanhood, however, she recedes too far into the background to qualify as a foil to her sister. It is repeatedly made clear that Magdalen is more interesting than her dull, largely offstage, counterpart, Norah.[34] Used up by her final attempt to gain control of her husband's last will, Magdalen collapses: "Her energy was gone; her powers of resistance were crushed" (672). Arriving just in time, Captain Kirke finds her hidden in the "squalid by-ways of London, . . . cast friendless and helpless, on the mercy of strangers, by illness which had struck her prostrate, mind and body alike" (701). When Kirke takes her up in his manly arms, her mind wanders "back to old days at home," and she mistakes him for her father (699). Safely infantilized, she can recuperate from the perversions wrought by her will power to begin a new life as Kirke's grateful wife. The traces of illness in her face leave "a delicacy in its outline which add[s] refinement to her beauty" (737). The strong, scheming young woman is cut down to size; the reformed wife is more delicate in her features as well as in her morals.

The novel's juxtaposition of manly ideals and successful men is more interesting. In contrast to Kirke, Magdalen's first suitor, Frank, is a failure abroad, although he becomes a successful sycophant in England. Indeed, his pathetic helplessness ensures his advancement as, in the words of his outspoken father, "one of the legislators of this Ass-ridden country" (541). Having returned to England stowed away on Kirke's ship, Frank marries a rich colonialist's widow old enough to be his grandmother and thus joins the other feeble members of the ruling classes. This contrast between enfeebling cultivation and a hard life in tropical or arid places that test manliness partly reasserts the ideologies of muscularity. Kirke's successes in the China Seas stand out against both Frank's pitiful flight from a dull position as clerk in China and with the armchair imperialist Noel, whose dressed-up, wizen body is more grotesque than any of his exotic "litter of curiosities" (282). Yet Kirke's true heroism manifests itself in his rescue of Magdalen, whom he marries, regardless of society's judgment of her former ruthlessness, and thereafter "nurses . . . with a woman's tenderness."[35] Even Kirke, Collins's most heroic hero, shares the tenderness, if not the susceptibilities, of Collins's increasingly delicate heroes.

In Collins's next novel, *Armadale* (1866), big, handsome Allan Armadale meets with fond ridicule; his empty-headed naïveté sets off the sympathetically portrayed emotional susceptibility and intellectual superiority of the novel's real hero Midwinter, Allan's secret namesake and double, "a slim, dark, undersized man."[36] In *The Moonstone* (1868), the biggest Englishman more pointedly figures as the morally weakest, most corrupt, character. The real thief of the moonstone is the eminently respectable, hypocritically pious philanthropist Godfrey Ablewhite. That this muscular Christian serves as the novel's villain paves the way for physically unprepossessing, often awkward heroes, whose delicacy contrasts forcefully with Godfrey's self-confident, grand exterior. By eulogizing his "magnificent head," "his charming voice and his irresistible smile," Miss Clack inadvertently parodies the "Christian Hero."[37] The ridicule of stereotyped big rosy Englishmen as part of the reaction against the ideologies and aesthetics of muscular Christianity generates a salutary exposure of the healthy hero. It is perfected in *Man and Wife*, as it takes up the "social question [of] the present rage for muscular exercises on the health and morals of the rising generation of Englishmen" (viii).

A controversial novel about the inconsistencies of marriage laws in Victorian Britain and about the moral as well as physical dangers of athleticism, *Man and Wife* witnesses a turning point in the development of Collins's heroes. Geoffrey Delamayn embodies the healthy muscular villain. Cultivated only physically, he is "a magnificent animal" (77): "The modern gentleman was young and florid, tall and strong. [His] features were as perfectly regular and as perfectly unintelligent as human features can be" (76). Sir Patrick is nostalgic for intellectually refined men of sense and sensibility, who in his judgment have vanished from society. Geoffrey's physical and moral demise proves him right. Having exhausted his "vital force" (489), he collapses during a race; he also plots the murder of his unwanted wife, who after his death marries the old, old-fashioned, but nostalgically idealized Sir Patrick. A second plot unites tearful Arnold to Sir Patrick's pretty niece. Frail and feeling men are the true heroes and deserving husbands of this novel.

In Collins's subsequent novels of the 1870s, the contrast between muscular men of the world and sentimental heroes recurs endlessly. In *Miss or Mrs.?* (1871), rough, robust, and self-made Turlington is outdone by his rival in love, the romantically named Launcelot Linzie, "a slim, nimble, curly-headed young gentleman," who discovers Turlington's dark past and saves the lives of the heroine and her incapacitated father.[38] In *Poor Miss Finch* (1872), Oscar Dubourg is not only beautiful in a girlish way, fragile and epileptic as well as lovesick and melancholic, but also more irresolute and sensitive than his nasty twin. "He was a little too effeminate for my taste," declares Madame Pratolungo, the delightful would-be revolutionary and first-person narrator through most of the book: "In common with all women, I like a man to be a man. There was, to my mind, something weak and womanish in ... this Dubourg.[39] Poor blind Miss Finch unfortunately relies on her temporarily restored ability to see and is tricked into marrying Nugent, the wrong twin, although she can tell the brothers apart by touching them. Nostalgia for the time before her sight was restored leads her to discover the deception. Eventually, she is united with Oscar. Madame Pratolungo has to acknowledge that her initial preference for the more resolute twin was the result of common prejudice in favor of energetic men:

> A man with delicately-strung nerves says and does things which often lead us to think more meanly of him than he deserves.... A man provided with nerves vigorously constituted is provided also with a constitutional health and hardihood which express themselves brightly in his manners, and which lead to a mistaken impression that his nature is what it appears to be on the surface.... In the last

of these typical men, I saw reflected—Nugent. In the first—Oscar. (vol. 2, 274)

The identical twin brothers of *Poor Miss Finch* pointedly exemplify the incongruity between surface attractions and hidden qualities, but it is an important theme in all of Collins's later novels. The prologue of *Man and Wife* highlights the "strong personal contrast" between "a dashing, handsome man" with "energy in his face" and "an inbred falseness under it," on the one hand, and the "steady foundation of honour and truth" of his "slow and awkward" counterpart (11–12) on the other hand. All further developments of the novel's tortuous plots reaffirm this alignment. Similarly, in *The New Magdalen* (1873), Horace Holmcroft is morally weak and physically handsome, with "his clear complexion, his bright blue eyes, and the warm amber tint in his light Saxon hair."[40] His physical largeness, which sets off his moral pettiness, contrasts sharply with his rival's slight stature: Julian Gray is "of not more than the middle height" (132–33). Like the aestheticized sickliness of the sentimental hero, his pallor highlights the "lustrous brightness of [his eyes]" (117) and indicates his deep nature. As expected, the pale, slight man of feeling is the desirable hero.

In *The Law and the Lady* (1875), the resolute heroine pushes her sensitive husband to the margins of the narrative as she strives to clear his name and restore his peace of mind. In fact, the novel boasts a female amateur detective as well as an interesting treatment of doubled weak men. Eustace Macallan, tried for the murder of his first wife, suffers under the Scottish verdict of "not proven." His second wife's resolute enterprise offsets his "state of nervous depression."[41] Indeed, Valeria's attraction to Eustace's gentleness and sweetness suggests a reversal of traditional gender roles: "He looks at me with the tenderest and gentlest eyes (of a light brown) that I ever saw in the countenance of a man. His smile is rare and sweet; his manner, perfectly quiet and retiring" (11). This resolute woman is no transgressive anti-heroine, but then she exerts her energies to save her husband. Similarly, androgynous Miserrimus Dexter externalizes Eustace's effeminacy: "He would have looked effeminate, but for the manly proportions of his throat and chest.... Never had a magnificent head and body been more hopelessly ill-bestowed than in this instance!" (173). Dexter's combination of vulnerability and violence, as well as his passion for both Valeria and her predecessor, marks him as the sensitive antihero's double. After Valeria's discovery that the first wife died not by a murderer's but by her own hand, convinced by Dexter of her husband's indifference, and after Dexter's destruction, Valeria and Eustace are reunited. Eustace's recuperation coincides, indeed is symbolized by, Dexter's death. The destruction of the androgynous madman reaffirms the happy marriage.

What is more important and indeed a transgression that is not retracted or modified is the novel's emphasis on Valeria's nostalgic obsession. Her love for Eustace and her nostalgia for the happy time before her discovery of her husband's dubious past enable her to succeed where the law has failed: "Let me see for myself, if his lawyers have left nothing for his wife to do. Did they love him as I love him?" (109). Nostalgia urges her to reclaim the love they once cherished: "My mind wandered backward once more, and showed me another picture in the golden gallery of the past" (15). Nostalgia is a transgressive desire in a society that values progress and energy. We have already seen how in *The Two Destinies* (1876) a susceptibility to visions is affirmed as spiritual and practical in restoring the love of the past in defiance of the physicians who have diagnosed it as a disease. In *The Fallen Leaves* (1879), empathy connects a feminized hero to the child-prostitute he rescues and eventually marries. *Jezebel's Daughter* (1880) lists a series of weak men who are victimized by a scheming foreign woman, but the novel is more important for its sympathetic portrayal of one Jack Straw, a version of the Holy Fool, who has become one of "the poor martyrs of the madhouse."[42] *The Black Robe* (1881) juxtaposes two sensitive, victimized men who are in love with the same woman. The death of the undeserving suitor facilitates a nostalgic return to the deserving, initially rejected, weaker man, after his counterpart's death has purged the negative qualities of his feminized emotionalism.[43] Increasingly, Collins's novels introduce new men (and women) of sensibility who resemble the feeling heroes and heroines of the novel of sensibility, but are confronted with Victorian ideologies of manly self-assertion. Emotional as well as physical delicacy are ambiguously presented in his earlier works, but become the protagonists' most redeeming qualities in the novels of the 1870s and 1880s—a development that culminates in Ovid Vere's fainting fit in *Heart and Science* (1883). Its use of medical discourses merits a close reading.

Overpowering Vitality: *Heart and Science*

The consummate realization of the new *fin-de-siècle* (anti-) hero is undoubtedly fainting, enervated, and nostalgic Ovid Vere in

Heart and Science. Aptly set when the "weary old nineteenth century had advanced into the last twenty years of its life," the novel opens with the delineation of a brilliant young man who has received a "warning from overwrought Nature."[44] Ovid's nervous exhaustion recalls the sickly heroes of the novel of sensibility while it engages late-nineteenth-century discourses on nervous diseases and psychological theories. Intended to be a novel about vivisection, *Heart and Science* is a mission novel that explores a series of other concerns as well. C. S. Wiesenthal has suggested that it is, in a sense, about experimental neurophysiology, "addressing issues at the very cutting edge, so to speak, of contemporary Darwinian science."[45] Detailing the heroine's partial catalepsy, her paralysis and temporary amnesia, it displays the entire symptomatology of hysteria as posited in contemporary psychiatric thought. To Wiesenthal, Wilkie Collins "seems to seize upon the reassuring possibility of the organic localization of hysterical disorder as a potential answer to the vexed 'mysteries' of psychosomatic pathology."[46] However, the propagators of theories of an "organic localization" of sensibility in the novel include the vivisectionist Dr Benjulia, the aptly named Mr. Null, and the villainous woman of science, Mrs. Gallilee. Ovid Vere, one of the few good physicians in sensation fiction and a sufferer from nervous exhaustion himself, cures his beloved more with devoted attention than with a vague new *deus ex machina* cure.

In a novel as tellingly titled as *Heart and Science*, it is not surprising that sensibility is not only reasserted as a symptom of moral superiority, but also reclaimed from medical narratives. The choice of the protagonists' names contributes to the stark contrast between heart and science and their transcendence in Ovid's treatment of Carmina. Ovid Vere is named after the Latin poet, probably because of his importance as a writer of love poetry, and the Latin word *vere* [true]. The name of the half-Italian heroine, Carmina, meaning "song" or "poem," links her to him. Mr. Null's name describes his status in the medical profession; Mrs. Gallilee's indicates her focus on a scientific worldview. Miss Minerva, the mannish governess, whose adoration of Ovid first turns her against Carmina and then induces her to defend her, is named after the Roman goddess of wisdom, poetry, and medicine. Ironically, she is neuralgic and nervous, qualities that place her in opposition to the fleshy amateur scientist Mrs. Gallilee, Ovid's mother. A staunch defender of love, Miss Minerva is physically frail and on the side of the sickly hero and heroine.[47]

The hero's fainting fit carries the promotion of the weepy, virtuously weak man of feeling to its logical conclusion. At the same time, it ties in with the novel's antivivisectionist mission in that it accentuates the moral difference between the physically strong, heartless villains, and the men and women of feeling. Shortly after his hysterical outburst over the squashing of a beetle, Ovid swoons in the arms of the heroine, who herself has been taken ill after seeing a stray dog run over in the street. Detailing Ovid's illness, the novel heavily draws on the late-Victorian concept of an exhaustible quantity of energy in nature as well as a corresponding depletion of energy in man, his *vis nervosa*. Ovid's collapse follows the killing of an animal as well as his stuttering attempts to tell Carmina that he likes her, but it is also attributed to the fact that "physically and mentally he had no energy left" (108). Yet what the novel makes clear is that reserves of vital forces, like those of physical strength, differ and, in sentimental fashion, reflect a reciprocal relationship with moral strength. The "overpowering vitality" of Ovid's mother, who shares a fondness for cold-hearted dissection with Benjulia, the Faustian vivisectionist, contrasts decisively with the high sensibility of the novel's hero and heroine:

> In her eagerness to facilitate [Ovid's] departure [to Canada], she proposed to superintend the shutting up of his house.... She even thought of the cat. The easiest way to provide for the creature would be of course to have her poisoned; but Ovid was so eccentric in some things, that practical suggestions were thrown away on him.... Mrs. Gallilee's overpowering vitality was beginning to oppress her son (127).

The juxtaposition of the sensitive, delicate young man with a powerful woman—in this case, his own mother—is of course a recurring topos in Wilkie Collins's fiction. In *Heart and Science*, the contrast between praiseworthy delicacy and heartlessness is an integral part of the novel's antivivisection mission and its criticism of amateur scientists in general. The ruthless zeal of a woman of science brings into focus ideologies of energy and will power as well as the invasion of the home by the craze for natural science in Victorian Britain. Mrs. Gallilee's "eagerness,... practical suggestions, [and] overpowering vitality" fulfill the criteria for the enterprising Victorian male, which the men in the novel (with the vivisectionist as the telling exception) notably lack. The mother's investment of her energies in amateur scientific events renders the Gallilee house uncomfortable as a home. That Mrs. Gallilee is styled as "complete a mistress of the practice of domestic virtue as of [science]" (66) sarcastically refers to her skill as a hostess of scientific dinner parties as well as to her suppression of her mild-tempered husband. Submerged "under her powder and paint," she plays the sociable hostess and perfect mother, and also eagerly seizes the role of Carmina's "second mother," "play[ing] the part to perfection" (69, 66). She endorses what is considered fashionable. Her guests appreciate the scientific events organized by this "tender nurse of half-developed tadpoles" (127), a characterization that again calls her motherly qualities into question while parodying her eagerness to play all her parts to perfection for fashionable society.

Mrs. Lecount, Noel's "domestic treasure" in *No Name*, has prefigured the scientific, powerful woman. This novel and *Heart and Science*, in fact, form revealing focus points of the development of Collins's (anti-) heroes, in that Captain Kirke exemplifies the topos of manliness tested abroad, while Ovid represents Collins's most outspoken endorsement of the new man of sensibility and sympathy. *Heart and Science*, furthermore, returns to issues central to the earlier novel. In *No Name*, written in 1862, but set years earlier, Magdalen first encounters Mrs. Lecount's aquarium in 1846, when "the art of keeping fish and reptiles as domestic pets had not [yet] been popularized in England" (200). Magdalen consequently recoils "in irrepressible astonishment and disgust, from the first specimen of an Aquarium that she had ever seen" (200). The headless frogs escaping into the corridors in *Heart and Science*, on the other hand, are part of a dinner party and only astonish skeptical servants. This novel was written and is set at a time when amateur infatuation with the natural sciences was a fashion. Mrs. Gallilee's cold-hearted dissections are not only condoned, but admired. While Benjulia attempts to conceal his laboratory, there is no such compunction at Mrs. Gallilee's dinner parties. As Barbara T. Gates puts it, "Collins seems to have liked Benjulia in the way that Dickens liked Fagin."[48] The downfall of Mrs. Gallilee, by contrast, is detailed with farcical relish.

Mrs. Gallilee's crushing energy allows her to combine her success at scientific social events with strict order at home, yet this energy is her most damning characteristic. In *Heart and Science*, as in *No Name*, will power is a central theme explicitly linked to the writing, influencing, and interpreting of the wills of weak men. The last will of Carmina's father appoints her aunt, Mrs. Gallilee, her guardian, who will receive her fortune if the girl dies childless. Stout, with "rather a round and full face" (74), Mrs. Gallilee is the strongest woman in the house, indeed the strongest, most vital member of the household, whereas the men are variations of sentimental men of feeling. Mr. Mool, the blushing lawyer—"a human anomaly" (70)—stands in stark contrast to the self-confident lawyers in the earlier novels as well as to his overpowering client, who prefers to dissect the flowers he tends and admires. Ovid, enfeebled by nervous exhaustion, is sentimental and romantic, qualities that his mother has long suppressed. His amiable but powerless stepfather is "a lazy, harmless old fellow" (48). In a household of women, where the father is treated like a child while all the real children are female, Carmina is at the mercy of the strongest woman once Ovid has been sent abroad for his health. Male authority is subverted to make way for a hierarchical matriarchy that at once accentuates and parodies the concept of the survival of the fittest. The father's reassertion of power at the novel's end seems at first a reactionary conclusion to its exploration of gender relations in the Victorian home. But it also marks the triumph of an old-fashioned anti-hero of sensibility over a modern woman of science.

Both *No Name* and *Heart and Science* set feeble men against powerful women who dictate and reinterpret the last wills of other feeble men. In both novels, these women's intriguing plots are unsuccessful, but whereas in *No Name* the disputed inheritance is eventually restored to a good (male) cousin who happens to marry the passive sister, in *Heart and Science* a group of feeble men rises up against the domineering society woman, who has attempted to misuse another feeble man's last will for financial gain. The crushing of Mrs. Gallilee's will power—and the battle over will power is closely linked to disputes over last wills—is not so much the domestication of a strong woman as a prison break from ideologies of energy and enterprise. Weak men and women reclaim their right to indulge in lovesickness and nostalgia. While susceptible heroes and, more frequently, heroines are of course obvious choices as the most useful protagonists in sensation novels, the significance of vitality in the characterization of strong villains, whatever their sex, also highlights the rejection of enterprising, muscular, assertive characters.

In Collins's subsequent novels, the heroes are unambiguously sentimental, sensitive, and full of exquisite sensibilities. In *I Say No* (1884), for example Alban Morris, a drawing teacher like Hartright in *The Woman in White*, is the heroine's lovesick lover, although his effeminate rival's pitiful end shows that the development of the sensitive hero is not always straightforward. Mirabel, an "effeminate pet of drawing-rooms and boudoirs," is a "weak womanish creature, with rings on his little white hands;" he "looks a poor weak creature, in spite of his big beard."[49] Yet he is only a coward, not a villain, and, as a pet parson, has much in common with Godfrey Ablewhite, the hypocrite in *The Moonstone*, including a manly, booming voice. Mirabel's fainting fit is moreover outdone by the lovesickness that induces Alban to shed "hot tears" (vol. 1, 82).

Even more strikingly, in *The Evil Genius* (1886), a sentimental lawyer counterpoises the selfishness exhibited by all the other protagonists. He saves a "wretched little fish" by putting it back into the water "with humane gentleness of handling"—although a little girl protests that "that's not sport!"[50] His contemplation of the adulterous love at the center of the tortuous plot brings into focus a recurring condemnation of conventions, of the rules of society: "Is there something wrong in human nature? Or something wrong in human laws? All that is best and noblest in us feels the influence of love—and the rules of society declare that an accident of position shall decide whether love is a virtue or a crime" (194). A novel about custody laws, *The Evil Genius* emphatically points out the soft, sensitive, and sentimental side of its good men. To separate even a weak man from his child is shown to be tragic, and many tears are shed over the cruel law. The hard mother-in-law is the evil genius of the title, not the young adulterous governess, whose own heartless mother has neglected her after her father's death. The end of the novel sees all fatherless children re-equipped with their lost fathers or, alternatively, with the father's good friend as a parental substitute. In the conclusion of this study, I shall further bring out the significance of this "re-domestication" of lost fathers—who double as new men of feeling—for Collins's recuperation of nostalgia. Like the revision of nostalgic reading pleasures, they become symbolic of important shifts in the representation of domesticity, privacy, and above all, nostalgic longing.

Published in the same year as *The Evil Genius*, *The Guilty River* (1886) returns to the frequently used device of a "double" to distinguish a hypersensitive hero from his androgynous, violently emotional counterpart. It is once again a story about love and clashing clan issues, as yet prefiguring the new, growing emphasis on domestic issues, on feeling family men rather than on lovesick would-be lovers. Gerard Roylake returns to England as the heir of an estate, "look[ing] more like a foreigner than an Englishman."[51] He spends his days catching moths for his studies until he retraces "woodland paths [that are] familiar to [him] in the by-gone time" (248) and meets Cristel, the miller's daughter. His nostalgia for his boyhood, for a time when his friendship with Cristel was not considered improper, suffuses their meetings: "Days, happy days that were past, revived. Again, I walked hand in hand with my mother, among the scenes that were round me" (314). His suppressed anxieties, however, become manifest in the mysterious figure of his nameless rival, a deaf mulatto:

To my thinking, [his eyes] were so entirely beautiful that they had no right to be in a man's face. I might have felt the same objection to the pale delicacy of his complexion, [and] to his finely shaped sensitive lips, but for two marked peculiarities in him which would have shown me to be wrong—that is to say: the expression of power about his head, and the signs of masculine resolution presented by his mouth and chin. (277)

The nameless man's deafness externalizes Gerard's sense of isolation in society; his mixed racial origin, Gerard's inability to reject his foreign education; his smoldering passion for Cristel, Gerard's hopeless attempts to suppress his growing love. His nervousness and effeminacy mirror Gerard's own so closely that it causes unease. Gerard repeatedly describes himself as "depressed." He monitors his own increasing depression by observing the other's "nervous irritability" (246) and "hysterical passion" (281). He watches his double "burst into tears" (292) and later "burst[s] out crying" (343) himself when he finds Cristel gone. His jealousy and ill humor trigger and are externalized as the "demoniacal rage and hatred" (259) that make his too-beautiful double look ugly. Like Dexter's in *The Law and the Lady*, the double's androgyny is an exaggerated version of the hero's feminine susceptibility. While Gerard's own languid way of life contrasts sharply with his double's will power, which is linked to his "vile temper" and suppressed "demoniacal rage" (259), he is at once repelled and attracted by the other's beauty. The recognition of his own features frightens, disgusts, and titillates him. As Gerard dwells on the double's "entirely beautiful" eyes and "pale delicacy," he remarks that such features have "no right" to be found in a man. His denunciation of course expresses his anxiety about his own masculinity. At the same time, the "expression of power [that makes] it impossible to mistake the stranger for a woman" (254) also threatens Gerard. After the double's death abroad, Cristel and Gerard eventually return from a self-imposed exile to be reunited at home. The mixture of attraction and repulsion that men of sensibility feel for their doubles clearly articulates their self-conscious struggles with themselves. These disconcerting negative examples underscore the complexity of Collins's representation of his sensitive heroes.

In short, the development of the new hero of sensibility can be nicely traced in the succession of Collins's novels. It is helped by the continual defense of socially unacceptable behavior, lack of will power, love at first sight, nostalgic lovesickness, and increasingly also yearning lost fathers. Physical pining and harking back to the unrealized possibilities of the past are reclaimed from conceptualizations of effeminacy as well as distinguished from pathologies; instead, they are praised as the virtues of the new hero. Ovid falls in love with Carmina at first sight during their chance meeting in the middle of the street, as Basil does on an omnibus in the earlier novel; unlike Basil, however, Ovid does not err. Most importantly, nostalgia is invested with new power—a power that, often together with emphatic love, can rescue helpless anti-heroes in two ways: through his own nostalgia and that of the similarly empowered heroine. In *The Legacy of Cain* (1888), Collins's novel about phrenology, Eunice's nostalgia for her happy days with her fiancé Philip, before her adoptive sister Helena seduced him, perhaps most pointedly forms an "all-powerful counter-influence" (10) to her visions of her murderous mother. The novel ends with a triumph of love. Philip, whose physiognomy and behavior define him as a weak man, is left to the good influence of the woman who has defeated inherited rage with nostalgic memories of love. In *Blind Love* (1890), completed by Walter Besant after Collins's death, it is likewise Lord Harry's helplessness, when the heroine finds him in a pool of blood after his suicide attempt, that makes her nurse and marry him. Unlike a sentimental hero, he is of a "coarser fibre than herself," which makes her regret that she seems to have "wrecked [her] life in a blind passion."[52] Nonetheless, even her marriage to his dull rival after his death does not kill her love for Lord Harry. Collins's last novel registers the death of his men of tender feelings in the figure of a man of consuming passion. The heroine's nostalgia, however, reaffirms a defense of nostalgic heroes and heroines and of nostalgia for men of feeling: "She has one secret—and only one—which she keeps from her husband. In her dark desk she preserves a lock of Lord Harry's hair. Why? I know not. Blind love doth never wholly die" (316).

The analysis of the self-conscious and critical revaluation of the symptoms and treatments of longing and the nostalgic hero in Wilkie Collins's novels forms an apt conclusion to a study that traces the changing understanding of nostalgia as a constructive emotion and as a way of remembering and imagining. Especially in his creation of new men of sensibility, the fictional treatment of nostalgia's pathology has come full circle. They hark back to the eighteenth-century cult of sensibility and anticipate the new *fin de siècle* antihero, as typified by Oscar Wilde's Dorian Gray or E. M. Forster's men of artistic sensibilities.[53] Nostalgia and its related afflictions are clearly variously treated in the traditional British novel. Longing becomes a clinically detailed pining that is idealized for its symptoms, a Romantic yearning, part of a rejected sentimentality, and then a self-consciously defended attitude that is itself recalled in nostalgia.

Conclusion: Nostalgia Revisited

A CREATIVE EMOTIONAL STATE AND FORM OF MEMORY, NOSTALGIA has been an important formative influence in the traditional eighteenth- and nineteenth-century British novel. Its various roles and functions in the analyzed texts prove that nostalgic fiction is about far more than a sentimentalizing of the past. As they deal differently and often critically with nostalgia, they show that it can be integrative as well as subversive, a virtue and part of individual self-expression. It shapes narratives, while it forms an important theme in the fictions, or fables, of modernity. Its growing pertinence in the course of the eighteenth century moreover sheds a fascinating light on the emergence of new ideals of personal happiness, of individuality and privacy. The eighteenth-century affective revolution changed psychophysical afflictions into emotional states and allowed indulgence in *personal* longing. Growing out of this association of emotional conditions with moral virtues and a contemporaneous interest in memory, nostalgia was essential to the experience of privacy, individuality, and what Roy Porter has termed a new hedonism. This concluding section aims to underline the significance nostalgia had for issues of privacy at the time, as it became primarily a personal, private longing, and played a crucial part in changing attitudes towards private reading habits and expressions of individual, even eccentric, longing. In this, the conclusion will newly highlight novels' re-representations of nostalgic reading pleasures and the nostalgia derived from the retrospective recollection of such private reading pleasures, and then move on to sum up the changing evaluation of the nostalgic imagination, the different answers to pivotal questions as to whose prerogative it is or what its creative potentials can hold.

When Dickens's most autobiographical novel, *David Copperfield*, was published in the middle of the nineteenth century, it not only detailed childhood experiences and celebrated a version of the "Romantic child" that was at once sentimentalized and linked to new theories of mesmerism, but it significantly counted among the narrator's fond retrospects a nostalgic account of his early reading experience. As the Murdstones keep him isolated from other children and increasingly also from his mother and their old servant (formerly the audience of his reading practice), young David Copperfield finds a source of consolation in a range of novels, his dead father's legacy. What follows is a nostalgic description of solitary reading. The Evangelical Murdstones may consider contact with fiction as well as with other children as corruptive, yet the narrator is nostalgic about his happy "escape" into consoling fantasies. His fond recollections of his childhood daydreams are far removed from earlier anxieties about fiction's tendency to confuse or corrupt, to lead to solipsism or inspire masturbatory and escapist fantasies. There are no such warnings in Dickens's description of either reading or daydreaming. On the contrary, David's solitary habits show him to be a sensitive and vulnerable child. The nostalgic description is meant to endear him to a similarly constituted reader, who is furthermore supposed to be sharing similar recollections of childhood reading. The passage needs to be quoted at some length:

> I believe I should have been almost stupefied but for one circumstance. It was this. My father had left a small collection of books in a little room upstairs, to which I had access (for it adjoined my own) and which nobody else in our house ever troubled. From that blessed little room, Roderick Random, Peregrine Pickle, Humphrey Clinker, Tom Jones, the Vicar of Wakefield, Don Quixote, Gil Blas, and Robinson Crusoe, came out, a glorious host, to keep me company. They kept alive my fancy, and my hope of something beyond that place and time,—they, and the Arabian Nights, and the Tales of the Genii,—and did me no harm; for whatever harm was in some of them was not there for me; *I* knew nothing of it. (*DC*, 55–56)

This reader is a "Romantic child," not the corruptive and corruptible child envisioned by the Murdstones. Even Tom Jones's escapades cannot do any harm: "[I] consoled myself under my small troubles (which were great troubles to me), by impersonating my favourite characters in them—as I did—and by putting Mr. and Miss Murdstone into all the bad ones—which I did too. I have been Tom Jones (a child's Tom Jones, a harmless creature) for a week together" (*DC*, 56). An innocent imagination, the narrator argues, cannot be corrupted. This attitude towards fiction contrasts sharply with the anxieties about involvement with fictitious characters that plagued moralists in the previous century and came newly to the fore in the Evangelical movements of the early Victorian age. By contrast, David's fantasies are at once comforting and liberating. His reading experience is solitary, secretive, and conducted in the private, almost hidden, spaces of the house, in a place "which nobody else in our house ever troubled" (*DC*, 55). It moreover fosters fantasies premised on the impersonation of characters, and yet there are no warnings against quixotic confusions of reality and fantasy. Instead, the projection of Mr. and Miss Murdstone into fictional bad characters is refreshing, amusing, and most importantly, fondly recalled by a narrator who has now become an author himself. It is *in retrospect* that this experience is so nostalgically dwelt upon. The remembering narrator fantasizes about the young boy, his younger self, indulging in fictions and fantasies. It forms part of his childhood nostalgia: "This was my only and my constant comfort. When I think of it, the picture always rises in my mind, of a summer evening, the boys at play in the churchyard, and I sitting on my bed, reading as if for life" (*DC*, 56). He ends with a direct appeal to the understanding reader: "The reader now understands, as well as I do, what I was when I came to that point of my youthful history to which I am now coming again" (*DC*, 56). The description of David "reading as if for life" testifies to his sensitivity and establishes an important link to a reader not only engaged in the process of reading at that very moment, but, it is clearly presumed, also able to remember a similar experience of absorbent reading.

David Copperfield is significantly not the only child in Victorian fiction who indulges in "escapist" reading habits that take them out of their miserable surroundings, console them, and give them hope for something "beyond that place and time." They are usually solitary and sensitive. They moreover seek solitude in order to read or fantasize as often as they turn to books to find consolation in their solitude. Most importantly, such episodes tend to recur in retrospective narratives as part of a nostalgically remembered childhood. In *Jane Eyre*, the titular heroine escapes from her tyrannical relatives by concealing herself behind drawn curtains in a window-seat with a book as her favorite companion. She is "shrined in double retirement" (1): "I was then happy: happy at least in my way. I feared nothing but interruption, and that came too soon." (3) Jane dreams over picture-books and particularly enjoys stories. She escapes into fantasies, and yet the reader is clearly led to sympathize with the solitary, self-concealed child and not with her big bullying cousins.

In her insightful article on "The Privacy of the Novel" and likewise more recently in a chapter of her latest book, *Privacy: Concealing the Eighteenth-Century Self*, Patricia Meyer Spacks points out that Jane Eyre's reading "creates a memorable image for reading's self-enclosure . . . a particularly nineteenth-century image."[1] Published in 1847, the novel thereby "draws on and helps to solidify the metaphors of Romanticism."[2] Linking this emergence of new reading habits to the far-reaching reconceptualizations of ideas of privacy and individuality, Spacks further emphasizes the significant changes in attitudes towards reading as a private pleasure that occurred in the course of the eighteenth and nineteenth centuries. If *Jane Eyre* had been published a century before, she argues, Jane "would not have inhabited the same setting or thought of reading in the same way.... If she read for the sake of imaginative stimulation in 1747 or thereabouts, her creator would probably have introduced even into a fictional text some warning about the danger of such stimulation."[3] The threat privacy was thought to pose in the eighteenth century resulted in stringent measures to police particularly women's reading habits and fantasies. Privacy was a social liability, even threat, and so was novel reading, as Roy Porter and Thomas Laqueur have amply pointed out. Increasingly, however, novelists charted imaginative possibilities of privacy.[4] The novel genre, Catherine Gallagher has similarly argued, created new emotional dispositions as readers had to be taught how to read fiction.[5] As it built on a new interest in individual experience and the recollection of the everyday, it also fostered the necessary predispositions. The cultivation of Romantic solitude moreover went hand in hand with the creation of more private spaces in bourgeois households. Recent accounts of eighteenth- and nineteenth-century reading practices have, in fact, stressed these changes in attitudes to privacy. Susan Stewart has argued that reading increasingly took place within a bourgeois domestic setting and therefore within "a milieu of interior space miming the creation of both an interior text and an interior subject."[6] J. Paul Hunter traces the growing need for privacy to urbanization and hence the greater proximity of individuals crowded in restricted spaces, and shows that moral sanctions on fiction ironically demanded more secrecy: cultural disapproval intensified the new phenomenology of solitude.[7] Yet, as we have seen, anxieties about solitary vices (including fiction and masturbation) also grew out of medical conceptualizations that linked physical debility to both solitude and indulgence in fiction. All these alignments gave moralists a range of grounds to oppose solitary reading.

While studies of reading practices have primarily rehearsed the concerns and admonitions of the time, they have given little attention to the positive, indeed pleasurable, aspects of reading, particularly private reading and its nostalgic remembrance. Spacks's analysis of the reader's assertion of privacy stands out in its emphasis on Jane Eyre's positively presented "double retirement" and creative use of picture books to make up her own stories, yet Spacks quickly moves away from this (post-) Romantic image of solitary reading to contrast it with the lack of private spaces in earlier fiction. When Elizabeth Bennet, for example, takes up a book in Austen's *Pride and Prejudice*, she does so in the company of relative strangers and is quickly accosted for doing so.[8] Yet, like Pamela and Clarissa before her, Elizabeth prefers to peruse letters in private, and as we have seen, her reflective rereading of both her sister's letters and later of Darcy's important self-justification are crucial to her reordering of memories. The interruptions of her reading and her solitary rambles only accentuate a need for privacy. While Elinor Dashwood attempts to prevent Marianne's solitariness by stressing the rules of social etiquette, and both sisters are shown to follow extremes in their reactions to society, Elizabeth is more self-possessed in her circumvention of tiresome company and resents the voluntary spies who feast on their neighbors' disgrace. She notably suggests that Lady Lucas "had better have stayed home" rather than coming to condole where "condolence [is] insufferable" (293). Elizabeth's own sociability is more an interest in intimacy and of course an ability to laugh at society's foibles, an amusement she has learned from her father. Her balanced desires for sociability and privacy anticipate Mr. Elliot's distinction between "good company" and "the best company" (150) in *Persuasion*. Like Frank Churchill in *Emma*, however, Mr. Elliot himself affects a false openness. The concealment of their real schemes shows that privacy can also lead to hypocrisy. Nonetheless, both Fanny Price and Anne Elliot find more time and space for private occupations, including reading. They combat and seek loneliness by reading, and their solitary pleasures are part of their individuality. It attests to a new Romantic solitariness that can be shared in a companionate marriage, but still isolates them from the insensible crowds.

With characteristic perspicacity, Austen of course poises affectations of reading pleasure and the solitariness it becomes associated with against the heroines' more balanced attitudes to both solitary withdrawal and reading. In *Pride and Prejudice*, Caroline Bingley takes up a book simply because it is the second volume to the one Darcy is reading. Failing to catch his attention although she is "quite as much engaged in watching Mr. Darcy's progress through his book, as in reading her own," she gives up her book with "a great yawn" (55). Elizabeth's doubts as to whether she could ever find Darcy a congenial reading companion even more pointedly articulate the significance of companionate reading as an intimate, still essentially private affair that could moreover reveal the readers' suitability: "Books—Oh!—no.—I am sure we never read the same, or not with the same feelings" (93). In *Persuasion*, Benwick and Louisa Musgrove fall in love over poetry, and Anne's conversations with Benwick raise Charles Musgrove's expectations as to their possible union simply because Benwick's "head is full of some books that he is reading upon [Anne's] recommendation, and he wants to talk to [her] about them" (131). Such intimacy cannot be accused of fostering solipsism, but it does not conform to ideals of a more general sociability either. In *Mansfield Park*, Fanny's resentment of the Crawfords partly arises from their disruption of her intimate stargazing, reading, and walking with Edmund. Forgotten by him, she withdraws more often into the remote east-room, where she is at least safe from "whatever her unreasonable aunts might require" (74). There she can dwell over the books Edmund has lovingly selected for her or contemplate other mementoes of the past. As I have shown, the east-room is a nostalgic space and remembered in nostalgia once Fanny is exiled to the crowded, urban household in Portsmouth. Her nostalgic duplication of this private space in exile testifies to her successful deployment of nostalgia as a survival strategy. She recreates her private space nostalgically in the small room she shares with her sister Susan:

> By sitting together up stairs, they avoided a great deal of the disturbance of the house; Fanny had peace, and Susan learnt to think it no misfortune to be quietly employed. They sat without a fire; but *that* was a privation familiar even to Fanny, and she suffered the less because reminded by it of the east-room. It was the only point of resemblance. In space, light, furniture, and prospect, there was nothing alike in the two apartments; and she often heaved a sigh at the remembrance of all her books and boxes, and various comforts there.... [A]fter a few days, the remembrance of the said books grew so potent and stimulative, that Fanny found it impossible not to try for books again. There were none in her father's house; but wealth is luxurious and daring—and some of hers found its way to a circulating library. (398)

Fanny's reading is remarkable for the central role nostalgia plays in its description. Nostalgia is stimulative, inducing Fanny to overcome her misery by attempting to reconstruct the most, perhaps only, truly pleasant room of her former home. Her recollections of her early reading pleasures are moreover nostalgic as well, and Fanny consequently "longed to give her [sister] a share in her own first pleasures" (398). They form an intimacy that guarantees the much desired peace and privacy for Fanny, and Susan learns the pleasure of quiet, secluded, and sedentary habits. This is the most positive description of a circulating library in the fiction of the time, although it is true that Fanny at least aims to restrict herself to poetry and biography. By contrast, Charlotte in *Sanditon* is a novel-reading heroine who immediately compares her expenses in the circulating library with the mounting financial distress of Frances Burney's Camilla. The Parkers of course lead her to the library in order to encourage expenses and to check the subscription list. They only find Mrs. Whitby "sitting in her inner room, reading one of her own Novels, for want of Employment" (389). She eagerly darts forward from her "Literary recess" (390) when company arrives. Fanny's plan to educate her sister is indeed described with a similar irony. She tends to dream of Mansfield instead, detailing a nostalgic picture to her eagerly listening sister. Nevertheless, nostalgia's functions are more complex than this disruption of Fanny's concentration might indicate. Tied up with memories of Edmund and of peaceful occupation removed from Aunt Norris's bullying, Fanny's fondness for books is in itself a nostalgic feeling.

Without such memories of early reading pleasures, Susan finds it difficult to settle down to the quiet, sedentary pursuit, and this is of course important in a novel concerned with the value of education: "The early habit of reading was wanting" (419). By contrast, Edmund detects in the child Fanny "a fondness for reading, which, properly directed, must be an education in itself" (22). He becomes so important to her partly by "recommend[ing] the books which charmed her leisure hours" (22). Without the benefit of fond affections, Maria and Julia Bertram lack the emotional disposition for reading, just as their uneducated cousin Susan does. Their governess cannot make up for an attachment to books, or to the tutor. Still, what Fanny and Susan indulge in most often is daydreams of Mansfield: "none returned so often, or remained so long between them, as Mansfield Park, a description of the people, the manners, the amusements, the ways of Mansfield Park." (419) Fanny of course "could not but indulge herself in dwelling on so beloved a theme" (419) as she alleviates homesickness with nostalgic daydreams, but Susan merely dreams of elegant refinement and grandeur. While her more mundane musings offset her sister's emotional attachment to Mansfield, which has comparatively little to do with the attractions of the fashionable world such as Everingham could boast as easily or indeed much better, Susan nonetheless sees her quixotic daydreams fulfilled. At the end of the novel, she is happily installed at the Park.

This defense of private reading and nostalgic dreaming over books has come very far from Arabella's embarrassing misinterpretations in Charlotte Lennox's *The Female Quixote* of 1752, one of the many eighteenth-century revisions of "quixotic" fictions. Arabella's "Foible" is to mistake seventeenth-century French romances for accurate histories of present-day society. Forced into a retired life by her father, she finds in them the only representation of men and women outside their extremely narrow circle of acquaintances. She is "wholly secluded from the World" and understandably models her behavior on what she finds in her favorite fiction.[9] As critics have been eager to point out, she contrasts favorably with the coquettish Miss Groves, "whose Reading had been very confined" (81), but who is "perfectly versed in the Modes of Town-Breeding, and *nothing-meaning* Ceremony" (68). Despite the ridicule heaped on her in the novel, Arabella is nonetheless a paragon of virtue. As opposed to fashionable women who have lived in the world, she is uncorrupted. What is strikingly different from later treatments of reading heroes and heroines, however, is Glanville's refusal to read the books that have been Arabella's earliest friends. Invited by his future wife to share her reading pleasures, he simply sits "rapt in Admiration at the Sight of so many huge Folio's, written, *as he conceived*, upon the most trifling Subjects imaginable [italics added]" (49). Irony in the novel flows in more than one direction.[10] Arabella's confusion of a fictional past with present-day society may be ridiculous, but she also feels a genuine regard for the heroes and heroines of her earliest pleasures, just as David Copperfield will later feel for Tom Jones. As Jane Austen puts it in *Northanger Abbey* in what is probably the most famous defense of novel reading in fiction, "if the heroine of one novel be not patronized by the heroine of another, from whom can she expect protection and regard?" (37).

In subsequent novels, the new ideal of the companionate marriage often includes shared pleasure in reading, and this is significant for redefinitions of this *solitary* vice as well as for nostalgic recollections of reading itself. In *Mansfield Park*, Fanny nostalgically remembers Edmund's role in the selection of her books. In *The Old Manor House*, Orlando secretly, and suspiciously, meets Monimia in the middle of the night in order to supervise her reading as the precursor of intimate conversations, but later novels carefully go around such glaring connections between lovemaking and companionate reading. The use of Inchbald's *Lovers' Vows*, a play adapted from Kotzebue's *Das Kind der Liebe* and first performed in Britain in 1798, in *Mansfield Park* externalizes this problem. The rehearsal of a coquette's proposal of love to her tutor becomes an emotionally charged scene for Edmund, Mary Crawford, and Fanny. Miss Crawford might imply that the cousins' relationship "makes all the difference" (168) if Fanny were to take her role, but Edmund's brotherly tutoring of Fanny only further complicates her already controversial love for her cousin, which Sir Thomas and Mrs. Norris have after all tried to guard against ever since her introduction into the household.[11]

Divorced from such outspoken sexual alignments, companionate reading becomes a sign of innocent intimacy in nineteenth-century domestic fiction. *Wives and Daughters* shows Molly cozily concealed in the Hamley library, reading Scott's novels. Only Roger ever uses the library, and when he begins to take an interest in Molly, he works on extending her reading pleasures. Their relationship is like "the bond between the Mentor and his Telemachus" (136–37). Later, Molly's love grows on nostalgic remembrances of his "brotherly kindness of old times" (243). Yet, as early as in *Northanger Abbey*, the heroine and her new friend, Miss Thorpe, admittedly "shut themselves up, to read novels together" (37), but it is important that reading becomes a subject of discussion between Catherine and Mr. Tilney, and not all their conversations are embarrassing. Catherine is by no means the first heroine to read novels, as Geraldine, for example, openly refers to the novels that "delighted [her] most" (202) in *Desmond*. But Mr. Tilney is undoubtedly one of the first unironically treated *men* in fiction who openly confess to indulging in enraptured readings of novels, and whose discussions of fiction with a young girl is more instructive than seductive.

Interpretations of *Northanger Abbey* that emphasize Catherine's quixotism frequently fail to make sufficient use of her hero's defense of reading. Countering her comments on men being too busy to read fiction (Glanville's facile excuse in *The Female Quixote*), Tilney asserts that "[t]he person, be it gentleman or lady, who has not pleasure in a good novel, must be intolerably stupid" (106). Remarkably, his reading habits are more asocial than Catherine's, who after all enjoys talking about her favorite books as much as reading them. His sister recollects that he disappeared with *The Mysteries of Udolpho*, the most contentious work of fiction in the novel: "I remember that you undertook to read it aloud to me, and that when I was called away for only five minutes to answer a note, instead of waiting for me, you took the volume into the Hermitage-walk, and I was obliged to stay till you had finished it" (107). Mr. Tilney turning temporary hermit to indulge in a Gothic novel makes him a congenial hero for Catherine, puts him in sharp contrast to the boorish Mr. Thorpe, who never reads novels as he has "something else to do" (48), and prefigures Austen's later revisions of desirable heroes.

By conventional standards, Mr. Tilney's heroic qualities are admittedly questionable. He is not only a second son who lives in a modernized parsonage, but he also lacks the more aggressive masculinity of his tyrannous father or his libertine brother. His "genius" in knowing muslin and particularly his attention to whether it "will wash well" almost induces Catherine to say out loud that she finds him rather "strange" (28). This is of course part of the novel's deliberate dismantling of clichés and expectations. His indulgence in solitary and companionate reading is part of his almost feminine character. While this disqualifies him from the role of a conventional romantic hero, he contrasts favorably with more aggressive and boorish men. In Austen's later novels, congenial partners regularly pore over a whole range of very different reading material together, including Navy lists as well as poetry. Even slightly boorish Mr. Martin makes an effort to read the Gothic novels Harriet Smith has recommended in *Emma*.

As attitudes to individualism, personal pleasure, and also romantic love changed at the end of the eighteenth century and progressively in the nineteenth century, prejudices towards solitary and companionate reading were, in fact, revised as well. In his "General Preface" to the *Waverley* novels, written in 1829, Walter Scott carefully distanced his own nostalgic recollection of his early reading pleasures from his hero's misguided absorption. Like David Copperfield, Scott entertained his schoolfellows with his stories:

> I must refer to a very early period of my life, were I to point out my first achievements as a tale-teller; but I believe some of my old schoolfellows can still bear witness that I had a distinguished character for that talent.... The chief enjoyment of my holidays was to escape with a chosen friend, who had the same taste with myself, and alternately to recite to each other such wild adventures as we were able to devise.... As we observed a strict secrecy on the subject of this intercourse, it acquired all the character of a concealed pleasure, and we used to select for the scenes of our indulgence long walks through the solitary and romantic environs . . . ; and the recollection of those holidays still forms an oasis in the pilgrimage which I have to look back upon.[12]

Indulging in fiction is an intimate "intercourse" conducted in "strict secrecy" and favorably during walks "through the solitary and romantic environs." Most importantly, Scott looks back nostalgically on such indulging. He goes back to "a very early period of [his] life" and dwells on the recollection as "an oasis." The absence of any warnings or admonitions against such intercourse with fictional characters and adventures is remarkable, and even more so considering the emphasis on the youth of the fictionalizing friends. What is more, their secret rambles lead to something productive. They are part of Scott's explanation of his creativity and indeed success. As Thomas Laqueur has pointed out, in the eighteenth century, fiction was commonly accused of failing to lead to anything productive, except personal pleasure. In addition, "[p]rivate reading also bore all the marks of masturbatory danger: privacy and secrecy, of course, but also the engagement of the imagination, self-absorption, and freedom from social constraint. The private reader was, at least for the moment, an autonomous if not autarkic being."[13] Increasingly, the understanding of pleasure and individual happiness changed (as the novels of the time show), and so did attitudes to solitary walks and the reading and writing of fiction.

In a recent study of the "invention" of the countryside that similarly occurred at the time, Donna Landry suggests that the newly valued "goods" produced by the countryside included recreation and retreat, aesthetic consumption and pleasure, and a withdrawal from crowded urban spaces.[14] When William Wordsworth formulated a definition of poetry that focused on the creative aspects of recalling events and emotions, he significantly had his walking tours in the Lake District in mind.[15] In his account of *Waverley*'s production, Scott paid tribute to this new interest in the nostalgic and indeed creative recollection of landscapes. His novel was the result of a deliberate attempt to take it into prose fiction: "My early recollections of the Highland scenery and customs made so favourable an impression in the poem called the *Lady of the Lake*, that I was induced to think of attempting something of the same kind in prose."[16] *Waverley* was thus a doubly nostalgic enterprise, or at least the retrospective preface nostalgically recalls a recollection for both the landscapes of Scott's youth and his youthful reading pleasures. Scott continues this nostalgic account by referring to an illness he suffered as a young man that excluded all activities except reading. He was "plunged into this great ocean of reading without compass or pilot," but apparently without any ill effects.[17] As an adult, he moreover recounts, he took up such absorbent reading once more in order to solace himself in his solitude:

> I was again very lonely but for the amusement which I derived from a good though old-fashioned library. The vague and wild use which I made of this advantage I cannot describe better than by referring my reader to the desultory studies of Waverley in a similar situation, the passages concerning whose course of reading were imitated from recollections of my own. It must be understood that the resemblance extends no farther.[18]

Waverley's "desultory" reading might be in the tradition of quixotic characters, but in his retrospective preface, Scott significantly distances his understanding of solitary reading and its much more productive results from his hero's misguided absorption.[19] This preface is the first crucial account of a nostalgically recalled, creative private reading. Fictional Victorian readers that are often also writers, like David Copperfield, increasingly refer nostalgically to their reading experience.[20] Even when a novelist sets out specifically to attack indiscriminate novel reading, as Mary Elizabeth Braddon attempts in her self-referential, partly parodic take on sensation fiction and, most intriguingly, its reception in *The Doctor's Wife* (1864), the critique has a tendency to shift onto the facile critic instead, deploring only naïve reading, not reading itself. Thus, Braddon's novel at once defends the art of a prolific writer of sensation fiction and turns the plot of the young married woman seduced by fiction—a thinly disguised borrowing from Gustave Flaubert's famous novel of adultery, *Madam Bovary* (1857)—into a developmental *Bildungsroman*. As critics have pointed out, the heroine's innocence, not her corruption, is attributed to her solitary reading pleasures: "Isabel Gilbert was not a woman of the world. She had read novels while other people perused the Sunday papers; and of the world out of a three-volume romance she had no more idea than a baby. She believed in a phantasmal universe, created out of the pages of poets and romancers."[21] Her innocence saves her, and ultimately she achieves a more discriminate level of reading that salvages even the consumption of, in Braddon's own words, "light literature" (253).

Most importantly, however, the significance of reading or daydreaming children becomes additionally pronounced and crucially revised as the Victorian sentimentalization of the "Romantic child" engenders idealizations of the child's imagination as well as childhood and childlikeness. In a pointed conclusion to my reading of nostalgic narratives, I thus additionally seek to emphasize how the representation of a new fatherhood is used as a link between nostalgia for childhood, idealizations of children, and the retention of a childlike imagination. By the late-Victorian age, the nostalgic imagination is given free reign, at least as far as children are concerned, though men of the world are often less indulged, as Wilkie Collins's later heroes have to discover.[22] As we have seen, in Charles Dickens's novels, children and praiseworthily childlike adults frequently live on nostalgic memories and imaginings, and often also manage to construct, or reconstruct, their dream homes. Floy Dombey in *Dombey &*

Son muses at length on her nostalgic imaginings of what once was and what might have been:

> [She] imagined so often what her life would have been if her father could have loved her and she had been a favourite child, that sometimes, for the moment, she almost believed it was so, and, born on by the current of that pensive fiction, seemed to remember how they had watched her brother in his grave together; how they had freely shared his heart between them; how they were united in the dear remembrance of him.... At other times she pictured to herself her mother yet alive. And oh, the happiness of falling on her neck, and clinging to her with the love and confidence of all her soul! And oh, the desolation of the solitary house again, with evening coming on, and no one there! (*D&S*, 313–14)

As chapter 3 has shown, such nostalgic dreams recur in Dickens's novels and are commonly the lauded prerogative of children and childlike adults. Victorian children's fiction feeds on such alignments, as I have briefly indicated in my analysis of fictional children in nineteenth-century novels. For example, in Burnett's *A Little Princess*, Sara Crewe is homesick and solitary, but her nostalgia fosters an imagination that prevents her from succumbing to resentment: "Her trick of pretending things was the joy of her life" (65). Like Fanny Price in Austen's sympathetic treatment of a child's anxieties in the opening chapters of *Mansfield Park*, Sara is banned to a desolate attic. She starts indulging in essentially escapist occupations that fail to be policed as solitary vices. On the contrary, she "found comfort in it and it was a good thing for her" (145). She pretends her attic is different, or "a place in a story" (108): "I can't help making up things. If I didn't, I don't believe I could live.... I'm sure I couldn't live here" (122). David Copperfield reads "as if for life" (*DC*, 56), when his stepfather shuts him out from family life. In the passages that recount Sydney's unhappy childhood in Wilkie Collins's *The Evil Genius* of 1886, the lonely girl is similarly banned to a lumber-room with her "bright imagination" as her only comfort: it is "a better protection against the cold" (59–60). Her fond recollections of her father and the nostalgia she feels for "a little memorial" forgotten by the nasty characters in the novel redeem her, while they also underline the importance of family life and domestic fathers: "Only some torn crumpled leaves from a book of children's songs that he used to teach me to sing; and a small packet of his letter, which my mother may have thrown aside and forgotten" (223). By the end of the nineteenth century, the nostalgically fantasizing child is clearly a cliché Collins can easily draw on when he wishes to redeem his adulterous antiheroine.

The Evil Genius, however, is even more remarkable for its contribution to a new understanding of the "family man" and its analysis of custody laws that undercut fathers' rights to their children than for its defense of solitary reading or daydreaming. Nevertheless, the connections it draws between new ideals of fatherhood and the significance of the childlike imagination cast an important light on adaptations of nostalgic narratives at the end of the nineteenth century.[23] Throughout the novel, nostalgic fathers and father-surrogates openly shed tears and sigh over children and particularly the children lost to them. In showing the combination of nostalgia's most easily sentimentalized and its most subversive elements, a reading of the novel indeed forms a good way to close a study of nostalgia's flexibility, while it opens up its functions in the changing fashions of masculinity and male domesticity to further discussion. The role nostalgia plays in dismantling and forming them addresses important aspects of its shifting definitions. In *A Man's Place: Masculinity and the Middle-Class Home in Victorian England*, John Tosh has significantly pointed out that in the course of the nineteenth century, the home became a man's place in a markedly new way: not as "his possession or fiefdom, but also as the place where his deepest needs were met."[24] This domestic masculinity markedly pinpoints reconfigurations of domesticity and privacy. The home as a new ideal after all went hand in hand with the emergence of the companionate marriage and later the nuclear family, and gave rise to corresponding changes in ideals of masculinity.

The roles of men *and* women were being redefined in the course of the eighteenth and nineteenth centuries. John Richetti reminds us that the traditional British novel, "whether written by a man or by a woman, presents domestic life as its recurring central subject and, with its focus on the interior and private lives of characters, moves dramatically away from the traditional concerns of literature with public life and masculine heroism," and that feminist critics have extended this development to an "establishment of a new modern self that is . . . gendered female."[25] This "feminizing transformation of British culture" tends to marginalize men unless they become important within the home.[26] Collins's domestic men of sensibility negotiate an intriguing twist. As this study has shown, nostalgia's function within these shifts was at once vital and inextricably intertwined with its own redefinition. The novel genre fascinatingly documented these changes while forming and being formed by them. A controversial novel meant to draw masculinity and domesticity into new debates, *The Evil Genius* reveals particularly well how these new ideals operated in the literature and culture of the time.

As the last chapter has shown in some detail, throughout Wilkie Collins's novels, redefinitions of fashionable masculinity are tied up with changing attitudes towards feeling and specifically nostalgic longing. Men of the world tend to ridicule the withdrawal to and immersion in apparently unproductive yearning that characterize the new domestic men of feeling, or even diagnose them as ill or insane. The mesmeric hero of *The Two Destinies* suffers from a nostalgic lovesickness that is diagnosed as a disease, as is young Hardie's in Reade's *Hard Cash,* because it contrasts with Victorian ideals of hardworking, energetic business men. As the nostalgic and lovesick hero of *The Two Destinies* follows his destiny, he needs to escape from home, and in marrying an unsuitable woman, he clearly defies moral strictures and goes against ideals of domesticity as well, and yet, the novel's framestory sees the reunited couple in a very comfortable and very bourgeois arrangement, despite the fact that society refuses to acknowledge their marriage. As we have seen, a series of pale, tearful, and fainting heroes follow in his wake.

Their subversive, even asocial, longings frequently end up in domestic settings after all, though of course with the necessary modifications installed, reminding us that Wilkie Collins himself enjoyed a form of non-marital bigamy with Caroline Graves and Martha Rudd in a bohemian domestic arrangement that he kept very private, indeed secret. He never married, but was a fond father, and apparently juggled his two families very successfully. Bigamy, adultery, the inconsistent divorce and custody laws feature repeatedly in his fiction, and hypocrisies never fare well, yet the private domestic home remains the prevailing ideal. Even the socialist who rescues the young prostitute in *The Fallen Leaves* wishes to settle down with her in a very bourgeois domestic arrangement. These men of feeling have been thoroughly domesticated, even while their sensitivities continue to offend against ideals of strong and energetic manhood, and their choices of partners against a range of moral hypocrisies.

In *Heart and Science* and *The Evil Genius*, new ideals of domesticity let men enjoy more domestic pleasures perhaps most decisive, but this enjoyment comes under a new threat. It consequently needs to be defended as well. Both privacy and nostalgia play an important role in Collins's essentially defensive description of his domesticated men of feeling in these two "mission" novels. Fathers' childlike behavior, their nostalgia for childhood and, after its temporary loss, for their role in their own children's childhood all contribute to this defense. As I have shown, his stepfather's feebleness underscores Ovid Vere's display of sensibility and exposes the mother's energy as heartless. Good men in *Heart and Science* seek domesticity and privacy. Ovid eventually has his fame thrust on him. Unlike the Faustian vivisectionist, he never seeks it. By contrast, the public events his mother organizes within the home dangerously collapse the realm of the private and the public. As a "lazy, harmless old fellow" (48), Mr. Gallilee is of course very different from his successful—if emphatically *not* ambitious—stepson, but his weakness renders him endearing. Even Benjulia is partly redeemed by his playful relationship with the youngest Gallilee daughter.

In many ways, the novel anticipates the treatment of fatherhood in *The Evil Genius*. Mr. Mool, the blushing lawyer, forms a tremulous alliance with Mr. Gallilee to "save" the children: "Out of their common horror of Mrs. Gallilee's conduct, and their common interest in Carmina, they innocently achieved between them the creation of one resolute man" (262). However, whereas Mr. Mool can still assure the "[a]mazed and distressed" father that he stands "on firm ground" (265) in his attempt to reclaim his daughters, the sentimental lawyer in *The Evil Genius* has this comfort no longer. In *Road To Divorce: England 1530–1987*, Lawrence Stone significantly speaks of a revolution in attitudes towards child custody. In 1857, the new Matrimonial Causes Court was empowered to allocate custody of children in divorce cases; in 1873 another act enabled Chancery to award custody as it saw fit; by 1886 it had become "morally accepted that it was only right to grant custody of young children to their mother."[27]

Lest we simply read Collins's exposure of custody laws in *The Evil Genius* as nothing more than a return to conservatism or the apex of an underlying mistrust of powerful women, it is important to pay attention to the juxtaposition of feeling and unfeeling men *and* women, and to keep Collins's interest in domestic men in mind. Instead of simply railing against new laws (rather than unreformed laws, as in his earlier novels), he does, in fact, something radically different in asserting a newly emerging father role that is fraught with ambiguities. Too much time spent in the nursery can easily lead to an infatuation with the governess, if not to incestuous desire, as the father's affair with Sydney shows. Nevertheless, the new father role fosters an expressive paternal love that is significantly different from a patriarch's pride in his offspring, and therefore testifies to the Victorian domestication of Romantic cults of the child and to men's growing interest in childhood and children. In *Heart and Science*, Mr. Gallilee enjoys being with children and behaving like a child. He is the indulgent father who is fond of eating ices and cakes himself, to the chagrin of the mannish governess. Uncles as well as fathers in *The Evil Genius* play with toys and take an eager interest in a new doll. In a chapter entitled "Kitty Keeps Her Birthday," which finely underscores the sentimentalization of the child and the growing interest in descriptions of toys and other paraphernalia of childhood, the new doll heartrendingly articulates the need for domestic fathers: "Kitty's arms opened and embraced her gift with a scream of ecstasy. That fervent pressure found its way to the right spring. The doll squeaked: 'Mamma!'—and creaked—and cried again—and said: 'Papa!'" (139)

The objects of the father's love in both *Heart and Science* and *The Evil Genius* are revealingly daughters. Brutish Mrs. Westerfield may favor her son, who might be a lord one day, this having been her sole reason for marrying the present lord's younger brother in the first place. Like Mr. Dombey in Dickens's novel, she resents her first child for being a girl. Good Victorian parents, by contrast, cherish their offspring without at all considering their possible future positions or their exchange value in the marriage market. It is for this interest in domesticity and domestic fathers, and most markedly, the new direction nostalgia for childhood and the happy home takes that *The Evil Genius* is important. In its sentimentality, it of course undercuts a more radical critique of domestic and public roles, and yet, there is a subversive element in even the most sentimental and domesticated uses of longing in the novel. It rather unconvincingly concludes with the remarriage of the divorced parents. The wife forgives the adulterous husband, and the father forgives the mother for inventing his death in order to deny him access to his daughter. A sentimental reunion of father and child shows him pale and tearful, a pitiful spectacle used to testify to his sensibility.

Just as "thin, pale, emaciated" (518) Fitz-Edward is redeemed in *Emmeline*, and Willoughby forfeits our compassion when he fails to pine properly, to contract "a habitual gloom of temper, or [to die] of a broken heart" (379), in *Sense and Sensibility*, Kitty's father is forgiven all when he pines nostalgically for what he has almost forfeited. The return of "poor lost papa" encapsulates the reconfiguration of men and of longing. This reformulation of nostalgia has turned a clinical disease caused by a delusive patriotism into a domestic, private, yearning for intimate relations in cozily confined surroundings. It has become a longing for home that is at once easily sentimentalized and often subversive in that it tends to go against laws and fashions, established or newly instituted alike. The sentimental reunion scene makes use of nostalgia to expose the cruelty and unfairness of what has been done to father and child:

> [H]e was so like—although he was thinner and paler and older—oh, so like her lost father! . . . She could only say: "You are so like my poor papa." In the instant when he kissed her, the child knew him. Her heart beat suddenly with an overpowering delight; she started back from his embrace. "That's how papa used to kiss me!" she cried. "Oh! You are papa! Not drowned not drowned!" She flung her arms round his neck, and held him as if she would never let him go again. "Dear papa! Poor lost papa!" His tears fell on her face; he sobbed over her. (342–43)

Papa indeed has not drowned, as his mother-in-law (the evil genius) would like to have it and makes her granddaughter believe, but he almost drowns in tears. As a result, he achieves a form of metaphorical rebirth. The sentimentality of this reunion scene of course shows the worst and unfortunately also the most notorious side of a sentimental nostalgia, but there are nonetheless subversive elements in the novel such as its treatment of adultery and more importantly for this analysis, of tearful and longing men. As in all of Collins's novels, nostalgia goes against fashions and new as well as old laws. At the same time, his fiction traces and contributes to nostalgia's redefinition, as a new clinical understanding of the nerves and the brain threatens personal desires and particularly men's private pining. Similarly, lapses into sentimentality may at times appear to disarm nostalgia's subversive aspects, but a triumphantly affirmed nostalgic longing for the eccentric or even unrespectable revises simple alignments between the domestic and the nostalgic. In this, they reclaim nostalgia's range and depths. The domestic happiness of Collins's adulterous, bigamous, and class- as well as gender-crossing protagonists pinpoints the difficulties nostalgia faces in distinguishing itself from a maudlin affectation of sensibility. It shows the impossibility of clearly demarcating its subversive from its conservative aspects.

Whether nostalgia is praised as comforting, liberating, and a symptom of sensibility, or feared as subversive and dangerously private clearly depends as much on changing fashions as on the ways both texts and contexts deploy it. Balancing its interest in the representation of the individual's experience with an emphasis on realist descriptions of the everyday, the genre of the novel keeps reassessing nostalgia's implications and potentials. Its uses of nostalgia shed an intriguing light on changing attitudes to this fascinatingly complex emotion and versatile cultural phenomenon, while nostalgia's history offers insight into the rise of the traditional novel. Not all novels resort to clinical conceptualizations as directly as the late-eighteenth-century novel of sensibility or the mid-Victorian sensation novel, but the slippages between literature and medical discourses reflect cultural homologies that enrich the descriptions of emotional experiences and are indeed vital for the development of nostalgia's dual sets of definitions.

This study has aimed to show how nostalgia operates as a theme in fiction and how it has helped to shape the traditional British novel. In this, its analysis has focused on the period of the novel's domination of the literary market, a period further demarcated by the rise of the sensibility cults in the eighteenth century and the reassessment of the Darwinian imagination at the end of the nineteenth century. In fulfilling essential roles in the "affective revolution" and the paradigm shifts prompted by evolutionary science, nostalgia becomes a central narrative in British fiction and contributes to the formation of Western modernity. The new genre of the novel not only calls attention to, but capitalizes on, nostalgia's cultural relevance and its unfortunately much-misunderstood creative elements. In this, it testifies to nostalgia's creativity and its vital centrality in modern, personal self-expression.

Notes

Longing, Yearning, Pining: An Introduction to Nostalgia

1. Wilkie Collins, *Man and Wife* (Oxford: Oxford University Press, 1995), 274. Hereafter cited parenthetically in the text.
2. See Roy Porter, *Bodies Politic: Disease, Death and Doctors in Britain, 1650–1900* (Ithaca: Cornell University Press, 2001), 61. In my discussions of the changing conceptualization of psychophysical maladies, I have taken up Porter's useful terminology.
3. Laura Brown, *Fables of Modernity: Literature and Culture in the English Eighteenth-Century* (Ithaca: Cornell University Press, 2001), passim. Brown devises a definition of the "cultural fable" that comes close to the Marxist notion of ideology in that it transcends particular writers and texts, but unlike ideology, it has a specific formal structure and an aesthetic distinctiveness (*Fables*, 2). Ian Watt speaks of "myths" and refers to a definition that arose in the Romantic period: "an apotheosis of the idea that there is a boundless validity in certain narrative fictions" (*Myths of Modern Individualism: Faust, Don Quixote, Don Juan, Robinson Crusoe* [Cambridge: Cambridge University Press, 1996], 191). In *The Sense of an Ending: Studies in the Theory of Fiction* (New York: Oxford University Press, 1967), Frank Kermode has significantly argued that "[f]ictions are for finding things out. . . . [T]hey change as the needs of sense-making change. Myths are the agents of stability, fictions the agents of change." (39) "Fictions" comes close to Brown's intriguing use of cultural fables. New historicism and cultural materialism notably agree on the distinctive myths (or fables) of contexts as well as texts, and my own work is similarly premised on a reading of cultural narratives that go beyond individual texts.
4. Compare Lynn Hunt and Margaret Jacob, "The Affective Revolution in 1790s Britain," *Eighteenth-Century Studies* 34, no. 4 (2001): 491–521. The most extensive synopsis of the age's "revolutions" can be found in Laura Brown's *Fables of Modernity*. Among a vast range of crucial changes that occurred in the eighteenth century, Brown lists the financial revolution and mercantile capitalism, the emergence of nationalism and imperialism, innovations in agriculture and the invention of the countryside, the creation of a bourgeois public sphere along with the consolidation of the middle classes, and also what has elsewhere been termed the "affective revolution:" fundamental changes in the structure of the family entailing companionate relationships among nuclear family members (*Fables*, 7–8).
5. Hunt and Jacob, "Affective," 496.
6. Johannes Hofer, "Medical Dissertation on Nostalgia by Johannes Hofer, 1688," trans. Carolyn Kiser Anspach, *Bulletin of the Institute of the History of Medicine* 2, no. 6 (1934): 380.
7. Hofer, "Nostalgia," 381.
8. Ibid., 383.
9. Ibid.
10. Immanuel Kant, *Anthropology from a Pragmatic Point of View*, trans. Victor Lyle Dowdell (Carbondale: Southern Illinois University Press, 1978), 69. In the original, Kant speaks of "Heimweh" (homesickness), "Sehnsucht" (longing), and "die Zurückrufung der Bilder der Sorgenfreiheit" (the recalling of images of a carefree existence). See Immanuel Kant, *Anthropologie in Pragmatischer*

Hinsicht (Frankfurt, 1799), 92. The Latin quotation is from Cicero, who translated a Greek remark, probably by Pacuvius. See Marcus Tullius Cicero, *Tusculan Disputations* (Cambridge, MA: Harvard University Press, 1966), 5, no. 37, l. 108: "Patria est, ubicumque est bene." (One's country is wherever one does well.)

11. Robert Burton, *The Anatomy of Melancholy* (New York: Random House, 1977), pt. 2, 175.

12. Samuel Taylor Coleridge, *Poetical Works* (Princeton: Princeton University Press, 2001), l. 16. All further references are to this edition.

13. Hofer, "Nostalgia," 380–81.

14. Thomas Trotter, *Observations on the Scurvy* (London: Longman, 1792), 44.

15. Trotter, *Scurvy*, 63.

16. Jonathan Lamb, *In the South Seas, 1680–1840* (Chicago: University of Chicago Press, 2001), 121, 125.

17. Jonathan Lamb, "'The Rime of the Ancient Mariner': A Ballad of the Scurvy," in *Pathologies of Travel*, eds. Richard Wrigley and George Revill (Amsterdam: Rodopi, 2000), 157–177.

18. Samuel Rogers, *The Pleasures of Memory* (Oxford: Woodstock, 1989), 20–21.

19. Joseph Banks, *Journal*, ed. Joseph Hooker (London: Macmillan, 1896), 329.

20. Charles Darwin, *The Voyage of the Beagle*, ed. L. Engel (Garden City, New York: Doubleday, 1962), 499. Compare Ann C. Colley, *Nostalgia and Recollection in Victorian Culture* (London: Macmillan, 1998), 17.

21. William Falconer, *A Dissertation on the Influence of the Passions upon Disorders of the Body* (London, 1796), 155–56.

22. Falconer, *Passions*, 45.

23. Thomas Arnold, *Observations on the Nature, Kinds, Causes, and Prevention of Insanity, Lunacy, or Madness* (London: 1782), 19, 265–66.

24. Arnold, *Insanity*, 270.

25. Helen Small, *Love's Madness: Medicine, the Novel, and Female Insanity* (Oxford: Oxford University Press, 1996), passim.

26. Arthur O'Shaughnessy, *Music and Moonlight: Poems and Songs* (London: Chatto & Windus, 1874), 17. Compare O. W. Holmes, "Cinders from Ashes," in *Pages from an Old Volume of Life: 1857–1881*. Project Gutenberg Oliver Wendell Holmes. ed. David Widger. Jun 2002 <http://promo.net/pg> Holmes looks back in nostalgia to his school years, describing himself as a "nostalgic boy." The term nostalgia is otherwise rarely used in fiction at the time, as "melancholy" and later "neurasthenia" or more simply "longing" take precedence. Nicholas Dames has suggested that nostalgia took a "terminological nap" (*Amnesiac Selves: Nostalgia, Forgetting, and British Fiction, 1810–1870* [New York: Oxford University Press, 2001], 253), just as the description of longing and memory became more central in the novel.

27. A. T. Thomson, "Lectures on Medical Jurisprudence," *The Lancet* (1837): 883.

28. Ibid.

29. Ibid.

30. Brown, *Fables*, 7.

31. Michel Foucault, *Madness and Civilization* (London: Tavistock Publications, 1967), 210. Robert Miles, *Gothic Writing 1750–1820: A Genealogy* (London: Routledge, 1993), 31. Compare also Dominick LaCapra, "Foucault, History and Madness," in *Rewriting the History of Madness: Studies in Foucault's* Histoire de la folie, eds. Arthur Still and Irving Velody (London: Routledge, 1992), 84.

32. William Wordsworth, *Lyrical Ballads* (Bristol: Biggs and Co, 1800), Preface.

33. David Lowenthal, *The Past is a Foreign Country* (Cambridge: Cambridge University Press, 1985), 11. Compare J. Starobinski, "The Idea of Nostalgia," trans. W.S. Kemp, *Diogenes* 54 (1966): 81–103, and George Rosen, "Nostalgia: A 'Forgotten' Psychological Disorder," *Clio Medica* 10 (1975): 29–51. For more recent references to nostalgia's medical history see Michael Roth, "Dying of the Past: Medical Studies of Nostalgia in Nineteenth-Century France," *History and Memory* 3, no. 1 (1991): 5–29; G. S. Rousseau, "War and Peace: Some Representations of Nostalgia and Adventure in the Eighteenth Century," in *Guerres et Paix: La Grande-Bretagne au XVIIIe siècle I–II*, ed. Paul-Gabriel Bouce (Paris: Universitè de la Sorbonne Nouvelle, 1998), 121–40; Colley, *Victorian*, 103; Dames, *Amnesiac*, 28–34; Svetlana Boym, *The Future of Nostalgia* (New York: Basic Books, 2001), 3–18. Compare also Lamb's recent work on "scorbutic nostalgia" ("Mariner," passim; Seas, 114–31).

34. Stanley Jackson, *Melancholia and Depression: From Hippocratic Times to Modern Times* (New Haven: Yale University Press, 1986), ix, 3. In *Black Sun: Depression and Melancholia* (New York: Columbia University Press, 1989), Julia Kristeva calls melancholia the "sombre lining of amatory passion" (5) and connects it to depression "without always distinguishing the particularities of the two ailments but keeping in mind their common structure" (11). Sigmund Freud's "Mourning and Melancholia" similarly stipulates a correlation between melancholia and mourning, stressing that both are reactions to the loss of a loved person or of an abstraction that has taken the place of one (*Works*, eds. James Strachey and Anna Freud et al. [London: Hogarth, 1995], vol. 14, 243–44).

35. Jackson, *Melancholia*, 352–72, 373–80.

36. Caryl Flinn, *Strains of Utopia: Gender, Nostalgia, and Hollywood Film Music* (Princeton: Princeton University Press, 1992), 93. The result of this "demedicalization" or "depathologization" has revealingly remained confused. Dames suggests that when nostalgia was "debunked" as a disease, it also "[lost] its dignity as a mode of memory" (*Amnesiac*, 47). Boym disputes the loss of nostalgia's pathological aspect. Quite the reverse, she argues, the Romantic age saw "its transformation from a curable disease into an incurable condition" (*Future*, 4).

37. Robert Hewison, *The Heritage Industry: Britain in a Climate of Decline* (London: Methuen, 1987), 29, 10.

38. David Lowenthal, "Nostalgia tells it like it wasn't," in *The Imagined Past: History and Nostalgia*, eds. Christopher Shaw and Malcolm Chase (Manchester: Manchester University Press, 1989), 20.

39. Janice Doane and Devon Hodges, *Nostalgia and Sexual Difference: The Resistance to Contemporary Feminism* (London: Methuen, 1987), xiii.

40. Raphael Samuel, *Theatres of Memory: Past and Present in Contemporary Culture* (London: Verso, 1994), 164.

41. Hofer, "Nostalgia," 380.

42. Linda Hutcheon, "Irony, Nostalgia, and the Postmodern," in *Methods for the Study of Literature as Cultural Memory*, eds. Raymond Vervliet and Annemarie Estor (Amsterdam: Rodopi, 2000), 195.

43. Lamb, *Seas*, 125; Winfried Schleiner, *Melancholy, Genius, and Utopia in the Renaissance* (Wiesbaden: Otto Harrassowitz, 1991), 14–15.

44. Homi Bhabha, "Introduction: Narrating the Nation," in *Nation and Narration*, ed. Homi Bhabha (London: Routledge, 1990), 2. See Nikos Papastergiadis, *The Turbulence of Migration: Globalization, Deterritorialization and Hybridity* (Cambridge: Polity, 2000) on the "negative movement that takes a

chauvinistic turn toward the homeland rather than the positive view which seeks to unhinge itself from notions of exclusivity and purity" (118). Compare also Gilles Deleuze and Félix Guattari, *What is Philosophy?* trans. Hugh Tomlinson and Graham Burchill (London: Verso, 1994) on the "homeland" of philosophy and the insight of psychosocial types like the exile, the stranger, or the migrant. Philosophy "is inseparable from a Homeland to which the a priori, the innate, or the memory equally attest," but its incommensurability turns the thinker into "an Exile" (68–69).

45. Ban Kah Choon, "Nostalgia and the Scene of the Other," in *Perceiving Other Worlds*, ed. Edwin Thumboo (Singapore: Singapore University Press, 1991), 3.

46. Rosemary Marangoly George, *The Politics of Home: Postcolonial Relocations and Twentieth-Century Fiction* (Cambridge: Cambridge University Press, 1996), 175. Raphael Samuel has provocatively suggested that what Edward Said has influentially termed orientalism is "by no means necessarily a pathological affair" (*Theatres of Memory: Island Stories* [London: Verso, 1998], 76.) I shall come back to Said's impact on the study of British domestic fiction.

47. Susan Stewart, *On Longing: Narratives of the Miniature, the Gigantic, the Souvenir, the Collection* (Durham: Duke University Press, 1984, repr. 2003), ix.

48. Ibid.

49. Ibid., 4.

50. Ian Watt, *The Rise of the Novel* (London: Peregrine Books, 1963), 23.

51. Watt, *Novel*, 14.

52. Michael McKeon, *The Origins of the English Novel 1600–1740* (Baltimore: John Hopkins University Press, 1987), 212, and "Generic Transformation and Social Change: Rethinking the Rise of the Novel," in *The Origin of the English Novel 1600–1740*, ed. Michael McKeon (Baltimore: Johns Hopkins University Press, 2000), 397.

53. J. Paul Hunter, *Before Novels: The Cultural Contexts of Eighteenth-Century Fiction* (New York: W. W. Norton & Co, 1990), xvi–xvii. Hunter further distinguishes between two "waves" of the novel's claims for novelty: one dating from the 1690s and the other from the 1740s. This second wave, after which I have also set the starting point for this study, involved specific claims for a "new species" or "new province" of narrative fiction (11). McKeon similarly emphasizes that in the mid–1740s "the novel has come to the end of its origins. And it begins to enter new territory" ("Generic," 379).

54. John Richetti's *Popular Fiction Before Richardson: Narrative Patterns 1700–1739* (New York: Oxford University Press, 1969) has been seminal for the study of early fiction, whereas his more recent *The English Novel in History 1700–1780* (London: Routledge, 1999) has been an important contribution to the study of subjectivity's significance in the novel.

55. Both new historicism and cultural materialism have been instrumental in this shift. Felicity Nussbaum and Laura Brown's introduction to *The New Eighteenth Century: Theory. Politics. English Literature* (New York: Methuen, 1987) constituted an important stepping-stone in this revision (1–22). Feminist accounts of the novel, such as Elaine Showalter's *A Literature of their Own: British Women Novelists from Brontë to Lessing* (Princeton: Princeton University Press, 1977), Jane Spencer's *The Rise of the Woman Novelist: From Aphra Behn to Jane Austen* (Oxford: Basil Blackwell, 1986), and Nancy Armstrong's *Desire and Domestic Fiction: A Political History of the Novel* (Oxford: Oxford University Press, 1987), also played a significant role. More recent studies include Catherine Gallagher's *Nobody's Story: The Vanishing Acts of Women Writers in the Marketplace, 1670–1820* (Oxford: Clarendon Press, 1994) and Margaret Anne Doody's ambitious *The True Story of the Novel* (New Brunswick:

Rutgers University Press, 1996). The latter employs the most flexible, perhaps too loose, definition of the novel: "A work is a novel if it is fictional, if it is in prose, and if it is of a certain length. Even these criteria are somewhat elastic" (16). In his introduction to *The Columbia History of the British Novel* (New York: Columbia, 1994), John Richetti suggests that "the novel can be described but never, it seems, adequately defined," but ventures a "minimalist description" that comes close to Doody's: "an extended (too long to read at one sitting) narrative in prose about imaginary but vividly particularized or historically specific individuals" (xi).

56. Benedict Anderson, *Imagined Communities: Reflections on the Origin and Spread of Nationalism* (London: Verso, 1983), 25. Raymond Williams's *Culture and Society 1780–1950* (London: Chatto & Windus, 1967) has also crucially contributed to these shifts in critical attention.

57. Anderson, *Communities*, 11.

58. Hunter, *Novels*, 24.

59. Gallagher, *Nobody*, passim, especially xvii and 172.

60. Hunter, *Novels*, 42. Hunter further argues that the concern with subjectivity in eighteenth-century fiction "finds a readier context among solitary readers than it would among a communal audience in a theatre or a group reading of the sort that became popular in Victorian times" (42). However, this group reading notwithstanding, Victorian reading experience remained indebted to Romanticism. See Patricia Meyer Spacks, "The Privacy of the Novel," *Novel* 31, no. 3 (1998): 304–16, and Patricia Meyer Spacks, *Privacy: Concealing the Eighteenth-Century Self* (Chicago: University of Chicago Press, 2003), 9–10, 29.

61. Roy Porter, "Forbidden Pleasures: Enlightenment Literature of Sexual Advice," in *Solitary Pleasures: The Historical, Literary, and Artistic Discourses of Autoeroticism*, ed. Paula Bennett and Vernon A. Rosario II (New York and London: Routledge, 1995), 87.

62. Thomas Laqueur, "Credit, Novels, Masturbation," in *Choreographing History*, ed. Susan Leigh Foster (Bloomington: Indiana University Press, 1995), 125. Compare Porter, *Bodies*, 28, and indeed Laqueur's extensive work on the subject in *Making Sex: Body and Gender from the Greeks to Freud* (Cambridge, MA: Harvard University Press, 1990), 227–30, "The Social Evil, the Solitary Vice, and Pouring Tea," in *Solitary Pleasures: The Historical, Literary, and Artistic Discourses of Autoeroticism*, eds. Paula Bennett and Vernon A. Rosario II (New York and London: Routledge, 1995), 155–61, and most recently, *Solitary Sex: A Cultural History of Masturbation* (New York: Zone Books, 2003), 302–58.

63. Suvir Kaul, *Poems of Nation, Anthems of Empire: English Verse in the Long Eighteenth Century* (Charlottesville: University Press of Virginia, 2000), 11, 15.

64. Kaul, *Empire*, 15–16.

65. Richetti, "Introduction," xii–xiii. Elsewhere Richetti has termed the contested nature of subjectivity "this fiction's obsessive theme. . . . The very nature of identity is a recurring philosophical dilemma, and the novel may be said to rehearse that problem at its own level of consciousness and within its particular frame of reference" (*Novel*, 3–4).

66. Richetti, "Introduction," xiv–xv.

67. Edward W. Said, *Orientalism* (Harmondsworth: Penguin, 1978) and *Culture and Imperialism* (London: Chatto & Windus, 1993).

68. See Nigel Leask's *British Romantic Writers and the East* (Cambridge: Cambridge University Press, 1992) and his recent *Curiosity and the Aesthetics of Travel Writing, 1770–1840* (Oxford: Oxford University Press, 2002). Compare also Felicity Nussbaum, *Torrid Zones: Maternity, Sexuality, and Empire in Eighteenth-Century English Narratives* (Baltimore: Johns Hopkins University

Press, 1995), Brown, *Fable,* passim. Jonathan Lamb's *In the South Seas, 1680–1840* (passim) has been of central interest to my analysis of nostalgia's origins. Although dealing with earlier material, Stephen Greenblatt's *Marvelous Possessions: The Wonder of the New World* (Chicago: University of Chicago Press, 1991), has similarly been important for its "recovery of the critical and humanizing power" of the marvelous (25). Leask similarly makes a point of moving away from retrospective assessments of an orientalist bias to a more historicized account of eighteenth-century aesthetics (*Curiosity,* passim).

69. Raymond Williams, *The Country and the City* (London: Hogarth Press, 1973, repr. 1985), 281.

70. Williams, *Country,* 12.

71. John Tosh, *A Man's Place: Masculinity and the Middle-Class Home in Victorian England* (New Haven: Yale University Press, 1999), 4. Compare also Janet and Peter Phillips's earlier study, *Victorians at Home and Away* (London: Croom Helm, 1978), 97–98.

72. Williams, *Country,* 12.

73. Friedrich Schiller, *Essays,* eds. Walter Hinderer and Daniel O. Dahlstrom (New York: Continuum Publishing, 1993), 181, 227.

74. Compare also Walter E. Houghton, *The Victorian Frame of Mind: 1830–1870* (New Haven: Yale University Press, 1957, repr. 1985), 344: Houghton has already pointed out that Victorian preoccupations with the past and with home—and in particular with the childhood home—form complementary aspects of one phenomenon. On the invention of the "Romantic child" see Peter Coveney's *Poor Monkey: The Child in Literature* (London: Richard Clay, 1957), xii. Coveney argues that "until the last decades of the eighteenth century the child did not exist as an important and continuous theme in English literature" (ix). The origin of this rising interest has been located in eighteenth-century poetry such as Blake's *Songs of Innocence and Experience* (1794), in which the figure of the child is situated within pre-Romantic idealizations of innocence, in a tradition of educational writings, and in a drop in the child mortality rate. Compare Lawrence Stone, *The Family, Sex and Marriage in England 1500–1800* (London: Weidenfeld and Nicolson, 1977). For a more recent overview see Linda A. Pollock's *Forgotten Children: Parent-Child Relations from 1500 to 1900* (Cambridge: Cambridge University Press, 1983) and Hugh Cunningham's *Children and Childhood in Western Society Since 1500* (London: Longman, 1995).

75. Stewart, *Longing,* 146.

76. Kaul, *Empire,* 15–16.

77. Although built on sweeping generalizations, Kaul's argument is convincing. Despite the reintroduction of colonial locations in late-Victorian fiction, they largely remained the site of adventure stories and romances that had more in common with Utopian narratives and the emergent science fiction genre than with the traditional novel. Compare Allienne R. Becker's *The Lost Worlds Romance: From Dawn till Dusk* (London: Greenwood, 1992) on narratives involving "lost worlds" such as the works of H. Rider Haggard. As we shall see, in realist novels, colonial locations, though central to the plot, are offstage or domesticated. John Richetti speaks of "[a]nother strain of fiction" initiated by *Robinson Crusoe* (1719), and which was opposed to the increasingly "feminized" domestic novel. Such fiction offers masculine adventure in exotic places, but, as Richetti admits, it "has tended, since Defoe's novel appeared, to be restricted to children's stories" ("Introduction," xiv–xv).

78. Roy Porter, "'In England's Green and Pleasant Land': The English Enlightenment and the Environment," in *Culture, Landscape, and the Environment: The Linacre Lectures 1997,* eds. Kate Flint and Howard Morphy (Oxford:

Oxford University Press, 2000), 34. Compare also Donna Landry, *The Invention of the Countryside: Hunting, Walking and Ecology in English Literature, 1671–1831* (Basingstoke: Palgrave, 2001), passim, particularly 16.

79. Alfred Tennyson, "In Memoriam," in Alfred Tennyson, *Poems* (Harlow: Longman, 1987), lvi, l. 15. All further references are to this edition.

80. Literary scholars have revealed that the impact of Charles Lyell's *Principles of Geology* (Chicago: University of Chicago Press, 1991), published between 1830 and 1833, and Robert Chambers's *Vestiges of the Natural History of Creation* (London: John Churchill, 1845) of 1844 on Victorian literature was at least as extensive as Charles Darwin's works. Compare Lionel Stevenson's *Darwin among the Poets* (Chicago: University of Chicago Press, 1932) and M. Millhauser's "Tennyson, Vestiges, and the Dark Side of Science," *VN* 35 (1969): 22–25. Gillian Beer's *Darwin's Plots: Evolutionary Narrative in Darwin, George Eliot and Nineteenth-Century Fiction* (London: Routledge & Kegan Paul, 1983) and George Levine's *Darwin and the Novelists: Patterns of Science in Victorian Fiction* (Cambridge, MA: Harvard University Press, 1988) have been influential in pointing out a Darwinian imagination in the British novel. My readings of mid-Victorian fiction in chapter 4 are indebted to their work.

81. J. A. Froude, *The Nemesis of Faith* (London: Chapman and Hall, 1849), 106.

82. Anderson, *Communities*, 11. In *Providence and Love: Studies in Wordsworth, Channing, Myers, George Eliot, and Ruskin* (Oxford: Clarendon Press, 1998), John Beer has traced the Romantic ideal of transcendent love to changes in the ways in which Providence was interpreted that occurred in the course of the nineteenth century. On the invention of the countryside see Landry, *Countryside*, passim.

83. George Steiner, *Nostalgia for the Absolute* (Toronto: CBC Publications, 1974), 2. In *Culture and Society*, Raymond Williams similarly locates the development of "distinctly modern" concepts in the last decades of the eighteenth century and in the first half of the nineteenth century (xvii). Compare also J. Hillis Miller's *The Disappearance of God* (Cambridge, MA: Belknap, 1963), 1–2, and Robert B. Pippin's more recent *Modernism as Philosophical Problem: On the Dissatisfaction of European High Culture* (Oxford: Basil Blackwell, 1991), 8–15.

84. See Novalis (Friedrich von Hardenberg), *Das Allgemeine Brouillon* (Hamburg: Felix Meiner, 1993): "Die Philosophie ist eigentlich Heimweh—Trieb überall zu Hause zu seyn" (194).

85. Simultaneously, a renewed interest in the sensation novel of the 1860s has unearthed literary productions that explicitly deal with anxieties about definitions of normalcy and wrongful incarcerations in asylums.

86. Studies of eighteenth- and nineteenth-century psychology have shown how important it is to approach writers "*not* from any modern psychological perspective, but from that of the psychology available to them in their own time" (Christopher Fox, "Defining Eighteenth-Century Psychology: Some Problems and Perspectives," in *Psychology and Literature in the Eighteenth Century*, ed. Christopher Fox [New York: AMS, 1987], 2). Compare Rick Rylance, *Victorian Psychology and British Culture* (Oxford: Oxford University Press, 2000), 7–8.

87. Elaine Showalter, *The Female Malady: Women, Madness, and English Culture* (London: Virago, 1987), 4.

88. Small, *Madness*, passim.

89. Interest in the representation of masculinity has increased ever since the publication of Eve Kosofsky Sedgwick's *Between Men: English Literature and Male Homosocial Desire* (New York: Columbia University Press, 1985). Michael Roper and John Tosh's *Manful Assertions: Masculinities in Britain*

since 1800 (London: Routledge, 1991) has opened new ground in making men visible as gendered subjects and emphasizing "the diversity and mutability of masculinity over time" (3). See chapter 1.

90. Studies of the relationship between medicine and literature have seen a boom since G. S. Rousseau's "Literature and Medicine: The State of the Field," *Isis* 72 (1981): 406–24. Compare Marie Mulvey Roberts and Roy Porter, eds. *Literature and Medicine during the Eighteenth Century* (London: Routledge, 1993), on what is now seen as the "essential compatibility between the medical and the literary enterprises" (1).

91. George E. Haggerty, *Men in Love: Masculinity and Sexuality in the Eighteenth Century* (New York: Columbia University Press, 1999), 89. On "muscular Christianity" see J. A. Mangan, *Athleticism in the Victorian and Edwardian Public School: The Emergence and Consolidation of an Educational Ideology* (Cambridge: Cambridge University Press, 1981); Norman Vance, *The Sinews of the Spirit: The Ideal of Christian Manliness in Victorian Literature and Religious Thought* (Cambridge: Cambridge University Press, 1985); Compare Donald E. Hall, ed., *Muscular Christianity: Embodying the Victorian Age* (Cambridge: Cambridge University Press, 1994), passim. See chapters 4 and 5.

92. John Mullan, "Hypochondria and Hysteria: Sensibility and the Physicians," *The Eighteenth Century: Theory and Interpretations* 25 (1984), 141. In particular the history of madness has been extensively studied ever since Michel Foucault's seminal *Madness and Civilization*, while his *History of Sexuality* (New York: Vintage, 1980) has inspired a range of works on sexuality, including the extensive works of Thomas Laqueur. See also George Rousseau's seminal article "Nerves, Spirits and Fibres: Towards the Origin of Sensibility," in R. F. Brissenden, ed. *Studies in the Eighteenth Century III* (Canberra: Australian National University Press, 1975), 137–57.

93. Laqueur, *Sex*, 149.

Chapter 1. The Aesthetics of Affliction

1. On account of the slippage of the terminology, I use the terms synonymously, unless a specific meaning is indicated. It has been pointed out that they meant "one and the same thing in the eighteenth century [and] were used by the writers of the period as interchangeable and synonymous" (B. S. Pathania, *Goldsmith and Sentimental Comedy* [New Delhi: Prestige Books, 1988], 18). Compare Jerome McGann, *The Poetics of Sensibility* (Oxford: Clarendon, 1996), 7.

2. In *Virtue in Distress* (London: Macmillan, 1974), R. F. Brissenden speaks of the "shallowness, insincerity, self-indulgent emotionalism" of literary sentimentalism (9–10); in *Sensibility: An Introduction* (London: Methuen, 1986), Janet Todd points out that sentimentality has become a byword for "debased and affected feeling, an indulgence in and display of emotion for its own sake beyond the stimulus and beyond propriety" (8).

3. Clara Tuite, *Romantic Austen: Sexual Politics and the Literary Canon* (Cambridge: Cambridge University Press, 2002), 8. A much-disputed term, "pre-Romantic" (or "preromantic") has been revived by Marshall Brown in *Preromanticism* (Stanford: Stanford University Press, 1991). Suggesting that the prefix should be understood "in its differentiating sense," Brown emphasizes that "preromantic" could be used to refer to the period preceding Romanti-

cism "precisely because it was *not yet* romantic" (2). More recently, Jennifer Keith has reassessed the influence of Northrop Frye, who initiated a still-prevalent label—the "Age of Sensibility"—in an important essay first published in 1956, as well as Brown's resuscitation of pre-Romanticism. Keith stresses the importance of freeing the pre-Romantics "from merely anticipating the Romantics," while appreciating what the Romantics learned from them ("'Pre-Romanticism' and the Ends of Eighteenth-century Poetry," in *The Cambridge Companion to Eighteenth-Century Poetry,* ed. John Sitter [Cambridge: Cambridge University Press, 2001], 286). Compare Northrop Frye, *Fables of Identity: Studies in Poetic Mythology* (New York: Harcourt, Brace & World, 1963), 130–37. I use the term "pre-Romantic" to refer to late-eighteenth-century novels, not simply as an alternative to calling them "novels of sensibility," but as an umbrella term that encompasses the Gothic novel and the early national tale as well. These novels anticipate full-blown Romantic fiction in experimenting with the themes, topoi, and styles that came to be associated particularly with the Romantic age. As Brown has put it, "[i]n many cases, the preromantics fashioned empty vessels that only their successors were able to fill" (*Preromanticism,* 7). The role of fiction in Romanticism has been repeatedly reassessed ever since Marilyn Butler's *Romantics, Rebels, and Reactionaries: English Literature and its Background, 1760–1830* (Oxford: Oxford University Press, 1981). Compare also Robert Kiely's *The Romantic Novel in England* (Cambridge, MA: Harvard University Press, 1972) and the collection *Beyond Romanticism: New Approaches to Texts and Contexts 1780–1832* (London: Routledge, 1992), edited by Stephen Copley and John Whale.

4. Frances Burney, *Camilla* (London: Oxford University Press, 1972), 807.

5. Brissenden, *Virtue,* 94.

6. Charlotte Smith, *Desmond* (London: Pickering & Chatto, 1997), 202. Hereafter cited parenthetically in the text.

7. Henry Mackenzie, *Works,* ed. Susan Manning (London: Routledge, 1996), 21–22. Hereafter cited parenthetically in the text.

8. Schleiner, *Melancholy,* 14. In *Visits to Bedlam: Madness and Literature in the Eighteenth Century* (Columbia: University of South Carolina Press, 1974), Max Byrd similarly analyses the Platonic and Aristotelian *loci classici* of the "inspired madman" (xii), but also emphasizes the contrast between Augustan conceptualizations of madness and its idealization in the cult of sensibility (57).

9. George Cheyne, *The English Malady* (London: 1733), 52.

10. Immanuel Kant, *Observations on the Feeling of the Beautiful and Sublime,* trans. John T. Goldthwait (Berkeley: University of California Press, 1960), 66.

11. Compare James Boswell, *The Hypochondriack,* 2 vols. (Stanford: Stanford University Press, 1928). Pinpointing a prevailing attitude, Boswell writes that he does "not dispute that men are miserable in a greater or lesser degree in proportion to their understanding and sensibility" (vol. 1, 137) and proceeds to analyze the connection between his own hypochondria and his high sensibility. As Haggerty has put it, "Boswell enjoys his hypochondria. He almost preens at times with satisfaction at the distress his sensibility causes him to suffer" (*Men,* 104).

12. Thomson, "Jurisprudence," 883.

13. Jane Austen, *Persuasion* (London: Oxford University Press, 1959), 68. Hereafter cited parenthetically in the text.

14. Thomson, "Jurisprudence," 883.

15. John Hill, *Hypochondriasis: A Practical Treatise on the Nature and Cure of that Disorder: Commonly called the Hyp and Hypo* (London, 1766), 3

16. Ibid., 6–7.

17. While this conflation of melancholy, madness, and genius has had a long history dating back to Pseudo-Aristotle's *Problem xxx*, what Schleiner terms the "humanist fascination with genial melancholy or melancholic genius" (*Melancholy*, 11) gains new impetus in the pre-Romantic cult of sensibility.

18. Robert Markley, "Sentimentality as Performance: Shaftesbury, Sterne, and the Theatrics of Virtue," in *The New Eighteenth Century: Theory. Politics. English Literature,* eds. Felicity Nussbaum and Laura Brown (New York: Methuen, 1987), 219.

19. On the middle-class redefinitions of the gentleman that occurred at the time see Robin Gilmour's *The Idea of the Gentleman in the Victorian Novel* (London: George Allen and Unwin, 1981) and Philip Carter's more recent *Men and the Emergence of Polite Society, Britain 1660–1800* (Harlow: Longman, 2001), passim. In the sensibility cults, women's afflictions came to the fore, and men had to combat allegations of effeminacy. I shall emphasize this gender split in my analysis of the sensibility cults below.

20. See Rousseau, "Nerves," 137–57, Mullan, passim, and Roy Porter, *Mind-Forg'd Manacles: A History of Madness in England from the Restoration to the Regency* (London: The Athlone Press, 1987), 31–32. On George Cheyne's influence see Roy Porter's *The Greatest Benefit to Mankind: A Medical History of Humanity from Antiquity to the Present* (London: Fontana, 1989), 258, and Porter, *Bodies*, 21. On the vulgarization of nervous illnesses see also Roy Porter and Dorothy Porter's *In Sickness and in Health: The British Experience, 1650–1850* (London: Fourth Estate, 1988), 71. Compare also Peter Melville Logan's *Nerves and Narratives: A Cultural History of Hysteria in Nineteenth-Century British Prose* (Berkeley: University of California Press, 1997), 7. See his reading of Thomas Trotter's *A View of the Nervous Temperament* (15–42).

21. Roy Porter, "*Barely Touching*: A Social Perspective on Mind and Body," in *The Language of Psyche: Mind and Body in Enlightenment Thought: Clark Library Lectures 1985–1986*, eds. G. S. Rousseau (Berkeley: University of California Press, 1992), 66.

22. Porter, "Perspective," 73. On "new hedonism" see also Roy Porter, "Enlightenment and Pleasure," in *Pleasure in the Eighteenth Century,* eds. Roy Porter and Marie Mulvey Roberts (Basingstoke: Macmillan, 1996), 1–18.

23. Porter, *Bodies*, 162.

24. Porter, *Manacles*, 84–88.

25. Compare Porter, "Pleasure," passim: Porter further emphasizes that this "rational hedonism, a faith that the pursuit of pleasure would advance the general good," was a belief in "a new human personality, the man of feeling," and thereby pointed towards Romanticism (17–18).

26. Elizabeth Inchbald, *A Simple Story* (London: Pandora, 1987), 169. Hereafter cited parenthetically in the text.

27. Kant, *Anthropology*, 69.

28. Invoking Kant's *Anthropology* (1798), Kristeva has stressed the dependence of nostalgia on a time rather than a place (*Depression,* 60). As part of its "demedicalization," this alleged shift to exclusively temporal aspects is often rehearsed in studies of the heritage industry.

29. Charlotte Smith, *The Old Manor House* (London: Pandora, 1987), 336. Hereafter cited parenthetically in the text.

30. Charlotte Smith, *Emmeline, The Orphan of the Castle* (London: Pandora, 1987), 42. Hereafter cited parenthetically in the text.

31. Mary Hays, *Memoirs of Emma Courtney* (Oxford: Oxford University Press, 2000), 33.

32. Charlotte Smith, *Montalbert* (London: S. Low, 1795), 49. Hereafter cited parenthetically in the text.

33. Charles Lamb, *Rosamund Gray* (Oxford: Woodstock, 1991), 96. Hereafter cited parenthetically in the text.

34. Compare Helen Small on the established iconography of love-madness in the staging of feeling: Ophelia set a standard for later madwomen (*Madness*, 8).

35. Compare Terry Eagleton, *The Rape of Clarissa: Writing, Sexuality and Class Struggle in Samuel Richardson* (Oxford: Basil Blackwell, 1982), 48.

36. Claudia Johnson, "A 'Sweet Face as White as Death': Jane Austen and the Politics of Female Sensibility," *Novel* 22, no. 2 (1989), 161–66.

37. Coveney, *Child*, xii.

38. As critics often point out, the naïveté of Harley, Yorick, or Primrose embodies the inherent irony of literary sentimentalism. See Barbara M. Benedict, *Framing Feeling: Sentiment and Style in English Prose Fiction 1745–1800* (New York, 1994), 50. Compare Chris Jones, *Radical Sensibility: Literature and Ideas in the 1790s* (London: Routledge, 1993), 33.

39. B. S. Hammond, "Mid-Century English Quixotism and the Defense of the Novel," *Eighteenth-Century Fiction* 10, no. 3 (1998): 259.

40. Catherine is the victim of a surfeit of Gothic novels. See Mavis Batey, *Jane Austen and the English Landscape* (London: Barn Elms, 1996), 8. In *The Madwoman in the Attic* (New Haven: Yale University Press, 1979), Sarah M. Gilbert and Susan Gubar speak of a redefinition of the Gothic as a subversive critique of patriarchy (135). Catherine is, as Barbara Hardy puts it in *A Reading of Jane Austen* (London: Owen, 1975), initiated into the horrors of social fact (180).

41. Frances Burney, *The Wanderer; Or, Female Difficulties* (Oxford: Oxford University Press, 1991), 117. Hereafter cited parenthetically in the text.

42. Haggerty, *Men*, 2. See also Haggerty's *Unnatural Affections: Women and Fiction in the Later Eighteenth Century* (Bloomington and Indianapolis: Indiana University Press, 1998), passim, in which he explores female subjectivity in women's novels, but also emphasizes "how male characters function in these novels" (2). Compare Claudia Johnson's *Equivocal Beings: Politics, Gender, and Sentimentality in the 1790s* (Chicago: University of Chicago Press, 1995) and Michele Cohen's *Fashioning Masculinity: National Identity and Language in the Eighteenth Century* (London: Routledge, 1996), passim. I have briefly discussed the influence of Laqueur and Sedgwick as well as the work of Tosh and Roper in the introduction.

43. Compare G. J. Barker-Benfield, *The Culture of Sensibility: Sex and Society in Eighteenth-Century Britain* (Chicago: University of Chicago Press, 1992), xxvi. Barker-Benfield has further shown that "[t]his tension between the high evaluation of refinement in men and the wish to square it with manliness permeated the eighteenth-century novel, whatever the sex of the writer" (*Sensibility*, 141). Jane Spencer has similarly argued that "the properly 'feminine' and the properly 'literary' were both being re-defined along the same lines" (*Woman*, 179). For a more recent discussion of the effeminacy created by "luxury" goods (including novels) see Liz Bellamy's *Commerce, Morality and the Eighteenth-Century Novel* (Cambridge: Cambridge University Press, 1998), passim.

44. See George Starr, "'Only a Boy': Notes on Sentimental Novels," in *The English Novel* 2 vols., ed. Richard Kroll (London: Longman, 1998), 29–54. Compare Haggerty, *Men*, 86–91. Barker-Benfield refers to "the popular misunderstanding of *The Man of Feeling*'s message and manhood" (147).

45. Patricia Meyer Spacks, *Desire and Truth: Functions of Plot in Eighteenth-Century English Novels* (Chicago: University of Chicago Press, 1990), 3.

46. Allan Ingram, *The Madhouse of Language: Writing and Reading Madness in the Eighteenth Century* (London: Routledge, 1991), 157.

47. Diane Long Hoeveler, *Gothic Feminism: The Professionalization of Gender from Charlotte Smith to the Brontës* (University Park: Pennsylvania State University Press, 1998), 38.

48. Charlotte Smith, *Marchmont* (London: Sampson Low, 1796), 8. Hereafter cited parenthetically in the text.

49. Frances Brooke, *Emily Montague* (Ottawa: Graphic Publishers, 1931), 44, 24.

50. Frances Brooke, *The Excursion* (Lexington: Kentucky University Press, 1997), 126.

51. Johnson, *Equivocal*, 148.

52. Samuel Richardson, *Clarissa* (New York: Viking, 1985), 673, 678.

53. Gerard A. Barker, *Grandison's Heirs: The Paragon's Progress in the Late-Eighteenth-Century English Novel* (Newark: University of Delaware Press, 1985), 49.

54. Barker, *Grandison*, 13, 47.

55. John Mullan, *Sentiment and Sociability: The Language of Feeling in the Eighteenth Century* (Oxford: Clarendon, 1988), 90, 81, 85.

56. Frances Burney, *Evelina* (New York: Chelsea House, 1988), 261. Hereafter cited parenthetically in the text.

57. Adam Smith, *The Theory of Moral Sentiments* (Indianapolis: Liberty Press, 1976), 209. J. G. A. Pocock has suggested that eighteenth-century economic man "was seen as on the whole a feminized, even an effeminate being, still wrestling with his own passions and hysterias and with interior and exterior forces let loose by his fantasies and appetites" (*Virtue, Commerce, and History* [Cambridge: Cambridge University Press, 1985], 114). Barker-Benfield has similarly pointed out that refined men were often thought to be "softened" by "luxury" goods (*Sensibility*, 49). Compare also Bellamy, *Commerce*, 13–38.

58. Kant, *Anthropology*, 160.

59. Johnson, *Equivocal*, 11. See also Haggerty on "the role of such gentle men in the construction of domesticated masculinity" (*Men*, 4).

60. Mary Brunton, *Emmeline* (London: Routledge, 1992). In this conservative sentimental story of a woman who has imprudently given in to her passion, regrets of the past have notably only a redemptive effect and, unlike in many earlier novels, fail to lead to anything constructive. The "bitter recollection" (4) of her happy first wedding already spoils the beginning of her second marriage: thinking of "friendship shown in her days of innocence, till the tears trickled down her cheeks," Emmeline realizes that she has "miserably forfeited the peace of innocence" (57–58).

61. Claudia Johnson, *Jane Austen: Women, Politics, and the Novel* (Chicago: Chicago University Press, 1988), 140–41.

62. See Johnson on the obligatory deaths of "lovely Woman" in conservative sentimental fiction, in which men serve as voyeurs ("Sensibility," 159–60). I shall come back to the significance of sick- and deathbeds in Austen's fiction.

63. Brissenden, *Virtue*, 94.

64. Frances Sheridan, *Sidney Bidulph* (Oxford: Oxford University Press, 1995), 7. Hereafter cited parenthetically in the text.

65. Margaret Anne Doody, "Frances Sheridan: Morality and Annihilated Time," in *Fetter'd or free? British Women Novelists 1670–1815*, eds. Mary Anne Schofield and Cecilia Macheski (Athens: Ohio University Press, 1987), 349.

66. As Barker has put it, Faulkland is at first patterned after Grandison, but a chain of circumstances misleads Sidney into believing him a virtual Lovelace (*Grandison*, 55).
67. Doody, "Sheridan," 345, 343.
68. Harold Bloom, ed. *Fanny Burney's Evelina* (New York: Chelsea House, 1988), xxvi.
69. Compare Ronald Paulson, "Evelina: Cinderella and Society," in *Fanny Burney's Evelina*, ed. Harold Bloom (New York: Chelsea House, 1988), 5–12. Paulson calls Evelina an outsider "sensitive enough to see the wrongness of the society she enters, but [who] still knows she must make common cause with it" (8). See also Huang Mei, *Transforming the Cinderella Dream: From Frances Burney to Charlotte Brontë* (New Brunswick: Rutgers University Press, 1990). Huang draws attention to the popularity of the Cinderella-plot in English novels, which is re-tailored by the story of Pamela's rise from obscurity.
70. Julia Epstein, "Marginality in Frances Burney's Novels," in *The Cambridge Companion to the Eighteenth-Century Novel*, ed. John Richetti (Cambridge: Cambridge University Press, 1996), 206.
71. Johnson, "Sensibility," 159–60. Compare Katharine Rogers's *Frances Burney: The World of "Female Difficulties"* (Hemel Hempstead: Simon & Schuster, 1990): Rogers maintains that the representation of Cecilia's illness aims "for simple emotional, rather than symbolic, effects" (66). Unlike Clarissa, Burney's heroines recover, but their illnesses nonetheless serve more than merely a melodramatic effect; they are central crises in the novels. I shall emphasize the significance of Austen's recovering heroines in the next chapter.
72. Frances Burney, *Cecilia* (Oxford: Oxford University Press, 1988), 291. Hereafter cited parenthetically in the text.
73. Maria Edgeworth, *Belinda* (London: Everyman, 1993). Edgeworth based the Virginia-subplot on the true story of her father's friend Thomas Day, a writer of nauseatingly didactic children's fiction, who educated two orphan girls in order to raise an ideal wife for himself.
74. Jane Austen, *Mansfield Park* (London: Oxford University Press, 1953), 19. Hereafter cited parenthetically in the text.
75. Although literary critics have often emphasized the "unimportance of children in Jane Austen's fiction" (David Grylls, *Guardians and Angels: Parents and Children in Nineteenth-Century Literature* [London, Faber, 1978], 114), it has traditionally been acknowledged that Fanny Price's situation stands out, as Jacqueline Banerjee has shown (*Through the Northern Gate: Childhood and Growing Up in British Fiction 1719–1901* [New York: Peter Lang, 1996], 24). Banerjee has also attempted to shed new light on the role of children in Austen's other fiction, pointing out that "she often champions them at the expense of those adults (like Lady Susan) who exploit and underestimate them" (*Childhood*, 22). Nonetheless, as Banerjee herself acknowledges, this role of children is still far removed from their centrality in mid-Victorian fiction. I shall come back to Dickens's revision of the child's original innocence in chapter 3.
76. M. O. Grenby, *The Anti-Jacobin Novel: British Conservatism and the French Revolution* (Cambridge: Cambridge University Press, 2001), 24. Grenby lists a vast number of anti-Jacobin novels written in the last decade of the eighteenth century that attests to their short, but culturally significant, predominance in the literary market. Chris Jones has similarly emphasized that "Evangelicalism adopted many of the reformist aims of moral and humanitarian sensibility, yet fostered a dependence on constituted authority" (*Radical*, 113). Compare Jones's juxtaposition of "Sensibility in Revolution" and "Sensibility in Reaction" (*Radical*, 59–107 and 108–35).

77. Compare Small, *Madness*, passim.

78. See Gary Kelly, *English Fiction of the Romantic Period* (London: Longman, 1989), 62. Todd and Blank have suggested that Smith "continued to publish fiction of a decidedly explosive nature," although she "did tone down the radicalism" in displacing the plot of the next novel, *The Old Manor House* (1793), into the past of the American War of Independence. Her fictional treatments of personal struggles that parallel public crises, in fact, largely remain true to her sympathies with the suppressed, even while the victims of persecution change. See Antje Blank and Janet Todd, "Introduction," Charlotte Smith, *Desmond* (London: Pickering & Chatto, 1997), xxi.

79. Patricia Meyer Spacks, "Novels of the 1790s: Action and Impasse," in *The Columbia History of the British Novel,* ed. John Richetti (New York: Columbia, 1994), 265.

80. As Hammond has put it, "it is usual to argue that in the early to mid-eighteenth century the treatment of Quixotism was satirical, whereas, as the century wore on, it was gradually romanticized" ("Quixotism," 262). Compare Susan Staves, "Don Quixote in Eighteenth-Century England," *Comparative Literature* 24 (1972): 193–215. See also Wendy Motooka, *The Age of Reasons: Quixotism, Sentimentalism and Political Economy in Eighteenth-Century Britain* (London: Routledge, 1998) on "the larger relation between sentimentalism and quixotism" (19).

81. Sarah Fielding, *David Simple* (Oxford: Oxford University Press, 1987), 96, 27.

82. Compare Burney, *Evelina*, 369.

83. Mary Wollstonecraft, *Political Writings*, ed. Janet Todd (Oxford: Oxford University Press, 1994), 41.

84. Compare Diana Bowstead, "Charlotte Smith's *Desmond*: The Epistolary Novel as Ideological Argument," in *Fetter'd or free? British Women Novelists 1670–1815,* eds. Mary Anne Schofield and Cecilia Macheski (Athens: Ohio University Press, 1987), 237–63. Bowstead suggests that Montfleuri's "reforms on his estate are an expression of his radical beliefs" (245).

85. Bowstead, *"Desmond,"* 250. Chris Jones has pointedly called Geraldine "a Trojan horse" that caters for a divided readership (*Sensibility*, 162–63).

86. Jane Austen, *Northanger Abbey* (London: Oxford University Press, 1959), 157, 161.

87. Ann Radcliffe, *The Castles of Athlin and Dunbayne: A Highland Story* (London: Folio Society, 1987), 88–89.

88. Ann Radcliffe, *The Mysteries of Udolpho* (Oxford: Oxford University Press, 1998), vol. 2, ch. 3; vol. 3, ch. 1, passim; vol. 2, ch. 5, 227. Hereafter cited parenthetically in the text.

89. Terry Castle, "Introduction," in Ann Radcliffe, *The Mysteries of Udolpho* (Oxford: Oxford University Press, 1998), ix.

90. Castle, "Introduction," xviii–xxiv. Castle compares Montoni's bullying to that exacted by "Richardson's depraved Harlowes" (xviii).

91. Terry Castle, *The Female Thermometer: Eighteenth-Century Culture and the Invention of the Uncanny* (Oxford: Oxford University Press, 1995), 123–24.

92. Miles, *Gothic*, 3. Miles further links the Gothic aesthetic to the period of crisis in the late-eighteenth century that Foucault has diagnosed which expressed itself, "partly, in the birth of 'nostalgia'. . . . Nostalgia is a recognition of difference (the past as irretrievable) married to an insistence on sameness (the past, we hope, will tell us what we still really *are*)" (*Gothic,* 31). George Haggerty suggests that the Gothic novel emerges at a crucial moment "when the battle lines of cultural reorganization are being formed in the later eighteenth century" ("The Gothic Novel," in *The Columbia History of the British Novel,*

ed. John Richetti [New York: Columbia, 1994], 221). In *Gothic Fiction / Gothic Form* (University Park: Pennsylvania State University Press, 1989), he speaks of "the affective nature of Gothic fiction" (4). Compare Spacks on the Gothic's "mode of effectiveness" (*Desire*, 156).

93. Anthony Vidler, *The Architectural Uncanny: Essays in the Modern Unhomely* (Cambridge, MA: Massachusetts Institute of Technology Press, 1992), ix–x.

94. Vidler, *Uncanny*, ix.

95. Freud, *Works,* vol. 17, 234. Intriguingly, Freud also posited the idea that love might be a form of homesickness. I shall come back to this insightful take on nostalgia in my reading of Dickens's fictions of home in chapter 3.

96. Bhabha, "Introduction," 2.

97. Janet Sorensen, "Writing Historically, Speaking Nostalgically: The Competing Languages of Nation in Scott's *The Bride of Lammermoor*," in *Narratives of Nostalgia, Gender and Nationalism,* eds. Jean Pickering and Suzanne Kehde (London: Macmillan, 1997), 31, 46. For a recent investigation of the *heimlich* and the *unheimlich* in Victorian fiction see particularly Carolyn Dever, *Death and the Mother from Dickens to Freud: Victorian Fiction and the Anxiety of Origins* (Cambridge: Cambridge University Press, 1998), passim. See chapter 3.

98. Consider also Laura Brown's analysis of eighteenth-century conceptualizations of alterity: Modernity, Brown argues, "is consistently involved with a problematic figure of difference," and as "others," both women and non-Europeans "provide a template, a catalyst, a reference point, a precedent, a strategy, of a conclusion for the imaginative exercises that these cultural fables undertake" (*Fables*, 10). Felicity Nussbaum similarly emphasizes that the "invention of the 'other' woman of empire enabled the consolidation of the cult of domesticity in England" (*Torrid*, 1). Home and the state of homelessness or "unhomely" experience associated with the exotic can be seen as manifestations of the new phenomenology of self and other. My reading of *The Wanderer* shows how the novel draws the association between the foreign and the female "other" into debates.

99. Margaret Anne Doody, "Deserts, Ruins and Troubled Waters: Female Dreams in Fiction and the Development of the Gothic Novel," *Genre* 10 (1977): 560–62.

100. Haggerty, *Gothic,* 7 and passim. Compare also Haggerty on the transgressive potential of the "female Gothic" of women writers: they "begin to give a sense of how 'female Gothic' is grounded in feminine sensibility and to what degree it can be read as a symptom of the denial of female desire in hegemonic culture" (*Unnatural*, 19).

101. Compare Robert Miles, "The 1790s: the effulgence of Gothic," in *The Cambridge Companion to Gothic Fiction*, ed. Jerrold E. Hogle (Cambridge: Cambridge University Press, 2002), 42. For a good overview of recent critical discussions see Jerrold E. Hogle, "Introduction: the Gothic in Western Culture," in *The Cambridge Companion to Gothic Fiction,* ed. Jerrold E. Hogle (Cambridge: Cambridge University Press, 2002), 13.

102. Elizabeth A. Bohls, "Disinterestedness and denial of the particular: Locke, Adam Smith, and the subject of aesthetics," in *Eighteenth-Century Aesthetics and the Reconstruction of Art,* ed. Paul Mattick (Cambridge: Cambridge University Press, 1993), 35. Compare Stephen Copley and Peter Garside, eds. *The Politics of the Picturesque: Literature, Landscape and Aesthetics since 1770* (Cambridge: Cambridge University Press, 1994) on the ahistorical and aestheticized use of buildings and settings such as ruins and dilapidated cottages, "which in other circumstances are the indicators of poverty or social deprivation" (6).

103. Bellamy, *Commerce*, 163.
104. Ibid., 165.
105. Grenby, *Anti-Jacobin*, 4.
106. Walter Scott, *Waverley* (Edinburgh: Adam & Charles Black, 1870), 153. See Kiely, *Romantic*, 143.
107. Maria Edgeworth, *The Absentee* (Oxford: Oxford University Press, 1988), 81, 80.
108. Lady Morgan (Sydney Owenson), *The Wild Irish Girl* (London: Pandora, 1986), 172.
109. Anderson, *Communities*, 13.
110. Thomas Nipperdey, "In Search of Identity: Romantic Nationalism, Its Intellectual, Political and Social Background," in *Romantic Nationalism in Europe,* ed. J. C. Eade (Canberra: Australian National University Press, 1983), 10–15.
111. Studies of colonial representations have emphasized the negative effects of such imagined, or fictional, communities and the new fiction of the nation. With a direct reference to Benedict Anderson, Homi Bhabha points out that those "who will not be contained within the *Heim* of the national culture . . . articulate the death-in-life of the idea of the 'imagined community' of the nation" ("DissemiNation: time, narrative, and the margins of the modern nation," in *Nation and Narration*, ed. Homi Bhabha [London: Routledge, 1990], 315). Laura Brown speaks of "fables" of a "new world," showing how Western modernity was "consistently involved with a problematic figure of difference:" women and non-Europeans (*Fables*, 10). In this analysis of the "fables" of alterity in Western modernity, Brown builds on her equally insightful earlier work on the representation of women in imperialist discourses. See Laura Brown, *Ends of Empire: Women and Ideology in Early Eighteenth-Century English Literature* (Ithaca: Cornell University Press, 1993). Compare also Nussbaum, *Torrid*, passim.
112. Leask, *Romantic*, 20. In his excellent study of the pastoral, *The Uses of Nostalgia: Studies in Pastoral Poetry* (London: Constable, 1972), Laurence Lerner has traced its creation and consolidation in Western literature up to its reduction to a convention. As the validity of traditional myths and their promises of the *locus amoenus* were drawn into question in post-Enlightenment Europe, nostalgic spaces became more personal. Paradise and Arcadia were reduced to clichés (35–40). In his more recent study on the aesthetics of travel writing, particularly accounts of antiquarian (or archaeological) travels, Leask similarly speaks of countries located in "torrid zones" that shared "the fate of being considered 'antique lands' by Europeans" despite their cartographic and cultural distance (*Curiosity*, 1).
113. Landry, *Countryside*, 16.
114. Sorensen, *"Lammermoor,"* passim.
115. Morgan, *Irish*, 172.
116. Maria Edgeworth, *The Absentee* (Oxford: Oxford University Press, 1988), 37.
117. Kelly, *Romantic*, 43.
118. Anne Mellor, "British Romanticism, Gender, and Three Women Artists," in *The Consumption of Culture 1600–1800: Image, Object, Text*, eds. Ann Bermingham and John Brewer (London: Routledge, 1995), 121–42.
119. Jane Austen, *Northanger Abbey* (London: Oxford University Press, 1959), 198.
120. Tracy Edgar Daugherty, *Narrative Techniques in the Novels of Fanny Burney* (New York: Peter Lang, 1989), 164–65.

121. Johnson, *Equivocal*, 167.
122. Deidre Lynch, "Domesticating Fictions and Nationalizing Women: Edmund Burke, Property, and the Reproduction of Englishness," in *Romanticism, Race, and Imperial Culture, 1780–1830*, eds. Alan Richardson and Sonia Hofkosch (Bloomington: Indiana University Press, 1996), 42, 59.
123. Boym, *Nostalgia*, 14.
124. Compare Margaret Anne Doody, *Frances Burney: The Life in the Works* (Cambridge: Cambridge University Press, 1988), 313–316; Kate Chisholm, *Fanny Burney: Her Life 1752–1840* (London: Chatto & Windus, 1998), 220.
125. Kelly, *Romantic*, 15–16.
126. Sara Salih, "'Her Blacks, Her Whites and Her Double Face': Altering Alterity in *The Wanderer*," *Eighteenth-Century Fiction* 11, no. 3 (1999): 301.
127. Salih, "Alterity," 307.
128. Johnson, *Equivocal*, 169.
129. Ibid., 169–70.
130. Nussbaum, *Torrid*, 1, 15–17, 73–74. See also Laura Brown's readings of earlier narratives in *Ends of Empire* and *Fables of Modernity* (passim). Brown significantly reassesses the representation of women in the contexts of mercantile capitalism, imperialism, and the growth of consumer society.
131. Smith, *Montalbert*, 50.
132. In Charlotte Smith's first novel, *Emmeline* (1788), by contrast, Frenchified manners and affected accents are simply ridiculed. "Something of a coxcomb" (363), the self-elected Frenchman Bellozane indulges in displays of "excessive vanity" (381) and "the volatility of his adopted country" (499). Compare Doody on false nationalities in *Evelina* (Burney, 52).
133. Lynch, "Domesticating," 59.
134. Edmund Burke, *Reflections on the Revolution in France* (London: Penguin, 1986), 120.
135. Epstein, "Marginality," 208. Johnson similarly suggests that *"The Wanderer* refutes Wollstonecraft as Burney stunningly misreads her" (*Equivocal*, 145). Compare Justine Crump, "'Turning the World Upside Down': Madness, Moral Management, and Frances Burney's *The Wanderer*," *Eighteenth-Century Fiction* 10, no. 3 (1998): 325–40. See also Claire Harman's *Fanny Burney: A Biography* (London: Harper Collins, 2000) on Harleigh's intellectually spineless pleadings with Elinor (324–27).

Chapter 2. Headaches or Heartaches

1. Lionel Trilling, *The Opposing Self* (London: Secker and Warburg, 1955), 212. Compare Paul Pickrel, "Lionel Trilling and *Mansfield Park*," *Studies in English Literature* 27, no. 4 (1987): 609–21, and also "'The Watsons' and the Other Jane Austen," *ELH* 55, no. 2 (1988): 443–67.
2. Nina Auerbach, "Feeling as One Ought about Fanny Price," in *Jane Austen's Mansfield Park*, ed. Harold Bloom (New York: Chelsea House Publisher, 1987), 104, 103, 106.
3. John Wiltshire, "*Mansfield Park, Emma, Persuasion*," in *The Cambridge Companion to Jane Austen*, eds. Edward Copeland and Juliet McMaster (Cambridge: Cambridge University Press, 1997), 60.
4. Elaine Jordan, "Jane Austen goes to the Seaside: *Sanditon*, English Identity and the 'West Indian' Schoolgirl," in *The Postcolonial Jane Austen*, eds. You-me Park and Rajeswari Sunder Rajan (London: Routledge, 2000), 43.

5. Tony Tanner, "Introduction," Jane Austen, *Mansfield Park* (Harmondsworth: Penguin, 1983), 9.
6. Nicholas Dames, "Austen's 'Nostalgics,'" *Representations* 73 (2001): 121.
7. John Wiltshire, *Jane Austen and the Body* (Cambridge: Cambridge University Press, 1992), 9. Compare Anita Gorman, *The Body in Illness and Health: Themes and Images in Jane Austen* (New York: Peter Lang, 1993), 184.
8. Wiltshire, *Body*, 8.
9. "Review of *Sense and Sensibility*," in *Jane Austen: Critical Assessments*, ed. Ian Littlewood (Mountfield: Helm Information, 1998), vol. 1, 264.
10. Jane Austen, *Sense and Sensibility* (London: Oxford University Press, 1960), 97. Hereafter cited parenthetically in the text.
11. Maaja Stewart, *Domestic Realities and Imperial Fictions: Jane Austen's Novels in Eighteenth-Century Contexts* (Athens: Georgia University Press, 1993); You-me Park and Rajeswari Sunder Rajan, eds. *The Postcolonial Jane Austen* (London: Routledge, 2000), passim.
12. Mary Waldron, *Jane Austen and the Fiction of her Time* (Cambridge: Cambridge University Press, 1999), passim. Important earlier attempts to situate Austen within the fiction of her time include Jocelyn Harris's *Jane Austen's Art of Memory* (Cambridge: Cambridge University Press, 1989) and Kenneth Moler's *Jane Austen's Art of Allusion* (Lincoln: University of Nebraska Press, 1968).
13. Tuite, *Romantic*, passim, particularly 100: "the association of Austen with green England is not simply a late nineteenth- or twentieth-century phenomenon. Austen's texts themselves participate in the Romantic-period cultural strategy of naturalizing the country, and its local social relations."
14. Marilyn Butler, *Jane Austen and the War of Ideas* (Oxford: Clarendon, 1987), passim. Marvin Mudrick's *Jane Austen: Irony as Defense and Discovery* (Princeton: Princeton University Press, 1952) is the most influential account of the cold and ironic Austen.
15. Johnson, *Austen*, 166.
16. Johnson, "Sensibility," 161–66. Compare also Johnson, *Austen*, xxii.
17. On the ways in which Elizabeth Bennet's "shamelessly athletic run" rewrites Burkean fiction and how Catherine Morland's extraordinary hunger and restful sleep after having been disappointed in her wishes to dance once more with Tilney comically offend conservative idealizations of woman's debility see Johnson, "Sensibility," 164.
18. Austen's parodic dismantling of anti-Jacobin fiction is central to Johnson's argument, but I refer particularly to her discussion of *Sense and Sensibility* in Johnson, *Austen*, 49, 23, 53, and "Sensibility," passim.
19. Johnson, *Austen*, 172. Johnson further remarks that "one of the deepest and most methodically contrived ironies of *Sense and Sensibility* is that not all of Elinor's skepticism can save her from erroneous conjectures, nor all her modesty preserve her from depending upon Edward" (*Austen*, 63).
20. Waldron, *Austen*, 77.
21. Small, *Madness*, 90, 99–100.
22. Johnson, "Sensibility," 167–68. Small emphasizes that Brandon tells Eliza's sentimental story "with a clear eye to its moral" (*Madness*, 100). A good caution against conceiving Brandon as too interesting while forgetting how much of his characterization is represented through the eyes and minds of other characters is Cheryl L. Nixon's article on the changes undergone by the novel's dull heroes in Emma Thompson's movie adaptation, "Balancing the Courtship Hero: Masculine Emotional Display in Film Adaptations of Austen's Novels," in *Jane Austen in Hollywood*, eds. Linda Troost and Sayre Greenfield (Lexington: UP of Kentucky, 1998), 35.
23. Stewart, *Domestic*, 79.

24. Glenda Hudson, *Sibling Love and Incest in Jane Austen's Fiction* (Basingstoke: Macmillan, 1992), 59. It has also been suggested that Marianne is linked to Clarissa Harlow through the device of the two Elizas. See also Harris, *Austen*, 59.

25. Tuite, *Romantic*, 67, Waldron, *Austen*, 82.

26. Waldron, *Austen*, 82.

27. As Jane Stabler has recently put it, "[o]ne of the great themes of Austen's fiction is moving house" (*Burke to Byron, Barbauld to Baillie, 1790–1830* [Basingstoke: Palgrave, 2002], 192).

28. Waldron has even suggested that Edward and Elinor's ridicule of Marianne "is a species of flirtation which is vibrant with emotional strain, and which leaves Marianne, whom they both snub unmercifully, isolated" (*Austen*, 72–73). This snubbing anticipates the bullying of Fanny Price in the later novel. It should also not be forgotten that Elinor admits that "that to avoid one kind of affectation, Edward here falls into another" (97).

29. In his analysis of the "unassimilable self," Dames similarly cautions against ascribing Marianne's "bout of remembrance to lovesickness rather than homesickness," but the contrast he establishes between an old plot of nostalgia and a modern, communal nostalgia is fraught with ambiguous overgeneralizations that obstruct his interesting reading of the novel (*Amnesiac*, 46).

30. Johnson, "Sensibility," 167–68.

31. Jane Austen, *Pride and Prejudice* (Oxford: Oxford University Press, 1988), 106. Hereafter cited parenthetically in the text.

32. Jane Austen, *Minor Works* (London: Oxford University Press, 1965), 318.

33. Pickrel, "Watsons," 449. Pickrel further speaks of Emma as "an exile in her own family" (450) and places her among a "series of important female characters in the later works—Emma Watson, Fanny Price, Jane Fairfax, and Anne Elliot," which he terms "the exiles:" "These characters share not only a common exile but also an extraordinarily complete psychological isolation" (451).

34. When Cassandra Austen retrospectively recollected her sister's plans for the novel, she suggested that "Mr. Watson was soon to die; and Emma to become dependent for a home on her narrow-minded sister-in-law and brother. She was to decline an offer of marriage from Lord Osborne, and much of the interest of the tale was to arise from Lady Osborne's love for Mr. Howard, and his counter affection for Emma, whom he was finally to marry" (James Edward Austen-Leigh, *A Memoir of Jane Austen* [London: Bentley, 1870], 364). This summary was passed down in the Austen family. Even before Austen-Leigh's publication of the *Memoir*, one of Jane's nieces, Catherine Hubback, published the first completion of an Austen novel, *The Younger Sister* (London: Thomas Cautley Newby, 1850). Hubback capitalized on the promises of further homesickness, regret, and endurance in the novel: "[T]here are times when all I have lost comes back to my memory, and seems quite to overpower me. My earliest friends lost to me, and with them the happy home where I had enjoyed every indulgence, and every pleasure that affection could procure" (vol. 3, 57).

35. Jane Austen, *Emma* (London: Oxford University Press, 1952), 5. Hereafter cited parenthetically in the text.

36. Johnson, *Austen*, 125.

37. Although Johnson has pointed out that Emma needs to learn "a proper regard for public opinion" (130) that is opposed to Mrs. Elton's presumption, she significantly stresses the "atypicality" and "eccentricity" of the final happy arrangement to suggest that a "conclusion which seemed tamely and placidly conservative then take an unexpected turn, as the guarantor of order himself cedes a considerable portion of the power which Austen has allowed him to expect. In moving to Hartfield, Knightley is sharing her home, and in placing

himself within her domain, Knightley gives his blessing to her rule" (*Austen*, 143).

38. Kelly, *Romantic*, 118.
39. Austen, *Minor Works*, 391.
40. Compare *Pride and Prejudice*, ch.10, specifically 154.
41. Sarah Tytler, *Jane Austen & Her Works* (London: Cassel, Petter, Galpin & Co, 1880), 92.
42. Alistair M. Duckworth, *The Improvement of the Estate: A Study of Jane Austen's Novels* (Baltimore: John Hopkins University Press, 1994), 125.
43. Isobel Armstrong, "Introduction to *Pride and Prejudice*," in *Jane Austen: Critical Assessments,* ed. Ian Littlewood (Mountfield: Helm Information, 1998), vol. 3, 407.
44. Among the many revisions and re-enactments of Darcy's tenderness to the weeping Elizabeth and their transpositions onto other eligible bachelors in sequels to Austen's fiction, one of the most obvious imitations can be found in Julia Barrett's *Presumption* (London: Michael O'Mara Books, 1993). When a new character, Leigh-Cooper, sees Elizabeth in distress, he repeats Darcy's reactions in the original: "'You are ill,' said he, with great gentleness. 'Let me call your maid; would you take a glass of wine? Or,' suddenly drawing back as he recollected himself, 'perhaps I am intruding.'" (124) The original runs thus: "[I]t was impossible for Darcy to leave her, or to refrain from saying, in a tone of gentleness and commiseration, 'Let me call your maid. Is there nothing you could take to give you present relief? A glass of wine; shall I get you one? You are very ill.'" (276). Compare my detailed reading of sequels to Jane Austen's novels, published from the mid-nineteenth century onwards: Tamara S. Wagner, "Rewriting Sentimental Plots: Sequels to Novels of Sensibility by Jane Austen and Another Lady," in *And Now for the Sequel: Examining Updates of Eighteenth-Century Works,* eds. Debra Bourdeau and Elizabeth Kraft (Newark: Delaware University Press forthcoming).
45. Said, *Imperialism*, 73. But compare also Susan Fraiman, "Jane Austen and Edward Said: Gender, Culture, and Imperialism," *Critical Inquiry* 21, no. 4 (1995): 805–21.
46. Franco Moretti, *Atlas of the European Novel* (London: Verso, 1999), 27. But compare Katie Trumpener, *Bardic Nationalism: The Romantic Novel and the British Empire* (Princeton: Princeton University Press, 1997), 163.
47. Fanny's refusal to act, but not to help in the preparations, should be compared with Elizabeth Bennet's attempts to prevent her youngest sister's excursion to Brighton by influencing her father behind that sister's back in *Pride and Prejudice*. When her sister elopes with the novel's villain, Elizabeth is proved right, just as Fanny is in her appraisal of the acting scheme, but while Fanny has repeatedly been called dull, prim, a creep-mouse, and also a killjoy, Elizabeth's interference, which so adroitly mirrors Darcy's meddling in Bingley's affairs, has excited astonishingly little comment.
48. Butler, *Austen*, 241.
49. Kathryn Sutherland has significantly called Fanny's "selective powers of memory" her "greatest survival strategy" ("Introduction," Jane Austen, *Mansfield Park* [London: Penguin, 1996], xiii).
50. Henry Austen's "biographical notice" was published in the posthumous publication of *Northanger Abbey* and *Persuasion*. See Jane Austen, *Northanger Abbey* and *Persuasion* (London: Oxford University Press, 1959), 7.
51. Mavis Batey pinpoints Austen's ambivalent stance towards literary and other fashions, suggesting that she uses "crosscurrents . . . in matters of 'Taste and Feeling,'" chronicling them "with amused detachment (*Austen*, 8).

52. The precise nature of Pemberley is never stated, indeed is perhaps deliberately left obscure. Critics have called it "Gilpinesque" (Batey, *Austen,* 80) as well as "virtually a paradigm of the picturesque" (Armstrong, "Introduction," 407). In *Jane Austen's England* (London: Hale, 1986), Maggie Lane rather incongruously styles it Austen's "most perfect Brownian creation" (23).

53. It is noteworthy that Fanny shares Marianne Dashwood's attachment to fine trees. It becomes clear that Norland has fallen into worse hands when Mr. John Dashwood plans to cut down old walnut trees to make way for a greenhouse. In Austen's novels, fine trees are an attribute of desirable estates. These are, as Sarah Gilbert and Susan Gubar have pointed out, "spacious, beautiful places almost always supplied with the loveliest fruit trees and the prettiest prospects" (*Madwoman*, 154). They invite consumption as well as aesthetic appreciation. In an article on the iconography of woodland, Stephen Daniels suggests that trees are as "rich a symbolic resource as a material one, frequently being exploited to represent ideas of social order" ("The political iconography of woodland in later Georgian England," in *The Iconography of Landscape: Essays on the Symbolic Representation, Design and Use of Past Environments*, eds. Denis Cosgrove and Stephen Daniels [Cambridge: Cambridge University Press, 1997], 43). Fashionable improvement for its own sake never fares well in Austen.

54. Stewart, *Domestic*, 27.

55. Sutherland sees the east-room as "the physical site of Fanny's and the house's memory," "a Romantic location, as laden with meaning and restorative power as the landscape above Tintern Abbey is for Wordsworth" ("Introduction," xiii). See Kenneth Muir, *The Romantic Period* (London: Macmillan, 1980), 1–3.

56. Katie Trumpener has pointed out that in Mary Crawford's hands this bardic instrument, "cherished vehicle of Irish, Welsh, and Scottish nationalism," is used for purely picturesque effect (*Nationalism*, 18–19). Tuite has recently reassessed Trumpener's argument critically, pointing out that "Austen's text does not engage the harp to produce this 'organic' relationship with any degree of national (that is, Irish and Scottish) specificity; the harp signifies an organic relationship understood as a generalized English country relationship. The organic is certainly a privileged figure for Austen, but it works to link and join, rather than to emphasize difference" (*Romantic*, 150).

57. Tanner, "Introduction," 22.

58. Jay Clayton, *Romantic Vision and the Novel* (Cambridge: Cambridge University Press, 1987), 60–61. Kelly speaks of Austen's "paradoxical status as a Romantic novelist" (*Romantic*, 111). Tuite's recent study significantly considers the Austen novel as "a specifically Romantic form of cultural production" (*Romantic*, 1).

59. Ibid., 70.

60. John Wiltshire, *Recreating Jane Austen* (Cambridge: Cambridge University Press, 2001), 138.

61. Compare Lillian Naydor, *Wilkie Collins* (London: Prentice Hall, 1997), 72. This introduction of the Gothic into the middle-class home constitutes an important disruption of ideals of domesticity, engendering different representations of homelessness, homesickness, and uncongenial homes. I shall come back to the significance of this subgenre in subsequent chapters.

62. Tanner, "Introduction," 17.

63. As Roger Sales puts it, the novel "offers both an optimistic and pessimistic answer to the question of who will win the peace" (*Jane Austen and Representations of Regency England* [London: Routledge, 1996], 199).

64. Walter Allen termed *Persuasion* "the tenderest of [Austen's] novels" (*The English Novel* [Harmondsworth: Macmillan, 1958], 110). More recently, Claude Rawson has agreed that it is "conspicuous for its tender and underisive treatment of its heroine's affections" (*Satire and Sentiment: 1660–1830* [Cambridge: Cambridge University Press, 1994], 267). Jocelyn Harris has further suggested that the contrast of genuine and artificial melancholy is a central theme in the novel (*Memory*, 193).

Chapter 3. Childhood Lost

1. Charles Dickens, *Christmas Books* (London: Chapman and Hall, 1878), 189.
2. Charles Dickens, *Bleak House* (Oxford: Oxford University Press, 1959), xiv. Hereafter cited parenthetically in the text. Compare also Robert Newsom's full-length study of the "Romantic" elements in *Bleak House* (*Dickens on the Romantic Side of Familiar Things:* BLEAK HOUSE *and the Novel Tradition* [New York: Columbia University Press, 1977], passim.)
3. Charles Dickens, *Dombey and Son* (Oxford: Clarendon, 1974), 313. Charles Dickens *Little Dorrit* (Oxford: Clarendon, 1979), 165. Hereafter cited parenthetically in the text.
4. On the "non-home" in Dickens's fiction compare Ephraim Sicher, "Bleak Homes and Symbolic Houses: At-Homeness and Homelessness in Dickens," in *Homes and Homelessness in the Victorian Imagination,* eds. Murray Baumgarten and H. M. Daleski (New York: AMS, 1998), 33–49.
5. Jackie Wullschläger, *Inventing Wonderland: The Lives and Fantasies of Lewis Carroll, Edward Lear, J. M. Barrie, Kenneth Grahame and A. A. Milne* (London: Methuen, 1995), 12. Compare Fred Kaplan, *Sacred Tears: Sentimentality in Victorian Literature* (Princeton: Princeton University Press, 1987), 7.
6. Penny Brown, *The Captured World: The Child and Childhood in Nineteenth-Century Women's Writing in England* (Hemel Hempstead: Harvester Wheatsheaf, 1993), 61.
7. See Banerjee, *Childhood*, 83–108. Compare also Pat Jalland's *Death in the Victorian Family* (Oxford: Oxford University Press, 1996) on a still-alarmingly high infant and child mortality rate in the Victorian age, and the ways the Victorian family faced the ever-present threat of this calamity.
8. Charles Dickens, *David Copperfield* (Oxford: Clarendon, 1981), 11. Hereafter cited parenthetically in the text.
9. Raymond Chapman, *The Sense of the Past in Victorian Literature* (London: Croom Helm, 1986), 145.
10. Charlotte Brontë, *Jane Eyre* (London: Zodiac, 1965), 34. Hereafter cited parenthetically in the text.
11. Coveney, *Monkey*, 74.
12. Catherine Waters, *Dickens and the Politics of the Family* (Cambridge: Cambridge University Press, 1997), 29.
13. Baruch Hochman and Ilja Wachs, *Dickens: The Orphan Condition* (Madison: Fairleigh Dickinson University Press, 1999), 14.
14. Dever, *Death*, 4.
15. Peter Ackroyd, *Dickens* (London: Sinclair-Stevenson, 1990), 232.
16. Ibid., 414.
17. Compare Ackroyd, *Dickens*, 414: "[Dickens's] real contribution to the depiction of Christmas lay in his talent for chiaroscuro. Beyond the hearth were

the poor, the ignorant, the diseased, the wretched; and do we not enjoy the flames of the Christmas fire more because of the very shadows which it casts? Dickens had an acute sense of, and need for, 'Home'—it sprang from his own experience of being banished from that blessed place." For an insightful overview of the "images of terror and threat" that are poised against and counterpoised by images of "restoration and restitution" see Baruch Hochman, "Bulrush and Harvest Home," in *Homes and Homelessness in the Victorian Imagination,* eds. Murray Baumgarten and H. M. Daleski (New York: AMS Press, 1998), 52.

18. Mildred Newcomb, *The Imagined World of Charles Dickens* (Columbus: Ohio State University Press, 1989), 99.

19. Malcolm Andrews, *Dickens and the Grown-up Child* (Iowa City: University of Iowa Press, 1994), 43.

20. The *Oxford English Dictionary* significantly defines sentimentality as an "affectation of sensibility." Thus, it forms a negative example or distortion of sensibility or a case of affected or diffuse sensibility.

21. Charles Dickens, *Oliver Twist* (Oxford: Oxford University Press, 1949), 216. Hereafter cited parenthetically in the text.

22. Fred Kaplan, *Dickens and Mesmerism: The Hidden Springs of Fiction* (Princeton: Princeton University Press, 1975), 152, 139.

23. Ibid., 107.

24. Franco Moretti, *The Way of the World: The* Bildungsroman *in European Culture* (London: Verso, 1987), 182–84. According to Moretti, this emphasis on childhood is one of "the many differences between the English *Bildungsroman* and the continental one" (182).

25. Alison Winter, *Mesmerized: Powers of Mind in Victorian Britain* (Chicago: University of Chicago Press, 1998), 11, 58: Winter analyzes Cruishank's illustration of Oliver's waking dream, suggesting that "Oliver's extended legs [are] reminiscent of the rigid postures of magnetic subjects in certain steps of the trance" (58). Compare John Sutherland, "Is Oliver dreaming?" John Sutherland, *Is Heathcliff a Murderer?* (Oxford: Oxford University Press, 1996), 35–45.

26. Charles Dickens, *Martin Chuzzlewit* (Oxford: Clarendon, 1982), 71. Hereafter cited parenthetically in the text.

27. Marcel Proust, *In Search of Lost Time,* trans. C. K. Scott Moncrieff and Terence Kilmartin (London: Vintage, 1996), vol. 1, 51.

28. Charles Dickens, *Nicholas Nickleby* (London: Oxford University Press, 1957), 758–59. Hereafter cited parenthetically in the text.

29. Rylance, *Psychology,* 66.

30. Dames, *Amnesiac,* 138, 4.

31. Ibid., 4. Walter Benjamin has already shown that Proust's involuntary recollection has more to do with forgetting than with remembering. Dames, however, speaks of a "genteel dialectic of nostalgia," which he sees as peculiarly Victorian. Although he admits that it is problematic to identify nostalgia with forgetting, he proceeds to build his argument on this generalization, joining the deriders of the heritage industry in their simplification of nostalgia. See Walter Benjamin, *Illuminations,* trans. Harry Zohn (London: Jonathan Cape, 1968), 204. Compare Milton L. Miller, *Nostalgia: A Psychoanalytical Study of Marcel Proust* (Dallas: Taylor, 1969), passim.

32. Moretti, *Bildungsroman,* 44. *David Copperfield* has notably been called a "Proustian novel of the shaping of life through the echoes and prophecies of memory" (Angus Wilson, *The World of Charles Dickens* [London: Secker & Warburg, 1970], 214).

33. Compare also Sally Shuttleworth's references to the story in "'The malady of thought': Embodied memory in Victorian psychology and the novel," in

Memory and Memorials, 1789–1914, Matthew Campbell et al. (London: Routledge, 2000), 46–59.

34. Patrick McCarthy, "Making for Home: David Copperfield and His Fellow Travellers," in *Homes and Homelessness in the Victorian Imagination,* eds. Murray Baumgarten and H. M. Daleski (New York: AMS Press, 1998), 27.

35. Charles Dickens, *Hard Times* (London: Oxford University Press, 1970), 287.

36. John Ruskin, *Works* (London: George Allen, 1908), 122.

37. Compare Frances Armstrong, *Dickens and the Concept of Home* (Ann Arbor: UMI Research Press, 1990) on the novel's (albeit comical) affirmation of Wemmick's fortified home. Armstrong has convincingly argued that "Wemmick's real strength is that he understands why fortifications are necessary around a home: not to keep the world out so much as to keep the fiction in" (138).

38. Samuel Butler's retrospective diatribe against the ideals of Victorian domesticity in *The Way of All Flesh* highlights this inverted version of homesickness as a being sick of a dysfunctional home: "This was how it came to pass that their children were white and puny; they were suffering from homesickness. They were starving, through being over-crammed with the wrong things." (Samuel Butler, *The Way of All Flesh,* ed. A. J. Hoppe [Dent: London, 1968], 95.)

39. Steven Mintz, *A Prison of Expectations: The Family in Victorian Culture* (New York: New York University Press, 1983), 10.

40. A. S. Byatt, *Possession* (London: Chatto & Windus, 1990), 210.

41. Sarah Waters, *Fingersmith* (London: Virago, 2002). Michael Faber, *The Crimson Petal and the White* (Edinburgh: Canongate, 2002). Compare also Waters's earlier novels, in particular *Affinity* (London: Virago, 1999), which focuses on the Victorian interest in mesmerism and the occult, while detailing a Victorian prison. Recent historical novels indeed reflect academic interest in nineteenth-century underworlds and subcultures, but the length and elaborate plot-twists of the above mentioned works closely, almost nostalgically, imitate the Victorian sensation genre.

42. Charles Dickens, *Our Mutual Friend* (London: Oxford University Press, 1959), 184. Hereafter cited parenthetically in the text.

43. Jeff Nunokawa, "For Your Eyes Only: Private Property and the Oriental Body in *Dombey and Son,*" in *Macropolitics of Nineteenth-Century Literature: Nationalism, Exoticism, Imperialism,* eds. Jonathan Arac and Harriet Ritvo (Philadelphia: University of Pennsylvania Press, 1991), 138–65.

44. Robert G. Stange, "Expectations Well Lost: Dickens's Fable for His Time," in *Dickens: Critical Assessments,* ed. Michael Hollington (Mountfield: Helm Information, 1995), 518.

45. Charles Dickens, *Great Expectations* (Oxford: Clarendon, 1993), 3–4. Hereafter cited parenthetically in the text.

46. See David Trotter, "Introduction," Charles Dickens, *Great Expectations* (London: Penguin, 1996): Magwitch is "an atmosphere, a condition, not a moral dilemma" (xi). Stange similarly points out a bond "between the child and the criminal; they are alike in their helplessness; both are repressed and tortured by established society, and both rebel against its incomprehensible authority" ("Expectations," 520).

47. Compare Geoffrey Thurley, *The Dickens Myth: Its Genesis and Structure* (London: Routledge & Kegan Paul, 1976), *passim.* As Thurley puts it, "the Dickens myth," a "primal wish-fulfillment fantasy," is "at first simply enacted with extraordinary power and richness, then raised to awareness, and finally subjected to criticism" (18). See Almansi, *"Expectations,"* 584–88.

48. Small, *Madness*, 209. Small remarks on the incongruity of Dickens's sentimentalism. While he was interested in the questionable status of eighteenth-century sentimental values seventy years on, revitalizing many set-pieces of sentimental fiction such as the lingering deathbed scene, the repentance of the prostitute, and the return of the lost child, the love-mad woman "singularly failed to attack his sympathy" (207).

49. The Victorian age saw increasing awareness of the necessary hygienic standards in sickrooms and hospitals, which also initiated reforms of hired nurses. See Alison Bashford, *Purity and Pollution: Gender, Embodiment and Victorian Medicine* (London: Macmillan, 1998): "The story of the shift between types of nurses—told not infrequently as the shift between Dickens's Sairey Gamp and Florence Nightingale—was one which gathered its meaning and significance within ideas about sanitary reform" (xv).

50. John Lucas, *The Melancholy Man: A Study of Dickens's Novels* (Brighton: Harvester Press, 1980), 49.

51. Dever, *Death*, 26, xi.

52. Dever, *Death*, xi. Dever further argues that mid-nineteenth-century texts express an epistemological crisis of origins through the representation of maternal loss, a concern most famously argued in Darwin's *The Origin of Species* (6). I shall return to the influence of Darwinian narratives on Victorian fiction in chapter 4.

53. Miriam Bailin, *The Sickroom in Victorian Fiction: The Art of Being Ill* (Cambridge: Cambridge University Press, 1994), 79. Bailin shows how "illness figures the involuntary emergence into visibility of the self, which, if read aright, makes legible its secret longings" (265). In her article on *Shirley*, she speaks of the sickroom "romance," with its private dreamlike intensities, its formal symmetries, its archetypal figures, its suspension of linear development, and . . . its capacity to grant a fulfilment equal to desire" ("'Varieties of Pain': The Victorian Sickroom and Brontë's *Shirley*," *MLQ* 48, no. 3 [1987]: 256). Compare Athena Vrettos, *Somatic Fictions: Imagining Illness in Victorian Culture* (Standford: Standford University Press, 1995), on the capacity of illness to reconfigure conceptions of the self (3). Fred Kaplan similarly suggests that "such illness represents a concentration of all the psychic diseases of the individual's life" (*Mesmerism*, 157).

54. Charles Dickens, *The Old Curiosity Shop* (Oxford: Clarendon, 1997), 557. Hereafter cited parenthetically in the text.

55. Robert M. Polhemus, "The Favorite Child: *David Copperfield* and the Scriptural Issue of Child-Wives," in *Homes and Homelessness in the Victorian Imagination*, eds. Murray Baumgarten and H. M. Daleski (New York: AMS Press, 1998), 3. Compare also Robert M. Polhemus, "Comic and Erotic Faith Meet Faith in the Child: Charles Dickens's *The Old Curiosity Shop*," in *Critical Reconstructions: The Relationship of Fiction and Life*, eds. Robert M. Polhemus and Roger B. Henkle (Stanford: Stanford University Press, 1994), 71–89.

56. Philip Collins, *Dickens and Education* (London: Macmillan, 1963), 84. Compare Newcomb, *Dickens*, 88.

57. James R. Kincaid, *Child-Loving: The Erotic Child and Victorian Culture* (London: Routledge, 1992), passim.

58. Dinah Craik, *Olive* (Oxford: Oxford University Press, 1999), 32.

59. Ellen Wood, *East Lynne* (New Brunswick: Rutgers University Press, 1984), 493.

60. Frances Hodgson Burnett, *The Secret Garden* (London: Folio Society, 1986), 225.

61. Humphrey Carpenter, *Secret Gardens: A Study of the Golden Age of Children's Literature* (London: George Allen & Unwin, 1985), 188.

62. Frances Hodgson Burnett, *Little Lord Fauntleroy* (Oxford: Oxford University Press, 1993), 54.

63. Johanna Spyri, *Heidi,* trans. Eileen Hall (London: Penguin, 1995), 199; 222.

64. Kenneth Grahame, *Dream Days* (London: Bodley Head, 1973), 17; Kenneth Grahame, *The Golden Age* (Edinburgh: Paul Harris, 1983), 13–14.

65. The magical Victorian garden in A. Philippa Pearce's 1958 *Tom's Midnight Garden* (London: Heinemann Educational, 1979) shows the persistence of this association. In Tom's reality, the dream-garden has been supplanted by "a narrow, paved space enclosed by a wooden fence, with a gateway on to the side-road at one end. . . . The place smelt of sun on stone and metal and the creosote of the fencing" (4). Late-twentieth-century environmentalist children's books have perpetuated such Romantic cults of nature and children. In Penelope Farmer's *Charlotte Sometimes* (Bath: Chivers, 1985), for example, Charlotte travels into the past to notice changes in the landscape with "nostalgic curiosity" (158): "The tree had been beautiful as a sailing-ship, its trunk stouter than a mast, its branches spread like sails, and she felt sad, even indignant that they should have thought to cut it down" (34).

66. Charles Dickens, *A Tale of Two Cities* (London: Oxford University Press, 1960), 358.

67. Thurley, *Dickens*, 11.

68. Angus Wilson, "The Heroes and Heroines of Dickens," in *Dickens: A Collection of Critical Essays,* ed. Martin Price (Englewood Cliffs, NJ: Prentice-Hall, 1967), 23.

69. As Dever suggests, Dickens's fictional houses evoke concepts of the *heimlich* [homely] and the *unheimlich* [uncanny] and the notion of love as homesickness, as posited in Freud's essay "The Uncanny" (*Death*, passim). Compare Newsom: "love may be homesickness after all" (*Romantic,* 86). Yet Bleak House also forms what Gaston Bachelard terms an "oneiric house" [*The Poetics of Space,* trans. Maria Jolas (Boston: Beacon, 1969), 16]. His topoanalysis sees the house as "a privileged entity for a phenomenological study of the intimate values of inside space" (3), an image for the localization of memories: "Thanks to the house, a great many of our memories are housed, and if the house is a bit elaborate, if it has a cellar and a garret, nooks and corridors, our memories have refuges that are all the more clearly delineated" (8). Bleak House is a nostalgic space that houses memories of the past in its elaborate corridors and cozy corners.

70. It has also been suggested that the symbolic burial of Esther's doll "repeats in literal form the psychological drama enacted by her own mother on her own birthday: a mother burying her dead baby" (Dever, *Death,* 90). The infant that provides the link in the unification of Lady Dedlock and the child she was made to believe dead and buried is covered with her handkerchief, literally marked as "Esther Summerson."

71. Hochman and Wachs, *Orphan,* 86. They further suggest that Esther's narrative "is the product of the repressions that survival mandates" (89). Compare also Anny Sadrin, "Charlotte Dickens: The Female Narrator of *Bleak House,*" in *Dickens: Critical Assessments,* ed. Michael Hollington (Mountfield: Helm Information, 1995): "[Critics] always sound as if they wish to apologise for not liking her as much as they should" or "tend to patronize her" (249–50).

72. Newsom, *Romantic,* 83–84.

73. Critics have rightly suggested that the "authorial approval of the at-homeness of *Bleak House* is unmistakable" (Sicher, "Homes," 37), that it is "probably the imaginary home dearest to [Dickens]" (David Parker, "Dickens at

Home," in *Homes and Homelessness in the Victorian Imagination,* eds. Murray Baumgarten and H. M. Daleski [New York: AMS Press, 1998], 66).

74. Frances Armstrong has even suggested that Wemmick's fortified abode is "perhaps the most loving and peaceful home" in Dickens's writing (*Dickens,* 136).

75. Waters has pointedly shown that "Fagin's den offers perhaps the most notable parody of the middle-class family in the novel" (*Dickens,* 34).

76. Wilkie Collins, *The Fallen Leaves* (London: Chatto & Windus, 1879), vol. 1, 163–64.

77. Gillian Beer, *Arguing with the Past: Essays from Woolf to Sidney* (London: Routledge, 1989), 27.

78. For a psychological study of Amy's suppressed resentment see Richard A. Currie, "'As if she had done him a wrong': Hidden Rage and Object Protection in Dickens's Amy Dorrit," *English Studies* 72, no. 4 (1991): 369.

79. Compare also Dames, *Amnesiac,* 141, 268, n. 41 on what he sees as a "forgetting" of the resentful characters: "One might almost say that the movement of a Dickens text is to eliminate these characters, or to restore them to some more normative version of health—in short, to *forget* them. Thus Satis House is razed and sold for scrap—transformed into a sort of utility—and thus Mrs. Clennam's house collapses on itself; the traumatic cathexes of some of Dickens's characters are not allowed to outlive the novel's conclusion, and the novel itself becomes an exercise in exorcism, in a *leaving behind*" (268).

80. Dr. Manette's amnesia in *A Tale of Two Cities* is even more frightening. Compare Thurley, *Dickens,* 11.

Chapter 4. Homesickness

1. Jerome Hamilton Buckley, *The Triumph of Time: A Study of the Victorian Concepts of Time, History, Progress, and Decadence* (Cambridge, MA: Harvard University Press, 1967), 13.

2. Chapman, *Past,* 4, 7.

3. Campbell, *Memory,* 1.

4. This topos, a sentimentalized version of the Romantic child, is central to George Eliot's *Silas Marner* (1861) as well as Craik's *Olive* and, as we have seen, many of Dickens's novels. As I have indicated in chapter 3, it is taken to its extremes in late-Victorian and Edwardian fiction.

5. Frances Hodgson Burnett, *A Little Princess* (London: Penguin, 1996), 134. Lewis Carroll's *Alice's Adventures in Wonderland* (1865) and *Through the Looking-Glass* (1871) are central to Victorian cults of the child, but while they express the author's nostalgia for childhood, there is little nostalgia in the texts. Late-Victorian and Edwardian children's fiction such as Burnett's novels, Grahame's *The Wind in the Willows* (1908), Barrie's *Peter Pan* (1911), and later Milne's *Winnie-the-Pooh* (1926) and *The House at Pooh Corner* (1928) not only expresses nostalgia more directly, but shows the influence of Victorian child cults on twentieth- and twenty-first-century conceptualization and perpetuation of children's "classics."

6. Charlotte Brontë, *Villette* (Oxford: Clarendon, 1984), 715. Hereafter cited parenthetically in the text.

7. Jenni Calder, *Women and Marriage in Victorian Fiction* (London: Thames and Hudson, 1976), 63.

8. Charlotte Brontë, *Shirley* (Oxford: Clarendon, 1979), 503. Compare Miriam Bailin's article on the novel: Bailin argues that in *Shirley*, "somatic disorder becomes the primary form of self-assertion, convalescence the measure of comfort, and physical dependency the enabling condition for intimacy" (*"Shirley,"* 257).

9. Sally Shuttleworth, "The Dynamics of Cross-Culturalism in Charlotte Brontë's Fiction," in *The Brontë Sisters: Critical Assessments,* ed. Eleanor McNees (Mountfield: Helm Information, 1996), 340.

10. Philip Momberger, "Self and World in the Works of Charlotte Brontë," in *The Brontë Sisters: Critical Assessments,* ed. Eleanor McNees (Mountfield: Helm Information, 1996), 179.

11. As Hsiao-Hung Lee puts it in *Possibilities of Hidden Things: Narrative Transgression in Victorian Fictional Autobiographies* (New York: Peter Lang, 1996), Lucy imagines herself "living through the lives of other women" (75–76).

12. Compare Robert Bernard Martin, *The Accents of Persuasion* (London: Faber and Faber, 1966), 183.

13. Compare Showalter, *Malady,* 136. Originally an American disease, neurasthenia was eagerly appropriated in Britain as a new name for what had been called spinal irritation, neuralgic disease, or nervous weakness. It was soon extended to include low spirits more generally.

14. Janet Oppenheim, *"Shattered Nerves:" Doctors, Patients, and Depression in Victorian England* (Oxford: Oxford University Press, 1991), 116.

15. Vrettos, *Somatic,* 29.

16. Sally Shuttleworth, *Charlotte Brontë and Victorian Psychology* (Cambridge: Cambridge University Press, 1996), 9. Compare Oppenheim, *Nerves,* 82. Dr. John's kindly meant, but rather insipid—solid, stable, and unmoved—letters similarly fail to fulfill the expectations raised by Lucy's loneliness. Her passionate clinging to a "simply good-natured" (*Villette,* 350) letter is understandable; her hysteria over its threatened loss symptomatic of her loneliness: "'Oh! They have taken my letter!' cried the grovelling, groping monomaniac." (*Villette,* 353) Robert Bernard Martin notes that the "infrequency of John's letters and the emotional turmoil that they arouse in Lucy are set in direct contrast to the letters that she receives from Paul" (*Persuasion,* 165).

17. On Brontë's use of phrenology see Sally Shuttleworth, "Psychological Definition and Social Power: Phrenology in the Novels of Charlotte Brontë," in *Nature Transfigured: Science and Literature 1700–1900,* eds. John Christie and Sally Shuttleworth (Manchester: Manchester University Press, 1989), 121–51. Compare also Shuttleworth, *Psychology,* 57–70, and Nicholas Dames, "The Clinical Novel: Phrenology and *Villette,*" *Novel* 29, no. 3 (1996): 367–90.

18. Charlotte Brontë, *The Professor* (London: Smith, Elder & Co, 1857), 197. Hereafter cited parenthetically in the text.

19. Moral capacity is seen as being mapped onto the surface of the skull. See T. R. Wright, "From Bumps to Morals: The Phrenological Background to George Eliot's Moral Framework," *Review of English Studies* 33, no. 129 (1982): 35–40. Wright speaks of the "moralization" of Gall, pointing out that cerebral physiology as conceived by the eighteenth-century Viennese neuroanatomist Franz Joseph Gall had nothing to do with morals. Gall's theory simply posits the brain as a "place of rendezvous of all the single organs, each innate disposition having an organ of its own, which is increased in proportion to the power residing in the disposition" (Charles A. Blöde, *Dr F. J. Gall's System of the Functions of the Brain,* ed. Nicholas J. Wade [London: Routledge, 2000], 14–15).

20. Bailin, "*Shirley,*" 256.

21. Deirdre D'Albertis, *Dissembling Fictions: Elizabeth Gaskell and the Victorian Social Text* (Basingstoke: Macmillan, 1997), 137. In his chapter on "Empire Stories: The Imperial and the Domestic" in *Island Stories*, however, Raphael Samuel has convincingly foregrounded the imperialist aspects of *Cranford* (1851): although it "is as provincial a novel as it would be possible to imagine," India is "quite an insistent pressure on the story" (74). Samuel goes on to emphasize that the absence of racism in the novel is striking, as is a belief in the goodness of the Indian people and a common humanity (76). As I shall show, the use of the similarly off stage Africa in *Wives and Daughters* is more complicated, but its critical, even satirical, representation of racism is similarly striking in a mid-Victorian novel.

22. Lynn L. Merrill, *The Romance of Victorian Natural History* (Oxford: Oxford University Press, 1989), 16. On the changes from an earlier ideal of naturalist field-work compare also Landry, *Countryside*, 30.

23. Anna Unsworth, *Elizabeth Gaskell: An Independent Woman* (London: Minerva, 1996), 219.

24. D'Albertis, *Dissembling*, 144.

25. Compare Terence Wright, *Elizabeth Gaskell: We are not angels: Realism, Gender, Values* (London: Macmillan, 1995): Wright calls Roger a "new lover and New Man" (45), but fails to explore the extent of Roger's "newness," his difference from languid sentimental heroes and from the new muscular men.

26. William Greenslade, *Degeneration, Culture and the Novel 1880–1940* (Cambridge: Cambridge University Press, 1994), 2.

27. Ibid., 1.

28. Kelly Hurley, *The Gothic Body: Sexuality, Materialism, and Degeneration at the Fin de Siècle* (Cambridge: Cambridge University Press, 1996), 6.

29. Henry Maudsley, *Sex in Mind and in Education* (New York: Miller, 1874), 5.

30. Gillian Beer, *Open Fields: Science in Cultural Encounter* (Oxford: Oxford University Press, 1996), 219.

31. H. G. Wells, *The Time Machine* (Harmondsworth: Penguin, 1946), 48, 31.

32. Francis Galton, "Kantsaywhere," in Karl Pearson, *The Life, Letters and Labours of Francis Galton* (Cambridge: Cambridge University Press, 1914–1930), 412.

33. Edward Bellamy, *Equality* (New York: D. Appleton, 1897), 364.

34. Mary E. Bradley Lane, *Mizora* (New York: G. W. Dillingham, 1890), 9, 193.

35. Most subsequent versions have intriguingly been Dystopian. Works such as *The Time Machine* moreover show that hope in evolution and eugenics was never uniform. Bellamy's works spawned a plethora of Dystopias, including Conrad Wilbrandt's *Mr. East's Experiences in Mr. Bellamy's World: Records of the Years 2001 and 2002* (New York: Harper & Brothers, 1891), in which Friedrich Ost [East] reads *Looking Backward* and is disturbed by the questions it leaves unanswered. Put in suspended animation, he is at first delighted to wake in the "golden age" (20) described by Mr. West in Bellamy's novel, but he soon discovers its drawbacks. The book ends on the eve of civilization's utter collapse. In Ignatius Donnelly's *Caesar's Column* of 1889 (Cambridge: Belknap, 1960), a countrified hero stays in a hotel called *The Darwin* in a gleaming twentieth-century New York only to find it "rotten at the core" (34): the "old question of the survival of the fittest" (32) has moulded the suppressed into well-endowed suppressers. William Morris's *News From Nowhere* of 1890 (Cambridge: Cambridge University Press, 1995) stands out among the Utopias

of the time as it reacts against Bellamy's industrial Utopia by creating a pre-industrial rural future. Mid-Victorian domestic novels anticipate concerns that are more explicitly tackled in later Utopian and Dystopian fiction by integrating them into the traditional plots of the British novel.

36. Levine, *Darwin*, 13, 3.
37. Beer, *Fields*, 173.
38. Ibid.
39. Beer, *Darwin*, 210.
40. Armstrong, *Desire*, 40.
41. Wilkie Collins, *No Name* (London: Sampson Low, 1862), 10. Hereafter cited parenthetically in the text.
42. Elizabeth Gaskell, *Wives and Daughters* (London: Smith, Elder and Co., 1866), 40; 83. Hereafter cited parenthetically in the text.
43. Since Margaret apparently left her childhood home for London even before the opening of the novel, her nostalgia for her parents' rural home is undercut; the repulsion she feels in the north as much the result of her life in the metropolis as of her longing for the southern countryside.
44. Compare Samuel Smiles's repeated invocation of "work, work, work" as he details the lives of those who engineered the empire through their industry and energy in his *Self-Help* of 1859 (London: John Murray, 1882): "youth must work in order to enjoy" (v).
45. Mangan, *Athleticism*, 106–7.
46. As Jenny Uglow points out, "[o]ne could see the novel as an interesting example of the limits of mid-Victorian thinking about race in the patronizing stereotypes and music-hall jokes applied by Mr. Gibson to the African peoples Roger encounters on his expedition" (*Elizabeth Gaskell: A Habit of Stories* [London: Faber and Faber, 1993], 586). D'Albertis has even suggested that Preston exhibits the "same animalistic characteristics" that are attached to African natives, which "should prompt us to consider anew the significance of Gaskell's redrafting of Darwin's theory of evolution" (146).
47. Moretti, *Atlas*, 27.
48. Compare Robert J. C. Young, *Colonial Desire: Hybridity in Theory, Culture and Race* (London: Routledge, 1995) on the mapping of colonial desire and especially his analysis of Victorian conceptualizations of race (passim).
49. Vrettos, *Somatic*, 147.
50. Roxann Wheeler, *The Complexion of Race: Categories of Difference in Eighteenth-Century British Culture* (Philadelphia: University of Pennsylvania Press, 2000), 2.
51. Young, *Desire*, 4.
52. Ibid., 169.
53. D'Albertis, *Dissembling*, 139. D'Albertis has further suggested that Roger Hamley is modeled on Charles Darwin, with whom Elizabeth Gaskell was personally acquainted (139). This comparison renders D'Albertis's subsequent analysis of "Gaskell's concentration on [Roger's] brute strength" (144) even more disturbing.
54. Jane Spencer, *Elizabeth Gaskell* (Basingstoke: Macmillan, 1993), 130.
55. See Michel Foucault, *Language, Counter-Memory, Practice*, ed. Donald F. Bouchard (Ithaca: Cornell University Press, 1977). In "Nietzsche, Genealogy, History," Foucault writes that "descent attaches itself to the body. It inscribes itself in the nervous system, in temperament, in the digestive apparatus" (147).
56. Greenslade, *Degeneration*, 28.
57. E. Holly Pike, *Family and Society in the Works of Elizabeth Gaskell* (New York: Peter Lang, 1995), 131.
58. Spencer, *Gaskell*, 130.

59. Unsworth, *Gaskell*, 183.
60. Ibid., 187.

Chapter 5. Nostalgia and Men of Sensibility

1. John Barlow, *On Man's Power over Himself to Prevent or Control Insanity* (London: William Pickering, 1849), 11.
2. George M. Beard, *A Practical Treatise on Nervous Exhaustion (Neurasthenia)* . . . (New York: Wood, 1880), v, 50. Compare A. Proust and Gilbert Ballet, *The Treatment of Neurasthenia* (London: Henry Kimpton, 1902) on nineteenth-century conceptualizations of "aboulia or enfeeblement of the will" (53).
3. Susan Stone-Blackburn points out that thought transference is both the *psi*-phenomenon that figures most frequently in Victorian fiction and the one that the Society for Psychical Research, founded in 1882, settled on as its most promising line of inquiry ("Consciousness Evolution and Early Telepathic Tales," *Science Fiction Studies* 20 [1993]: 241–50). It was the society's founding member, F. W. H. Myers, who introduced the term "telepathy," alongside "telesthesia." Compare W. F. Barrett et al, *Proceedings of the Society for Psychical Research* (London: Trubner, 1883): "We venture to introduce the words *Telesthesia* and *Telepathy* to cover all cases of impression received at a distance without the normal operation of the recognized sense organs." (147) As Nicholas Royle shows, this "creation" of telepathy does not indicate that an analysis of its roles in literature has to be "confined to literary texts published since 1882" (*Telepathy and Literature: Essays on the Reading Mind* [Oxford: Basil Blackwell, 1991], 3). "Mesmerism" and "mesmeric rapport" are the most frequently used terms that describe a form of telepathic link or communication in pre-1882 texts.
4. I have engaged in a more detailed analysis of the functions of mesmerism and clinical conceptualizations of neurasthenia in *The Two Destinies* elsewhere. See Tamara S. Wagner, "Victorian Fictions of the Nerves: Telepathy and Depression in Wilkie Collins's *The Two Destinies*," *Victorian Institute Journal* 32 (2004), forthcoming. For an overview of Victorian conceptualizations of healthy and diseased minds, brains, and souls as well as forms of memory see Rylance, *Psychology*, passim. Emphasizing the role of mesmerism in Victorian medicine, Winter likewise sees mesmerism "as a diagnostic tool to study Victorian culture" (*Mesmerized*, 11). Compare also Shuttleworth, "Malady," 46–59.
5. Wilkie Collins, *The Two Destinies* (London: Chatto & Windus, 1876), 35; 63. Hereafter cited parenthetically in the text.
6. Compare Barlow, *Insanity*, 20–28.
7. Wilkie Collins, *The Legacy of Cain* (London: Chatto & Windus, 1889), 10.
8. Wilkie Collins, *The Woman in White* (London: Folio Society, 1992), 361. Hereafter cited parenthetically in the text.
9. Lyn Pykett, *The "Improper" Feminine: The Women's Sensation Novel and the New Woman Writing* (London: Routledge, 1992), 41. Compare Nayder, *Collins*, 72.
10. Alex J. Tuss, *The Inward Revolution: Troubled Young Men in Victorian Fiction, 1850–1880* (New York: Lang, 1992), 2.
11. Tuss, *Inward*, 64.
12. Lyn Pykett, *The Sensation Novel from* THE WOMAN IN WHITE *to* THE MOONSTONE (Plymouth: Northcote House, 1994), 41.

13. In *Wilkie Collins and Other Sensation Novelists: Walking the Moral Hospital* (Basingstoke: Macmillan, 1991), Nicholas Rance suggests that the best sensation novels "derive their effects from subverting a diversity of early and mid-Victorian ideologies" (1). Jenny Bourne Taylor's *In the Secret Theatre of Home: Wilkie Collins, Sensation Narrative, and Nineteenth Century Psychology* (London: Routledge, 1988) similarly analyzes "the ways in which nineteenth-century ideas about the workings of the mind transform and are transformed in Collins's fiction" (2).

14. Vrettos, *Somatic*, 134.

15. Mangan, *Athleticism*, 106–7.

16. Compare Hall, *Muscular*, 4.

17. Thomas Hughes, *Tom Brown's School Days* (Cambridge: Macmillan, 1858), 106.

18. Alec Waugh, *The Loom of Youth* (London: Methuen, 1984), 12, 10. Compare Vance's *Sinews of the Spirit* on mid-Victorian novels that endorse the ideals of muscular Christianity, such as George A. Lawrence's *Guy Livingstone* (1857) and *Sword and Gown* (1859) and Frank E. Smedley's *Frank Fairlegh* (1850).

19. Kaplan, *Mesmerism*, 19.

20. Smith, *Sentiments*, 209.

21. As Vance puts it, "[t]he official, manly ideology that the healthy body will foster a healthy mind and a healthy morality seems increasingly wide of the mark" (*Sinews*, 192).

22. E. M. Forster, *The Longest Journey* (London: Penguin, 1989), 51.

23. Recent reassessments of the sensation novel suggest a connection between, or at least parallel development of, popular genres that focus on the representation as well as the invocation of emotions. Compare Ann Cvetkovich, *Mixed Feelings: Feminism, Mass Culture, and Victorian Sensationalism* (New Brunswick, NJ: Rutgers University Press, 1992): "Despite their difference," notes Cvetkovich, "genres such as the Gothic novel, the sentimental novel, the novel of sensibility, the Newgate novel, the domestic novel, and the detective novel are similar to the sensation novel in their ability to produce affect" (15). See also Pykett, *Feminine*, 27.

24. Sally Shuttleworth, *Charlotte Brontë and Victorian Psychology* (Cambridge: Cambridge University Press, 1996), 50.

25. Charles Reade, *Hard Cash: A Matter-of-Fact Romance* (London: Sampson Low, Son, and Marston, 1863), 47.

26. Mary Elizabeth Braddon, *Lady Audley's Secret* (Oxford: Oxford University Press, 1987), 39.

27. Oppenheim, *Nerves*, 149.

28. Peter Thoms, "Escaping the Plot: The Quest for Selfhood in *The Woman in White*," in *Wilkie Collins to the Forefront: Some Reassessments*, eds. Nelson Smith and R. C. Terry (New York: AMS, 1995), 192.

29. Wilkie Collins, *Hide and Seek* (London: Bentley, 1854), 273.

30. Wilkie Collins, *Basil: A Story of Modern Life* (London: Bentley, 1852).

31. Compare D. A. Miller, "*Cage aux Folles*: Sensation and Gender in Wilkie Collins's *The Woman in White*," in *The Making of the Modern Body: Sexuality and Society in the Nineteenth Century*, eds. Catherine Gallagher and Thomas Laqueur (Berkeley: University of California Press, 1987): Miller speaks of a "case of feminization via the nerves" (115).

32. Compare Naydor, *Collins,* 72: "Sensation novels dramatize marital strife and domestic horror within the middle-class Victorian home . . . . Undermining the ideal of middle-class domesticity, they represent the private sphere as a place of Gothic strife and suffering rather than a healthy and harmonious refuge from the conflicts of public life."

33. Wilkie Collins, *No Name* (Oxford: Oxford University Press, 1986), 5, 291. Hereafter cited parenthetically in the text.

34. Compare Deirdre David, "Rewriting the Male Plot in Collins's *No Name* (1862): Captain Wragge Orders an Omelette and Mrs. Wragge Goes into Custody," in *The New Nineteenth Century: Feminist Readings of Underread Victorian Fiction*, eds. Barbara Leah Harman and Susan Meyer (London: Garland, 1996), 33–44.

35. Pykett, *Novel*, 26.

36. Wilkie Collins, *Armadale* (London: Smith, Elder, 1866), 342. Christopher Kent points out how both Allan and Midwinter pale in comparison with the strong, scheming, villainous woman: "The adventuress Lydia Gwilt, by contrast with both the Armadales, is a bold risk taker and a calculator of the odds, who takes advantage of circumstance and accident to shape the perceptions of probability of men to meet her own requirements" ("Probability, Reality, and Sensation in the Novels of Wilkie Collins," in *Wilkie Collins to the Forefront: Some Reassessments*, eds. Nelson Smith and R. C. Terry [New York: AMS, 1995], 61). Intriguingly, Lydia is also "the dubious beneficiary of the male chauvinism of public opinion which declares [that beautiful women cannot commit murder]" (71).

37. Wilkie Collins, *The Moonstone: A Romance* (London: Folio Society, 1992), 232–33, 183. Julian Symons points out that Count Fosco's obesity in *The Woman in White* likewise "was in opposition to the recognized type of villain," since "in Victorian days fat men were jolly" (*Bloody Murder: From the Detective Story to the Crime Novel* [London: Pan, 1994], 59).

38. Wilkie Collins, *Miss or Mrs.?* (London: Richard Bentley, 1873), 10.

39. Wilkie Collins, *Poor Miss Finch* (London: Bentley, 1872), vol. 1, 85.

40. Wilkie Collins, *The New Magdalen* (London: Bentley, 1873), 100.

41. Wilkie Collins, *The Law and the Lady* (Oxford: Oxford University Press, 1992), 367.

42. Wilkie Collins, *Jezebel's Daughter* (London: Chatto & Windus, 1880), vol.3, 17–18.

43. Wilkie Collins, *The Black Robe* (London: Chatto & Windus, 1881). Through such doubling ideal sensitive men can easily be set apart from their extreme, or negative, versions. In many of Collins's later novels, it serves as a way to save his new heroes from allegations of moral weakness or disconcerting androgyny.

44. Wilkie Collins, *Heart and Science* (Peterborough, Ont.: Broadview, 1996), 45. Hereafter cited parenthetically in the text.

45. C. S. Wiesenthal, "From Charcot to Plato: The History of Hysteria in *Heart and Science*," in *Wilkie Collins to the Forefront: Some Reassessments*, eds. Nelson Smith and R. C. Terry (New York: AMS, 1995), 257.

46. Wiesenthal, "Hysteria," 260.

47. Collins's naming of characters is seldom arbitrary. In *No Name*, as we have seen, Magdalen lives up to her name in the end. In *The New Magdalen*, the redeemed woman and her false counterpart are named Mercy and Grace, respectively, and while Mercy embodies both qualities, Grace possesses neither. Consider also Hartright ("heart-right") in *The Woman in White*.

48. Barbara T. Gates, "Wilkie Collins's Suicides: 'Truth As It Is in Nature,'" in *Wilkie Collins to the Forefront: Some Reassessments*, eds. Nelson Smith and R. C. Terry (New York: AMS, 1995), 252.

49. Wilkie Collins, *I Say No* (London: Chatto and Windus, 1884), vol. 3, 165, vol. 1, 216, vol. 3, 167.

50. Wilkie Collins, *The Evil Genius* (Peterborough, Ont.: Broadview, 1994), 193.

51. Wilkie Collins, *The Guilty River*, eds. Norman Page and Toru Sasaki (Oxford: Oxford University Press, 1999), 247.

52. Wilkie Collins, *Blind Love* (London: Chatto and Windus, 1890), 140, 260.

53. While the role of the antihero in Victorian sensation fiction has recently been brought to the fore, the continuous legacy of the eighteenth-century man of feeling, filtered by the Romantic and the Victorian novel, has been largely ignored. Murray Roston's recent *The Search for Selfhood in Modern Literature* (Houndmills: Palgrave, 2001) dates the emergence of the antihero in the mid-twentieth century. Victor Brombert's *In Praise of Antiheroes: Figures and Themes in Modern European Literature, 1830–1980* (Chicago: Chicago University Press, 1999) provides a general overview of nineteenth- and twentieth-century European anti-heroes.

Conclusion

1. Spacks, "Novel," 305; *Privacy*, 29. Drawing on recent anthropological definitions of privacy that see it as the capacity to exercise, experience, and discover one's own uniqueness, Spacks further emphasizes that reading novels "permits and facilitates all these activities, at the level of fantasy. Through imaginative processes of identification and differentiation in relation to fictional characters, fictional actions, one learns to be more grandly oneself." ("Novel," 305)

2. Spacks, *Privacy*, 29.

3. Ibid. Compare also Spacks, "Novel," 305.

4. As Spacks pointedly puts it, "the idea of privacy as authenticity, as a space of self-discovery, proves intensely relevant to the meditations of poets, fictional characters, and diarists of this earlier period. Indeed, one might reformulate the eighteenth-century concern with what I have been calling 'psychological privacy' as an effort to discern, comprehend, and properly place the individual reflection of the authentic. Privacy is above all an imaginative category. If a remarkable act of imagination was required to conceive of back stairs, figuring out how to use the new possibilities of new architecture demanded comparable imaginative force. . . . The connection between the increasing individualism of the eighteenth century and intensifying stress on privacy is obvious enough." (8) Nostalgic imaginings, though not touched upon by Sparks, are markedly central to this development, and this conclusion will foreground this significance.

5. Gallagher, *Nobody*, xvii.

6. Stewart, *Longing*, xi.

7. Hunter, *Novels*, 40–41.

8. Spacks, *Privacy*, 30–31. Compare also Terry Lovell's "Subjective powers? Consumption, the reading public, and domestic woman in early eighteenth-century England," in *The Consumption of Culture 1600–1800: Image, Object, Text*, eds. Ann Bermingham and John Brewer (London: Routledge, 1995), 27.

9. Charlotte Lennox, *The Female Quixote* (Oxford: Oxford University Press, 1989), 7. Hereafter cited parenthetically in the text.

10. As Laurie Langbauer pointedly puts it, the novel at once mocks and lauds Arabella's quixotism ("Romance Revised: Charlotte Lennox's *The Female Quixote*," *Novel* 18 [1984], 30). Spacks speaks of "the possibility of a double community" that is implicitly raised by subversive readings of the novel, but carefully sets them against accounts of readers' perceptions at the time: "What eighteenth-century female readers thought about the matter we can only surmise. . . . The most prominent male readers—Samuel Johnson, Henry Fielding—found Lennox's book a triumph of orthodoxy, warning young women against excessive indulgence in the reading of romances" (*Privacy*, 42–43). Compare Hammond, "Quixotism," passim, and Leland Warren, "Of the

Conversation of Women: *The Female Quixote* and the Dream of Perfection," *Studies in Eighteenth-Century Culture* 11 (1982), 367–80.

11. Compare Hudson, *Sibling*, 22.

12. Walter Scott, "General Preface," in *Waverley; Or, 'Tis Sixty Years Since* (New York: A. L. Burt, 1892), 11–12.

13. Laqueur, *Solitary*, 323–314. Compare also Laqueur, "Credit," 124–25; *Sex*, 227–30.

14. Landry, *Countryside*, 2.

15. William Wordsworth, *Lyrical Ballads* (Bristol: Biggs and Co, 1800), Preface.

16. Scott, "Preface," 15.

17. Scott, "Preface," 13.

18. Ibid., 13–14.

19. Kiely has significantly shown that the journeys undertaken by the aptly named Waverley negotiate a transition from his incipiently bookish approach to a romantic vision that eventually becomes reality after all (*Romantic*, 143). Like most "foibles" of eighteenth-century quixotic figures, his delusion is shown to be understandable, endearing, and even laudable rather than simply ludicrous.

20. As Ian Watt has shown, in *Emile* (1762), Rousseau recommends *Robinson Crusoe* as a book for "that happy age" of childhood, but for educational purposes, not for solitary pleasures. Individualism and solitariness of course play a crucial role in Rousseau's concepts of a natural education, but as Watt has importantly pointed out, the choice of Defoe's novel is part of a new cultural myth premised on a misreading. While "the moral subject of the myth is essentially solitude," Defoe "was no islomaniac; his basic ecological ideal was, alas, not nature and the natural life, but the urbanization of the countryside" (*Myths*, 175–76).

21. Mary Elizabeth Braddon, *The Doctor's Wife* (Oxford: Oxford University Press, 1998), 253. Hereafter cited parenthetically in the text. Compare Kate Flint, *The Woman Reader, 1837–1914* (Oxford: Oxford University Press, 1993), 291, 283. Lyn Pykett, "Introduction," in Mary Elizabeth Braddon, *The Doctor's Wife* (Oxford: Oxford University Press, 1998), xiii.

22. Much has recently been written on the difference between Victorian children's fiction written by men and by women: while men indulged nostalgia for childhood, women, already infantilized by society, preferred to use fantasy to explore possibilities of power and transgression. See Edith Lazaros Honig's *Breaking the Angelic Image: Woman Power in Victorian Children's Fantasy* (New York: Greenwood, 1988), passim. Compare also Catherine Robson's *Men in Wonderland: The Lost Girlhood of the Victorian Gentleman* (Princeton: Princeton University Press, 2001), passim.

23. Collins's critical analysis of divorce and custody laws anticipates Henry James's better known *What Maisie Knew* (1897) by almost ten years. Graham Law has summed up Collins's intriguing take on late-Victorian custody laws in his introduction to the novel ("Introduction," in Wilkie Collins, *The Evil Genius* [Peterborough: Broadview Press, 1998], passim.) Compare also Lawrence Stone's *Road To Divorce: England 1530–1987* (Oxford: Oxford University Press, 1992), 390.

24. Tosh, *Masculinity*, 1.

25. Richetti, "Introduction," xiv.

26. Richetti shows how cultural historians have argued that the novel "represents and promotes a feminizing transformation of British culture" (*English*, 197).

27. Lawrence Stone, *Divorce*, 390. See also Tosh, *Masculinity*, 159.

Bibliography

Ackroyd, Peter. *Dickens*. London: Sinclair-Stevenson, 1990.

Allen, Walter. *The English Novel*. London, Harmondsworth: Penguin, 1958.

Almansi, Guido. "*Great Expectations*." In *Dickens: Critical Assessments*, edited by Michael Hollington, 584–88. Mountfield: Helm Information, 1995.

Anderson, Benedict. *Imagined Communities: Reflections on the Origin and Spread of Nationalism*. London: Verso, 1983.

Andrews, Malcolm. *Dickens and the Grown-University Press Child*. Iowa City: University of Iowa Press, 1994.

Arac, Jonathan and Harriet Ritvo, eds. *Macropolitics of Nineteenth-Century Literature: Nationalism, Exoticism, Imperialism*. Philadelphia: University of Pennsylvania Press, 1991.

Armstrong, Frances. *Dickens and the Concept of Home*. Ann Arbor: UMI Research Press, 1990.

Armstrong, Isobel. "Introduction to *Pride and Prejudice*." In *Jane Austen: Critical Assessments*, edited by Ian Littlewood, 398–412. Mountfield: Helm Information, 1998.

Armstrong, Nancy. *Desire and Domestic Fiction: A Political History of the Novel*. Oxford: Oxford University Press, 1987.

Arnold, Thomas. *Observations on the Nature, Kinds, Courses, and Prevention of Insanity, Lunacy, or Madness*. London: 1782.

Auerbach, Nina. "Feeling as One Ought about Fanny Price." In *Jane Austen's Mansfield Park*, edited by Harold Bloom, 103–116. New York: Chelsea House Publisher, 1987.

Austen, Jane. *Emma*. Ed. R. W. Chapman. Oxford: Oxford University Press, 1988.

———. *Mansfield Park*. Ed. R. W. Chapman. London: Oxford University Press, 1953.

———. *Minor Works*. Ed. R. W. Chapman. London: Oxford University Press, 1965.

———. *Northanger Abbey* and *Persuasion*. Ed. R. W. Chapman. London: Oxford University Press, 1959.

———. *Pride and Prejudice*. Ed. R. W. Chapman. Oxford: Oxford University Press, 1988.

———. *Sense and Sensibility*. Ed. R. W. Chapman. London: Oxford University Press, 1960.

Austen-Leigh, James Edward. *A Memoir of Jane Austen*. London: Bentley, 1870.

Bachelard, Gaston. *The Poetics of Space*. Trans. Maria Jolas. Boston: Beacon, 1969.

Bailin, Miriam. "'Varieties of Pain': The Victorian Sickroom and Brontë's *Shirley*." *Modern Language Quarterly* 48, no. 3 (1987): 254–78.

———. *The Sickroom in Victorian Fiction: The Art of Being Ill*. Cambridge: Cambridge University Press, 1994.

Ban, Kah Choon. "Nostalgia and the Scene of the Other." In *Perceiving Other Worlds*, edited by Edwin Thumboo, 1–12. Singapore: Times Academic Press, 1991.

Banerjee, Jacqueline. *Through the Northern Gate: Childhood and Growing Up in British Fiction 1719–1901*. New York: Peter Lang, 1996.

Banks, Joseph. *Journal*. Ed. Joseph Hooker. London: Macmillan, 1896.

Barker, Gerard A. *Grandison's Heirs: The Paragon's Progress in the Late Eighteenth-Century English Novel*. Newark: University of Delaware Press, 1985.

Barker-Benfield, G. J. *The Culture of Sensibility: Sex and Society in Eighteenth-Century Britain*. Chicago: University of Chicago Press, 1992.

Barlow, John. *On Man's Power over Himself to Prevent or Control Insanity*. London: William Pickering, 1849.

Barrett, Julia. *Presumption*. London: Michael O'Mara Books, 1993.

Barrett, W. F. et al. *Proceedings of the Society for Psychical Research*. London: Trubner, 1883.

Bashford, Alison. *Purity and Pollution: Gender, Embodiment and Victorian Medicine*. London: Macmillan, 1998.

Batey, Mavis. *Jane Austen and the English Landscape*. London: Barn Elms, 1996.

Baumgarten, Murray, and H. M. Daleski, eds. *Homes and Homelessness in the Victorian Imagination*. New York: AMS Press, 1998.

Beard, George M. *A Practical Treatise on Nervous Exhaustion (Neurasthenia). . . .* New York: Wood, 1880.

Becker, Allienne R. *The Lost Worlds Romance: From Dawn till Dusk*. London: Greenwood, 1992.

Beer, Gillian. *Arguing with the Past: Essays from Woolf to Sidney*. London: Routledge, 1989.

———. *Darwin's Plots: Evolutionary Narrative in Darwin, George Eliot and Nineteenth-Century Fiction*. London: Routledge & Kegan Paul, 1983.

———. *Open Fields: Science in Cultural Encounter*. Oxford: Oxford University Press, 1996.

Beer, John. *Providence and Love: Studies in Wordsworth, Channing, Myers, George Eliot, and Ruskin*. Oxford: Clarendon, 1998.

Bellamy, Edward. *Equality*. New York: D. Appleton, 1897.

Bellamy, Liz. *Commerce, Morality and the Eighteenth-Century Novel*. Cambridge: Cambridge University Press, 1998.

Benedict, Barbara M. *Framing Feeling: Sentiment and Style in English Prose Fiction 1745–1800*. New York: AMS, 1994.

Benjamin, Walter. *Illuminations*. Trans. Harry Zohn. London: Jonathan Cape, 1968.

Bermingham, Ann, and John Brewer, eds. *The Consumption of Culture 1600–1800: Image, Object, Text*. London: Routledge, 1995.

Bhabha, Homi. "DissemiNation: time, narrative, and the margins of the modern nation." In *Nation and Narration*, edited by Homi Bhabha, 291–322. London: Routledge, 1990.

———. "Introduction: Narrating the Nation." In *Nation and Narration*, edited by Homi Bhabha, 1–7. London: Routledge, 1990.

———, ed. *Nation and Narration*. London: Routledge, 1990.

Blöde, Charles A. *Dr F. J. Gall's System of the Functions of the Brain*. Ed. Nicholas J. Wade. London: Routledge, 2000.

Bloom, Harold, ed. *Jane Austen's* MANSFIELD PARK. New York: Chelsea House Publisher, 1987.

———, ed. *Fanny Burney's Evelina*. New York: Chelsea House, 1988.

Boswell, James. *The Hypochondriack*. 2 vols. Stanford: Stanford University Press, 1928.

Bowstead, Diana. "Charlotte Smith's *Desmond*: The Epistolary Novel as Ideological Argument." In *Fetter'd or free? British Women Novelists 1670–1815*, edited by Mary Anne Schofield and Cecilia Macheski, 237–263. Athens: Ohio University Press, 1987.

Braddon, Mary Elizabeth. *Lady Audley's Secret*. Oxford: Oxford University Press, 1987.

———. *The Doctor's Wife*. Oxford: Oxford University Press, 1998.

Brissenden, R. F. *Virtue in Distress: Studies in the Novel of Sentiment from Richardson to Sade*. London: Macmillan, 1974.

———, ed. *Studies in the Eighteenth Century III*. Canberra: Australian National University Press, 1975.

Brombert, Victor. *In Praise of Antiheroes: Figures and Themes in Modern European Literature, 1830–1980*. Chicago: Chicago University Press, 1999.

Brontë, Charlotte. *Jane Eyre*. London: Zodiac, 1965.

———. *The Professor*. London: Smith, Elder & Co, 1857.

———. *Villette*. Ed. Herbert Rosengarten and Margaret Smith. Oxford: Clarendon, 1984.

Brooke, Frances. *Emily Montague*. Ed. Lawrence J. Burpee and F. P. Grove. Ottawa: Graphic Publishers, 1931.

———. *The Excursion*. Ed. Paula R. Backscheider and Hope D. Cotton. Lexington: Kentucky University Press, 1997.

Brown, Laura. *Ends of Empire: Women and Ideology in Early Eighteenth-Century English Literature*. Ithaca: Cornell University Press, 1993.

———. *Fables of Modernity: Literature and Culture in the English Eighteenth-Century*. Ithaca: Cornell University Press, 2001.

Brown, Marshall. *Preromanticism*. Stanford: Stanford University Press, 1991.

Brown, Penny. *The Captured World: The Child and Childhood in Nineteenth-Century Women's Writing in England*. Hemel Hempstead: Harvester Wheatsheaf, 1993.

Brunton, Mary. *Emmeline*. Ed. Caroline Franklin. London: Routledge, 1992.

Buckley, Jerome Hamilton. *The Triumph of Time: A Study of the Victorian Concepts of Time, History, Progress, and Decadence*. Cambridge, MA: Harvard University Press, 1967.

Burke, Edmund. *Reflections on the Revolution in France*. Ed. Conor Cruise O'Brien. London: Penguin, 1986.

Burnett, Frances Hodgson. *Little Lord Fauntleroy*. Oxford: Oxford University Press, 1993.

———. *A Little Princess*. London: Penguin, 1996.

———. *The Secret Garden*. London: Folio Society, 1986.

Burney, Frances. *Camilla*. Ed. Edward A. and Lillian D. Bloom. London: Oxford University Press, 1972.

———. *Cecilia*. Eds. Peter Sabor and Margaret Anne Doody. Oxford: Oxford University Press, 1988.

———. *Evelina*. Ed. Harold Bloom. New York: Chelsea House, 1988.

———. *The Wanderer*. Ed. Margaret Ann Doody, Robert L. Mack and Peter Sabor. Oxford: Oxford University Press, 1991.

Burton, Robert. *The Anatomy of Melancholy*. Ed. Holbrook Jackson. New York: Random House, 1977.

Butler, Marilyn. *Jane Austen and the War of Ideas*. Oxford: Clarendon, 1987.

———. *Romantics, Rebels, and Reactionaries: English Literature and its Background, 1760–1830*. Oxford: Oxford University Press, 1981.

Butler, Samuel. *The Way of All Flesh*. Ed. A. J. Hoppe. London: Dent, 1968.

Byatt, A. S. *Possession: A Romance*. London: Chatto & Windus, 1990.

Byrd, Max. *Visits to Bedlam: Madness and Literature in the Eighteenth Century*. Columbia: University of South Carolina, 1974.

Calder, Jenni. *Women and Marriage in Victorian Fiction*. London: Thames and Hudson, 1976.

Campbell, Matthew et al., eds. *Memory and Memorials, 1789–1914*. London: Routledge, 2000.

Carpenter, Humphrey. *Secret Gardens: A Study of the Golden Age of Children's Literature*. London: George Allen & Unwin, 1985.

Carter, Philip. *Men and the Emergence of Polite Society, Britain 1660–1800*. Harlow: Longman, 2001.

Castle, Terry. *The Female Thermometer: Eighteenth-Century Culture and the Invention of the Uncanny*. Oxford: Oxford University Press, 1995.

———. "Introduction." In Ann Radcliffe, *The Mysteries of Udolpho*, vii–xxvi. Oxford: Oxford University Press, 1998.

Chapman, Raymond. *The Sense of the Past in Victorian Literature*. London: Croom Helm, 1986.

Cheyne, George. *The English Malady; Or, a Treatise of Nervous Diseases of all Kinds, as Spleen, Vapours, Lowness, and Hysterical Distempers, etc.* London: 1733.

Chisholm, Kate. *Fanny Burney: Her Life 1752–1840*. London: Chatto & Windus, 1998.

Christie, John and Sally Shuttleworth, eds. *Nature Transfigured: Science and Literature 1700–1900*. Manchester: Manchester University Press, 1989.

Cicero, Marcus Tullius. *Tusculan Disputations*. Cambridge, MA: Harvard University Press, 1966.

Clayton, Jay. *Romantic Vision and the Novel*. Cambridge: Cambridge University Press, 1987.

Cohen, Michele. *Fashioning Masculinity: National Identity and Language in the Eighteenth Century*. London: Routledge, 1996.

Coleridge, Samuel Taylor. *Poetical Works*. Ed. J. C. C. Mays. Princeton: Princeton University Press, 2001.

Colley, Ann C. *Nostalgia and Recollection in Victorian Culture*. London: Macmillan, 1998.

Collins, Philip. *Dickens and Education*. London: Macmillan, 1963.

Collins, Wilkie. *Armadale*. London: Smith, Elder and Co, 1866.

———. *Basil*. London: Richard Bentley, 1852.

———. *The Black Robe*. London: Chatto & Windus, 1881.

———. *Blind Love*. London: Chatto and Windus, 1890.

———. *The Evil Genius*. Ed. Graham Law. Peterborough, Ont.: Broadview, 1994.

———. *The Fallen Leaves*. London: Chatto & Windus, 1879.

———. *The Guilty River*. Eds. Norman Page and Toru Sasaki. Oxford: Oxford University Press, 1999.

———. *Heart and Science*. Ed. Steve Farmer. Peterborough: Broadview, 1996.

———. *Hide and Seek*. London: Richard Bentley, 1854.

———. *I Say No*. London: Chatto & Windus, 1884.

———. *Jezebel's Daughter*. London: Chatto & Windus, 1880.

———. *The Legacy of Cain*. London: Chatto & Windus, 1889.

———. *Man and Wife*. Oxford: Oxford University Press, 1995.

———. *Miss or Mrs?* London: Richard Bentley, 1873.

———. *The Moonstone*. London: Folio Society, 1992.

———. *The New Magdalen*. London: Richard Bentley, 1873.

———. *No Name*. London: Sampson Low, 1862.

———. *Poor Miss Finch*. London: Richard Bentley, 1872.

———. *The Two Destinies*. London: Chatto & Windus, 1876.

———. *The Woman in White*. London: Folio Society, 1992.

Conger, Syndy McMillen, ed. *Sensibility in Transformation: Creative Resistance to Sentiment from the Augustans to the Romantics*. Rutherford: Fairleigh Dickinson University Press, 1990.

Copeland, Edward, and Juliet McMaster, eds. *The Cambridge Companion to Jane Austen*. Cambridge: Cambridge University Press, 1997.

Copley, Stephen, and Peter Garside, eds. *The Politics of the Picturesque: Literature, Landscape and Aesthetics since 1770*. Cambridge: Cambridge University Press, 1994.

Copley, Stephen, and John Whale, *Beyond Romanticism: New Approaches to Texts and Contexts 1780–1832*. London: Routledge, 1992.

Cosgrove, Denis, and Stephen Daniels, eds. *The Iconography of Landscape: Essays on the Symbolic Representation, Design and Use of Past Environments*. Cambridge: Cambridge University Press, 1997.

Coveney, Peter. *Poor Monkey: The Child in Literature*. London: Richard Clay, 1957.

Craik, Dinah. *Olive*. Oxford: Oxford University Press, 1999.

Crump, Justine. "Turning the World Upside Down: Madness, Moral Management, and Frances Burney's *The Wanderer*." *Eighteenth-Century Fiction* 10, no. 3 (1998): 325–40.

Cunningham, Hugh. *Children and Childhood in Western Society since 1500*. London: Longman, 1995.

Currie, Richard A. "'As if she had done him a wrong': Hidden Rage and Object Protection in Dickens's Amy Dorrit." *English Studies* 72, no. 4 (1991): 368–76.

Cvetkovich, Ann. *Mixed Feelings: Feminism, Mass Culture, and Victorian Sensationalism*. New Brunswick: Rutgers University Press, 1992.

D'Albertis, Deirdre. *Dissembling Fictions: Elizabeth Gaskell and the Victorian Social Text*. Basingstoke: Macmillan, 1997.

Dames, Nicholas. *Amnesiac Selves: Nostalgia, Forgetting, and British Fiction, 1810–1870*. New York: Oxford University Press, 2001.

———. "Austen's 'Nostalgics,'" *Representations* 73 (2001): 117–43.

———. "The Clinical Novel: Phrenology and *Villette*." *Novel* 29, no. 3 (1996): 367–90.

Daniels, Stephen. "The political iconography of woodland in later Georgian England." In *The Iconography of Landscape: Essays on the Symbolic Representation, Design and Use of Past Environments,* edited by Denis Cosgrove and Stephen Daniels, 43–82. Cambridge: Cambridge University Press, 1997.
Darwin, Charles. *The Voyage of the Beagle.* Ed. L. Engel. Garden City, New York: Doubleday, 1962.
Daugherty, Tracy Edgar. *Narrative Techniques in the Novels of Fanny Burney.* New York: Peter Lang, 1989.
David, Deirdre. "Rewriting the Male Plot in Collins's *No Name* (1862): Captain Wragge Orders an Omelette and Mrs Wragge Goes into Custody." In *The New Nineteenth Century: Feminist Readings of Underread Victorian Fiction,* edited by Barbara Leah Harman and Susan Meyer, 33–44. London: Garland, 1996.
Deleuze, Gilles, and Félix Guattari. *What is Philosophy?* Trans. Hugh Tomlinson and Graham Burchill. London: Verso, 1994.
Dever, Carolyn. *Death and the Mother from Dickens to Freud: Victorian Fiction and the Anxiety of Origins.* Cambridge: Cambridge University Press, 1998.
Devlin, D. D. *The Novels and Journals of Fanny Burney.* Basingstoke: Macmillan, 1987.
Dickens, Charles. *Bleak House.* Ed. Osbert Sitwell. Oxford: Oxford University Press, 1959.
———. *Christmas Books.* London: Chapman and Hall, 1878.
———. *David Copperfield.* Ed. Nina Burgis. Oxford: Clarendon, 1981.
———. *Dombey and Son.* Ed. Alan Horsman. Oxford: Clarendon, 1974.
———. *Great Expectations.* Ed. Margaret Cadwell. Oxford: Clarendon, 1993.
———. *Hard Times.* Ed. Dingle Foot. London: Oxford University Press, 1970.
———. *Little Dorrit.* Ed. Harvey Peter Sucksmith. Oxford: Clarendon, 1979.
———. *Martin Chuzzlewit.* Ed. Margaret Cadwell. Oxford: Clarendon, 1982.
———. *Nicholas Nickleby.* Ed. Sybil Thorndike. London: Oxford University Press, 1957.
———. *The Old Curiosity Shop.* Ed. Elizabeth M. Brennan. Oxford: Clarendon, 1997.
———. *Oliver Twist.* Ed. Humphrey House. Oxford: Oxford University Press, 1949.
———. *Our Mutual Friend.* Ed. E. Salter Davies. London: Oxford University Press, 1959.
———. *A Tale of Two Cities.* Ed. John Shuckburgh. London: Oxford University Press, 1960.
Doane, Janice, and Devon Hodges. *Nostalgia and Sexual Difference: The Resistance to Contemporary Feminism.* London: Methuen, 1987.
Donnelly, Ignatius. *Caesar's Column.* Ed. Walter B. Rideout. Cambridge: Belknap, 1960.
Doody, Margaret Anne. "Deserts, Ruins and Troubled Waters: Female Dreams in Fiction and the Development of the Gothic Novel." *Genre* 10 (1977): 529–72.
———. *Frances Burney: The Life in the Works.* Cambridge: Cambridge University Press, 1988.
———. "Frances Sheridan: Morality and Annihilated Time." In *Fetter'd or free?*

British Women Novelists 1670–1815, edited by Mary Anne Schofield and Cecilia Macheski, 324–58. Athens: Ohio University Press, 1987.

———. "Introduction." In Fanny Burney, *The Wanderer.* Eds. Margaret Ann Doody, Robert L. Mack and Peter Sabor, vii-xxxvii. Oxford: Oxford University Press, 1991.

———. *The True Story of the Novel.* New Brunswick: Rutgers University Press, 1996.

Duckworth, Alistair M. *The Improvement of the Estate: A Study of Jane Austen's Novels.* Baltimore: John Hopkins University Press, 1994.

Dyson, A. E., ed. *Dickens: Bleak House.* Basingstoke: Macmillian, 1969.

———, ed. *Charlotte Brontë: Jane Eyre and Villette.* Basingstoke: Macmillan, 1973.

Eade, J. C., ed. *Romantic Nationalism in Europe.* Canberra: Australian National University Press, 1983.

Eagleton, Terry. *The Rape of Clarissa: Writing, Sexuality and Class Struggle in Samuel Richardson.* Oxford: Basil Blackwell, 1982.

———, ed. *Raymond Williams: Critical Perspectives.* Cambridge: Polity, 1989.

Easson, Angus. *Elizabeth Gaskell.* London: Routledge & Kegan Paul, 1979.

———. "Introduction." In Elizabeth Gaskell, *Wives and Daughters.* Ed. Angus Easson, ix–xxiv. Oxford: Oxford University Press, 1987.

Edgeworth, Maria. *The Absentee.* Ed. W. J. McCormack and Kim Walker. Oxford: Oxford University Press, 1988.

———. *Belinda.* Ed. Eiléan Ní Chuilleanáin. London: Everyman, 1993.

Epstein, Julia. "Marginality in Frances Burney's Novels." In *The Cambridge Companion to the Eighteenth-Century Novel,* edited by John Richetti, 198–211. Cambridge: Cambridge University Press, 1996.

Faber, Michel. *The Crimson Petal and the White.* Edinburgh: Canongate, 2002.

Falconer, William. *A Dissertation on the Influence of the Passions upon Disorders of the Body.* London, 1796.

Farmer, Penelope. *Charlotte Sometimes.* Bath: Chivers, 1985.

Ferguson, Moira. *Colonialism and Gender Relations from Mary Wollstonecraft to Jamaica Kincaid.* New York: Columbia University Press, 1993.

Fielding, Sarah. *David Simple.* Ed. Malcolm Kensall. Oxford: Oxford University Press, 1987.

Fletcher, Loraine. *Charlotte Smith: A Critical Biography.* London: Macmillan, 1998.

Flinn, Caryl. *Strains of Utopia: Gender, Nostalgia, and Hollywood Film Music.* Princeton: Princeton University Press, 1992.

Flint, Kate. *The Woman Reader, 1837–1914.* Oxford: Oxford University Press, 1993.

Forster, E. M. *The Longest Journey.* London: Blackwood, 1907.

Foster, James R. *History of the Pre-Romantic Novel in England.* London: Oxford University Press, 1949.

Foster, Susan Leigh, ed. *Choreographing History.* Bloomington and Indianapolis: Indiana University Press, 1995.

Foucault, Michel. *The History of Sexuality.* Trans. Robert Hurley. New York: Vintage, 1980.

———. *Language, Counter-Memory, Practice: Selected Essays and Interviews.* Ithaca: Cornell University Press, 1977.

———. *Madness and Civilisation.* London: Tavistock Publications, 1967.

Fox, Christopher. "Defining Eighteenth-Century Psychology: Some Problems and Perspectives." In *Psychology and Literature in the Eighteenth Century,* edited by Christopher Fox, 1–22. New York: AMS, 1987.

———, ed. *Psychology and Literature in the Eighteenth Century.* New York: AMS, 1987.

Fraiman, Susan. "Jane Austen and Edward Said: Gender, Culture, and Imperialism." *Critical Inquiry* 21, no. 4 (1995), 805–821.

Freud, Sigmund. *Works.* Eds. James Strachey and Anna Freud et al. London: Hogarth, 1995.

Froude, J. A. *The Nemesis of Faith.* London: Chapman and Hall, 1849.

Frye, Northrop. *Fables of Identity: Studies in Poetic Mythology.* New York: Harcourt, Brace & World, 1963.

Gallagher, Catherine. *Nobody's Story: The Vanishing Acts of Women Writers in the Marketplace, 1670–1820.* Oxford: Clarendon, 1994.

Gallagher, Catherine, and Stephen Greenblatt, eds. *Practicing New Historicism.* Chicago: Chicago University Press, 2000.

Gallagher, Catherine, and Thomas Laqueur, eds. *The Making of the Modern Body: Sexuality and Society in the Nineteenth Century.* Berkeley: University of California Press, 1987.

Galton, Francis. "Kantsaywhere." In *The Life, Letters and Labours of Francis Galton,* edited by Karl Pearson, 411–25. Cambridge: Cambridge University Press, 1914–1930.

Gaskell, Elizabeth. *North and South.* London: Chapman and Hall, 1855.

———. *Wives and Daughters.* London: Smith, Elder and Co., 1866.

George, Rosemary Marangoly. *The Politics of Home: Postcolonial Relocations and Twentieth-Century Fiction.* Cambridge: Cambridge University Press, 1996.

Gilbert, Sarah M., and Susan Gubar. *The Madwoman in the Attic: The Woman Writer and the Nineteenth-Century Literary Imagination.* New Haven: Yale University Press, 1979.

Gilmour, Robin. *The Idea of the Gentleman in the Victorian Novel.* London: George Allen and Unwin, 1981.

Gorman, Anita. *The Body in Illness and Health: Themes and Images in Jane Austen.* New York: Peter Lang, 1993.

Grahame, Kenneth. *Dream Days.* London: Bodley Head, 1973.

———. *The Golden Age.* Edinburgh: Paul Harris, 1983.

Green, Martin. *Dreams of Adventure, Deeds of Empire.* London: Routledge, 1980.

Greenblatt, Stephen. *Marvelous Possessions: The Wonder of the New World.* Chicago: Chicago University Press, 1991.

Greenslade, William. *Degeneration, Culture and the Novel 1880–1940.* Cambridge: Cambridge University Press, 1994.

Grenby, M. O. *The Anti-Jacobin Novel: British Conservatism and the French Revolution.* Cambridge: Cambridge University Press, 2001.

Grey, J. David, ed. *The Jane Austen Handbook with a Dictionary of Jane Austen's Life and Works.* London: Athlone, 1986.

Griffiths, M. "Great English Houses/New Homes in England." *Span* 36 (1993): 488–503.

Grylls, David. *Guardians and Angels: Parents and Children in Nineteenth-Century Literature*. London, Faber and Faber, 1978.

Haggerty, George E. *Gothic Fiction / Gothic Form*. University Park: Pennsylvania State University Press, 1989.

———. "The Gothic Novel." In *The Columbia History of the British Novel*, edited by John Richetti, 220–246. New York: Columbia, 1994.

———. *Men in Love: Masculinity and Sexuality in the Eighteenth Century*. New York: Columbia University Press, 1999.

———. *Unnatural Affections: Women and Fiction in the Later Eighteenth Century*. Bloomington and Indianapolis: Indiana University Press, 1998.

Hagstrom, Jean H. *Sex and Sensibility: Ideal and Erotic Love from Milton to Mozart*. Chicago: University of Chicago Press, 1980.

Hall, Donald E., ed. *Muscular Christianity: Embodying the Victorian Age*. Cambridge: Cambridge University Press, 1994.

Hammond, B. S. "Mid-Century English Quixotism and the Defence of the Novel." *Eighteenth-Century Fiction* 10, no. 3 (1998): 247–68.

Hardy, Barbara. *A Reading of Jane Austen*. London: Owen, 1975.

Harman, Barbara Leah, and Susan Meyer, eds. *The New Nineteenth Century: Feminist Readings of Underread Victorian Fiction*. London: Garland, 1996.

Harman, Claire. *Fanny Burney: A Biography*. London: Harper Collins, 2000.

Harris, Jocelyn. *Jane Austen's Art of Memory*. Cambridge: Cambridge University Press, 1989.

Hays, Mary. *Memoirs of Emma Courtney*. Oxford: Oxford University Press, 2000.

Heilman, Robert. "Charlotte Brontë's 'New' Gothic in *Jane Eyre* and *Villette*." In *Charlotte Brontë: Jane Eyre and Villette*, edited by A. E. Dyson, 195–204. Basingstoke: Macmillan, 1973.

Hewison, Robert. *The Heritage Industry: Britain in a Climate of Decline*. London: Methuen, 1987.

Hill, John. *Hypochondriasis: A Practical Treatise on the Nature and Cure of that Disorder: Commonly called the Hyp and Hypo*. London, 1766.

Hilles, Frederick W., and Harold Bloom, eds. *From Sensibility to Romanticism*. New York: Oxford University Press, 1965.

Hobsbawm, E. J. *Nations and Nationalism since 1780: Programme, Myth, Reality*. Cambridge: Cambridge University Press, 1990.

Hochman, Baruch. "Bulrush and Harvest Home." In *Homes and Homelessness in the Victorian Imagination*, edited by Murray Baumgarten and H. M. Daleski, 51–64. New York: AMS Press, 1998.

———, and Ilja Wachs. *Dickens: The Orphan Condition*. Madison: Fairleigh Dickinson University Press, 1999.

Hoeveler, Diane Long. *Gothic Feminism: The Professionalization of Gender from Charlotte Smith to the Brontës*. University Park: Pennsylvania State University Press, 1998.

Hofer, Johannes. "Medical Dissertation on Nostalgia by Johannes Hofer, 1688." Trans. Carolyn Kiser Anspach. *Bulletin of the Institute of the History of Medicine* 2, no. 6 (1934): 376–91.

Hogle, Jerrold E. "Introduction: the Gothic in Western Culture." In *The Cam-

bridge Companion to Gothic Fiction, edited by Jerrold E. Hogle, 1–20. Cambridge: Cambridge University Press, 2002.

———. *The Cambridge Companion to Gothic Fiction*. Cambridge: Cambridge University Press, 2002.

———, ed. Hochman, Baruch. "Bulrush and Harvest Home." In *Homes and Homelessness in the Victorian Imagination*, edited by Murray Baumgarten and H.M. Daleski, 51–64. New York: AMS Press, 1998.

Hollington, Michael, ed. *Dickens: Critical Assessments*. 4 vols. Mountfield: Helm Information, 1995.

Holmes, O. W. "Cinders from Ashes." *Pages from an Old Volume of Life*: 1857–1881. *Project Gutenberg Oliver Wendell Holmes*. Ed. David Widger. Jun 2002 <http://promo.net/pg>

Honig, Edith Lazaros. *Breaking the Angelic Image: Woman Power in Victorian Children's Fantasy*. New York: Greenwood, 1988.

Houghton, Walter E. *The Victorian Frame of Mind: 1830–1870*. 1957. New Haven: Yale University Press, 1957, reprinted 1985.

Huang, Mei. *Transforming the Cinderalla Dream: From Frances Burney to Charlotte Brontë*. New Brunswick: Rugters University Press, 1990.

Hubback, Catherine. *The Younger Sister*. London: Thomas Cautley Newby, 1850.

Hudson, Glenda A. *Sibling Love and Incest in Jane Austen's Fiction*. Basingstoke: Macmillan, 1992.

Hughes, Thomas. *Tom Brown's School Days*. London: Macmillan, 1858.

Hunt, Lynn, and Margaret Jacob. "The Affective Revolution in 1790s Britain." *Eighteenth-Century Studies* 34, no. 4 (2001): 491–521.

Hunter, J. Paul. *Before Novels: The Cultural Contexts of Eighteenth-Century Fiction*. New York: W. W. Norton & Co, 1990.

Hurley, Kelly. *The Gothic Body: Sexuality, Materialism, and Degeneration at the Fin de Siècle*. Cambridge: Cambridge University Press, 1996.

Hutcheon, Linda. "Irony, Nostalgia, and the Postmodern." In *Methods for the Study of Literature as Cultural Memory*, edited by Raymond Vervliet and Annemarie Estor, 189–207. Amsterdam: Rodopi, 2000.

Inchbald, Elizabeth. *A Simple Story*. Ed. Jeanette Winterson. London: Pandora, 1987.

Ingram, Allan. *The Madhouse of Language: Writing and Reading Madness in the Eighteenth Century*. London: Routledge, 1991.

Jackson, Stanley. *Melancholia and Depression: From Hippocratic Times to Modern Times*. New Haven: Yale University Press, 1986.

Jalland, Pat. *Death in the Victorian Family*. Oxford: Oxford University Press, 1996.

Johnson, Claudia L. *Equivocal Beings: Politics, Gender, and Sentimentality in the 1790s*. Chicago: Chicago University Press, 1995.

———. *Jane Austen: Women, Politics, and the Novel*. Chicago: Chicago University Press, 1988.

———. "A 'Sweet Face as White as Death': Jane Austen and the Politics of Female Sensibility." *Novel* 22, no. 2 (1989): 159–74.

Jones, Chris. *Radical Sensibility: Literature and Ideas in the 1790s*. London: Routledge, 1993.

Jordan, Elaine. "Jane Austen goes to the Seaside: *Sanditon*, English Identity and the 'West Indian' Schoolgirl." In *The Postcolonial Jane Austen,* edited by You-me Park and Rajeswari Sunder Rajan, 29–55. London: Routledge, 2000.

Kant, Immanuel. *Anthropologie in Pragmatischer Hinsicht.* Frankfurt, 1799.

———. *Anthropology from a Pragmatic Point of View.* Trans. Victor Lyle Dowdell. Carbondale: Southern Illinois University Press, 1978.

———. *Observations on the Feeling of the Beautiful and Sublime.* Trans. John T. Goldthwait. Berkeley: University of California Press, 1960.

Kaplan, Fred. *Dickens and Mesmerism: The Hidden Springs of Fiction.* Princeton: Princeton University Press, 1975.

———. *Sacred Tears: Sentimentality in Victorian Literature.* Princeton: Princeton University Press, 1987.

Keith, Jennifer. "'Pre-Romanticism' and the Ends of Eighteenth-Century Poetry." In *The Cambridge Companion to Eighteenth-Century Poetry,* edited by John Sitter, 271–90. Cambridge: Cambridge University Press, 2001.

Kelly, Gary. *English Fiction of the Romantic Period 1789–1830.* London: Longman, 1989.

Kent, Christopher. "Probability, Reality and Sensation in the Novels of Wilkie Collins." In *Wilkie Collins to the Forefront: Some Reassessments,* edited by Nelson Smith and R. C. Terry, 53–74. New York: AMS, 1995.

Kermode, Frank. *The Sense of an Ending: Studies in the Theory of Fiction.* New York: Oxford University Press, 1967.

Kiely, Robert. *The Romantic Novel in England.* Cambridge, MA: Harvard University Press, 1972.

Kincaid, James R. *Child-Loving: The Erotic Child and Victorian Culture.* London: Routledge, 1992.

Kristeva, Julia. *Black Sun: Depression and Melancholia.* New York: Columbia University Press, 1989.

Kroll, Richard, ed. *The English Novel.* 2 vols. London: Longman, 1998.

Lamb, Charles. *Rosamund Gray.* Oxford: Woodstock, 1991.

Lamb, Jonathan. *In the South Seas, 1680–1840.* Chicago: University of Chicago Press, 2001.

———. "'The Rime of the Ancient Mariner': A Ballad of the Scurvy." In *Pathologies of Travel,* edited by Richard Wrigley and George Revill, 157–77. Amsterdam: Rodopi, 2000.

LaCapra, Dominick. "Foucault, History and Madness." In *Rewriting the History of Madness: Studies in Foucault's* HISTOIRE DE LA FOLIE, edited by Arthur Still and Irving Velody, 78–85. London: Routledge, 1992.

Landry, Donna. *The Invention of the Countryside: Hunting, Walking and Ecology in English Literature, 1671–1831.* Basingstoke: Palgrave, 2001.

Lane, Maggie. *Jane Austen's England.* London: Hale, 1986.

Lane, Mary E. Bradley. *Mizora.* New York: G. W. Dillingham, 1890.

Langbauer, Laurie. "Romance Revized: Charlotte Lennox's *The Female Quixote.*" *Novel* 18 (1984): 29–49.

Lansbury, Coral. *Elizabeth Gaskell: The Novel of Social Crisis.* London: Paul Elek, 1975.

Laqueur, Thomas W. "Credit, Novels, Masturbation." In *Choreographing History,* edited by Susan Leigh Foster, 119–28. Bloomington and Indianapolis: Indiana University Press, 1995.

———. *Making Sex: Body and Gender from the Greeks to Freud.* Cambridge, MA: Harvard University Press, 1990.

---. "The Social evil, the Solitary vice, and pouring tea." In *Solitary Pleasures: The Historical, Literary, and Artistic Discourses of Autoeroticism*, edited by Paula Bennett and Vernon A. Rosario II, 155–61. New York and London: Routledge, 1995.

---. *Solitary Sex: A Cultural History of Masturbation*. New York: Zone Books, 2003.

Layton, Susan. *Russian Literature and Empire: Conquest of the Caucasus from Pushkin to Tolstoy*. Cambridge: Cambridge University Press, 1994.

Leask, Nigel. *British Romantic Writers and the East*. Cambridge: Cambridge University Press, 1992.

---. *Curiosity and the Aesthetics of Travel Writing, 1770–1840*. Oxford: Oxford University Press, 2002.

Leavis, F. R. and Q. D. *Dickens: The Novelist*. London: Chatto & Windus, 1970.

Lee, Hsiao-Hung. *Possibilities of Hidden Things: Narrative Transgression in Victorian Fictional Autobiographies*. New York: Peter Lang, 1996.

LeFanu, Alicia. *Memoirs of Mrs Frances Sheridan*. London: Whittaker, 1824.

Lenard, Mary. *Preaching Pity: Dickens, Gaskell, and Sentimentalism in Victorian Culture*. New York: Peter Lang, 1999.

Lennox, Charlotte. *The Female Quixote*. Ed. Margaret Dalziel. Oxford: Oxford University Press, 1989.

Lerner, Laurence. *The Uses of Nostalgia: Studies in Pastoral Poetry*. London: Constable, 1972.

Levine, George. *Darwin and the Novelists: Patterns of Science in Victorian Fiction*. Cambridge, MA: Harvard University Press, 1988.

Littlewood, Ian, ed. *Jane Austen: Critical Assessments*. 4 vols. Mountfield: Helm Information, 1998.

Logan, Peter Melville. *Nerves and Narratives: A Cultural History of Hysteria in Nineteenth-Century British Prose*. Berkeley: University of California Press, 1997.

Lonsdale, Roger, ed. *History of Literature in the English Language*. 4 vols. London: Barroe & Jenkins, 1971.

Lovell, Terry. "Subjective powers? Consumption, the reading public, and domestic woman in early eighteenth-century England." In *The Consumption of Culture 1600–1800: Image, Object, Text*, edited by Ann Bermingham and John Brewer, 23–41. London: Routledge, 1995.

Lowenthal, David. *The Heritage Crusade and the Spoils of History*. Cambridge: Cambridge University Press, 1998.

---. "Nostalgia tells it like it wasn't." In *The Imagined Past: History and Nostalgia*, edited by Christopher Shaw and Malcolm Chase, 18–32. Manchester: Manchester University Press, 1989.

---. *The Past is a Foreign Country*. Cambridge: Cambridge University Press, 1985.

Lucas, John. *The Melancholy Man: A Study of Dickens's Novels*. Brighton: Harvester P, 1980.

Lynch, Deidre. "Domesticating Fictions and Nationalising Women: Edmund Burke, Property, and the Reproduction of Englishness." In *Romanticism, Race, and Imperial Culture, 1780–1834*, edited by Alan Richardson and Sonia Hofkosh, 40–71. Bloomington: Indiana University Press, 1996.

Kaul, Suvir. *Poems of Nation, Anthems of Empire: English Verse in the Long Eighteenth Century*. Charlottesville: University Press of Virginia, 2000.

McCarthy, Patrick. "Making for Home: David Copperfield and His Fellow Travellers." In *Homes and Homelessness in the Victorian Imagination*, edited by Murray Baumgarten and H. M. Daleski, 21–52. New York: AMS Press, 1998.

Mackenzie, Henry. *Works*. Ed. Susan Manning. London: Routledge, 1996.

McGann, Jerome. *The Poetics of Sensibility: A Revolution in Literary Style*. Oxford: Clarendon, 1996.

McGavran, James Holt, ed. *Romanticism and Children's Literature in Nineteenth-Century England*. Athens: University of Georgia Press, 1991.

McKeon, Michael. "Generic Transformation and Social Change: Rethinking the Rise of the Novel." In *The Origin of the English Novel 1600–1740*, edited by Michael McKeon, 382–99. Baltimore: Johns Hopkins University Press, 2000.

———. *The Origins of the English Novel 1600–1740*. Baltimore: Johns Hopkins University Press, 1987.

———, ed. *Theory of the Novel: A Historical Approach*. Baltimore: Johns Hopkins University Press, 2000.

McNees, Eleanor, ed. *The Brontë Sisters: Critical Assessments*. 4 vols. Mountfield: Helm Information, 1996.

Mangan, J. A. *Athleticism in the Victorian and Edwardian Public School: The Emergence and Consolidation of an Educational Ideology*. Cambridge: Cambridge University Press, 1981.

Marcus, Stephen. *Dickens: From Pickwick to Dombey*. New York: Basic Books, 1965.

Markley, Robert. "Sentimentality as Performance: Shaftesbury, Sterne, and the Theatrics of Virtue." In *The New Eighteenth Century: Theory. Politics. English Literature*, edited by Felicity Nussbaum and Laura Brown, 210–230. New York: Methuen, 1987.

Marsden, Gordon, ed. *Victorian Values: Personalities and Perspectives in Nineteenth-Century Society*. London: Longman, 1990.

Martin, Robert Bernard. *The Accents of Persuasion*. London: Faber and Faber, 1966.

Matus, Jill L. *Unstable Bodies: Victorian Representations of Sexuality and Maternity*. Manchester: Manchester University Press, 1995.

Maudsley, Henry. *Sex in Mind and in Education*. New York: Miller, 1874.

Mellor, Anne K. "British Romanticism, Gender, and Three Women Artists." In *The Consumption of Culture 1600–1800: Image, Object, Text*, edited by Ann Bermingham and John Brewer, 121–42. London: Routledge, 1995.

Merrill, Lynn L. *The Romance of Victorian Natural History*. Oxford: Oxford University Press, 1989.

Meyer, Susan. "Colonialism and the Figurative Strategy of Jane Eyre." In *Macropolitics of Nineteenth-Century Literature: Nationalism, Exoticism, Imperialism*, edited by Jonathan Arac and Harriet Ritvo, 159–83. Philadelphia: University of Pennsylvania Press, 1991.

———. *Imperialism at Home: Race and Victorian Women's Fiction*. Ithaca: Cornell University Press, 1996.

Miles, Robert. *Gothic Writing 1750–1820: A Genealogy*. London: Routledge, 1993.

———. "The 1790s: the effulgence of Gothic." In *The Cambridge Companion to Gothic Fiction*, edited by Jerrold E. Hogle, 41–62. Cambridge: Cambridge University Press, 2002.

Miller, D. A. *"Cage aux folles*: SENSATION AND GENDER IN WILKIE COLLINS'S *The Woman in White*." In *The Making of the Modern Body: Sexuality and Society in the Nineteenth Century,* edited by Catherine Gallagher and Thomas Laqueur, 107–136. Berkeley: University of California Press, 1987.

Miller, J. Hillis. *The Disappearance of God.* Cambridge, MA: Belknap, 1963.

———. "Introduction." In Charles Dickens, *Bleak House*, 11–36. London: Penguin, 1985.

Miller, Milton L. *Nostalgia: A Psychoanalytical Study of Marcel Proust*. Dallas: Taylor, 1969.

Millhauser, M. "Tennyson, Vestiges, and the Dark Side of Science." *Victorian Newsletter* 35 (1969): 22–25.

Mintz, Steven. *A Prison of Expectations: The Family in Victorian Culture*. New York: New York University Press, 1983.

Moler, Kenneth. *Jane Austen's Art of Allusion*. Lincoln: University of Nebraska Press, 1968.

Momberger, Philip. "Self and World in the Works of Charlotte Brontë." In *The Brontë Sisters: Critical Assessments,* edited by Eleanor McNees, 179–96. Mountfield: Helm Information, 1996.

Moretti, Franco. *Atlas of the European Novel*. London: Verso, 1999.

———. *The Way of the World: The* BILDUNGSROMAN *in European Culture*. London: Verso, 1987.

Morgan, Lady (Sydney). *The Wild Irish Girl*. Ed. Brigid Brophy. London: Pandora, 1986.

Morris, William. *News From Nowhere*. Ed. Krishan Kumar. Cambridge: Cambridge University Press, 1995.

Motooka, Wendy. *The Age of Reasons: Quixotism, Sentimentalism and Political Economy in Eighteenth-Century Britain*. London: Routledge, 1998.

Mudrick, Marvin. *Jane Austen: Irony as Defence and Discovery*. Princeton: Princeton University Press, 1952.

Muir, Kenneth. *The Romantic Period*. London: Macmillan, 1980.

Mullan, John. "Hypochondria and Hysteria: Sensibility and the Physicians." *The Eighteenth Century: Theory and Interpretation* 25, no. 2 (1984): 141–74.

———. *Sentiment and Sociability: The Language of Feeling in the Eighteenth Century*. Oxford: Clarendon, 1988.

Naydor, Lillian. *Wilkie Collins*. London: Prentice Hall, 1997.

Newcomb, Mildred. *The Imagined World of Charles Dickens*. Columbus: Ohio State University Press, 1989.

Newsom, Robert. *Dickens on the Romantic Side of Familiar Things: Bleak House and the Novel Tradition*. New York: Columbia University Press, 1977.

Nipperdey, Thomas. "In Search of Identity: Romantic Nationalism, Its Intellectual, Political and Social Background." In *Romantic Nationalism in Europe*, edited by J. C. Eade, 1–15. Canberra: Australian National University Press, 1983.

Nixon, Cheryl L. "Balancing the Courtship Hero: Masculine Emotional Display in Film Adaptations of Austen's Novels." In *Jane Austen in Hollywood*, edited by Linda Troost and Sayre Greenfield, 22–43. Lexington: University Press of Kentucky, 1998.

Novalis (Friedrich von Hardenberg), *Das Allgemeine Brouillon*. Hamburg: Felix Meiner, 1993.

Nunokawa, Jeff. "For Your Eyes Only: Private Property and the Oriental Body in *Dombey and Son*." In *Macropolitics of Nineteenth-Century Literature: Nationalism, Exoticism, Imperialism,* edited by Jonathan Arac and Harriet Ritvo, 138–58. Philadelphia: University of Pennsylvania Press, 1991.

Nussbaum, Felicity. *Torrid Zones: Maternity, Sexuality, and Empire in Eighteenth-Century English Narratives.* Baltimore: Johns Hopkins University Press, 1995.

Nussbaum, Felicity, and Laura Brown, eds. *The New Eighteenth Century: Theory. Politics. English Literature.* New York: Methuen, 1987.

Oppenheim, Janet. *"Shattered Nerves": Doctors, Patients, and Depression in Victorian England.* Oxford: Oxford University Press, 1991.

O'Shaughnessy, Arthur. *Music and Moonlight: Poems and Songs.* London: Chatto & Windus, 1874.

Ousby, Ian. *The Englishman's England: Taste, Travel and the Rise of Tourism.* Cambridge: Cambridge University Press, 1990.

Papastergiadis, Nikos. *The Turbulence of Migration: Globalisation, Deterritorialisation and Hybridity.* Cambridge: Polity, 2000.

Park, You-me, and Rajeswari Sunder Rajan, eds. *The Postcolonial Jane Austen.* London: Routledge, 2000.

Parker, David. "Dickens at Home." In *Homes and Homelessness in the Victorian Imagination,* edited by Murray Baumgarten and H. M. Daleski, 65–75. New York: AMS Press, 1998.

Pathania, B. S. *Goldsmith and Sentimental Comedy.* New Delhi: Prestige Books, 1988.

Pattison, Robert. *The Child Figure in English Literature.* Athens: University of Georgia Press, 1978.

Paulson, Ronald. "Evelina: Cinderella and Society." In *Fanny Burney's Evelina,* edited by Harold Bloom, 5–12. New York: Chelsea House, 1988.

Pearce, A. Philippa. *Tom's Midnight Garden.* London: Heinemann Educational, 1979.

Pearlman, Elihu. "Inversion in *Great Expectations.*" In *Dickens: Critical Assessments,* edited by Michael Hollington, 549–61. Mountfield: Helm Information, 1995.

Pearson, Karl. *The Life, Letters and Labours of Francis Galton.* Cambridge: Cambridge University Press, 1914–1930.

Phillips, Janet and Peter. *Victorians at Home and Away.* London: Croom Helm, 1978.

Pickering, Jean, and Suzanne Kehde, eds. *Narratives of Nostalgia, Gender and Nationalism.* London: Macmillan, 1997.

Pickrel, Paul. "Lionel Trilling and *Mansfield Park.*" *Studies in English Literature* 27, no. 4 (1987): 609–621.

———. "'The Watsons' and the Other Jane Austen." *ELH* 55, no. 2 (1988): 443–67.

Pike, E. Holly. *Family and Society in the Works of Elizabeth Gaskell.* New York: Peter Lang, 1995.

Pinch, Adela. *Strange Fits of Passion: Epistemologies of Emotion, Hume to Austen.* Stanford: Stanford University Press, 1996.

Pippin, Robert B. *Modernism as Philosophical Problem: On the Dissatisfaction of European High Culture.* Oxford: Basil Blackwell, 1991.

Pocock, J. G. A. *Virtue, Commerce, and History.* Cambridge: Cambridge University Press, 1985.

Polhemus, Robert M. "Comic and Erotic Faith Meet Faith in the Child: Charles Dickens's *The Old Curiosity Shop.*" In *Critical Reconstructions: The Relationship of Fiction and Life,* edited by Robert M. Polhemus and Roger B. Henkle, 71–89. Stanford: Stanford University Press, 1994.

———. "The Favourite Child: *David Copperfield* and the Scriptural Issue of Child-Wives." In *Homes and Homelessness in the Victorian Imagination,* edited by Murray Baumgarten and H. M. Daleski, 3–20. New York: AMS Press, 1998.

Polhemus, Robert M., and Roger B. Henkle, eds. *Critical Reconstructions: The Relationship of Fiction and Life.* Stanford: Stanford University Press, 1994.

Pollock, Linda A. *Forgotten Children: Parent-Child Relations from 1500 to 1900.* Cambridge: Cambridge University Press, 1983.

Porter, Roy. "*Barely Touching*: A Social Perspective on Mind and Body." In *The Language of Psyche: Mind and Body in Enlightenment Thought: Clark Library Lectures 1985–1986,* edited by G. S. Rousseau, 45–80. Berkeley: University of California Press, 1992.

———. *Bodies Politic: Disease, Death and Doctors in Britain, 1650–1900.* Ithaca: Cornell University Press, 2001.

———. "Enlightenment and Pleasure." In *Pleasure in the Eighteenth Century,* edited by Roy Porter and Marie Mulvey Roberts, 1–18. Basingstoke: Macmillan, 1996.

———. "Forbidden Pleasures: Enlightenment Literature of Sexual Advice." In *Solitary Pleasures: The Historical, Literary, and Artistic Discourses of Autoeroticism,* edited by Paula Bennett and Vernon A. Rosario II, 75–98. New York and London: Routledge, 1995.

———. *The Greatest Benefit to Mankind: A Medical History of Humanity from Antiquity to the Present.* London: Fontana, 1998.

———. "'In England's Green and Pleasant Land': The English Enlightenment and the Environment." In *Culture, Landscape, and the Environment: The Linacre Lectures 1997,* edited by Kate Flint and Howard Morphy, 15–43. Oxford: Oxford University Press, 2000.

———. *Mind-Forg'd Manacles: A History of Madness in England from the Restoration to the Regency.* London: The Athlone Press, 1987.

Porter, Roy, and Dorothy Porter. *Patient's Progress: Doctors and Doctoring in Eighteenth-century England.* Cambridge: Polity Press, 1989.

———, eds. *In Sickness and in Health: The British Experience, 1650–1850.* London: Fourth Estate, 1988.

Porter, Roy, and Marie Mulvey Roberts, eds. *Pleasure in the Eighteenth Century.* Basingstoke: Macmillan, 1996.

Price, Martin, ed. *Dickens: A Collection of Critical Essays.* Englewood Cliffs: Prentice-Hall, 1967.

Proust, A. and Gilbert Ballet. *The Treatment of Neurasthenia.* London: Kimpton, 1902.

Proust, Marcel. *In Search of Lost Time*. Trans. C. K. Scott Moncrieff and Terence Kilmartin. London: Vintage, 1996.

Pykett, Lyn. *The "Improper" Feminine: The Women's Sensation Novel and the New Woman Writing*. London: Routledge, 1992.

———. "Introduction." In Mary Elizabeth Braddon, *The Doctor's Wife*, vii–xxv. Oxford: Oxford University Press, 1998.

———. *The Sensation Novel From* THE WOMAN IN WHITE *to* THE MOONSTONE. Exeter: BPC Wheatons Ltd, 1994.

Radcliffe, Ann. *The Castles of Athlin and Dunbayne: A Highland Story*. London: Folio Society, 1987.

———. *The Mysteries of Udolpho*. Oxford: Oxford University Press, 1998.

Rajan, Rajeswari Sunder. "Austen in the World: Postcolonial Mappings." In *The Postcolonial Jane Austen,* edited by You-me Park and Rajeswari Sunder Rajan, 3–25. London: Routledge, 2000.

Rance, Nicholas. *Wilkie Collins and Other Sensation Novelists: Walking the Moral Hospital*. Basingstoke: Macmillan, 1991.

Rawson, Claude. *Satire and Sentiment: 1660–1830*. Cambridge: Cambridge University Press, 1994.

Reade, Charles. *Hard Cash: A Matter-of-Fact Romance*. London: Sampson Low, Son & Marston, 1863.

Reed, Amy Louise. *The Background of Gray's Elegy: A Study in the Taste for Melancholy Poetry 1700–1751*. New York: Columbia, 1962.

"Review of *Sense and Sensibility.*" In *Jane Austen: Critical Assessments,* edited by Ian Littlewood, 263–66. Mountfield: Helm Information, 1998.

Richardson, Alan. *Literature, Education, and Romanticism: Reading as Social Practice 1780–1832*. Cambridge: Cambridge University Press, 1994.

Richardson, Alan, and Sonia Hofkosh, eds. *Romanticism, Race, and Imperial Culture, 1780–1834*. Bloomington: Indiana University Press, 1996.

Richardson, Samuel. *Clarissa*. Ed. Angus Ross. New York: Viking, 1985.

Richetti, John, ed. *The Cambridge Companion to the Eighteenth-Century Novel*. Cambridge: Cambridge University Press, 1996.

———, ed. *The Columbia History of the British Novel*. New York: Columbia, 1994.

———. "Introduction." In *The Columbia History of the British Novel,* edited by John Richetti, ix–xix. New York: Columbia, 1994.

———. *The English Novel in History 1700–1780*. London: Routledge, 1999.

———. *Popular Fiction Before Richardson: Narrative Patterns 1700–1739*. New York: Oxford University Press, 1969.

Roberts, Marie Mulvey, and Roy Porter, eds. *Literature and Medicine during the Eighteenth Century*. London: Routledge, 1993.

Robson, Catherine. *Men in Wonderland: The Lost Girlhood of the Victorian Gentleman*. Princeton: Princeton University Press, 2001.

Rogers, Katharine M. *Frances Burney: The World of "Female Difficulties."* Hemel Hempstead: Simon & Schuster, 1990.

Rogers, Samuel. *The Pleasures of Memory*. Oxford: Woodstock, 1989.

Roper, Michael, and John Tosh, eds. *Manful Assertions: Masculinities in Britain since 1800*. London: Routledge, 1991.

Rosen, George. "Nostalgia: A 'Forgotten' Psychological Disorder." *Clio Medica* 10 (1975): 29–51.

Roston, Murray. *The Search for Selfhood in Modern Literature*. Houndmills: Palgrave, 2001.

Roth, Michael. "Dying of the Past: Medical Studies of Nostalgia in Nineteenth-Century France." *History and Memory* 3, no. 1 (1991): 5–29.

Rouner, Leroy S., ed. *The Longing for Home*. Notre Dame: University of Notre Dame Press, 1996.

Rousseau, G. S. ed. *The Language of Psyche: Mind and Body in Enlightenment Thought: Clark Library Lectures 1985–1986*. Berkeley: University of California Press, 1992.

———. "Literature and Medicine: The State of the Field." *Isis*: 72 (1981), 406–24.

———. "Nerves, Spirits and Fibres: Towards the Origin of Sensibility." In *Studies in the Eighteenth Century III*, edited by R.F. Brissenden, 137–57. Canberra: Australian National University Press, 1975.

———. "War and Peace: Some Representations of Nostalgia and Adventure in the Eighteenth Century." In *Guerres et Paix: La Grande-Bretagne au XVIIe siècle I–II,* edited by Paul-Gabriel Bouce, 121–40. Paris: Universitè de la Sorbonne Nouvelle, 1998.

Royle, Nicholas. *Telepathy and Literature: Essays on the Reading Mind*. Oxford: Basil Blackwell, 1991.

Ruskin, John. *Works*. Eds. E. T. Cook and Alexander Wedderburn. London: George Allen, 1905.

Rylance, Rick. *Victorian Psychology and British Culture 1850–1880*. Oxford: Oxford University Press, 2000.

Sadrin, Anny. "Charlotte Dickens: The Female Narrator of *Bleak House*." In *Dickens: Critical Assessments*, edited by Michael Hollington, 248–559. Mountfield: Helm Information, 1995.

Said, Edward W. *Culture and Imperialism*. London: Chatto & Windus, 1993.

———. "Jane Austen and Empire." In *Raymond Williams: Critical Perspectives,* edited by Terry Eagleton, 150–64. Cambridge: Polity, 1989.

———. *Orientalism*. Harmondsworth: Penguin, 1978.

Sales, Roger. *Jane Austen and Representations of Regency England*. London: Routledge, 1996.

Salih, Sara. "'Her Blacks, Her Whites and Her Double Face': Altering Alterity in The Wanderer." *Eighteenth-Century Fiction* 11, no. 3 (1999): 301–15.

Samuel, Raphael. *Theatres of Memory Vol.1: Past and Present in Contemporary Culture*. London: Verso, 1994.

———. *Theatres of Memory Vol.2: Island Stories*. London: Verso, 1998.

Schiller, Friedrich. *Essays*. Eds. Hinderer, Walter and Daniel O. Dahlstrom. New York: Continuum Publishing, 1993.

Schleiner, Winfried. *Melancholy, Genius, and Utopia in the Renaissance*. Wiesbaden: Otto Harrassowitz, 1991.

Schofield, Mary Anne, and Cecilia Macheski, eds. *Fetter'd or free? British Women Novelists 1670–1815*. Athens: Ohio University Press, 1987.

Schor, Hilary M. *Scheherezade in the Marketplace: Elizabeth Gaskell and the Victorian Novel*. Oxford: Oxford University Press, 1992.

Scott, Walter. *Waverley*. Edinburgh: Adam & Charles Black, 1870.

Sedgwick, Eve Kosofsky. *Between Men: English Literature and Male Homosocial Desire*. New York: Columbia University Press, 1985.

Shaw, Christopher, and Malcolm Chase, eds. *The Imagined Past: History and Nostalgia.* Manchester: Manchester University Press, 1989.

Sheridan, Frances. *Sidney Bidulph.* Eds. Patricia Köster and Jean Coates Cleary. Oxford: Oxford University Press, 1995.

Showalter, Elaine. *The Female Malady: Women, Madness, and English Culture 1830–1980.* London: Virago, 1987.

———. *A Literature of their Own: British Women Novelists from Bronte to Lessing.* Princeton: Princeton University Press, 1977.

Shuttleworth, Sally. *Charlotte Brontë and Victorian Psychology.* Cambridge University Press, 1996.

———. "The Dynamics of Cross-Culturalism in Charlotte Brontë's Fiction." In *The Brontë Sisters: Critical Assessments,* edited by Eleanor McNees, 340–52. Mountfield: Helm Information, 1996.

———. "'The malady of thought:' Embodied memory in Victorian psychology and the novel." In *Memory and Memorials, 1789–1914,* edited by Matthew Campbell et al., 46–59. London: Routledge, 2000.

———. "Psychological definition and social power: phrenology in the novels of Charlotte Brontë." In *Nature Transfigured: Science and Literature 1700–1900,* edited by John Christie and Sally Shuttleworth, 121–51. Manchester: Manchester University Press, 1989.

Sicher, Ephraim. "Bleak Homes and Symbolic Houses: At-Homeness and Homelessness in Dickens." In *Homes and Homelessness in the Victorian Imagination,* edited by Murray Baumgarten and H. M. Daleski, 33–49. New York: AMS Press, 1998.

Sisk, David W. *Transformations of Language in Modern Dystopias.* Westport: Greenwood, 1997.

Small, Helen. *Love's Madness: Medicine, the Novel, and Female Insanity.* Oxford: Clarendon, 1996.

Smiles, Samuel. *Self-Help.* London: John Murray, 1882.

Smith, Adam. *The Theory of Moral Sentiments.* Indianapolis: Liberty Press, 1976.

Smith, Charlotte. *Desmond.* Eds. Antje Blank and Janet Todd. London: Pickering & Chatto, 1997.

———. *Emmeline: The Orphan of the Castle.* Ed. Zoe Fairbairns. London: Pandora, 1987.

———. *Marchmont.* London: Sampson Low, 1796.

———. *Montalbert.* London: S. Low, 1795.

———. *The Old Manor House.* Ed. Janet Todd. London: Pandora, 1987.

———. *The Wanderings of Warwick.* Ed. Caroline Franklin. London: Routledge, 1992.

Smith, Nelson, and R. C. Terry, eds. *Wilkie Collins to the Forefront: Some Reassessments.* New York: AMS, 1995.

Snell, K. D. M., ed. *The Regional Novel in Britain and Ireland 1800–1990.* Cambridge: Cambridge University Press, 1998.

Sorensen, Janet. "Writing Historically, Speaking Nostalgically: The Competing Languages of Nation in Scott's *The Bride of Lammermoor.*" In *Narratives of Nostalgia, Gender and Nationalism,* edited by Jean Pickering and Suzanne Kehde, 30–51. London: Macmillan, 1997.

Spacks, Patricia Meyer. *Desire and Truth: Functions of Plot in Eighteenth-Century English Novels.* Chicago: University of Chicago Press, 1990.

BIBLIOGRAPHY

———. "Novels of the 1790s: Action and Impasse." In *The Columbia History of the British Novel*, edited by John Richetti, 247–74. New York: Columbia, 1994.

———. "The Privacy of the Novel." *Novel* 31, no. 3 (1998): 304–16.

———. *Privacy: Concealing the Eighteenth-Century Self.* Chicago: Chicago University Press, 2003.

Spencer, Jane. *Elizabeth Gaskell.* Basingstoke: Macmillan, 1993.

———. *The Rise of the Woman Novelist: From Aphra Behn to Jane Austen.* Oxford: Basil Blackwell, 1986.

———. "Women writers and the eighteenth-century novel." In *The Cambridge Companion to the Eighteenth-Century Novel*, edited by John Richetti, 212–35. Cambridge: Cambridge University Press, 1996.

Spyri, Johanna. *Heidi.* Trans. Eileen Hall. London: Penguin, 1995.

Stabler, Jane. *Burke to Byron, Barbauld to Baillie, 1790–1830.* Basingstoke: Palgrave, 2002.

Stafford, William. *Socialism, Radicalism, and Nostalgia: Social Criticism in Britain 1775–1830.* Cambridge: Cambridge University Press, 1987.

Stange, G. Robert. "Expectations Well Lost: Dickens's Fable for His Time." In *Dickens: Critical Assessments*, edited by Michael Hollington, 517–26. Mountfield: Helm Information, 1995.

Starobinski, J. "The Idea of Nostalgia" Trans. W. S. Kemp. *Diogenes* 54 (1966): 81–103.

Starr, George. "'Only a Boy': Notes on Sentimental Novels." In *The English Novel*, edited by Richard Kroll, 29–54. London: Longman, 1998.

Staves, Susan. "Don Quixote in Eighteenth-Century England." *Comparative Literature* 24 (1972): 193–215.

Steiner, George. *Nostalgia for the Absolute.* Toronto: CBC Publications, 1974.

Stern, Rebecca. "'Personation' and 'Good Marking-Ink': Sanity, Performativity, and Biology in Victorian Sensation Fiction." *Nineteenth Century Studies* 14 (2000): 35–62.

Stevenson, Lionel. *Darwin among the Poets.* Chicago: Chicago University Press, 1932.

Stewart, Maaja A. *Domestic Realities and Imperial Fictions: Jane Austen's Novels in Eighteenth-Century Contexts.* Athens: University of Georgia Press, 1993.

Stewart, Susan. *On Longing: Narratives of the Miniature, the Gigantic, the Souvenir, the Collection.* Baltimore: John Hopkins University Press, 1984.

Still, Arthur, and Irving Velody, eds. *Rewriting the History of Madness: Studies in Foucault's* HISTOIRE DE LA FOLIE. London: Routledge, 1992.

Stone, Lawrence. *The Family, Sex and Marriage in England 1500–1800.* London: Weidenfeld and Nicolson, 1977.

———. *Road To Divorce: England 1530–1987.* Oxford: Oxford University Press, 1992.

Stone-Blackburn, Susan. "Consciousness Evolution and Early Telepathic Tales." *Science Fiction Studies* 20 (1993): 241–50.

Strickland, Charles. *Victorian Domesticity: Families in the Life and Art of Louisa May Alcott.* Alabama: University of Alabama Press, 1985.

Sutherland, John. *Is Heathcliff a Murderer?* Oxford: Oxford University Press, 1996.

Sutherland, Kathryn. "Introduction." In Jane Austen, *Mansfield Park*, vii–xxi. London: Penguin, 1996.

Symons, Julian. *Bloody Murder: From the Detective Story to the Crime Novel: A History*. London: Pan Books, 1994.

Tanner, Tony. "Introduction." In Jane Austen, *Mansfield Park*, 7–35. Harmondsworth: Penguin, 1983.

Tave, Stuart M. "From 'The Sensibility of Marianne and the Exertion of Elinor Dashwood.'" In *Jane Austen: Critical Assessments*, edited by Ian Littlewood, 222–27. Mountfield: Helm Information, 1998.

Taylor, Jenny Bourne. *In the Secret Theatre of Home: Wilkie Collins, Sensation Narrative, and Nineteenth Century Psychology*. London: Routledge, 1988.

Tennyson, Alfred. *Poems*. 3 vols. Ed. Christopher Ricks. Harlow: Longman, 1987.

Thomas, Donald. *The Post-Romantics*. London: Routledge, 1990.

Thomas, Ronald R. *Detective Fiction and the Rise of Forensic Science*. Cambridge: Cambridge University Press, 1999.

Thoms, Peter. "Escaping the Plot: The Quest for Selfhood in *The Woman in White*." In *Wilkie Collins to the Forefront: Some Reassessments*, edited by Nelson Smith and R. C. Terry, 183–207. New York: AMS, 1995.

Thomson, A. T. "Lectures on Medical Jurisprudence." *The Lancet* (1837): 881–89.

Thumboo, Edwin, ed. *Perceiving Other Worlds*. Singapore: Times Academic Press, 1991.

Thurley, Geoffrey. *The Dickens Myth: Its Genesis and Structure*. London: Routledge & Kegan Paul, 1976.

Tillotson, Kathleen. *Novels of the Eighteen-Forties*. Oxford: Clarendon, 1983.

———. "Dombey and Son." In *Dickens: A Collection of Critical Essays*, edited by Martin Price, 115–34. Englewood Cliffs: Prentice-Hall, 1967.

Todd, Janet. *Sensibility: An Introduction*. London: Methuen, 1986.

Tosh, John. *A Man's Place: Masculinity and the Middle-Class Home in Victorian England*. New Haven: Yale University Press, 1999.

Trilling, Lionel. *The Opposing Self*. London: Secker and Warburg, 1955.

Troost, Linda, and Sayre Greenfield, eds. *Jane Austen in Hollywood*. Lexington: University Press of Kentucky, 1998.

Trotter, David. "Introduction." In Charles Dickens. *Great Expectations*, vii-xx. London: Penguin, 1996.

Trotter, Thomas. *Observations on the Scurvy*. London: Longman, 1792.

Trumpener, Katie. *Bardic Nationalism: The Romantic Novel and the British Empire*. Princeton: Princeton University Press, 1997.

Tuite, Clara. "Domestic Retrenchment and Imperial Expansion: The Property Plots of *Mansfield Park*." In *The Postcolonial Jane Austen*, edited by You-me Park and Rajeswari Sunder Rajan, 93–115. London: Routledge, 2000.

———. *Romantic Austen: Sexual Politics and the Literary Canon*. Cambridge: Cambridge University Press, 2002.

Tuss, Alex L. *The Inward Revolution: Troubled Young Men in Victorian Fiction*. New York: Peter Lang, 1992.

Uglow, Jenny. *Elizabeth Gaskell: A Habit of Stories*. London: Faber and Faber, 1993.

Unsworth, Anna. *Elizabeth Gaskell: An Independent Woman.* London: Minerva, 1996.

Vance, Norman. *The Sinews of the Spirit: The Ideal of Christian Manliness in Victorian Literature and Religious Thought.* Cambridge: Cambridge University Press, 1985.

Vervliet, Raymond, and Annemarie Estor, eds. *Methods for the Study of Literature as Cultural Memory.* Amsterdam: Rodopi, 2000.

Vidler, Anthony. *The Architectural Uncanny: Essays in the Modern Unhomely.* Cambridge, MA: Massachusetts Institute of Technology Press, 1992.

Vrettos, Athena. *Somatic Fictions: Imagining Illness in Victorian Culture.* Standford: Standford University Press, 1995.

Wagner, Tamara S. "Victorian Fictions of the Nerves: Telepathy and Depression in Wilkie Collins's *The Two Destinies.*" *Victorian Institute Journal* 32 (2004), forthcoming.

———. "Rewriting Sentimental Plots: Sequls to Novels of Sensibility by Jane Austen and Another Lady." In *And Now for the Sequel: Examining Updates of Eighteenth-Century Works,* edited by Debra Bourdeau and Elizabeth Kraft (Newark: Delaware University Press), forthcoming.

Waldron, Mary. *Jane Austen and the Fiction of her Time.* Cambridge: Cambridge University Press, 1999.

Warren, Leland. "Of the Conversation of Women: *The Female Quixote* and the Dream of Perfection." *Studies in Eighteenth-Century Culture* 11 (1982): 367–80.

———. "The Conscious Speakers. Sensibility and the Art of Conversation Considered." In *Sensibility in Transformation: Creative Resistance to Sentiment from the Augustans to the Romantics,* edited by Syndy McMillen Conger, 25–42. Rutherford: Fairleigh Dickinson University Press, 1990.

Waters, Catherine. *Dickens and the Politics of the Family.* Cambridge: Cambridge University Press, 1997.

Waters, Sarah. *Affinity.* London: Virago, 1999.

———. *Fingersmith.* London: Virago, 2002.

Watt, James. "The Medical Bequest of Disaster at Sea." *Journal of Royal College of Physicians* 32, no. 6 (1998): 572–79.

Watt, Ian. *Myths of Modern Individualism: Faust, Don Quixote, Don Juan, Robinson Crusoe.* Cambridge: Cambridge University Press, 1996.

———. *The Rise of the Novel.* 1957. London: Peregrine Books, 1963.

———, ed. *The Victorian Novel: Modern Essays in Criticism.* Oxford: Oxford University Press, 1971.

Waugh, Alec. *The Loom of Youth.* 1917. Reprint, London: Methuen, 1984.

Wells, H. G. *The Time Machine.* Harmondsworth: Penguin, 1946.

Wheeler, Roxann. *The Complexion of Race: Categories of Difference in Eighteenth-Century British Culture.* Philadelphia: University of Pennsylvania Press, 2000.

White, Allan H. "Language and Location in Charles Dickens's *Bleak House.*" In *Dickens: Critical Assessments,* edited by Michael Hollington, 214–30. Mountfield: Helm Information, 1995.

Wiesenthal, C. S. "From Charcot to Plato: The History of Hysteria in *Heart and Science.*" In *Wilkie Collins to the Forefront: Some Reassessments,* edited by Nelson Smith and R. C. Terry, 257–68. New York: AMS, 1995.

Wilbrandt, Conrad. *Mr East's Experiences in Mr Bellamy's World*. Trans. Mary J. Safford. New York: Harper & Brothers, 1891.
Williams, Gareth D. *The Curse of Exile: A Study of Ovid's Ibis*. Cambridge: Cambridge University Press, 1996.
Williams, Raymond. *Culture and Society 1780–1950*. London: Chatto & Windus, 1967.
———. *The Country and the City*. London: Hogarth Press, 1973, reprinted 1985.
Wilson, Angus. *The World of Charles Dickens*. London: Secker & Warburg, 1970.
———. "The Heroes and Heroines of Dickens." In *Dickens: A Collection of Critical Essays*, edited by Martin Price, 16–23. Englewood Cliffs: Prentice-Hall, 1967.
Wiltshire, John. *Jane Austen and the Body*. Cambridge: Cambridge University Press, 1992.
———. "*Mansfield Park, Emma, Persuasion*." In *The Cambridge Companion to Jane Austen*, edited by Edward Copeland and Juliet McMaster, 58–83. Cambridge: Cambridge University Press, 1997.
———. *Recreating Jane Austen*. Cambridge: Cambridge University Press, 2001.
Winter, Alison. *Mesmerized: Powers of Mind in Victorian Britain*. Chicago: University of Chicago Press, 1998.
Wood, Ellen. *East Lynne*. Ed. Sally Mitchell. New Brunswick: Rutgers University Press, 1984.
Wordsworth, William. *Lyrical Ballads*. Bristol: Biggs and Co, 1800.
Wright, Terence. *Elizabeth Gaskell: "We are not angels:" Realism, Gender, Values*. London: Macmillan, 1995.
Wright, T. R. "From Bumps to Morals: The Phrenological Background to George Eliot's Moral Framework." *Review of English Studies* 33, no. 129 (1982), 35–40.
Wrigley, Richard and George Revill, eds. *Pathologies of Travel*. Amsterdam: Rodopi, 2000.
Wullschläger, Jackie. *Inventing Wonderland: The Lives and Fantasies of Lewis Carroll, Edward Lear, J. M. Barrie, Kenneth Grahame and A. A. Milne*. London: Methuen, 1995.
Young, Robert J. C. *Colonial Desire: Hybridity in Theory, Culture and Race*. London: Routledge, 1995.

Index

adoption: fantasies of, 127–28, 130, 138, 140–51, 158–59, 168, 185; of homes, 111–12, 144, 151–52, 155, 168, 172; informal 82–83, 85, 102, 185
affective revolution, 13–14, 23, 27, 28, 176, 216, 234, 235 n. 4
Alcott, Louisa May: *Little Women*, 145
alterity, 26, 71, 80–83, 106, 165, 170–71, 181–82, 214, 249 n. 98, 250 n. 111. *See also* orientalism
American War of Independence, 13, 248 n. 78
amnesia, 192, 198, 209, 261 n. 79; and nostalgia, 131–32, 192–93, 257 n. 31
androgyny, 200, 207–8, 213–14, 267 n. 43
anti-Jacobin fiction, 51, 60, 62, 72–84, 90, 99, 247 n. 76, 252 n. 18
Arnold, Thomas (1), 18
Arnold, Thomas (1795–1842), 179
associationism, 131–32
Austen, Cassandra, 253 n. 34
Austen, Jane, works of: *Emma*, 51, 101–2, 105–6, 110, 196, 220, 225; *Mansfield Park*, 30–31, 40, 51, 62, 77, 85–89, 98–119, 124, 196, 220–24, 228, 247 n. 75; *Northanger Abbey*, 43, 69–70, 77, 98–99, 110, 223–25; *Persuasion*, 35, 51–52, 86, 88–89, 99–100, 106, 108, 118–24, 196, 220–21; *Pride and Prejudice*, 31, 88, 90–91, 98–99, 103–6, 110, 112–14, 124, 219–20; *Sanditon*, 102, 221–22; *Sense and Sensibility*, 44, 88–89, 91–99, 103, 108, 110, 114, 119, 142, 220, 232; *The Watsons*, 100, 110, 118

Banks, Joseph, 17
Barlow, John, 190–92
Barrie, James, 261 n. 5
Bellamy, Edward, 175, 263–64 n. 35
Besant, Walter, 215
Bildungsroman, 130, 153, 227, 257 n. 24

Boswell, James, 243 n. 11
Braddon, Mary Elizabeth, works of: *The Doctor's Wife*, 227; *Lady Audley's Secret*, 194, 198–99
Brontë, Anne: *Agnes Grey*, 202
Brontë, Charlotte, works of: *Jane Eyre*, 126, 145, 164–65, 201–2, 218–19; *The Professor*, 165, 169–70; *Shirley*, 164–65, 259 n. 53; *Villette*, 32, 163–72
Brooke, Frances, 48
Brunton, Mary, 51, 246 n. 60
Burke, Edmund, 65, 67, 72, 75, 78, 83
Burkean fiction. *See* Jacobin fiction
Burnett, Frances Hodgson, 261 n. 5; works of: *Little Lord Fauntleroy*, 162–64; *The Little Princess*, 163, 228; *The Secret Garden*, 146–47
Burney, Frances, 78; works of: *Camilla*, 34, 48, 51, 56–64, 222; *Cecilia*, 56, 59–61, 247 n. 71; *Evelina*, 49, 56–59, 64, 67, 82, 251 n. 132; *The Wanderer*, 30, 43, 51, 57, 59–62, 64, 74–84, 251 n. 135
Burton, Robert, 15, 16
Butler, Samuel, 135, 258 n. 38

Carroll, Lewis (Charles Lutwidge Dodgeson), 261 n. 5
catharsis, 141, 150. *See also* sickroom: rebirth in
Cervantes, Miguel de: *Don Quixote*, 66. *See also* quixotism
Chambers, Robert, 28, 241 n. 80
Cheyne, George, 35
child death, 138, 144–45
childhood: nostalgia for. *See under* nostalgia; orphans; Romantic child
Coleridge, Samuel Taylor, 15–17
Collins, William Wilkie, 11–13, 32, 230; works of: *Armadale*, 205; *Basil*, 200, 215; *The Black Robe*, 208; *Blind Love*, 215; *The Evil Genius*, 213, 228–33; *The Fallen Leaves*, 159, 208, 230; *The Guilty River*, 213–14; *Heart and Science*, 194, 208–12, 215, 230–32; *Hide and Seek*, 199–200; *I Say No*, 212;

293

Collins, William Wiklie (*continued*)
Jezebel's Daughter, 208; *The Law and the Lady*, 207–8; *The Legacy of Cain*, 192, 215; *Man and Wife*, 11, 180, 193–97, 205–7; *Miss or Mrs?*, 206; *The Moonstone*, 205, 212; *The New Magdalen*, 207; *No Name*, 176–77, 194, 200–5, 211–12; *Poor Miss Finch*, 206–7; *The Two Destinies*, 191–92, 208, 230; *The Woman in White*, 192, 194, 199–201
consumer: consumerism, 36–37, 44–45, 245 n. 43, 246 n. 57; revolution 37, 45; society, 13, 251 n. 130
Cook, James, 17
Cowper, William, 108, 115
Craik, Dinah (nee Mulock): *Olive*, 145, 162, 261 n. 4
custody laws, 213, 229, 231, 233, 269 n. 23. *See also* adoption

d'Arblay, Alexandre, 78
d'Arblay, Frances. *See* Burney, Frances
Darwin, Charles, 17, 259 n. 52, 264 n. 46, 264 n. 53
Darwinian imagination, 28–29, 173–77, 209, 241 n. 80, 259 n. 52, 264 n. 46. *See also* evolution
Darwinism, social, 195. *See also* eugenics
Defoe, Daniel, 269 n. 20
Degeneration, 32, 163, 172–84. *See also* entropy
Dickens, Charles, 13, 31, 62–63, 227–28; works of: *Bleak House*, 125, 128, 134, 145, 151–56; *Christmas Carol, A*, 137; *David Copperfield*, 62, 128–31, 133, 138–41, 147–48, 155–56, 172, 216–18, 225, 227–28; *Dombey and Son*, 125, 128–29, 136–38, 144–45, 156, 232, 227–28; *Great Expectations*, 128, 131, 134–36, 139–42, 156, 161, 197; *Hard Times*, 133, 136, 150; *The Haunted Man*, 125, 132, 144, 161; *Little Dorrit*, 125, 128–29, 133–34, 149, 156–61; *Martin Chuzzlewit*, 130–31, 133, 136–37, 142, 156; *Nicholas Nickleby*, 131, 137, 144; *The Old Curiosity Shop*, 128, 144–45, 148; *Oliver Twist*, 125, 128–33, 143–44, 148, 153, 155–56, 158; *Our Mutual Friend*, 125, 136–37, 143, 147–50, 156, 197; *The Tale of Two Cities*, 148
divorce, 51, 231–32, 269 n. 23
Donnelly, Ignatius, 263–64 n. 35
double, 52, 65, 69–70, 116, 118, 140–41, 143, 148, 151–53, 180, 189, 192–93, 203–8, 213–14, 260 n. 70
dystopia, 174–75, 263–64 n. 35

Edgeworth, Maria, works of: *The Absentee*, 75–77; *Belinda*, 61, 247 n. 73; *Ennui*, 75
effeminacy: anxieties of, 29, 36–38, 43–51, 178–80, 192, 194–208, 212, 214, 244 n. 19, 245 n. 43, 245 n. 44, 246 n. 57. *See also* androgyny
Eliot, George, works of: *Middlemarch*, 178; *Silas Marner*, 261 n. 4
entropy, 174–75, 210
eugenics, 175, 177, 184
evolution, 28, 32, 162–63, 172–89, 195, 234, 264 n. 46. *See also* Darwinian imagination; eugenics

Falconer, William, 18
fatherhood, Victorian, 137–38, 213–14, 227–33
Fielding, Henry, 39, 217
Fielding, Sarah, 66
Flaubert, Gustave: *Madam Bovary*, 227
Forster, E. M.: *The Longest Journey*, 197, 215
Foucault, Michel, 19, 29, 44, 242 n. 92, 248–49 n. 92, 264 n. 55
French Revolution, 13, 62–84
Freud, Sigmund, 70–71
Froude, J. A.: *The Nemesis of Faith*, 28

Galton, Francis, 175, 177. *See also* eugenics
Gaskell, Elizabeth, works of: *Cranford*, 172, 263 n. 21; *Mary Barton*, 172; *North and South*, 172, 179; *Wives and Daughters*, 32, 163, 172–74, 177–89, 224
Gilpin, William, 114
Gilpinesque, 255 n. 52. *See also* picturesque
Goethe, Johann Wolfgang: *The Sorrows of Young Werther*, 47

INDEX

Gothic, 43, 69, 70–73, 95, 98, 174, 224–25, 245 n. 40, 248–49 n. 92, 249 n. 102, 266 n. 23; and Victorian domesticity, 136, 161, 201, 255 n. 61, 266 n. 32
Grahame, Kenneth, 147, 263 n. 5
Graves, Caroline, 230

Hardenberg, Friedrich von (pseud. Novalis), 29
Hill, John, 36
Hofer, Johannes, 14–17, 21
homesickness. *See under* nostalgia
Hubback, Catherine, 253 n. 34
Hughes, Thomas, 195–96
humoralism, 36
hybridity, 78, 82–83, 182, 214; and miscegenation 81, 182
hypochondria, 18–19, 25, 33, 35–37, 102, 121, 168, 199, 243 n. 11
hysteria, 209–10, 214

illegitimacy, 47, 58–59, 65, 82–83, 92, 133–34, 153–57, 160, 201–2. *See also* orphans
imperialism, 74–84, 180–1, 195–96, 235 n. 4, 263 n. 21; micropolitics of, 86, 90, 106–7, 117, 137, 154–55, 171, 205, 187; and science, 163, 180–83, 189. *See also* orientalism
Inchbald, Elizabeth, works of: *Lovers' Vows*, 223; *A Simple Story*, 38, 49–50, 52
individuality, 13, 20, 22–23, 26, 37, 71–72, 163, 216, 218, 225, 269 n. 20
Industrial Revolution 13, 23, 27
industrialization, 147, 179
insanity: in medical discourses, 14, 18–19, 35–36, 191–92, 242 n. 92, 244 n. 17; in novels of sensibility, 41, 59–61, 63, 66; in sensation fiction, 136, 192–200, 208, 230. *See also* monomania; neurasthenia

Jacobin fiction, 56, 60–74, 78–79, 83–84, 90–91, 98
James, Henry: *What Maisie Knew*, 269 n. 23

Kant, Immanuel, 15–16, 18, 35, 38, 50, 235–36 n. 10

Lamb, Charles (*Rosamund Gray*), 40–43, 45
Lane, Mary E. Bradley, 175
Lennox, Charlotte: *Female Quixote*, 43, 222–23
locus amoenus, 76, 143–44, 250 n. 112
lovesickness: and insanity, 18, 141, 198, 230, 245 n. 34, 259 n. 48; in medical discourses 18–20, 34, 169, 200; and nostalgia, 18, 20, 44–46, 51, 55–65, 85–87, 91–99, 103–6, 111, 113, 118–24, 160–61, 164, 169, 212, 214–15, 230, 249 n. 95, 253 n. 29; parody of, 141, 160–61 (*see also* melancholy: affectation of); and pining, aesthetics of, 44–51, 58–59, 202
Lyell, Charles, 28, 241 n. 80

Mackenzie, Henry: *The Man of Feeling*, 34–35, 45, 47–48
melancholy: affectation of, 46, 121–22, 161, 196–197, 203; in medical discourses, 15, 17, 19–20, 191, 197; and nostalgia, 16–20, 27, 33, 35–37, 40–42, 46, 58, 94, 117, 121, 196, 236 n. 26, 237 n. 34, 244 n. 17; and Romanticism. *See* Romanticism: Romantic longing
maternity: and death, 58, 138, 143, 147, 152–54, 185–86; and evolution, 184–85, 188–89; failure of, 78, 145, 185, 187; of maternal surrogates, 65, 130, 143, 155, 159, 164, 259, 185–86 (*see also* adoption)
mesmerism, 126, 129–32, 144, 158, 161–63, 165, 180, 191, 216, 230, 257 n. 25, 258 n. 41, 265 n. 3, 265 n. 4
miscegenation. *See* hybridity
modernity, 13, 19, 26, 71, 216, 229, 234, 235 n. 3, 235 n. 4, 241 n. 83, 249 n. 98, 250 n. 111
monomania, 160, 192, 199, 262 n. 16
Morgan, Lady. *See* Sydney Owenson
Morris, William: *News From Nowhere*, 263–64 n. 35
motherhood. *See* maternity
muscular Christianity, 32, 174, 177–80, 193–96, 205–6, 242 n. 91, 266 n. 18

nationalism, 24, 57, 64–84, 235 n. 4, 237–38 n. 44, 255 n. 56; and imagined communities, 24–25, 71, 75–76, 250 n. 111
neurasthenia, 168, 174–76, 178, 190–92, 195, 209–12, 236 n. 26, 262 n. 13
New Man, 32, 172–89, 263 n. 25. *See also* muscular Christianity; sensibility: man of
nostalgia: for childhood, 27–28, 31, 41–42, 55–57, 61–64, 68, 125–61, 162–63, 167–68, 187, 227–29, 240 n. 74; etymology of, 14–17, 236 n. 26, 237 n. 33, 237 n. 36; for heritage, 21–22; as homesickness 14–16, 19–22, 34, 44, 56–65, 71, 94–100, 106–9, 112, 115–16, 118–20, 129, 131, 138, 151–61, 162–69, 172, 185–88, 191–92, 225, 227–28, 256–57 n. 17; in medical discourses, 14–21, 30–32, 33–38, 50, 52, 55–56, 87–88, 107, 168–69, 190–93, 237 n. 33, 237 n. 36, 244 n. 28 (*see also under* lovesickness); in relation to sentimentality 13, 30–31, 33, 35–38, 40–74, 125–29, 134–35, 139, 142–50, 163–64, 215–16, 227, 229, 232–34
Novalis. *See* Hardenberg, Friedrich von

orientalism, 26, 76–77, 80–82, 106–7, 238 n. 46, 239–40 n. 68, 240 n. 77, 263 n. 21. *See also* alterity; imperialism
orphans, 40–46, 60, 74, 101, 126–150; and abandonment, 127–29, 132, 140, 152–59, 165. *See also* adoption
O'Shaughnessy, Arthur, 18
otherness. *See* alterity
Owenson, Sydney (Lady Morgan), 75, 77

pathetic fallacy, 164
Pearson, Karl, 175. *See also* eugenics
phrenology, 169–70, 176, 192, 215, 262 n. 17, 262 n. 19
picturesque, 65, 68–70, 72–73, 77, 95, 114, 255 n. 56
pre-Romanticism, 74, 240 n. 74, 242–43 n. 3, 244 n. 17. *See also* sensibility
primogeniture, 184

privacy: concepts of, 13, 25–26, 124, 218–20, 225, 229–30, 232–33; and imagination 25, 72, 219, 226, 268 n. 4; and individuality 86–89, 110, 115–16, 124; and masturbation 25, 217, 219, 226, 239 n. 62; and reading, 24–26, 112, 115–16, 213, 216–29, 239 n. 60, 268 n. 1; and solipsism 217, 221; and space 115–16, 124, 171, 219, 221, 230
Proust, Marcel, 131, 257 n. 31, 257 n. 32

quixotism, 43, 57, 66–67, 80, 248 n. 80, 222–24, 227, 268–69 n. 10, 269 n. 19

Radcliffe, Ann, works of: *The Castles of Athlin and Dunbayn*, 69; *The Mysteries of Udolpho*, 69–70, 95, 224
Reade, Charles, 195; works of: *Hard Cash*, 194, 197–98, 230
rebirth. *See under* sickroom
Richardson, Samuel, works of: *Clarissa*, 41, 49, 52, 91, 220, 247 n. 66; *Pamela*, 47, 49, 52, 220, 247 n. 69, 247 n. 71; *Sir Charles Grandison*, 48–49, 247 n. 66
Rogers, Samuel, 17
Romantic child, 27–28, 42, 125–26, 128–30, 138–39, 146–48, 155–56, 163, 216–18, 227, 231, 240 n. 74, 247 n. 75, 261 n. 4
Romanticism, 20, 31, 86, 88, 90, 117, 129, 218–19, 242–43 n. 3, 244 n. 25; and fiction 20, 33, 74, 76, 89–90, 112, 117, 171, 242–43 n. 3, 255 n. 58; and individualism 37, 75, 77, 89, 219–20, 225 (*see also* individuality); and longing 15–16, 31, 37, 77, 85–124, 128, 190, 215; and nationalism 74–76, 79, 84 (*see also* nationalism)
Rousseau, Jean Jacques, 61, 63, 269 n. 20
Rudd, Martha, 230
Ruskin, John, 135

Schiller, Friedrich, 27
sensation novel, Victorian, 136, 145–46, 174, 190–215, 227, 230,

241 n. 85, 258 n. 41, 266 n. 13, 266 n. 23, 266 n. 32
sensibility: cults of, 30, 33–89, 215, 234, 243 n. 8, 244 n. 19; man of, 43–51, 245 n. 42, 245 n. 43, 245 n. 44, 246 n. 59; new man of, 178–180, 184, 190–215, 229–33, 267 n. 43, 268 n. 53; novel of, 12–13, 30, 33–89, 242–43 n. 3, 266 n. 23; parody of, 88–91
St. Pierre, Bernardin de: *Paul and Virginia*, 62
Scott, Walter, 71, 75, 224–27; works of: *The Bride of Lammermoor*, 77; "General Preface," 225–27; *Waverley*, 75, 226–27
Sheridan, Frances: *Sidney Bidulph*, 30, 47, 51–56, 93, 98, 142
sickroom, 32, 63, 97, 140–50, 163–72, 197, 246 n. 62, 259 n. 48, 259 n. 49, 259 n. 53; failure of, 143, 148–49, 164–72; rebirth in, 140–44, 148–50
Smiles, Samuel, 179, 264 n. 44
Smith, Adam, 50, 197
Smith, Charlotte, works of: *Desmond*, 30, 34, 53, 62, 65–74, 224; *Emmeline*, 39, 43, 44–48, 98, 232, 251 n. 132; *Marchmont*, 48, 89; *Montalbert*, 39–40, 82; *The Old Manor House*, 39, 223, 248 n. 78
somatics: cultural fictions of 169, 181, 190–95; of desire, 59; of distress 87, 169; of longing, 56, 190–91

Spyri, Johanna: *Heidi*, 146
Sterne, Laurence, 45, 47, 50
Stoker, Bram (*Dracula*), 175
suicide, 41, 47, 53, 58, 63, 83, 98, 191, 201, 208

telepathy. *See* mesmerism
Tennyson, Alfred, 28
Thackeray, William Makepeace: *Pendennis*, 172
thermodynamics. *See* entropy
Thomson, A.T., 18–19, 35
Trotter, Thomas, 16

uncanny, 70–71, 152–53, 249 n. 97, 249 n. 98, 260 n. 69. *See also* double
unheimlich. *See* uncanny
utopia, 16, 21, 32, 67, 151, 174–75, 189, 240 n. 77, 263–64 n. 35. *See also* dystopia

vis nervosa. *See* neurasthenia
vivisection, 194, 209–10, 231

Waugh, Alec: *The Loom of Youth*, 196
Wells, H. G.: *The Time Machine*, 175, 263–64 n. 35
Wilbrandt, Conrad: *Mr. East's Experiences in Mr. Bellamy's World*, 263–64 n. 35
Wilde, Oscar: *Dorian Gray*, 215
Wollstonecraft, Mary, 62, 67
Wood, Ellen: *East Lynne*, 145–46
Wordsworth, William, 20, 226